The Cosmic Experience of One

An awareness-expanding course for human beings

A later 6th sub-density united group

&

Jasun Ether

∞
Source

A Source paperback

The Cosmic Experience of One
An awareness-expanding course for human beings

Published by Source 2026

Cover design by Chris Brignola

www.jasunetherbooks.com

Library of Congress Cataloging-in-Publication Data
Names: Ether, Jasun, author
Title: The Cosmic Experience of One : An awareness-expanding course for human beings
Identifiers: LCCN 2026906972
ISBN (hardcover) 978-1-7348334-7-8
ISBN (paperback) 978-1-7348334-8-5
ISBN (eBook) 978-1-7348334-6-1
Subjects: Nonfiction | Spirituality | Spiritual growth

1 2 3 4 5 6 7 ∞

The Cosmic Experience of One

An awareness-expanding course for human beings

101.1 – Introduction & The 3 Big Questions

Hello and welcome to the Cosmic Experience of One. This is an awareness-expanding course for human beings. It could also be considered a life manual for Earthlings. First an introduction for this educational course will be given. After that we will address the big questions everyone asks: Is there a God, and if so, what is God? What is the purpose of life? And what happens after death? Surprisingly, the answers for these elementary questions still elude most of humanity today. Not only will these elementary questions be answered, but this course also shares a treasure trove of the most important and fundamental information about life and beyond that offers a great expansion of awareness.

Here is a summary of what this course covers: understanding the big picture, the structure and ways of the Cosmos, the history of the solar system Earth resides in which includes life on other planets, all the densities (which humans often mistakenly call dimensions) in this Cosmos are explained and the types of life-forms that reside in them, how dualism and paradoxes play a major role in the Cosmos, how higher-density beings in the outer planes and inner planes guide and assist human beings and other 3rd density beings in expanding their awareness, methods for balancing the chakras that pave the path for advancement in the Cosmos, the dance of pre-incarnate plans (destiny) and free will, the reason for the veil of forgetfulness being placed on 3rd density beings (which includes human beings on Earth), the history of religions and their origins, the human condition, the nature of sexuality and sexual energy, past civilizations on Earth, the strategies used by negative and negatively oriented beings and how they are effective, the harvest, coming Earth changes, the transition of Earth and humans into the 4th density, meditation techniques, mysteries on Earth—all of these topics and others offer the missing puzzle pieces to strengthen your understanding of the big picture and potentially provoke determination for self-work that assists you on your journey. It is time for it to be known.

This course is set up and structured like a university course, where information builds upon itself, understanding 101 subjects in order to more fully comprehend 102 topics, then 103 topics, and lastly 104 concepts. If you jump ahead to a certain subject without having absorbed the preceding subjects, you will be doing yourself a great disservice. The subjects should be understood and learned in order. If you skip ahead to a certain subject of your interest, you will most likely misunderstand the concepts, or worse, think you have grasped the concepts and walk away with a skewed version of the topics, and some of these concepts are hard enough to understand even when laid out in sequential order, so do yourself a favor and absorb them in order.

This consciousness-expanding course answers the most important questions humanity has been asking or ought to be asking, and since answers always lead to more questions, it also answers questions most have not thought to ask yet. The knowledge covered, even if only partially understood, has the power to change your perception about life and almost all its facets, giving you the opportunity to be liberated from the many prisons of the mind.

Some of the non-transitory information offered in this course has been conveyed piece by piece throughout the ages, falling on uncomprehending ears or hidden away by selfish human beings who lust after power in order to assert control over others. Although such information in this course isn't new, it will be new to your current focal point of awareness. Knowledge is power, and I assure you that you're about to embark on the most powerful journey of your life if you apply your mind to this awareness-expanding course, which is meant for all human beings.

In secret societies arcane knowledge is taught much like in a school: members aren't taught certain information until they get high enough in the order. This method either unfairly holds back information from those who aren't deemed privileged enough, or because information can't be grasped properly unless one learns it in sequential order. One can't jump eight steps of stairs at once; they ascend the flight of stairs by taking the next step in the staircase and proceed one step at a time. One of the reasons humanity has been held back is because these secret societies' arcane knowledge has been reserved for only the few that perceive themselves to be the elite. We are going to end that now; it's time to make this information known to all on Earth. There should be no information reserved for a select few on Earth. If you have the curiosity and determination, you have the right to be privy so you may expand your awareness. If a certain percentage of human beings on this planet understood and practiced the information presented in this course, it would be shared within the collective and naturally bring about sane civilizations working toward harmony instead of the current disharmony on planet Earth. This course not only presents secret societies' arcane knowledge for all human beings, but reveals far more knowledge and wisdom than secret societies know.

A drawback in presenting this information in this way is that there's no regulation in making sure one has mostly understood a concept before moving onto the next subject. So please, if you don't feel you've understood a subject adequately, go over it again and ruminate and meditate on it before proceeding to the next subject. This information is meant to be ruminated on and practiced rather than merely taken in quickly and abandoned. It's your responsibility to regulate and test yourself to evaluate if you're ready to take the next step up the ascension staircase. The keys to the Cosmos are in your hands, as they always were, you just didn't know it.

Who I am isn't important because none of this information came through solely by myself. This information, knowledge, and wisdom has been brought through in a team effort. Instead of being the sole founder of this course's information, think of me as a dedicated messenger who has utilized experience and time on Earth to understand human beings' mindsets and ways to understand the human condition in order to more aptly explain these concepts with specific sentence structure, examples, metaphors, and analogies that most human beings can relate to and understand.

I'm not going to share my personal profound experiences I've had on my path of remembering who I am because those experiences are for me, as yours are for you, and I'm not going to use them in an attempt to persuade you to believe the information shared in this awareness-expanding course. It's your task to discern; I and we have no wish to infringe upon your free will.

My personal experiences helped me remember what I already knew. Every being knows everything at some level in the tree of mind, but it's harder for one to remember if they've been veiled from it for a long time, just as one feels it's extremely difficult or even seemingly impossible to remember what happens in the beginning of a long dream—not even mentioning all the cryptic symbolism within. You'll remember the ending of a dream more easily, but with dedication, willpower, practice, and tools, you can remember more of your dreams. This is a literal statement about dreaming, but it's also an analogy that'll help you grasp the concept of recalling knowledge that has been stored in your subconscious mind after the veil of forgetfulness was enacted when you incarnated into 3rd density (known incorrectly to human beings as the 3rd dimension).

Some spiritual teachers have shared their profound experiences and it was suitable to do so, but with the very wide scope of information, knowledge, and wisdom shared in this course, it's more suitable to offer the information without persuasion, letting you truly decide for yourself what's true or not. Whether it rings true or not to you, it's as it should be on your current destination on the long journey. No information or truth should be forced, no matter how accurate or important it may be.

It's more prudent and important to tell you what I'm not rather than who I am. I'm not for or against any particular race, nation, political party, religion, ideology, or any other category that human beings use to identify and separate themselves from each other. The knowledge and wisdom presented here is for every single being on Earth, and not on Earth. As a dedicated messenger, it is my honor and duty to assist in your growth of awareness.

"How is the information found in this educational course procured, and how can I get information like it myself?" you may ask. This is covered in future topics, but in short, the best way is to do the inner work that assists self-growth: observing yourself internally as much as you observe others and the ways of the planet, and practicing meditation, which can open the door to your own connection to your higher self and potentially Source energy and mind. There are many ways to pierce the veil of forgetfulness that's placed upon the 3rd density: balancing your chakras and opening up the flow of energy to your indigo chakra (third eye) and connecting to Source energy or mind through the violet (crown) chakra, so-called astral projecting, remote viewing, channeling through a trance state, regression hypnotherapy, and balancing out your lower chakras in order to allow dream teachings are just a few examples.

Another method is to listen to someone else, as you're doing right now, but be careful when you do this because most human beings are in it for the money, fame, status, or power, because that's what Earth's current broken system breeds the desire for. Humans are taught and socially conditioned to believe that acquiring these things is success—that these things make one content, but the opposite is usually the case.

Humanity is still wallowing in unconsciousness because most human beings haven't been thinking for themselves and instead readily going along with the status quo. Through self-work you'll balance your lower chakras, and then start working on your higher chakras. Once one has balanced their chakras adequately, from their indigo chakra they may go through their violet crown chakra to connect to their higher self and Source energy and mind. Then one is able to glean information for themselves, but it may take a being more than one lifetime. Even halfway through this process, when one's lower chakras are adequately balanced and their green heart chakra has been activated and actively being worked on, they not only may understand what stable happiness (contentment) is, but feel it, as it will be their state of being. This course not only assists you on this path, it also unearths a treasure trove of other knowledge and wisdom that offers a quickened pace along your journey.

Even when you have adequately balanced all your chakras and connect to your higher self and become aware of the Oneness, you won't be perfect or fully enlightened. It's impossible to be perfect or fully enlightened while incarnate in the 3rd density, so don't beat yourself up about your setbacks, and there will be many because you live on a planet where the things that aren't important are taught and socially conditioned to be the most important things in life. Some of you are aware of this, if not consciously, unconsciously; either way, it promotes discontent and apathy as one's years go by. The carefree child all too often becomes a discontent or dispassionate adult when exposed to distorted experience after experience in a non-nourishing society. The pace of this effect has been accelerated in recent times, which will be explained.

Besides the big three questions that we focus on in this introduction, the other topics related to the big three questions in this intro are only briefly covered, or not at all; they, along with certain terms you may not fully understand, are covered and expanded upon within the many subjects and topics throughout this course. Some of these topics won't even be covered until 103 educational levels because learning—as well as un-learning the many falsities taught in your Earthly societies—requires a step by step process, where the steps ascend and allow you to expand your awareness.

Knowledge needed to begin your journey of going inside yourself and connecting with the information you seek is also eventually covered. Of course it'll take a considerable amount of time and dedication to get there, but no teacher or guru is a worthy guide if they don't intent to prepare you and lift you up to where they reside so you no longer need to rely on them and can be spiritually self-sufficient. Those who say you'll always need them as a guru, teacher, preacher, etc. should be avoided, as they are human beings caught up in the illusory game of feeding their ego by using others to do it, or practicing selfish actions disguised as altruistic actions, sometimes even mentally deceiving themselves about their motives.

Understanding the human condition is key to offering assistance. Let me use an example to convey how understanding the human condition is of the upmost importance if one wants to help themselves and humanity. Let's say you live on a planet that's very advanced spiritually and technologically. You decide to take an altruistic mission to another planet that's behind yours in its spiritual advancement. You are advanced enough to scan the planet and instantly learn their languages, but you can't just land your spacecraft and start teaching them due to the potential fear factor of such contact. Even though you know their language, you can't effectively teach them until you understand their ways of life, society, and mindset, because you won't be able to use analogies, metaphors, and comparative topics they are familiar with in order to help them understand topics they're not familiar with, nor will you be able to construct sentences that are easily understood. You need to know their mental struggles and dispositions in order to know how you can best assist them. Not only do you need to know all this, but you have to live among them and live their ways yourself firsthand as one of them in order to truly experience what they experience from an unbiased viewpoint. Only then can you truly understand them and know how to best assist them. This has been the problem when 3rd density beings—Earthlings in this case—channel information from higher-density beings. Even though higher-density beings are advanced enough to use Earth languages to share information, their information almost reads like a different language because they don't know how to properly use vocabulary, sentence structure, or use analogies and metaphors to be effective. Even if they did, they still wouldn't be effective without living among the beings and knowing the aforementioned things. Therefore, 4th, 5th, and 6th density beings take on the mission to incarnate back down on 3rd density planets—Earth being one of them—to assist in the growth of awareness, especially during pivotal times like now. They have been called wanderers. But I'm getting ahead of myself; we'll talk about wanderers in a later subject.

Before closing this introduction, even after all that has been stated, I reiterate that you should discern for yourself what is true and what is not; be a freethinker. Telling you to mindlessly believe the information in this educational course would make me no different from the unconscious controlling authorities on Earth.

Now that we are done with the introduction, let's cover the big three questions.

101.2 – Is there a God, and if so, What is God?

You have most likely lived enough years on Earth to have formed an opinion on this topic through religion, science, or other forms of social conditioning. Some human beings have a rigid idea whether God exists and what is God. So much has been invested and distorted in the label "God" that it would be better not to use this label. Instead we will use a label that is not so charged and does a more accurate job at explaining what we are talking about. Labels like the All, Oneness, the Great Central Sun, the One Beingness, or Source are all more useful terms because they already describe what God is: everything. We typically use the labels "Oneness" or "Source" instead of "God" for this awareness-expanding course, but they are also just words, just labels.

Yes, God (Source) does exist, but what is Source? That is the real question. We are not here to tell you that what you have been taught in your specific way of life or religion is wrong. Rather, what human beings call enlightened beings have brought forward knowledge and wisdom that later was transcribed into different religions or ways of life by human beings were originally in collaboration and agreement. These higher-density beings incarnated on Earth at different time periods and within different geographical areas and cultures, so the language and customs of the place were used to teach the same knowledge and wisdom, but their words were either misinterpreted from the moment it left their mouths, translated to another language inaccurately, or had their meanings twisted by powerful individuals and groups throughout history in the name of control. Since religions were the most important aspect of a human's life in the past—and to some it still is—dictating what humans thought and how they lived their lives, naturally those who wanted power and control over others used religions to their advantage as a tool, because nothing controlled human beings more effectively than the "word of God".

If you disagree about what we are saying, that is understandable because much more needs to be explained regarding such an impactful subject. Religions and their origins are covered in a later subject. Right now we will stay on topic and answer the main question about what is Source/Oneness. Source is not an angry old man in the sky. Source is not a he or a she. Source is beyond gender or any dualistic aspect in the Cosmos. Source never judges or looks down upon you, as you are a part of Source. Everything is Source. There is nothing that is not Source/Oneness.

Freely, of their own volition, not forced, all beings seemingly fragmented from Source to play a part in the Cosmos, the methodical illusion. We say "seemingly" because even though it may appear like you are separate from Source, it is an illusion; at no time is anything separate from Source in reality, as everything is connected in Oneness. Everything from a human being, a plant, water, dirt, a planet, a sun, a rock, a table—everything is Oneness and is connected through the ether with Source, just like how all Internet-capable devices are invisibly connected to the global network via Wi-Fi. The global Internet being Source, Wi-Fi being the ether, and all beings and things being the Internet-capable devices in this comparison. In the Cosmos, the illusion, everything initially appears to be separate, but upon deeper analysis—which progressive, non-dogmatic science hypothesizes—we understand that everything is connected, whether it can be seen or not with the naked eye. So what appears to be fragments or parts of Source acting separately is an illusion. The separation is an illusion, but the illusion is necessary in order to have the experiences that Source is seeking through the countless roles It plays in the Cosmos. Nothing can be separate from Source, as everything is Source/Oneness, including you. The materials of Source are in every thing and every being—everyone and everything in the Cosmos. Even a table has some of this material. A table or any inanimate object is not a self-aware being like a human being, but it still has some of Source materials and is a part of Source or it would not be in existence.

When Source wanted to experience different roles and focal points of consciousness, Source, which is intelligent and infinite, had to use parts of itself because nothing but Source exists. The only building blocks to take from and use were from itself. You could picture Source as a big ball of clay. (More to reality Source would be an infinitely large ball of intelligently aware clay.) Pieces of the clay need to be taken from the big ball to create anything since nothing exists but the big ball of clay. And only in the finite physical world does it appear like the pieces of clay are separate from the whole. It only appears to the naked eye that there is not something in the metaphysical/unseen inner planes that is keeping a connection to all the seemingly separate pieces of Source in the physical outer planes. All rivers flow towards and are connected to the ocean.

In order for Source to experience something other than its natural blissful state of being that is love, joy, and peace, Source plays different roles like actors in a theatrical play. You may ask: "If you're in a blissful state full of love, joy, and peace, why would you want to do something else?" It is similar to a human being having a great meditation session that lasts many hours or days, but at some point they realize: "This is great, but now it is time to do or experience something else, something different."

Since Source's state of being is purely loving, joyful, and peaceful in an unending fashion, an illusion needs to be constructed to experience other states of being, an illusion where the pieces of Source have forgotten they are Source/Oneness. Since you are both a piece/spark of Source and Source at the same time (since the concept of time is an illusion, but we will get into that later), you can stay in touch with that loving, joyful, peaceful state of being while you are playing your part on the illusory game board in the Cosmos. You do this by staying present and keeping a portion of your awareness as Source inside yourself while you are doing whatever in the illusion.

This is not wishful thinking, as you are a part of Source that is connected to Source, which also makes you Source at the same time, so your true state of being is also love, joy, and peace; all discontent states of being are the illusion. This state of being of Source is more recognizable in children who have not lived long enough in a broken societal system that has skewed their reality into thinking that being discontent or dispassionate—or anything less than pure love, joy, and peace—is their natural state. Although, a child is full of energy, so they may not be peaceful at this stage, as any human parent knows. Once a being lives long enough and has enough experiences in a non-nurturing/broken society, they begin to bury their natural state of being that is love, joy, and peace until it is forgotten. Thus, the child who is full of life typically becomes the dispassionate adult at some point in adulthood.

You are what you think you are. Your state of being is what you tell it to be. The state of mind of most adults is a clear indicator that you are living in a broken societal system; meaning, a societal system that does not nurture and serve the planetary whole. You come onto this planet as a loving and joyful child and through the hardships of the broken societal system—that human beings collectively decided to create as their experience on Earth—a child ends up displaying the state of mind of your typical adult. If a child is not carefree, it is because their surroundings have been so harsh that they are starting to lose carefree feelings earlier than other children. As the dysfunctional societal system becomes more broken, one tends to bury their natural state of love, joy, and peace and becomes dispassionate younger in their age development.

Heaven and hell are not places, they are extreme states of mind you choose to experience while playing your part, as well as experiencing all the states of mind in between these two extremes. Higher-density beings conveyed this through channels or while they were incarnate on Earth as wanderers, but at some point or right from the beginning, as with many beliefs in religions, their meanings were misunderstood or twisted.

If you are going to play a sport or any multiperson game, you need many players to do it. You cannot do it with one player. So Source puts some of its essence in different players and even a smaller amount of its essence in the unconscious-of-self things like the field, ball, and such, and an experience is had. Since Source is everything, even the roles that make up the villains—"evil" human beings and other malevolent beings—are all Source as well. Remember, everything and every being is Source; there is absolutely nothing that is not Source. At the heart of the illusory game board there is a constant struggle between the forces of "good" and "evil", but all are sparks of Source. The Devil, Lucifer, or whatever or whomever cannot beat God because they are a part of God/Source. There is nothing that is not Source—no exceptions. The parts of Source on the game board playing the roles of the villains may be in control and winning at certain times on certain planets, just as the roles of Source playing the heroes may be winning, but either way, eventually all roles merge back with Source fully and all their experiences are collected by Source.

If you still do not understand exactly what God/Source is or think the explanations given so far are too basic, do not worry; as we move along, more is offered so that a greater understanding may be held. One cannot properly talk about the details of Source without first laying down the groundwork to comprehend Source/Oneness, like taking 101 courses in university before taking 102 courses and so on, but you will be offered quite a good understanding by the end of the 101 courses alone, which also build upon each other in sequential order. Even the sentence structure and terms used in this educational course are less simplistic as the subjects move along. Since Source is everything, all future topics covered in this awareness-expanding course further explain Source. Every topic offers a greater understanding of Source/Oneness, and in doing so, you understand yourself more, as you are a part of Source and Source in totality in a timeless state.

You may ask: "Why does Source do it?" That brings us to the next question: What is the purpose of life? Why did Source create the Cosmos? What is the point?

101.3 – What is the Purpose of Life?

There is a phrase you may have heard: As above, so below; as below, so above. This phrase is accurate. Even if you have not spent decades or lifetimes balancing your chakras up to stimulating your indigo (third eye) chakra to utilize the pathway through your violet (crown) chakra which grants access to the energy and mind of Source to more fully comprehend this phrase, you can still put enough of the countless available pieces of the grand puzzle together to recognize the reoccurring pattern and design by using this accurate and meaningful phrase: as above, so below; as below, so above. It means there is a correspondence between the physical outer planes and the metaphysical inner planes, and the microcosm mirrors the macrocosm, and the macrocosm mirrors the microcosm in all realms in existence. One finds the same or similar patterns and relations repeated in both the metaphysical inner planes and the physical outer planes, the invisible and the visible, the big and small things and functions in the Cosmos.

The golden ratio's spiraling shape can be seen in small things like shells and pine cones (microcosm) and is the same spiraling pattern of a hurricane and a spiral galaxy (macrocosm), all of which corresponds and comes from the spiraling shape of life-force energy, which flows in a manner depicted in the golden ratio. The layout of an atom (microcosm) with its nucleus, neutrons, protons, and electrons, resembles the layout of a solar system (macrocosm) with its stars, planets, dwarf planets, and debris. Just like the same basic functions of code can be seen repeated in a computer program, the basic codes of life are repeated throughout what can be seen and what cannot be seen in the Cosmos.

Let us use human beings—one of countless examples—as an example of the below and Source as the above. There is nothing more above or macro than Source, as It is everything. Everything is a microcosm of Source's macrocosm. When God created human beings in the image of God (paraphrasing the *Bible*), it means Source used parts of itself to create human beings, as well as the countless other things and beings in the Cosmos. We can see Source's image in the countless examples throughout the Cosmos—especially within self-aware beings like humans—because as above, so below; as below, so above.

Example: a human is having a profound meditation session where they are experiencing extreme peace, love, and joy for hours or even days, but at some point the human knows that the wise action is to get up and do something else because the human is aware that there is more to experience than meditation. Meditation is very important, but there are other things to do, be, and experience in life. Just as Source in its natural state of pure love, joy, and peace, could simmer in its own bliss for what could be an unfathomable amount of Earthly time before Source thinks: This is great, but let us try something else, something different to more fully understand myself and what I am capable of.

Let us say you have been home alone for months. You may keep enjoying your solitude, knowing you do not need anything outside yourself, but it would be fun to do something with friends. You decide to create a game, a board game, a sport, a multiplayer video game, a theatrical production, etc. to interact in different situations to learn, enjoy, be entertained, and to know yourself more fully by acting or deciding what to do in different situations you have never been in before. You do it because you like having new experiences. Human beings create games for enjoyment, entertainment, and learning because they are mirroring what Source does. After Source enjoys its blissful state of being for countless eons, Source decides to do something else to know itself more fully. Source puts itself in countless different roles and situations to see how It would react, and these experiences are revealing, enjoyable, educational, and entertaining at the same time.

Source wanting to know more about itself conveys the idea that Source does not know everything. Human beings are heavily programmed to believe that God/Source knows everything, but this is not the reality. Source does know every single minute detail within the Cosmos, not only in real-time but before the players know because Source is all players and of the nature of time in the illusion, but Source does not know everything outside of the Cosmos. What is outside of the Cosmos? The same thing that is inside the Cosmos: only Source, as Source is everything. There is nothing that is not Source. So the only thing that Source does not know fully is itself. What would a wise being do to learn more about itself? It would create experiences where It could not only learn more about itself, but enjoy the process of doing it at the same time. This enjoyment could also be seen as entertainment. Do you not enjoy being entertained? We can see that being entertained is one of the most enjoyable things for human beings. Just as human beings create a wide range of entertainment that includes all matter of light to dark material in all types of mediums, so does Source. Where do you think human beings got this attribute from?

The more comprehensive an experience or game is, the longer it lasts and the more knowledge of self is gained and the more entertaining it is. Human beings have created live action role play games that can be played day after day for years. Human beings create all kinds of games for entertainment and learning: card games, board games, video games, sports, theatrical plays, movies, fictional stories shared verbally or in books, etc. Human beings are mirroring Source because they are a chip off the old block.

Source creates the Cosmos. (How Source does this will be covered in a later subject.) The Cosmos, an infinitely comprehensive experience that offers countless eons of illusory time for entertainment and the chance to know itself more fully when It is experiencing countless different roles in an infinite array of situations.

Just like a human needs other humans to play its games, so does Source. But since Source is the only thing that exists, It rectifies this issue by using parts of itself to be all the players. All games, once they have been played for a while, can be changed a bit, made more comprehensive, fair, balanced, and difficult to ensure more fun, entertainment, learning, and discovery of self.

The Cosmos was not created all at once, it keeps being built upon. At first the players, the sparks of Source, were aware of themselves as being a part of Source and their connection to Source. There was no veil of forgetfulness in 3rd density at this point. These were some of the first solar systems created, and at some point variations were made in proceeding solar systems and galaxies to add aspects to the game that would make it more comprehensive, more enjoyable, and add more experiences that create more cause-and-effect scenarios to possibly reduce stagnation, which consequentially offers more learning while also quickening the pace back to Source. Source had the variations of its players, sparks of itself, forget that they were Source in totality and a part of Source at the same time, and so the veil of forgetfulness in 3rd density was imagined and applied to the mental projection of the Cosmos. This is why you only remember your current incarnation in each of your 3rd density incarnations. This variation in the Cosmos provided countless different experiences and situations to encounter. It allows Source to know aspects of itself much more fully. In this iteration, free will was also greatly expanded upon, which is covered in a future topic. One could consider this a major upgrade in the coding or engine of the illusory game within the Cosmos. As human beings are aware, a harder and more comprehensive game with a diverse range of experiences is more enjoyable, educational, and entertaining, especially in the long run. And most importantly, Source could know itself a great deal more from such a range of experiences It put itself into.

Now, let us look at a video game created by human beings to make it easier to understand Source's game/experience that human beings have labeled the Cosmos. The good old saying as above, so below; as below, so above will assist us yet again.

There are levels in a video game you progress through as you gain experience, overcome many challenges, and defeat the end boss for every level. You may ask: "But why do we need to have challenges and an evil end boss?" Because without them, you would not learn much and it would be quite boring. Imagine Mario blissfully skipping through fields of strawberries and stopping for an occasional picnic before he casually walks across the finish line at the end of every level, not even needing to see how high he can jump onto a pole at the end to assess what he has learned for that level. It would be quite meaningless and boring. Anyone would get bored of this game, most quite quickly. Players would express, "There is no point to this game! Why am I playing it?"

"Why does God allow such suffering and evil to exist?" many have asked. Do you understand now? Without challenges there is no growth, no change, no learning, less entertainment ... boring. You may say, "But I would be fine strolling through strawberry fields forever and having the occasional picnic here, there, and everywhere." Well, after a while you would get very bored of it and want to experience something different, even if the different thing was something deemed unpleasant for a period of time, because it is something different. However, God/Source does not create suffering on a planet. Human beings are given free will, and as co-Creators in the experience, they can choose to collectively and singularly create suffering. Human beings and all other sparks of Source may choose to create suffering; it is not forced upon any spark of Source. Unlike a big government, Source does not limit experiences by taking away everyone's free will and rights in a particular area because of the few, and the actions of these few are necessary for the experience to be effective.

Every level in a human being's video game could be seen as a sub-density in Source's cosmic game/experience. (We cover and explain how many densities there are and each aspect and goal of each density in a later subject.) In every level of a video game, just like in every sub-density, a certain amount of obstacles and challenges need to be overcome, lessons learned, growth acquired, and not letting the "evil" end boss stop your progression. (Players that make up the "good" and "bad" side and their roles are extensively covered in later subjects.)

You have heard or even uttered yourself at some point: "God, if you're really there and claim to care, why don't you come down and end suffering and make Earth a paradise?" or simply "God, why do you allow suffering to exist?" As we stated, Source does not create suffering; the collective on each planet may choose to create it for themselves. To expand on this idea, suppose a highly intelligent and creative human being put much thought into creating a game for a group of their friends to play. At some point in the game, the creator of the game is not going to halt the game and finish challenges for the players or interject and interact in any way because they would be ruining the game they created for the players. The players are able to create experiences they choose to have without being interrupted. What would be the point of making a game in the first place if you did that? In Source's perspective it makes even more sense why It would not intervene in its game, the Cosmos, because It is playing the game itself, as It is the pieces on the board game and the One that created the board. Source is doing itself a favor and is not going to ruin the experience for itself, which includes parts of itself, by intervening.

At no point does Source directly intervene in the cosmic experience, the illusory game board called the Cosmos. Help is given to players who need it and ask for it, but only from other players on the game board, whether they be in the same or of a higher density. And then there are the players who choose to play the roles to assist and guide every single player—both of which will be covered in a future subject. (Please be patient when we say material will be covered later, as this introduction would never end if we did not break the topics up into parts, and more importantly, most parts would not be understood or fully grasped unless preceding material is covered first.)

Source created the experience for you and itself to enjoy, play, and learn from. We say "you and itself" because Source is you and you are Source. Source is not going to ruin the game, the grand experience. Source ruining the game would not be a benevolent act, it would be quite the opposite. It would be robbing the players of their free will, which is the first and most important rule for the cosmic experience. For without free will, there is no experience to be had in the first place.

Source is not separate from you or any other being. To be more exact, there is no separate being called Source or God that created the Cosmos. Every being and thing is a part of Source and that is what constitutes Source. Before the Cosmos was made and experienced, all beings were Oneness with Source as Source and collectively created the Cosmos. Therefore, you and all other beings collectively created the Cosmos, and continue to co-create it as it is experienced. There is no separate being to blame for what happens on your planet or on any planet. If there was anyone to blame, it would be the collective of beings, which includes you, that took part in creating the Cosmos, or what happens on a planet. Your higher self, being more aware than the focal point that is your present consciousness, is pleased with Earth and the Cosmos because it understands the grand experience from a higher viewpoint. It would benefit an individual to cease pointing a blaming finger at some fictional being called God that is separate from the individual and become aware enough to know that they and the collective are Source and created the Cosmos. Typically, to not know this or not know it fully until later densities is how the experience was intentionally set up. Why we are revealing it now to you in 3rd density will be understood later.

Some of you may have been expecting some grand answer to the purpose of life or think we are belittling existence by calling it a mere game. The grand answers and experiences are all in the grand game, and we have merely labeled it a game for better understanding as it mirrors the games human beings create, but of course the cosmic experience is infinitely more comprehensive and profound than the best game a human being could fathom and create. If you had to apply a human label to explain existence in the Cosmos, a game would be the most accurate and revealing label. Although, the Cosmos is more like an infinite set of game boards that interact with each other in varying degrees and capacities. A player, a spark of Source, journeys through countless experiences and profundities before the player finishes the game, merging back with Source in their entire capacity. There is nothing more grand or profound than this journey, and if you were to understand only 5% of the Cosmos, you would not hesitate to agree.

The cosmic experience is infinitely more profound and awe-inspiring than living one life on Earth and then spending eternity in a place called heaven and hell. A single human being can create much better games than that, so of course Source would come up with a game that is infinitely more comprehensive, profound, entertaining, educational, and so on. If anything was blasphemous, it would be thinking Source could only create a game that is worse than a game a single human being could create. Having one life on Earth would be akin to having one try at a video game, only being able to play it once and then being judged for your single performance and being forced to spend forever in some ambiguous place called heaven or hell. That does not make much sense and even a neophyte would probably come up with something better. Such a statement might come across as condescending to some, but we are simply relaying reality. Human beings who make video games want you to play them over and over again for enjoyment, entertainment, to learn and get better at them. And when you are thoroughly done with it, you can play a different video game. The same is for the Cosmos: when you are finished with this Cosmos, you can play the next profound and entertaining cosmic game, or even play a major assisting or caretaking role in the present cosmic game before moving onto the next Cosmos/experience. And after that there will be another Cosmos (or whatever label besides "Cosmos" the entities playing it decide to call it), and so on into infinity. Source is infinite, so the act of knowing itself is also infinite. Thus, the experiences to do so are also infinite.

Some may say: "Well, if it's just a game and heaven and hell don't exist and God doesn't judge anyone, I can do whatever I want without repercussions." This assumption is incorrect. As you know, there are rules for every game so it can be fair and properly enjoyed by all its players. You cannot do whatever you want in a human-created game because the game would not function. In Source's comprehensive game, you can do whatever you want, but there are rules for the game and consequences for performing certain actions. The universal law of balancing energy, which humans have labeled karma, could be seen as one of the major rules of the game. Unlike the corrupt justice systems on Earth, the universal law of balancing has no loopholes and is all knowing, meaning no one gets away with anything. Everything that is in need of balancing will have to be balanced out at some point in a beings journey back to Source no matter what, and from your higher-self's viewpoint, it is not considered judgment, something to be feared, or a hassle; instead, it is seen as the right thing to do, an honor and a duty to set things right for what you have done to yourself. We say "yourself" instead of another because all are One in the Oneness, so what one does to another, they are also doing to themselves in the highest viewpoint. All are One being.

The kindergarten-like explanations presented in religions is why so many human beings in your current time have turned to science and have lost interest in religions that tout a holier than thou God, teach that human beings are insignificant sinners, and teach that you only live one lifetime. When humans lose interest in religions, they sometimes take the new viewpoint that God does not even exist. They are actually closer to the truth than the unrealistic God that is depicted in holier-than-thou-God religions, so their new viewpoint is understandable, but still incorrect. It is comical to hear a being say that God does not exist, because they, being a piece of God, would not exist if God did not exist.

As the saying goes: "Life is a journey, not a destination." The Cosmos provides the journey, and the destination is merging back with Source in full capacity. Source created the journey and offers all the experiences within it to enjoy, not to solely focus on the destination and ignore the journey. When one realizes the destination is the same place where one starts, the journey is the thing, the profound experience to enjoy. If you did not want to enjoy the journey, you would have never left the destination. But here you are, so you did choose to enjoy the journey.

Source creates each Cosmos to know itself more fully, and in doing so is also given enjoyment and entertainment. You, as a part of Source, willingly chose to play many parts, have many experiences—what you would label good and bad experiences—to learn and grow, and understand yourself more fully by playing a seemingly separate part of Source to understand itself more fully. As above, so below; as below, so above. As Source can only know itself more fully by looking into itself as pieces of the whole with free will, those pieces, or beings, can only know themselves more fully by having experiences and looking into themselves, which is observing oneself internally and doing the inner work.

This is the purpose of life, the grand journey, the profound cosmic experience. There are more specific purposes and goals in each density, which we will cover later.

101.4 – What Happens after Death?

There is no such thing as death, the idea that you cease to exist, leaving the physical for good and entering oblivion, or going to a mythical location called heaven and hell. The good news is: these concepts are incorrect. What human beings call death is simply a transition that is as natural as breathing. It has happened many times and will happen countless more times for every individual. Human beings fear what they do not understand. If you understand our words before this subject is through, you will know there is nothing to fear about "death". There is so much more possible pain and hardship to experience while living in a physical incarnation than after you "die" or even while you are "dying", so if you do not fear living, you definitely should not fear "dying".

The spirit is energy and energy cannot die nor be destroyed, it can only transition. The one known as Albert Einstein said, "Energy cannot be created or destroyed, it can only be changed from one form to another." A most accurate statement. Source is an awareness that uses intelligently conscious love energy to inspirit light, which makes all physical forms visible in the cosmic experience. You discard your 3rd density body after the transition as you would discard a car after utilizing it for a period of time. Both the 3rd density body and car are made up of the basic chemicals on your periodical table, nothing more, and they are recycled back to the planet where they came from, but your spirit and mind are never discarded and always reside in a type of physical body that is made up from the building blocks of the density or plane you currently reside in while you are in the Cosmos. When you transition, your spirit and mind simply utilize one of your other potential bodies. Your brain was merely the organ your mind utilized to make the 3rd density body function, but your mind is not your brain and continues on with you after the transition, as does your spirit. When a being eventually merges back with Source after countless incarnations and ascending the densities, the totality of their spirit and mind keep existing within the collective, but a physical body is not needed at that point. Thus, it is the mind and spirit of a being that

God/Source made human beings and all beings in the Cosmos in its image, not the physical body. The physical body is only necessary to experience the Cosmos.

We will explain the process of transitioning/dying. A feeling of coldness is felt right before one shifts out of the 3rd density body and into the etheric body, the 6th density body, which is the same form-making body used during "astral projection", which should be called etheric projection because it is the etheric body being utilized and not the astral body. The astral body is the physical body used in the 4th density. Those who first projected out of their 3rd density body thought they were utilizing the lighter 4th density body, which humans have called the astral body, so they mistakenly called the act astral projection. The etheric body is associated with the indigo (third eye or pineal) chakra. It is the form-making body and is the body that is always used in the metaphysical inner planes, which is where you go after transitioning/dying when you leave the physical outer planes. Your spirit and mind shift directly into the etheric body after you transition/die, leaving your 3rd density body. The etheric body is always used in the inner planes no matter what density you reside in.

Upon transitioning/dying, you automatically etheric project out of your 3rd density body. When the shift happens, a heavy weight is lifted, so it feels great. In the etheric body—which is not your spirit, but rather a much lighter physical body—you float out of and notice your 3rd density body, the body human beings simply call the physical body. Like all of your 7 potential physical bodies, the etheric body is physical but so full of love and light energy that its vibratory state is too high to be seen by 3rd density beings; it is automatically invisible to 3rd density beings. Your mind and consciousness are still intact as if nothing has happened. The shift is as painless and quick as the twinkling of an eye. Because there is no interruption in the streaming of your mind and thoughts, it usually takes one a moment to fully comprehend that they are still thinking and still themselves as they look down at their 3rd density body, the physical body that some human beings think is the only thing they are. From your floating etheric body, you look down and see the grieving human beings at the hospital or wherever you are. These human beings are devastated and frantic at your passing, but you feel great, so it might be a little confusing for you to see your loved ones or hospital workers in such a frantic state when you feel so good and know nothing is wrong. You may not fully comprehend that you are not in your 3rd density body anymore and wonder why they are so frantic, as you are all right and feel wonderful, having shed the illusory problems and worries accumulated in your 3rd density body. Then you notice the 3rd density body you used to inhabit and think: "Is that me? But how can that be me if I am here and looking at me, or is that what used to be a part of me?"

The transition can be painless. Pain is only felt for a period of time before exiting the 3rd density body if the human being's higher self wishes to feel pain to learn a lesson or experience it, like anything else in one's incarnation.

It is then your mind's perception as to how you transition to the inner planes, as the universe is mental, or of the mind. The tunnel of light is the standard approach for those who are not set on imagining another experience for the transition.

You may ask: "But what about the humans who have died and said they went to hell before they were resuscitated at the hospital?" That was their mental construct. If one believes strongly that they were naughty enough to go to hell, or gives much power to the idea due to fear of going to hell, they may go to their own mentally constructed hell, because hell does not actually exist unless you mentally create it for yourself. Beings, whose chosen role is to assist in the inner planes, make attempts and eventually mentally get through to the being and guide them out of their mental construct of a hell, much the same as when a being is stuck on the Earth surface planes as a ghost when refusing to enter the light, refusing to move on to the next phase of existence. There is always assistance in any case of need during the transition, as there are many beings whose role in the inner planes is to aid transitioning entities. Even if a being refuses to enter the light or move on and becomes a ghost, it does not mean they are stuck being a ghost forever; assisting inner planes beings will always be there and eventually mentally reach and guide the being to the inner planes so they can continue their journey.

If one strongly believes they will board a pirate ship that will bring them to the inner planes, that is what will happen. In the past, the boatman or ferryman was a mental construct many beings mentally created to cross over to the inner planes because they were used to unknown lands across the vast oceans which were reached by boat. When they transitioned/died they were entering an unknown land and so mentally constructed a boat to do so, as was fitting for them. The tradition of putting coins over the eyes to pay the boatman is silly, as coins or any financial system is no longer in play in the inner planes, or any physical density above 3rd density. The "boatman" has chosen this role and their reward is service to the Oneness. Financial systems are only used on 3rd density planets that are not spiritually developed enough to realize that such a system typically leads to a few enslaving the majority. The mental transitional journey is varied, but the destination is always the inner planes.

Within the tunnel of light—or however the transitioning being wants to mentally make their way to the inner planes—after one has been exposed to enough powerful love and light energy, the silver cord that attaches the etheric body to the 3rd density body is severed, officially ending that particular 3rd density incarnation. This same silver cord can be seen when one is temporarily etheric projecting out of their 3rd density body while incarnate.

The chemical elements used or borrowed from the planet to construct the 3rd density body are no longer inspirited with one's love and light signature and are returned to the planet. Like a book borrowed from a library and eventually returned, the book was never yours, only rented for a period of time to experience and learn. The returned chemical elements are now no different from any other chemical elements on the planet and have nothing to do nor hold any significance to the being that once borrowed it. Keeping or disposing these returned chemical elements to a particular place is spiritually meaningless. The transitioned being, no matter what their thoughts on the matter were while incarnate, no longer cares what happens to these returned chemical elements, as they now hold no more significance than the dirt that could be found anywhere on the planet. The mind and spirit move on and the physical matter than makes up the 3rd density body is abandoned and returned to the planet where it came from.

If it is not the proper time to transition yet, the transitioning being who is not set to transition yet goes back to their 3rd density body so the silver cord is not severed and they become conscious back in their 3rd density body again, resuscitated at the hospital, or wherever. The transitioning one might be told it is not their time yet by loved ones in their life that have already passed over, or by whomever greets them and tells them they had planned to experience more in that specific incarnation. Like waking up from a dream, the human being might remember the experience and be one of the countless human beings to tell their life after death experience.

This is a life-changing experience because the individual now knows there is life after "death", it feels great, and there is nothing to fear about it. Scientists might tell these human beings that their near-death experience was only an imaginary trip from the body releasing chemicals like endorphins, serotonin, or DMT to ease the transition into death, which they may believe is nonexistence. This scientific theory does not matter to the near-death experiencer because having experienced it firsthand, they simply know that it was real. It may be a negative life-changing experience to the individual that creates a mental hell for themselves, as they may think hell exists and that is where they would have gone. Although, this can turn out to be a beneficial life-changing experience as well if the individual strives to change their ways in their incarnation to avoid such a destination since they are not aware it was only a mental construct.

Regarding the silver cord that attaches the 3rd density body to the 6th density etheric body: the silver cord cannot be broken by malevolent beings or by mistake, so one need not produce fear in it intentionally or accidently being severed. Think of it more as an etheric cord rather than a physical cord that can be snipped like an umbilical cord. So whether in a transitioning state or practicing etheric projection, you do not need to worry about the silver cord being severed before it is your time. The silver cord assures that there is still a portion of one's spirit and mind in the 3rd density body while one is occupying their 6th density etheric body. Etheric projection typically happens spontaneously due to experiences and abilities acquired in past incarnations. It is typically not an experience one can learn by merely meditating in their bed. Human beings interested in relearning etheric projection may find The Gateway Experience by Robert Monroe to be beneficial. Again, most human beings are not able to learn to etheric project unless they have a rare past incarnation experience and are relearning the ability, but this audio-guided experience by the wanderer known as Robert Monroe offers mental and audio techniques that provide a high probability for one to expand their awareness to some degree and deepen their meditation and mental-focusing skills, which is an important achievement in itself, as meditation and mental focus are fundamental for progression.

If a human being has a strong belief they will meet a particular entity while transitioning, that being's energy signature will be there to guide them through the transition to the inner planes. If a human being strongly believes they will meet Jesus, Buddha, or any other higher-density being, they will. At least, they meet the projected energy signature of that being. Being of positive polarity, such beings are pleased to be of service.

There are always beings to greet you while transitioning. If it is not the pre-incarnate planned time for transitioning, there may be a slight delay in the greeting, but it always happens. You will be assisted; there is nothing to fear or worry about in regards to transitioning. You might meet a being you had no contact with in the incarnation you just lived, but as the veil of forgetfulness lifts and past incarnations are recalled, you remember who they are and all your experiences with them as past incarnations come flooding back into your consciousness from your subconscious mind, where they are stored all along. Regression hypnotherapy may be used to remember these past lives while still incarnate.

During the tunnel of light, or whatever the mentally chosen transition method, a being goes as far into the love and light energy of Source as they are comfortable, meaning they climb the ladder of sub-densities and possibly densities until the love and light energy of Source becomes too powerful for their current state of consciousness. Where they stop climbing is the sub-density the being has so far advanced to on their journey back to Source. You may think of it like an elevator ride where you are automatically let out on the correct floor of the inner plane's sub-density level that aligns with your current advancement, or grade level so to speak.

Next, the being heals in what has been called the void or the deep resting place to transmute built-up traumatic energy stored from intense or emotional experiences during the last incarnation. The being rests there until the traumatic energy is distilled and transmuted. The more trauma, the longer the rest in the deep resting place. You may think of it as the most comfortable bed in existence. Just as one may relinquish troubles from day-to-day living by sleeping every night, the deep resting place relinquishes built-up traumatic energy from a whole incarnation/lifetime. It is a releasing of unneeded strong emotions from traumas and intense experiences and is collected by Source.

Nothing of value is lost during the transition, or at any time on one's journey back to Source, or when one merges back with Source. A being does not lose their spirit, mind, experiences, or their personality/character. Though, a being's personality continues to grow and change throughout incarnations in all the densities infinitely more than how much a being's personality changes during growing from a child to an adult during a single incarnation. Beings retain all that is needed, as that is what Source and every part of Source intends. Why would Source send a part of itself to have experiences to know itself more fully and then delete the mind with all its experiences? That would make no sense and be counterproductive. Each spark of Source is a part of Source and so cannot become nonexistent, and every single experience is gifted and collected by Source. Using your computer references may assist with this understanding: Think of each experience as data that is stored on Source's infinite databank. Since there is infinite space and every piece of data assists Source at knowing itself more fully, there is no reason whatsoever to delete any experience, no matter how insignificant or terrible it may seem to beings who have not merged back with Source.

After the deep resting in the void, and before the learning and planning for one's next incarnation, another resting period is spent in the inner planes that matches one's level of awareness so they can acclimate to their new surroundings and to simply take a conscious resting break, a relaxing vacation so to speak. This break time will be expanded upon later in this subject.

After the being adjusts to its new state in the inner planes and has had their vacation-like break, they go to the school grade level they are advanced enough to reside in. Like grade levels in Earth schools, one cannot skip to a grade where things are taught that are not understood or only partially grasped. Each level has an adequate amount of advanced beings to teach, guide, and assist with planning for one's next incarnation. Just as you are currently playing the role of experiencing incarnations on a certain planet in the physical outer planes, some of these beings are currently playing the role of guide or teacher in the metaphysical inner planes. You may choose to be one of these guides or teachers at some point along your journey back to

Source. Some of these beings assisting in the inner planes have never personally experienced a physical incarnation in the outer planes, and may never do so. There are countless roles to play and experience in the grand cosmic experience.

The inner planes beings, who specialize in objectively viewing the life lived and assist you at understanding experiences in regards to growth and what can be done to balance karma and progress in your next incarnation, lovingly and willingly aid the Oneness by serving/assisting in this capacity. Besides the inner planes beings, the most assistance comes from one's higher self, which is their future self. There is no judgment whatsoever. No being in the inner planes judges you or shames you for anything you have done. Even the one known as Adolf Hitler was not judged. We use this example because this being is well known for the widespread death and suffering he caused, and to reiterate that no being is judged no matter how much suffering they caused. No being is ever judged, punished, shamed, or shown anything less than loving-kindness, even if they have generated a lot of karma to balance out. The only being who might judge you is you in your lower focal point of awareness, and doing so would serve no purpose as it does not assist you in balancing your karma.

Some beings choose to transition/die in groups in order to deal with group karma. What appears to be a great accident, natural disaster, or otherwise, can be used by these groups to accomplish the plans they set up before incarnating, their pre-incarnate plans.

An individual may think: "This is all great to know. Thank you. Now that I understand it and you make it sound so great, I'm going to go commit suicide now. Bye." The transition need not be feared, but there is nothing to gain from committing suicide. It only creates more karma and adds lessons to be learned, creating more work instead of less. One does not avoid anything with suicide; instead, they make more work for themselves because they have to learn the lesson of fortitude, seeing an incarnation through on top of the other lessons they prepare for themselves for their next incarnation. They are not judged for committing suicide, but they have to go back and do it all again anyway, compounded with adding the lesson of fortitude, which is usually learned in a suffering incarnation that a being also wishes to leave. They return to that which they so desperately fled.

Of course, at any time one can do the inner work and abandon the suffering in any incarnation. It is not an experience they have to have for the entire incarnation.

A being plans out each incarnation for specific reasons, even what can be perceived as an incarnation filled with strife has a reason. An incarnation with much strife gives one the opportunity to balance out a lot of accrued karma. It benefits one to leave when they planned on leaving in the plan they set up before their current incarnation. "But I have free will, you can't stop me. And if no one will judge me, sounds like a winner to me. Where's that razorblade?" Yes, you have the free will to do it and no one will judge you, but as stated already, it is not an easy way out, as you will only be creating more hard work for yourself the next go around, prolonging and adding to the suffering instead of cutting it short. You are not getting out of anything, as you will be going right back into a similar type of life so you can learn the lesson of fortitude.

2nd density beings like insects, plants, trees, animals, and such, automatically reincarnate without partaking in the preparation for the next incarnation, as they are conscious/aware beings but not self-aware beings yet. Early 3rd sub-density human beings who are still working on base lessons like fear and the mental pain threshold only need a very small preparation in the form of advice offered and automatically reincarnate. For 3rd density beings who are past the early sub-density stages—beings who have at some point activated the heart chakra—they prepare and learn in the inner planes for their next incarnation at what some have called the School of Knowledge, so we will use this label from here on to refer to it.

In the inner planes, one thoroughly goes through their last incarnation with a more detached and unbiased viewpoint to assess everything: reactions to stimuli, mental and emotional effects from experiences and how they were handled, actions taken and why, one's motivations, attitude toward experiences, how one handled victories and defeats, did one recognize their faults or did they use self-deception to justify their actions?, did one help others when the appropriate opportunities arose?, did one think for themselves?—everything is covered.

If one has a question or wants further guidance on a certain matter, one of the guides assists in that area. One's higher self has more experience to draw from and can view one's incarnation with even more removed objectivity. As we stated, no shaming or judgment is ever made by these advanced beings; after all, they are advanced. Such negativity is realized and abandoned by beings who are finished with the 3rd density experience and have graduated to 4th density positive.

When it is all done, one has learned many lessons and is aware of the steps to be taken in their next incarnation to balance karma and continue spiritually progressing as a being, a spark of Source. The guides aid at matching beings up with other beings who will interact with each other in the next incarnation. One may incarnate with the same beings over and over again because of the built-up karma acquired in past incarnations. You may be their child in one incarnation and their parent in another. The greater good for all beings is worked out and plans are made that give you the opportunities to balance karma and learn lessons to grow in awareness.

Just as the being, the spark of Source, was not forced to seemingly separate from Source to initially play roles in the Cosmos, nothing is forced upon a being during these planning stages for their next incarnation. One never has to experience anything they did not agree upon. That may sound like a surprise in your current focal point of awareness, especially if you are not enjoying your present incarnation, but your higher self is not surprised in the least. Since balancing karma is part of the requirement for progression, and every being is aware they want to progress while in the inner planes, experiences and situations are willingly signed up for so that spiritual progression may occur and the next sub-densities or density be reached.

Every being wants to advance, so they choose plans or willingly accept the recommendations given from the more experienced, advanced beings assisting them, even if the challenges planned for their next incarnation are significant. One does not remember their pre-incarnate planned challenges and goals after being incarnated into 3rd density because of the veil of forgetfulness placed upon 3rd density and to avoid abridging free will. It would be too easy and boring if one remembered their goals and mission. If one remembered and consciously adhered to a step-by-step plan all along the way, that would be infringement upon free will, and also make for quite a dispassionate player on the game board of life, knowing what is going to happen and what to do about it all along the way. This would not create the experiences needed to assist Source's knowing of itself more fully, and so therefore would be seen as holding little value, as well as lacking in enjoyment, entertainment, and true growth for the spark of Source.

If a human being is born with a defect of some kind, or has an accident during an incarnation that leaves them paralyzed from the waist down or some other debilitation, they are not aware they may have planned for it to happen before incarnating, and if one enlightened them to this reality, they would most likely get mad and say: "Why would I choose this suffering, this horrible situation for myself? God must hate me!" or "There isn't a God because why would God allow this to happen to me!"

Sometimes a being makes a pre-incarnate plan to have a disability—like losing the ability to walk or see—if they stray down a certain non-positive path. This is a way to balance accrued karma within the same incarnation, a pre-set balancing plan only to be set off in an incarnation if triggered.

If a being accepts their unchangeable situation, their temporary limitations, forgive other human beings who might have had a hand in it, abandon their victimhood and/or anger and live life to the fullest despite their circumstances, much karma is balanced out, much growth is made. Think of these incarnations or periods of an incarnation as an opportunity for much growth instead of looking at them as a punishment for deeds in a past incarnation; as we have stated, there is no judgment or punishment along a being's journey back to Source, only the need to balance karma. If other human beings treat you poorly due to your disability because they think you deserve what you got in this incarnation because of your deeds in a previous life, or they are simply being unkind, their actions toward you may generate karma for them. Forgive them and ignore their negativity while accepting your temporary limitations at the same time, as they know not what they do or say. It is possible that these adverse situations may also have been pre-incarnate planned with these other beings so that one's karma may be balanced out.

This balancing of energy and experiences human beings have labeled karma exists for two reasons: 1: It is a cosmic rule that ensures all players play fair before the end and do not ruin the overall game experience for other players. 2: Since all players, sparks of Source, are in reality One being—the Oneness/Source—doing anything negative to another player is the same as doing it to oneself and that oneself needs to make up with themselves before the experience is finished because one cannot exist in totality with themselves—merged back with Source—without doing such.

The debate of whether nature or nurture shapes a human being in an incarnation is one example of many similar debates where both sides are seen as one in a higher-density viewpoint where dualism, paradoxes, or functions are known to be part of the same mechanism. This dualistic debate is very similar to that of pre-incarnate plans (destiny) and free will. Nature is the sum total of all one's incarnations. Nurture, those beings and experiences that have a hand in it, might have been pre-planned or an act of free will. Nurture can play a large role in an incarnation if one allows it to, and one's nature is typically what grants it to or not. Once one has expanded their awareness adequately, the argument of nature versus nurture, and so many other dualistic thoughts based on confusion, fall by the wayside as truth is found on both sides and is rather part of the same function instead of being opposing ideas.

The Earthly saying, "You can't choose your parents" or "You can't choose your children" is inaccurate. In the planning for your next incarnation, you do choose your parents, and they choose you. And as we stated, the roles could be reversed in a different incarnation. All is agreed upon and planned in advance once you make it past the early stages of the 3rd sub-densities. One chooses their family, friends, lovers, rivals, and all in their incarnation that offers possible growth and spiritual progression. Life is not random chances of occurrences. Though, because of the universal law of free will, chance in circumstances is always a possibility. Without the universal law of free will, all pieces on the multilayered chessboard would move automatically in a predetermined way and not much would be learned for Source to know itself more fully, and the sparks of Source would not find the experience that enjoyable, entertaining, and so on.

If a human being continues putting off their pre-incarnate major plans or mission due to free will, their spirit guides, and the spirit guides of other human beings whether it is a group plan or not, orchestrate serendipitous circumstances to offer the human being(s) the opportunity to get on the pre-set path. Every incarnation is a dance of pre-incarnate planning (destiny) and free will.

One may ask: "If you learn the lessons in the inner planes, why incarnate in the outer planes to learn them again?" One needs to experience and live the lessons, not just know them. If one reads a book about enlightenment and says, "That makes sense, I agree with that. I'm enlightened now," and then goes out into the world making the same mistakes and not living what they learned, what they agreed with, it would not matter much would it? Knowing can be powerful, but only applying and practicing it in one's life offers liberation and grants true growth.

—∞—

We will expand upon what a 3rd density being experiences in the inner planes after transitioning/dying. Human beings are merely one example of the countless versions of beings currently in 3rd density. We will present three generalizations of what happens in the inner planes for 3rd density beings: the early/lower, the middle, and the later/upper sub-densities. There are 7 sub-densities within every density, thus, 3rd density has 7 sub-densities within it.

Some of the beings who are meant to go to the early inner planes temporarily get stuck on the Earthly plane as ghosts and hang around low-level activities that emanate low-level energies. These are activities and energies they engaged in and created while they were incarnate. They are still craving and wanting certain vices to the degree that they strongly feel they have unfinished business or wants on Earth. They hang around incarnate human beings who have similar wants and cravings, soaking up the energy and living out the experiences vicariously. They hang around heavy drug users, heavy drinkers of alcohol, rape and lustful activities (orange-ray and yellow-ray chakra sexual acts), violence, murder, etc. They have been called hungry ghosts in some Asian cultures. In these cultures, the practice of offering them food or performing other acts is useless, especially burning material that pollutes the air the beings breathe. To avoid them is simple: do not perform the acts we have listed or similar negative acts and they will not be drawn to you or the locations where you dwell.

Some of these ghosts are aware they have started the transition away from their last incarnation but are postponing the transition to the inner planes for a number of different reasons.

Some of these ghosts are not fully aware they have transitioned and left their last incarnation and are so focused on the physical Earthly planes and the repeating situation they are locked into that they are not aware of the spirit guides trying to assist them to the inner planes. At some point they will recognize they have left the Earthly physical plane and the assisting guides are there to guide them to the inner planes so they can reincarnate.

When ghosts have had enough or at least realize they are not getting enough gratification in experiencing the cravings voyeuristically, they are guided to the inner planes to reincarnate. Since they are still in the early 3rd sub-density planes, their preparation time is considerably shorter than those beings who have passed the early 3rd sub-density stages. In comparison, these early 3rd sub-density beings reincarnate automatically, as the lessons they are still facing do not take much explaining or preparing.

These particular early 3rd sub-density beings are only one type of ghost scenario. Sometimes the spirit guides of an incarnate human being work with a loved one who has recently transitioned so the transitioned loved one can appear as a projected echo in the physical planes to deliver a parting message they feel is important. Some transitioned beings may do this to comfort the one they have left so they will stop grieving. A certain period of grieving for missing a being one is close to is understandable, but heavy, continual grieving can hold a transitioned being closer to the physical Earthly plane and hinder their progression. Strong continual grieving is a hindrance for both the griever and the one being grieved over. We understand a close loved one is missed, so we offer these words: Displaying a level of sadness for a period of time for missing the company of another being is understandable and fine, but know that there is no reason to be sad for the transitioned being, as they are very well in the inner planes and doing as they intended, continuing their journey. To continually grieve strongly is seen as selfish because it hinders the grieved-over being's progression. Some human beings choose to celebrate one's life in positivity instead of having a somber ceremony after their transition. This we align with because it makes sense and is positive for all beings, incarnate and disincarnate.

Another ghost scenario is when a being dies suddenly and is mentally confused about their current state. If it was not the pre-incarnate planned time or way for transitioning/dying, the being's subconscious mind, knowing it planned more time for balancing karma and achieving goals, may temporarily lock the conscious mind into a loop. A comparison would be when a human being is having a nightmare or an agitated dream and they partially wake up and toss and turn and go right back into the same or a similar agitated situation in the next dream or a continuation of the same dream. The mind is caught between the subconscious and conscious state in an agitated loop where negativity is charged and played out. As with all ghost scenarios, guides eventually reach these beings mentally and they make their way to the inner planes to reincarnate, just as the human being eventually wakes from their nightmare(s).

Early 3rd sub-density beings who do not get caught up as shells of their physical selves—ghosts—on the Earthly physical plane go directly to the quick preparation and automatically reincarnate back into 3rd density. There are libraries for learning in the inner planes for these early 3rd sub-density beings, but they are not visited much, as the beings on this plane typically do not gravitate toward such type of learning material.

Now we will cover the beings who go to the middle 3rd sub-density inner planes after they transition. They are past the early stages of the 3rd sub-density experience so they have much more learning and preparing to do for their next incarnation. Their experience is the same as already mentioned—they are greeted at the start of the death transition, heal in the deep resting place, take a vacation-like break in their particular sub-density inner plane, and guides assist them in reviewing their last incarnation and they learn and prepare for their next incarnation. Middle 3rd sub-density beings acclimate to the inner planes while taking a vacation-like break in settings they were used to on Earth. They rest and relax in a house where the interior is entirely constructed by their imagination; after all, the universe is mental. Their house may overlook a lake or something pleasant, or reside in a nice suburban setting. They may spend time there with family and friends. Time does not exist in the inner planes, as the inner planes are situated in time in space rather than the physical outer planes which are moving through space in time. If karma needs to be balanced out with beings still incarnate, the disincarnate being may vacation or learn until the beings they have accrued karma with have transitioned into the inner planes as well.

Eventually guides pay them a visit at their vacation-like areas and nudge them to start preparing for their next incarnation. Eventually they are persuaded to start preparing for their next incarnation in order to progress and continue their journey back to Source.

The libraries in the School of Knowledge in the middle 3rd sub-density inner planes provide books for learning any topic that is useful for the being. Unlike books on Earth, these books are activated by thought, going straight to the topic or lesson that the being is mentally seeking. One of these books that has gained notoriety on Earth by those who are able to etheric project and visit this library while still incarnate is the Book of Life, which is more well-known on Earth in some circles as the "Akashic Records". Lives and events can be looked up and used for examples in learning a specific lesson, topic, or experience. This offers the being an example they can draw from that helps them understand a similar experience or situation from their last incarnation and/or to prepare for their next incarnation. All beings' incarnations are recorded in the Book of Life. Each specific being's section in the Book of Life has been called their little book. When the little book is studied and digested, it may taste both bitter and sweet, as are the positive and negative actions one performed in their incarnations.

Now we will cover the beings who go to the later 3rd sub-density inner planes after their transition. As already covered, they are greeted in their transition, heal and rest in the deep resting place, have a vacation-like break, and then learn and prepare for their next incarnation. They do not need as much time acclimating to the inner planes because they have done it enough times, but time to rest and decompress is still useful before preparing for one's next incarnation. Their living conditions during their vacation-like break are akin to the wondrous locations on Earth: views of gorgeous mountains, deep canyons, oceans, waterfalls, grand lakes, etc.

Their School of Knowledge is more complex because they are ready for more advanced learning and preparation. Besides books and other learning material, viewing rooms are available—a room where the being can more thoroughly view their past life and prepare for their next incarnation by also viewing parts of other beings' lives that are relevant for learning lessons and concepts. This is much like utilizing the Book of Life, but more advanced concepts are able to be conveyed and learned, and done in a more immersive manner. It is like a room with a full circle wrap-around visual screen where one can jump to any time in others or one's life or display visual concepts to be explained. One's higher self assists in utilizing viewing rooms and aiding in explanations and understanding learning concepts.

Since 3rd density beings who are in the later stages of the 3rd sub-density experience cover higher concepts and create more advanced learning plans, they require more sophisticated tools to adequately learn and be prepared. They have these tools available to them for this reason, not because they are superior to early or middle 3rd sub-density beings. No being is superior or more valuable than another; all beings are seen as equal parts of Source in the Oneness on their journey back to Source, back to the totality of themselves. A being's particular focal point of awareness may be further along the path back to Source than another, but that does not make a being superior to another.

Again, the School of Knowledge in the later 3rd sub-density inner planes is more expansive, as learning and preparing for higher concepts requires more preparatory settings, materials, and tools. It has lush gardens with foliage that far surpass even the most prestigious university campuses or the most beautiful parks on Earth. There are many different complexes to visit in these inner planes—many different rooms, buildings, and facilities. One that is notable is the Tapestry room. The Tapestry could be seen as the most brilliant piece of art ever to grace a museum. It continues horizontally down the hall, being lit up from light flooding through windows on the opposite side of the hall. It is quite expansive. Within the spiritual Tapestry is a thread-like cord for every being who experiences a 3rd density incarnation on a certain originating planet during its grand cycle and that group or wave of beings' continued spiritual progress is recorded on it throughout the higher densities no matter what planets these group of beings may reside on in their journey back with Source. Each possibility/timeline has its own Tapestry. A being's thread is seen to entangle with other beings' threads that had a connection or some type of shared experience. If a being is very influential and has a hand in many other beings' experiences, their thread can be seen interacting with many other threads and can be thicker. The color of one's thread-like cord is also an indicator of one's vibration, their development.

Even those still incarnate can visit these inner planes via etheric projection if their vibration—current grade level in the Cosmos school—allows them access. Rooms and facilities can be accessed, like the libraries, healing rooms, Temple of Light, Temple of Wisdom, Tapestry room, and gardens, but some places are off limits to etheric projectors, as it is appropriate for some things to be kept secret while one is currently incarnate. The caretakers and guides can recognize that you are etheric projecting while still residing in a 3rd density physical body because they can see your silver cord trailing off to your 3rd density body; it has not been severed yet like those who are currently disincarnate. Besides this indicator, the caretakers and guides simply know if you are currently incarnate or disincarnate because your aura is completely visible to them like an open book. You are only allowed in the Tapestry room and other rooms if your vibration permits it, automatically granting you access. The Tapestry room caretakers greet you with loving-kindness and answer your questions, but they know it is not in your benefit to look into your future, so they do not permit you looking at your thread-like cord into your future. This would infringe upon your free will and could alter your perception of the future, thus possibly changing your choices in your current incarnation.

Tapestry caretakers have light-energy crystals that interact and light up different threads on the Tapestry to assist in teaching about different incarnate experiences, scenarios, and events. If you were to see the end of the Tapestry, it would be a brilliant shining white, as white is the color of all the color spectrums combined into One when the group of beings merge back with Source.

Books in the libraries for these inner planes are as mentioned already: they are not like books on Earth you have to flip through manually, but are rather accessed mentally and open up to what you want to view or learn. Your vibration determines what you have access to in books. This is for your own benefit and is not a stringent hierarchical system that limits knowledge like a caste system on Earth does. It is like the school system on Earth, but every being raises their vibration and graduates grades based on their own motivation and chosen speed. A third-grader is simply not shown university-level material because they are not ready to properly digest or learn it yet. If a being wants to experience 3rd density for a much longer period than other beings, it is absolutely fine and as it should be. Free will creates variation for a reason. An Earthly caste system attempts to keep groups of human beings in the same place permanently and actively works against their progression instead of for it. A caste system is one of many methods negatively oriented 3rd density beings utilize to keep others under them in a controlled pecking order.

We end this subject with a return to the video game analogy to assist in explaining the 3rd density experience in the Cosmos. As when you play a video game on your console of choice at home, after you die in the game, an inexperienced player jumps right back into the game and tries again with little thought or planning as to what they are going to do differently, maybe only quickly taking into account one specific challenge or obstacle needing to be overcome.

After a more advanced video game player dies, they take more time to contemplate their errors and think more deeply into strategies that may be used to get further in the game before dying. Even though they develop a plan, sometimes with the help of another human who has already beaten the level they are playing, it does not always work out as planned while playing the game again. These other players on the sidelines offering tips on how to succeed are like spirit guides—which we will talk about in a later subject—but most of the time the player is so wrapped up in the game that they do not hear the advice or understand it.

All this is strikingly similar to what happens in 3rd density, which is also played over and over again till graduating to 4th density, then onward progressing through all the densities, and eventually the cosmic experience is finished and the player merges in full capacity back with Source after their high vibration grants them access to traverse a black hole within the Cosmos. And that is not the end of it; one does not simply bliss out as Source forever at that point. This would become boring. There is no end, the experiences are infinite, as Source is infinite. Just as the video game player enjoys a different game after they have finished one, a being may enjoy the next Cosmos. There are always more experiences to be had, either in the outer planes, or inner planes where one can assist other sparks of Source in their journey, or have a caretaker or creative role in a local, galactic, or universal Council. Doing so would be akin to the video game player enjoying a particular cosmic game so much that they replay it in a certain fashion or capacity to assist others who have not beaten the game yet. When the being wishes to move on to the next cosmic game, or move onto the next expansive cosmic game directly after finishing one, they do so. As Source is infinite, the amount of Cosmoses to be experienced, enjoyed, entertained by, and learn from is infinite. Source is infinite, so learning about itself more fully is infinite, the process never ends.

Look at how many different video games have been created on Earth, or all the diverse amount of entertainment human beings have created on Earth; Source creates infinitely more than that for itself to play, enjoy, and learn from. As above, so below; as below, so above. Just as there are countless experiences to be had on Earth, there are endless experiences to be had in your infinite existence. Source is infinite, and since you are a spark of Source and Source at the same time in a timeless state, you are also infinite. You will never stop existing. "Death" is only a change of experiences, a transition from one experience to another. Let go of the weight that is the fear of death and allow yourself to fly while incarnate. Best to unshackle the illusory chains of fear that keep you a prisoner of your own mental making.

Before the Cosmos you are experiencing now, there was a previous grand cosmic experience created by Source. After the Cosmos you are currently experiencing is finished, there is another different grand cosmic experience to enjoy and progress through. There is no end to the enjoyment, no end for Source to know itself more fully through infinite experiences. The duration of each cosmic experience by Source and merging back with itself—the expanding creation and the eventual coalescing—could be seen as Source exhaling and then inhaling, over and over again. One mere exhale and inhale from Source is experienced as unfathomable eons of time for the players, the sparks of Source in each cosmic experience.

101.5 – The Creation & Structure of the Cosmos

Human beings used to think planet Earth was flat before finding out it was spherical because it looked flat from their vantage point of standing on the surface. Spiral galaxies like the Milky Way galaxy may be spread out on a mostly flat-like disc area and may seem to be moving in its entirety in a straight line or plane through space, but they are traveling along a topology shaped similar to an apple, which is the shape of the universe and is quite vast in size. The universe has a toroidal flow and pattern that is shaped like an apple—not a donut—with the seed of the apple being in the middle—the Great Central Sun, which became a black hole after completing the initial mental work of creating the original thought that is the Cosmos. All came into existence from the seed and all will eventually coalesce and return to the seed, which is Source.

The Cosmos, or each universe within it, is not the shape of a donut; this is misdirection/disinformation by negatively oriented beings. The Cosmos is the shape of an apple with a self-containing flow that is similar to what has been labeled on Earth a toroidal flow or pattern where spiraling energy moves continuously through the center and around its surface, with energy flowing endlessly inwards and outwards in a self-contained manner. Though, it is not only one continuously flowing direction like that in a donut shape; the electromagnetic field of the Cosmos, or each universe within it, is shaped like two superimposed apples where energy is spiraling and flowing in opposite directions. Within one apple shape, the flow of energy moves from the center seed to the top and fountains down around the surface to the bottom where it reverse fountains inward back to the seed and continues in this flow in a spiraling manner. The apple that superimposes the other flows in the same manner, but the energy flows from bottom to top. All love and light energy vibrates and spirals around these fields, arcing out in an expanding manner, reaching the outmost middle part of the field, and then arcing back in a collapsing manner as it journeys closer to moving through the center and back into the very middle where the concentration of Source resides before continuing on in a similar manner again. Some galaxies are closer to the center and some are farther away as they move through the apple-shaped universe. It is a closed system where all life-force is recycled, ever changing and shifting and never being wasted or destroyed. This is where the infinity sign originates from. All material is assembled by the dynamic tension of the electromagnetic fields of these two superimposed apple-shaped fields.

The same apple shape and flow of energy can be found in the electromagnetic fields around a galaxy, a star/solar system, a planet, and a human being. As above, so below; as below, so above. The electromagnetic field nurtures and protects everything within its apple-shaped field. The green-ray heart chakra of a human being resides in the middle of a human being's 7 chakra system and is comparative to the nurturing heartbeat of a star or a black hole—both of which are a Logos—that lies in the middle of a solar system or galaxy and up to the most macro example of the Great Central Sun Logos (which is now a black hole) in the middle of the universe, acting as the heartbeat for each universe within the Cosmos. Since these same flowing and spiraling apple-shaped fields make up the electromagnetic fields around a universe down to being around a planet and around a human being, nodes, ley lines, or energy centers (different terms for where they reside throughout a universe, planet, or being) exist where the spiraling life-force energy crisscrosses like braided hair. These nodes can be used like portals to hop around the universe. One does not need to travel in a spacecraft the whole distance to a location far away, such is linear thinking. In the apple shape of a Cosmos, or each universe, all throughout the ether is connected like crisscrossing roads on a map or the neural pathways in the brain, allowing connection and communication throughout the cosmic web. As above, so below; as below, so above.

The energy flowing topology of the Cosmos is similar to the shape of an apple, with each universe being within it. Each universe is a possible outcome of events, or a timeline, which has become the popular term used on Earth. Every timeline is a universe within its own dimension. Since there are an infinite amount of possibilities/timelines, there are an infinite amount of universes within the Cosmos. Since your focal point of awareness is always in a single timeline, and each timeline is in its own dimension, the universe and the Cosmos are the same thing from an individual's focal point of awareness or vantage point in a single possibility/timeline/universe.

The Cosmos is infinite, but not how a human typically thinks of the term "infinite"—spreading out with no end in the physical outer planes. In the outer planes, each universe may be seen as unfathomably expansive, but it is a closed system that begins by exiting the apple's seed, Source, and eventually returning to the seed. The infinite aspect of the Cosmos lies within the infinite universes—each possible timeline in its own dimension. The possibilities/timelines may be infinite, but a being's incarnations within each Cosmos comes to an end when one's focal point of awareness merges back with Source, merging back with a being's totality, as one part of Source and Source at the same instance in a state of timelessness outside of an illusory Cosmos. After a time of rest, the sparks of Source journey out again in the next Cosmos and continue in this manner within the infinite array of Cosmoses.

The illusion of time operates in the physical outer planes as a being moves through space in time. The metaphysical inner planes do not move through space in time and inhabit the invisible realms in time in space where time does not operate how it does in the physical outer planes. And the aspect of Source that exists outside of the illusory Cosmoses is in a state of timelessness that can only be understood after a being merges with its totality—merges back with Source. There are no words or images to describe this state, nor do we fully understand this state of being since our current focal point of awareness resides in the later 6th sub-density within the illusory Cosmos. 7th density is where beings in a united group work toward merging with their totality and after the 7th density is the merging back with Source. (We will cover the different densities in a future subject.)

Beings' experiences and incarnations in this particular Cosmos was not the beginning and will not be the end. There was a Cosmos before this Cosmos. Source used all that It learned about itself in previous Cosmoses to progressively create the Cosmos you currently reside in, and after you are done with this Cosmos, you will experience the next Cosmos. But before moving onto the next Cosmos after merging back with Source, a being may decide to assist in some manner within this particular

Cosmos for a period of time before moving onto the next Cosmos. There are infinite Cosmoses, so your experiences never end.

We have summed up the overall structure of the Cosmos. Now we will summarize the creation of the Cosmos, and in doing so cover more of the structure as well. Describing the Cosmos's creation cannot be done sufficiently with words, but we attempt to be as accurate as possible given the limitations.

For a Cosmos, a particular methodical illusion, first there is the Logos. A star and a black hole are both Logoi (plural for Logos), as a star and a black hole are the same thing but in a different phase. This should not be a surprise to human beings, as scientists on Earth know that stars have the possibility of turning into black holes. The Logoi are the Source's exhales and inhales for creation, the seeds in which mental projections come forth and return to. Source exhales and breathes life into a mental illusion using the form of a star Logos, and Source inhales and breathes life back inside itself using the form of a black hole Logos. The Logoi—stars and black holes—are entrances and exits for the Cosmos, which is a mental projection from Source. Only beings in the last 7th sub-density can use black holes to merge back with Source. All beings below this highest sub-density level would transition/die if they entered a black hole because the intense love and light energy they would face is not yet equal to the love and light energy that these beings consists of. Their spiritual mass has not phased or taken in an adequate amount of intelligently conscious love and light energy.

Through a star Logos, Source exhales part of its life force, which is intelligently conscious love energy. Therefore, a Logos could be considered this very love energy. This life force, or love energy, is projected out into and throughout the Cosmos, forming and creating the metaphysical or invisible structure of the Cosmos, the inner planes. This vibrating love energy could be seen as the spirit that animates and allows the physical to form. All physical matter is vibrating light, never being still or solid, starting with the base form of a photon. The vibrating love energy inspirits and cultivates light vibration, which is all matter that makes up the physical structure of the Cosmos. All physical matter is vibrating intelligently conscious light energy, which is made from vibrating intelligently conscious love energy that inspirits light energy, all of which is projected from Source, and is

Source at the same time because everything is Source and is never actually separate from Source.

The first star Logos, the Great Central Sun, appeared while Source's mental projection of the original thought was brought forward into existence. The Great Central Sun Logos, located in the center of the Cosmos, or each universe, projected intelligently conscious love energy and created the metaphysical inner planes. The inner planes have structured densities like the outer planes do.

Then the Great Central Sun Logos, using intelligently conscious love energy, inspirited intelligently conscious light energy, which cultivated the light to form so physical matter could exist. Then the aspect of Source that is the Great Central Sun Logos was done with its work/exhale and phased into a black hole Logos. At this point the physical outer planes existed in a chaotic form or dance for an unfathomable amount of time. Since Source in its totality does not interact directly within the Cosmos after this point, the upper densities of the inner planes act as a type of administrative and caretaker role for the physical outer planes, with the 6th and 7th density inner planes consisting solely of positively polarized beings. The beings in the 7th density inner planes act as the highest administrative positions for Source.

Then free will aspects of Source in the form of star Logoi for each galaxy continued the process of shaping the outer planes, each adding their own slight differences to Source's original thought projection. Then these star Logoi in the middle of each galaxy phased into black hole Logoi after their work was done. Then each star Logoi for each solar system or cluster of materials within its respected galaxy continued the process of using their free will to shape the outer planes for their specific area, adding their own slight differences that they see as a progression/upgrade to the original thought. When these star Logoi are done with their work, they might phase into a black hole Logos or eventually return to Source in another manner. After what may appear to be a countless unfathomable amount of time, all within the Cosmos coalesces back where it came from—the Great Central Sun Logos, which is the present black hole in the middle of the universe that inhales everything out of the mental projection that is the illusory Cosmos and back into itself, Source.

The primary rule or way of the Cosmos is free will. Without this game board rule, the profound cosmic experience would not be able to be played, as all pieces of Source would do the same thing or a predestined function, both not expanding on Source knowing itself more fully, and both would be pretty boring from a player's perspective in a game or experience. All pieces of Source are given free will so they can experience something different than Source's eternal state of being: pure love, joy, and peace. Since Source is infinite, Source is never done with knowing itself fully, which means sparks of Source—beings like yourself—never cease experiencing.

Logoi do not experience the densities in the cosmic experience; they do not play the game, so to speak. They help create each part of the experience, their respected galaxy or solar system area. Logoi are always fully aware of being Source and are the most concentrated parts of Source in the Cosmos. The Great Central Sun, which is now a black hole, being the most concentrated part of Source of all the Logoi. All the beings who experience the densities within the Cosmos co-create the different possibilities/timelines by using free will, so they are co-Creators from their seemingly separate from Source focal points of awareness. Even though the Logoi do not experience the densities in the illusion, free will starts with them because each Logos creates an adaptation in their respected galaxy or solar system and utilizes free will to do so. Each Logos of a galaxy creates their own addition as to what they see is a progression/upgrade of the cosmic experience. Each Logos/star of a solar system creates its own enhancements in the name of progression as well. So when a spacecraft from one solar system enters a different solar system, its occupants might notice a little difference, a minor tweak to the physics or nature they are used to. Perhaps the travelers do not even notice the changes.

The creation of solar systems in a galaxy follow the flow of life force—intelligently conscious love energy inspiriting and cultivating intelligently conscious light energy vibrations—so that the solar systems near the center of a galaxy are the oldest, and the farther the golden ratio shaped spiral of this life-force energy goes out, the newer the solar systems. The star/solar system planet Earth resides in is more towards the rim of the Milky Way galaxy, so it is one of the newer star systems, comparatively speaking.

The veil of forgetfulness in 3rd density was an adaptation a Logos created and it was implemented in the Milky Way galaxy later on in the spiral, so the solar systems toward the center of this galaxy do not experience the veil of forgetfulness and do not forget their 3rd density incarnations or that they are a part of Source always connected to Source. It was found that the beings in this experience did not strive very much toward graduating to 4th density because of their knowledge of being a part of Source. Their existence is that of being in a cozy bed that one does not feel the need to get out of. There are no service-to-self beings to fight and challenge the service-to-others beings because when a being knows they and all other beings are One as a part of Source and are always sharing that loving, joyful, and peaceful connection with Source, the illusion does not create service-to-self beings.

These beings know they will eventually graduate to 4th density, but they are enjoying 3rd density so much that there is not much of a desire to strive to graduate quicker. They tend to enjoy university life and are not pushed to do homework or things they do not want to do and know they will graduate at some point, but the when mostly does not matter. These beings do not face many challenges and hardships of the off-branching river shoots that galvanize striving toward the pathway back to the ocean. In this way, Source does not expand its knowledge of itself that much, nor is the experience challenging enough to be highly entertaining. Source expanding its knowledge of itself and having a highly entertaining experience/game to play are synonymous.

Looking to increase the striving toward the ocean and adding many challenging experiences that one can learn from, a Logos created its alterations/upgrade to Source's original thought by adding the veil of forgetfulness to 3rd density so that beings in its area of influence do not remember their past incarnations and do not initially know they are part of Source or that Source even exists. This is when 3rd density beings became more complex and confused. There was already a complex of the mind for 3rd density beings that partitioned Source mind from the rest of the tree of mind so that beings could seemingly experience separation from Source and have free will. After the veil of forgetfulness was placed on 3rd density beings, their mind complex became even more complex, adding another partition that separated the conscious mind from the subconscious mind. Since there is no fixed known connection with Source and knowing who they are, nor ensuring the continued state of love, joy, and peace that comes with such a connection, choosing to be a service-to-self being became an option, a temporary role to be played within the cosmic experience.

The great choice was born in 3rd density of being able to choose to graduate to 4th density by playing the role of a service-to-self negatively polarized being or the role of a service-to-others positively polarized being. This change creates a striving and seeking by beings to know who they are and why they are here that had not existed before. It is seen as most beneficial and effective because it greatly expands the nature of one's experiences and the whole journey back to Source.

Since all Logoi are mentally connected, this beneficial adaptation/upgrade was seen and adopted by other Logoi and became the new default setting for their solar systems, with continued enhancements/upgrades being made upon it by each Logos. After polarity was created, many refinements were made along the way by Logoi before getting to what human beings are experiencing on planet Earth. The experience is seen as being not too easy, far more exciting, and has more challenges, quests, and goals for the players to accomplish, all of which offers more learning opportunities. For a human being, this is the kind of game a dedicated gamer enjoys playing, and since one could consider Source a game creator and a game player at the same time, the thought is mutual. As above, so below; as below, so above.

We will give you an idea of how expansive the universe is and how abundant with life it is. In the Milky Way galaxy alone, there are approximately 248 billion stars. One third of these stars have orbiting planets. Approximately 7% of these approximately 248 billion stars have clustered materials instead of planets that some density life inhabit.

—∞—

Now we will focus in on the beginnings and the development of a single planet that eventually hosts 3rd density life and has a high probability to host higher-density life as it progresses. We will focus on planet Earth for this example. From the Logos/star Earthlings call the Sun, the intelligently conscious life-force energy continued spiraling out to shape the outer planes in its area with the slight alterations/upgrade it deemed progressive.

Physical matter continued to dance chaotically for an unfathomable period of time and eventually started to randomly form unique patterns, akin to how a random number generator functions. Then physical matter coalesced and patterns and cycles became set in an ordered manner.

All material in the Cosmos is shaped by the dynamic tension of the electromagnetic field, the two apple-shaped fields superimposed over each other, one field flowing one direction and the other the opposite direction. So as it is for every galaxy, solar system, planet, and being.

First there was fire and wind on planet Earth that eventually shaped earth and water—1st density life: atoms, molecules, the elementals (fire, wind, earth, & water), all conscious/aware life but not self-aware beings. The Earth began to stabilize and single-celled water life began to evolve and continued on up to beings such as lower water life, insects and lower plant life—early to middle 2nd density life. Then eventually this evolution grew into life-forms such as higher plant life, trees, and animals—middle to later 2nd density life, which is still conscious/aware life but not self-aware beings. Billions of years later, when planet Earth began its cycle of being able to naturally host 3rd density life-forms, a species of later 2nd sub-density life-forms was selected by the local Logos, the Sun, to graduate to a 3rd density experience; in this case it was apes. Intelligently conscious love and light energy was sent and focused on this selected species and the life-forms who received and utilized it transformed with a quick evolutionary leap forward into primitive humanlike bodies through a span of approximately 1,340 years.

Planet Earth is approximately 5.4 billion to 6.4 billion years old. This is a very rough estimation because as the Earth was forming, it is hard to consider when it officially became a planet in a human being's perspective, similar to the argument of when a fetus becomes a human being. There was only 1st density life on Earth for its first 900 million to 1.9 billion years approximately—starting with the elementals (wind, fire, earth, & water), atoms, and molecules. (The wide range being given due to the aforementioned reason at the start of this paragraph.) 2nd density life on Earth started approximately 4.5 billion years ago with early 2nd sub-density life-forms slowly evolving over billions of years to later 2nd sub-density life-forms. Dinosaurs also existed within this time frame but they did not naturally evolve on Earth. They were a genetic experiment placed on Earth hundreds of millions of years ago by a 3rd density reptilian race from a different solar system. Apes started rapidly evolving into primitive 3rd density human beings approximately 75,525 years ago. At this time, there was another group of 3rd density beings who were genetically altered in an assisting manner by the local Guardians and placed on Earth to continue their interrupted 3rd density experience on their original planet that became inhospitable due to warfare. (This will be covered in a later subject about your solar system's history.)

If a planet ends up hosting 3rd density beings, the later 2nd sub-density beings within a particular species who have spiritual advanced enough are the selected species by the local Logos to evolve into 3rd density beings. Only the beings in this species who are ready to graduate to 3rd density make this quick evolutionary leap forward at this cyclical time, which took approximately 1,340 years in Earth's case. This quick evolutionary leap forward is a onetime occurrence that coincides with the planet moving its core vibration to 3rd density—and so being able to host 3rd density life-forms—and the beginning of a new grand cycle, which consists of three major cycles. This is why later on when other apes and all other 2nd density beings become advanced enough to graduate to 3rd density, they do not go through the process of the quick leap forward in evolution. Instead, when later 2nd sub-density beings have experienced many incarnations and are ready to graduate after they transition/die, they incarnate as early 3rd sub-density beings—human beings in Earth's case—through the typical birthing process. This is why there are still apes on Earth and why other 2nd density beings on Earth have not and will not make the quick leap in evolution like the advanced apes did starting approximately 75,525 years ago.

Most 3rd density life-forms in this universe evolve into having a head, two legs, and two arms. One of the exceptions are the life-forms who evolve on water planets. There are 3rd density bipedal birds, cats, reptiles, dogs, trees, and so on throughout the later 2nd sub-density life-forms found on Earth and not on Earth that exist throughout the universe. Approximately 5% of 3rd density beings from other planets in this universe may pass as human beings in a crowd if not focused on adequately.

Creation and evolution are both factors for life and the growth of life in the Cosmos. Evolution is not mechanical like scientists think. Creation is not spontaneous like the religious think.

Evolution versus creation is another dualistic argument where both are true to some degree and work hand in hand as the same function, like nature and nurture we already covered.

The shape and look of 3rd density beings is carried with them into 4th density. Minor adaptations through evolution during their 3rd density experience may occur depending on their changing environment, but the general form and look stays the same. In 5th density, the density of light and wisdom, beings are able to shape their form however they want. Since it is the density of light, and light is what makes up all physical matter, 5th density beings can alter their physical bodies using thought alone.

The intelligently conscious love energy, or life-force energy for short, flows outward from Logoi/stars and is directed by a planet's apple-shaped electromagnetic field to be collected through the poles of a planet. The life-force energy is then distributed outward from the planet's core in a spiral fashion and has been called prana by human beings, which could be considered recycled life-force energy. This outward and upward life-force energy creates striving for growth for all beings up through the densities instead of random growth occurring. Just like the sunflower can be seen striving to face the flowing life-force energy from the Sun, all beings follow this set pathway for their conscious growth up through the densities. All beings, aware and self-aware, follow the life-force energy back to Source. All pathways lead to Source eventually, with some roads taking longer than others. Prana could be seen as the loving gentle hand of Source guiding the way back home.

101.6 – Densities & Mind/Body/Spirit Beings

Human beings have used the word "dimension" when talking about the different levels of planes beings reside in, lower and higher planes. This term is being used inaccurately in this way because a being in one dimension cannot be seen or interact with another being in a different dimension. Due to this, "dimension" is an accurate term when speaking about different possibilities/timelines/universes. But "dimension" is not an accurate term to use when speaking about the different levels of planes beings reside in because 4th, 5th, and 6th density beings can interact and be seen by 3rd density beings—such as human beings—if these beings in the higher planes permit their lighter physical bodies to be seen. Beings in all the density levels reside in the same dimension. In the beginning of the 4th density, 4th density beings would be completely visible to 3rd density beings if they were in sight of each other. 4th density beings have to learn how to become invisible to 3rd density beings; it is not automatic. "Density" is an accurate term when speaking about the physical outer planes and the metaphysical inner planes because as a being moves up the planes of awareness they become denser with intelligently conscious love and light energy as they ascend.

Being denser with this life-force energy makes the mind, body, spirit complex of a being gain spiritual mass and lose physical mass, so being denser with life-force energy makes a being's physical body lighter, so it weighs less. Since intelligently conscious love and light energy vibrates, a being's vibration increases as it moves up the densities on its journey back to Source. The term "density" as we are using it may sound like it is being used oppositely as to how human beings use this word because humans use the term solely to speak of the density of physical matter, where the denser something's physical matter is, the possibility of it being heavier and weighing more. We are speaking of the density of life-force energy and not of physical matter. So when a being is denser with life-force energy, it means there is more life-force energy in the being, which makes the being have a higher concentration of spiritual mass and less of a concentration of physical mass, so the physical body weighs less.

All matter is constantly vibrating/moving because it is inspirited by its metaphysical enabler, the intelligently conscious love energy projected into the cosmic experience by Source and is of Source. All is connected. All is unity. All is One.

There are 7 densities, not including 8 which is not considered a density but once reconfigured on its side to make ∞, it represents merging back with infinite Source. There are 7 sub-densities within every density and 7 sub-sub-densities within each sub-density, and so on to a mathematical infinity. Since the delineation of experience becomes slight and for simplicity's sake, we only refer to densities and sub-densities, and break up the sub-density groups into early, middle, and later.

As there are 7 densities, there are 7 physical bodies of a being to operate in each of the 7 densities. Typically only 1 physical body is activated at a time. Human beings are currently in the 3rd density and so utilize the 3rd density body, also known as the yellow-ray body. Some human beings think they will not have a physical body when they ascend to the next density, but this is not the case. Each physical body used in the next higher density becomes lighter in weight due to the gain of spiritual mass and the loss of physical mass, but the lighter bodies are still physical bodies because they are made from vibrating light energy. There is less physical matter in the physical bodies used as one ascends the densities, but they still contain physical matter and are physical bodies. When a 3rd density being graduates to 4th density, they utilize the lighter 4th density physical body, also known as the astral body or green-ray body, and so on till the very light 7th density physical body is used in the 7th density before merging back with Source in mind and spirit and not needing a physical body.

As there are 7 densities and 7 physical bodies to be utilized in each density, every being also has 7 energy centers, also known as chakras. The 7 chakras correlate with the 7 densities. Their relationship to each other will become clearer after we cover the densities in this subject and cover the 7 chakras in the first 103 subject, as learning about chakras is to learn about spiritual progression. 103 subjects focus on growth, spiritual progression, and inner work, and are understood more thoroughly after knowing more of the bigger picture of the Cosmos and Earth in subjects 101 and 102.

In order to function and take part in the experience of the Cosmos, a being always possesses three aspects of themselves: the mind, the body, and the spirit. Each of these is considered a complex because each has different sections or aspects within them, like the body complex having 7 aspects for the 7 densities we just mentioned. Thus, a human being, or any 3rd density being or higher, could also be called a mind, body, spirit complex. A being always utilizes all three complexes together while in the Cosmos, even during transitions—there are no exceptions. A being cannot exist in the Cosmos without having all three complexes.

Beings in the metaphysical inner planes also must have all three complexes—mind, body, and spirit—to experience the Cosmos in time in space. Though, they do not function in space in time and so only utilize the 6th density etheric body, or the 7th density body if they are in the 7th density inner planes. Thus, even an inner planes being in 3rd density uses the 6th density etheric body, and so is invisible to human beings in the 3rd density outer planes. The 6th density body, also known as the indigo-ray body or etheric body, is always used in the inner planes by disincarnate outer planes beings because it is the form-making body and can easily shift from one form to another in its love and light unity, being that it is very dense with love and light energy and therefore is high in spiritual mass, so it is the go-between body during transitions for outer planes beings. The 6th density etheric body is also used by outer planes beings during their incarnations when in the 6th density in the physical outer planes.

We have already spoken of the mind complex and how it was partitioned from Source mind at the beginning of the Cosmos in order to create free will, and later partitioned again in the tree of mind that separated the conscious mind from the hidden or subconscious mind so that free will and the experience could be enhanced for the progression of the cosmic experience.

The physical body is made up from the elements available in the density of the planet one incarnates onto. The mind is used for a being to experience thoughts, feelings, emotions, and further down the tree of mind toward Source mind, intuition is also available to those who are balanced and spiritually advanced enough to reliably tap into it. The greater the link, the greater the intuition. The spirit is the life-force energy that connects a being to Source and is a concentrated aspect of Source that resides in the being as the being at the same time. The more spiritually advanced a being is as they ascend the densities, the greater amount and flow of this life-force energy there is that not only connects a being to Source but dwells inside the physical body. An individual does not need to invite Source into their physical body, as Source is always in the individual and connects the individual to Source, even if the being is a negatively polarized being. If Source was not in you, you would simply not exist, as nothing exists but Source.

All three complexes—mind, body, and spirit—work in unison, are connected, and overlap. If a being continues to create a disturbance or an unbalancing mechanism in their mind due to negative thoughts, feelings, or emotions, the result is not only felt in the mind, it is felt in the body and spirit as well. The body attempts to relay this unbalance to you through ways such as tiredness, aches, pains, cancer, and transitioning/death as a last result. Likewise, if a being does not treat their body with love, appreciation, and nutrition by way of healthy foodstuffs and water, not only may a being experience the aforementioned symptoms, but the mind suffers as well by degrading the ability of critical thought and assisting negative feelings and emotions to arise. All three complexes are connected. An individual cannot do one thing to one of them and not affect the other. They are all complexes in the trinity complex that allows a being to experience the Cosmos.

To further explain how the mind, body, and spirit work together, we will offer a comparison of them to your computer. The body is like all the physical parts and hardware of the computer. The processor chip being like the brain and the circuitry system like the veins. All these physical parts give the spirit and the mind something to work with.

The mind is like the operating system. Without it, the physical parts would not perform actions. One could also consider the subconscious mind to be the code embedded behind the operating system. The subconscious mind uses dreams to teach lessons, but if the individual is not versed in understanding the symbolism, it means nothing or little to them. A dream interpreter is like a coder who understands what the code means. This code is gibberish to those who have not studied coding, as the dream is baffling to those who do not understand dream symbolism.

The spirit is like the electricity that creates pathways to the hardware and the operating system of the computer. Without the spirit, nothing happens, no work or experience can be done or had. Electricity flowing through the circuitry in the computer is like the energy flow of spirit through the body, or chi as it is called in parts of Asia. The electricity for the computer is localized in the computer, but it is also connected all the way to the power plant that creates the electricity and where it is most concentrated—like a Logos. It is connected to the power plant, but you do not see the pathway and consider your computer separate. Just like your spirit is localized in your body, but is also always connected to Source, that which is everything and powers everything. This is also similar to one considering all Internet-capable devices to be separate—like each human being—but they are all connected.

We expand past the mind, body, spirit complex. Then there is the Internet, which is like the cosmic web. Connecting to the Internet/web is similar to a human being using their mind to call out for assistance from higher-density beings. The user/caller may be in a dead zone or doing it incorrectly and getting nothing, no Internet or information. Or they may connect to the Internet and receive a load of possible information: accurate information, inaccurate information with good intentions (or misinformation), and/or inaccurate information with bad intentions (being made wrong on purpose or disinformation), for all is available to the seeker. It depends on what sites one resonates with and their intentions that lead them to particular sites in the first place. There are service-to-others beings and service-to-self beings in the 3rd density and higher densities that both want to spread their particular information and strengthen their views and followers. A VPN (virtual private network) is akin to using so-called magical exercises/rituals in order to protect the user/caller from unwanted visitors who stick their ugly noses in your business and mess with your actions and collect your private information to use against you.

These comparisons are simply meant to explain how the mind, body, spirit complex works together and how all is connected through the cosmic web, but the free will and spiritual power of a mind, body, spirit complex that is a being cannot be duplicated by a computer or any other technology, no matter how advanced.

—∞—

We will summarize each density. 1st density is the density of awareness. It is the first density that is experienced when a part of Source chooses to seemingly separate from Source to experience the cosmic illusion. The red-ray physical body is used in this density. Some of which that can be found in 1st density are the elementals (wind, fire, earth, & water, which could be seen as caretakers for 1st density), atoms, molecules. This is the density of awareness but not self-awareness. The upward flow of prana from a planet subtly provides a striving to the next density. You might have heard the saying "life finds a way" when speaking about the miraculous resilience of life and how it springs forward in even the harshest conditions; prana is the life-force energy behind life finding its way on a planet. It may take millions to billions of years to do so in 1st density, but beings in this density do not have a concept of time; they are aware (not self-aware) in the moment and that is all they experience. There is no difference between one day and a billion years for them.

—∞—

2nd density is the density of growth, growth of the physical body and of awareness. The orange-ray physical body is used in this density. Some of which that can be found in 2nd density you are familiar with on Earth are single-celled organisms, viruses, insects, fish, plants, trees, animals. Like 1st density, this density is aware/conscious, but it is not yet self-aware. Again, the upward flow of prana subtly provides a striving for growth to the next density that may take millions to billions of years. Again, 2nd density beings do not recognize time and live in the moment, so the duration of time passing by is meaningless to them. They are driven by survival and necessity for themselves and their pack or group. Plant life and trees experience this community by connecting through the soil, where they can communicate with each other and possibly share nutrients and water in the soil. The 2nd density experience is a group existence because self-awareness and individualization has yet to be reached. The beings in your myths such as fairies, gnomes, sprites, elves, and such are real and are the caretakers/spirit guides for 2nd density beings, looking out for them and guiding them. Most human beings' myths are built upon some kind of reality. Except for rare occasions and with human beings with certain rare abilities, these 2nd density spirit guides/caretakers cannot be seen because they reside in the inner planes of a planet, existing in time in space instead of in space in time like human beings. Just as 3rd density human beings have spirit guides in the inner planes, 2nd density beings have these spirit guides for their groups. After 3rd density life-forms have evolved and start having 2nd density beings as pets, this gives the 2nd density pet's growth an opportunity to be fast-tracked and graduate from 2nd density much sooner. This is the case because the 2nd density pet spends much time with individualized self-aware 3rd density being(s) and their vibration. This can be the case with not just animals but with plants and trees as well. They are given the opportunity to observe and adapt somewhat to their new individualized family and their different ways of life, or simply be effected by the human being's vibration. The more love a pet is given and time invested, the more their opportunity grows for graduation. If a pet adopts a unique character apart from its species and exhibits humanlike characteristics, it is a sign that the 2nd density being has grown and may be ready to graduate to 3rd density after its next transition.

3rd density is the density of self-awareness. The yellow-ray physical body is used in this density. This is the density where human beings reside. The local Logos's selected 2nd density species that has strived and grown in consciousness makes an evolutionary leap forward and graduates to the 3rd density experience. In Earth's case, apes to human beings. 3rd density beings that are not water-based adhere to a universal template where the 2nd density being rapidly evolves into a type of 3rd density being with a head, two legs, and two arms. This template was designed because it allows the self-aware being to properly function, have experiences, and grow as a being. This is the first density experience where self-awareness is in play, fully conscious of their individuality and so able to express more free will. The veil of forgetfulness is used for this density, and only in this density. This means a 3rd density being does not remember their previous density experiences—1st and 2nd—and also do not remember their previous 3rd density incarnations. This veil, or way of confusion, greatly enhances a being's free will. This is where the seeking of the journey begins, where beings start out on their self-aware striving and seeking. Although the upward flow of prana continues to provide life-force energy that channels up the being's chakras to subtly provide directional growth, it is the experiences, motivation, willpower, and how one reacts to experiences that progresses a being in this density, because beings in 3rd density have become self-aware and have taken up the mantle of self-responsibility. Progression toward the next density and all higher densities is no longer solely assisted by the subtle striving forward by the upward flow of prana. The 3rd density experience is by far the most intense and difficult of all the densities. This is because self-awareness being obtained throws the being into a sea of countless experiences and choices. The duration of time for this density is the shortest of all the densities. (The reason for this will be explained in the next subject.) A grand cycle experience differs from planet to planet depending on where the planet resides in the cycles/orbit or gears of the big cosmic clock that sets the duration of space in time for each cycle in 3rd density. For planet Earth, a grand cycle experience is approximately 75,510 years, but a being could graduate to 4th density sooner or later than the completion of this grand cycle. Some beings choose the long road, some choose the short road, but all roads lead back to Source and are all seen as valuable experiences. If a being graduates sooner, they have options. They could incarnate on a different planet where the 4th density is in play. Another option is continuing to reincarnate on the same 3rd density planet to assist others toward their graduation. Another option is to spend time in the inner planes as a spirit guide for an incarnate 3rd density being or to assist disincarnate 3rd density beings while they learn and prepare for their next incarnation back into 3rd density. The cosmic experience provides countless positions, roles, and experiences for beings in the journey back to Source.

—∞—

4th density is the density of love and understanding. The veil of forgetfulness ends when a being graduates 3rd density, so a being understands more of who they are and how the Cosmos works but is still far from knowing the grander bigger picture. Beings learn the lessons of love in this density—either love for others and self or love for self solely. (This distinction and most about 4th density will be further expanded upon in the next subject.) For now we will give a description of where most beings choose to go: 4th density positive, the service-to-others path, the positive polarity path. 4th density beings utilize the green-ray body, also known as the astral body, to experience this density. Unlike the heavy chemical body used in 3rd density, the astral body is lighter because it contains more intelligently conscious love and light energy, but it still resembles the look of its particular 3rd density body appearance—the evolution from the particular 2nd density species that a being came from. The 4th density body still needs to ingest foodstuffs to be sustainable, but the process of growing and preparing food is simpler than it is in 3rd density. The food is also of a higher vibration and easier on the system to that of foodstuffs in 3rd density. Eating in the 4th density is seen as merely a necessity and is done perfunctorily. 4th density beings are thoroughly invested in their work and would rather not take time out to consume foodstuffs, so taking the time to eat for them teaches the lesson of patience. Thoughts, feelings, emotions, and one's aura and vibration are seen clearly to others in this density. Telepathy is used and so talking and languages are not a necessity. Unlike 3rd density, the 4th density is experienced as a group, learning and progressing forward as a harmonious team until they have created a united group. A united group is a collection of beings who have mentally melded together enough to have created a shared mind, where all beings in the group have access to this group mind due to their shared intention. They utilize this group mind as well as their individual minds to learn and progress. The united group graduates to 5th density together when they are ready instead of like in 3rd density where individual beings grow and graduate on their own terms separately. Individual differences are expressed and are readily harmonized by the whole group; in this way, all voices and opinions are heard and considered. A 4th density positive being is compassionate, displays acts of loving-kindness, and is in harmony with themselves and with other beings in the united group. Just as 3rd density beings had to learn a partial amount of the early lessons of universal love to graduate to 4th density positive, 4th density beings learn a partial amount of the early lessons of wisdom in their later sub-densities to graduate to 5th density, because 5th density is the density of wisdom and light. From 4th density and higher, a grand cycle is no longer set by the specific location of a planet in its orbit; it is regularized and is approximately what would be considered 30 million years of Earth time, but the united group may graduate sooner or much later depending on their progression. This may seem like a long duration of time when compared to Earth's 3rd density grand cycle of approximately 75,510 years, but the illusion of time is only intensely focused on and so experienced in slow motion, so to speak, in the 3rd density experience. The illusion of time still exists in 4th density and higher, but it is not focused on as important because beings live in the present, and time becomes less of an illusion through the densities on a being's journey back to Source.

—∞—

5th density is the density of wisdom and light. Beings in this density focus on learning wisdom and the ways of light energy. In their later sub-densities they learn a little of the next density's focus—the merging of love and wisdom—in order to graduate to 6th density. Every density has its focus of learning and also learns a partial amount of the early lessons of the next density's focus in their later sub-densities in order to graduate to the next density of experience. Later 5th sub-density beings learn a partial amount of the early lessons in 6th density of uniting and balancing love and wisdom before graduating to 6th density. As words are a poor substitute in describing 4th density, there are simply no words to properly describe 5th density or higher, but we can disseminate some information. This density can be experienced in a group or individually. The blue-ray body is used for this density. The physical body used in the 5th density is fueled by a type of light nectar broth that is prepared by thought alone. Much of what is done and accomplished in 5th density is with thought alone. The form of the 5th density body is whatever the 5th density being makes it to be with thought alone. Approximately 25% of 5th density beings have adequately advanced to utilize their indigo-ray chakra to travel throughout the universe with thought projection and do not require a spacecraft. 5th density positive beings serve and aid positive polarity by beaming love and light to 3rd and 4th density beings who ask for and could use assistance. A grand cycle's duration of time in 5th density is hard to express because it may be experienced and graduated as an entire group or individually, but we will say that it is approximately averaged out roughly to what would be considered 55 million years of Earth time. Again, graduation may come sooner or much later than this average approximation.

——∞——

6th density is the density of uniting and balancing love and light energy, universal love and wisdom. First a being learns love in the 4th density, then wisdom in the 5th density, and then how to unite the two in an adequately balanced and harmonious manner in the 6th density. The indigo-ray body, also known as the etheric body, is used in 6th density. Foodstuffs for this body is pure love and light energy. The form of a 6th density body is seen as shimmering light rather than a form, if it chooses to be seen at all. However, like 5th density beings, 6th density beings can use thought to create any type of body form they want, which they typically do when phasing to visibility in order to interact with density levels below them. This density is experienced in a group and graduates to 7th density when the united group is ready. 6th density beings can mentally project their consciousness and travel throughout the universe without needing a spacecraft or any type of vehicle or technology. Later 6th sub-density beings may send love and light energy to lower-density beings who mentally call for aid. At some point the later 6th sub-density united group chooses to leave their home planet and inhabits a Logos/star in order to learn a partial amount of the early lessons in 7th density so they can be prepared to graduate to 7th density. All beings need to learn a partial amount of the early lessons in the next density before graduating to the next density. The united group then adds to the love and light energy from a Logos/star that is provided to its orbiting planets, serving and assisting the solar system. A grand cycle's duration of time in 6th density is approximately what would be considered 75 million years of Earth time, but a united group can graduate sooner or much later.

We are a later 6th sub-density united group that has chosen to inhabit the Logos/star that provides love and light energy to planets in the solar system that includes planet Earth. Thus, the Logos/star we inhabit is what human beings call the Sun.

——∞——

7th density is the density of traversing the gateway, the hallway that narrows, working toward merging back with Source. The violet-ray body is used in this density. A being reaches its totality of being in this density before it merges back with its infinite totality with and as Source.

——∞——

These are all the physical densities that make up the outer planes. The metaphysical densities that make up the inner planes have a very similar structure from 1st to 7th density and then merge back with Source. Whereas the physical densities are located in space in time, the inner planes are located in time in space, so they do not experience time like the physical outer planes. The timeless state inner planes beings experience is not the same as the timelessness Source experiences that cannot be fathomed until one merges back with Source. We will provide two examples of the timeless state of the inner planes a physical outer planes being experiences. The second example given you may recognize. 1: When an outer planes being is in the inner planes while disincarnate, they review their past incarnation and learn and study for their next incarnation. This may take what would be considered a long time if it were spent in the physical outer planes, but a being may do this in the inner planes for what would be considered years or decades in the outer planes and then reincarnate only six months or less in physical outer plane's time after their last transition/death. 2: A human being may have a dream that seemed like it would have taken an hour or two's worth of time to have, but they wake up and look at the clock and only ten minutes have passed since they last fell asleep. This is because dreams happen in the inner planes and so are not limited to the construct of space in time that is perceived in the outer planes.

Human beings who have had interactions with beings from the inner planes have called these beings angels or demons/devils. Many accurate drawings have been made to portray them. As with the physical outer planes densities, the metaphysical inner planes densities developed negative and positive inner planes realms after the dualism of polarities (positive and negative) was added/upgraded to the cosmic experience. One notable difference is that negatively polarized beings can reside in the early to middle 6th sub-densities in the outer planes before having to switch to positive polarity to further progress, but only positively polarized beings can reside in the 6th density inner planes. We already listed some inner planes beings in the summarized 1st to 3rd densities of the physical outer planes. We reiterate: In 1st density, the elementals that reside in wind, fire, earth, and water are inner planes beings. They do not have polarity, as polarity starts in the 3rd density for both the inner and outer planes. The elementals can be used as tools for so-called magical acts/rituals (mental acts focusing on love and/or light energy), performed by either positive or negative beings. Elementals indifferently carry out a task they are instructed to perform that could be perceived as positive or negative. In 2nd density, the group spirit guides/caretakers for animals, plants, trees, etc. we spoke of are inner planes beings. For 3rd density, we spoke of the inner planes beings who act as spirit guides for individual human beings. There are positive and negative 3rd density inner planes spirit guides or influencers.

The positively polarized 3rd, 4th, 5th, 6th, and 7th density inner planes beings are those that may resemble angels. The negatively polarized 3rd, 4th, and 5th density inner planes beings are those that may resemble demons/devils. These positively and negatively polarized inner planes beings have been indirectly responsible for some of the religions that have sprung up on Earth. Positively polarized inner planes beings do not intend on their information being used to create religions that foster separation between human beings, so if their information is turned into a religion, it was indirectly done and not intended by them. Negatively polarized inner planes beings tend to offer information that is intended to create religions that foster separation between human beings, but they are still indirectly responsible for their information turning into religions because it is the free will of the human being who decides and follows through with creating the religion or not. Fictitious places called heaven and hell were created from human beings' confusion when they interacted with these higher-density positive and negative inner planes beings. (This will be expanded upon in the subject about religions and their origins.)

A being's vibration increases as it moves up the densities. Each density is a vibratory spectrum that coincides with the energy center/chakra system: red, orange, yellow, green, blue, indigo, and violet—all being listed in order starting with the 1st density red-ray spectrum. As a being climbs the densities on its journey back to merging with Source, its mind, body, spirit complex increases its holding capacity of intelligently conscious love and light energy, so with each density a being climbs, their physical body used in that density increases in vibration and loses physical mass and so is lighter in weight and denser with life-force energy, which is the same as saying an increase in spiritual mass.

We reiterate: The connected mind, body, spirit complex that is a being becomes denser with life-force energy that increases its spiritual mass. This is why the term "density" is used for the planes/levels of existence. Beings in all densities would be seen with the naked eye of a 3rd density being in some shape or form if beings in the densities 4th and higher allowed themselves to be visible, because they are all in the same dimension. 4th density outer planes beings are visible to the naked eye of 3rd density outer planes beings in the beginning of their 4th density experience and have to learn how to be invisible to 3rd density beings. Densities 4th and higher eventually learn and intentionally make themselves invisible to the density directly below them so as to not interfere with each density's experience, not infringing upon their free will. They may make themselves invisible, but they are not like ghosts; a 3rd density being would bump into an invisible 4th density being if they walked in the same space. The same thing would happen with 3rd and 5th density beings, but at some point in a 5th density beings progression, they learn enough of the ways of wisdom and light and so would be able to morph as needed to avoid being bumped into.

When a planet progresses through the density experiences it offers—if it does so at all—it may have more than one density experience in play at the same time, but the experiences for 3rd density beings and higher are seemingly separate because the higher-density beings make themselves invisible and dwell in a different location on or in the planet that is being shared. The only time period the two densities would be visible to each other is during the shift from one density experience to the next, where the higher-density beings have just shifted to the next density and have not learned how to make themselves invisible to the density below them yet. A 3rd density being resides in the same dimension as a 4th density being, and all higher-density beings as well. "Dimension" is an accurate term when referring to different possibilities/timelines/universes since they are automatically separate from each other without choice because they exist in different times in space where their particular space in time operates. Beings in different dimensions, no matter what density they are in, cannot see or interact with each other because they are separated by design. There would be no point of having different dimensions if the beings in the dimensions were always interacting with each other. There are ways a being can transfer themselves to a different dimension, but they cannot reside in two dimensions at once. Such a transfer would be stagnation for a being because all their pre-incarnate plans for growth, spiritual progression, and balancing karma would be in the dimension they left, the opportunities abandoned. Each possibility/timeline/universe exists in its own dimension, thus separate from each other. There are infinite possibilities/timelines/universes.

Planet Earth is currently hosting 1st, 2nd, and 3rd density beings, and will soon host the 4th density experience in full capacity. Many decades ago, Earth's 3rd density experience started to overlap into a 4th density vibration and continues increasing toward this vibration more fully as the years go by, which has already caused Earth to realign its electromagnetic field, and will continue to do so to match the magnetism for the 4th density experience.

101.7 – The Choice & Higher-Density Influences

We will speak about the choice in 3rd density and summarize the roles of each density in the physical outer planes with an emphasis on how higher-density beings influence and affect 3rd density beings since this course is meant for the expansion of awareness for human beings, who are 3rd density beings.

The 1st and 2nd density experiences lay the groundwork, the foundation for the self-aware 3rd density being so they can make the choice of polarity: service to others (positive polarity) or service to self (negative polarity). The duration of time taken to make the choice is up to the 3rd density being. After the choice has been made, the 3rd density being graduates to 4th density positive or negative and continues polarizing on their chosen path up to the middle 6th sub-density where the dualistic experience of the two polarities ends and only the positive polarity path remains. From there, only a path of unity exists and is pursued where beings continue to polarize toward the positive through the rest of 6th density, then 7th density, and then merge back with Source.

For perspective, we reiterate: The duration of 2nd density is billions of years—it was approximately 4.5 billion years on Earth. The duration of 4th density is approximately 30 million years. The duration of 3rd density on Earth is approximately 75,510 years. The duration of 3rd density on any planet is by far the shortest of any density for two reasons. 1: It is a period for a being to make a choice of what they want to experience on their journey back to Source. It is akin to spending only four years in your university to choose the career you will possibly do for the rest of your life. Once you have chosen your career and graduated university, there is no reason to stay in university. Instead of a multitude of career choices one can choose in university, there are only two choices in the 3rd density for the journey back to Source: the positive or negative path. 2: 3rd density is the most intense and challenging of any density, where extreme highs and lows are experienced, much like on your roller coaster rides. A being is not given more than they can handle for any experience. This applies to a duration of time for a single incarnation and it also applies to the duration of time in an entire density.

A 3rd density being set on advancing toward the negatively polarizing service-to-self path is one that does things solely for their own sake. They live the truly selfish existence. When they do appear to be helping other beings, it is only because it serves/benefits themselves in some way. This is a challenging role to play because it goes against the biased nature of Source, which is love in unity. These beings do practice love—they are not loveless—but they mostly or only practice love by loving themselves. They concentrate on what satisfies and aids themselves in the experience and care not about what satisfies or aids others, as they see themselves as separate and not part of a whole. They believe, consciously or unconsciously, that this method of separation is the most efficient way to progress for the individual. They practice the art of separation and teach the method to others, directly or indirectly. They work with others on the same negatively advancing team because it benefits their desire for power and control, as power in numbers increases the probability of control over the majority. Unlike the positive path, the negative path throws other members under the bus, as the human saying goes, if it serves or protects the individual. There is no honest loyalty on the negative path.

A 3rd density being set on advancing toward the positively polarizing service-to-others path is interested in assisting others and themselves. When they help themselves, it is not to the detriment of others. They end up assisting many more beings than themselves because they are only one and there are many others, or you could say there are many other-selves and yourself is only one self, because in reality all are One being, all are of the self which is Source. Therefore, assisting others is to assist yourself. A self who is advancing toward the service-to-others path learns something and wants other-selves to benefit as they have, so they teach as many others as they can. Some human beings are confused and think a being advancing toward service to others only helps out others and does not help themselves. This is a falsity. One cannot assist others until they have first helped themselves. One cannot teach another to build a house unless they first learn how to build a house themselves. A being advancing toward the service-to-others path believes this method of unity to be the most efficient way to progress, both individually and as a whole. They realize that helping others in their community makes a more harmonious community that is more enjoyable to live in, and since they are living in the community, it benefits themselves as well. They practice the art of unity and teach the method to others, directly or indirectly.

These are the two examples of beings mostly toward either side of polarity, positive or negative. They may be close to finalizing their choice to graduate to 4th density positive or negative. Before one comes close to making the choice, their shade is closer to gray or neutral. Since no being is perfect in any density, especially in 3rd density, all beings are different shades of gray; no being is purely white or black in regards to their polarity. The goal of 3rd density is to make the choice, which is to move one's shade as far away from neutral gray and as close to a lighter or darker shade as possible. All beings are a shade of gray. The question is: what is your shade?

Because the veil of forgetfulness is used for the 3rd density experience, a being wakes up in 3rd density and does not remember who they are, their past incarnations, nor that they are a part of Source, they awake like an infant and are thrown into self-awareness where an infinite array of experiences and choices are available. These experiences range from intense joy and bliss to intense pain and sorrow. The range of emotions and feelings felt in 3rd density is by far the widest of any density. This can make 3rd density both a complete delight and complete suffering. The experience of 3rd density is in the mind of the one who experiences it, as many different beings can experience the same thing but have a wide range of different thoughts and emotional reactions about it.

Instead of a few moments to decide what path to take along a hiking trail, the 3rd density choice takes longer because it is a choice the being typically does not even know they need to make, since the veil obscures their past, and in doing so obscures their future. This is as it is intended. A being is thrown into countless experiences and the results of the cause and effect of these experiences offers the being a direction in their life—how they want to live their incarnation. How one decides to live the collection of their 3rd density incarnations is the choice—the countless choices made during incarnations that eventually makes the choice of which polarity path is chosen. This choice can be made in a few incarnations or numerous incarnations; it depends on each being. As seen by Source, the highest viewpoint possible, there is no incorrect choice, as all paths—short and long, positive and negative—serve Source. All paths were created to provide roles that need to be played in order to have the intended experiences along the journey. Thus, it would be a falsity to say that one path is wrong, at least from a very high viewpoint. From a lower viewpoint in 3rd density, there is typically a clear opinion that one path is wrong and the other is right. This is the prime paradox of the Cosmos that is resolved in the early to middle 6th sub-densities when negative polarity ends and only positive polarity remains.

Remember the video game comparison we presented in subject 101.3: The best games need heroes as well as villains to offer challenges, lessons, and growth. We cannot have the experience or theatrical play without a few characters choosing to play the villainous roles. From the game creator's viewpoint (Source and the Logoi), there is no such thing as wrong and right in the game; there is only what makes the experience comprehensive and worth having, and so what may be considered wrong and right to those playing the game, was purposefully designed by the intelligent and creative mind of Source and the Logoi. A game creator and an unbiased player both recognize that a game would be boring if the "good" or "bad" side always won, so anything is possible in the 3rd density experience.

Somewhere between the early to the middle 6th sub-densities, the dualism of polarity ends, the dualistic part of the experience ceases for all the players, sparks of Source. All the roles gave the players and the audience the experience they intended and are relinquished like an actor giving up a character's role when the theatrical play or movie ends. The curtain comes down on the play's ending and all the actors congratulate each other on how well they played their roles. This happens somewhere in the early to middle 6th sub-densities for each group or wave of beings. Then the curtain rises and the audience claps and shows their appreciation. There is always a happy ending for all, no matter what transpired during and at the end of the theatrical play. All sparks of Source are satisfied from their higher-density viewpoints and continue their experience in love and unity without paradoxes or any aspect of dualism and continue journeying toward merging with Source.

We have clarified that there is no wrong and right within the game from a very high viewpoint of 6th density and higher. That both protagonists and antagonists are needed for the cosmic experience. But from within the experience or game, there is a wrong and right stance perceived by the players, especially in 3rd density. The wise hero does not put their sword down and let the villain kill them because they know they are both part of Oneness, parts of Source. The game is to be played and cannot be avoided, as the only way out of the experience or game is to finish it. The hero chose their role and should play it as well as an actor tries to play their role. Their civilization or planet would fall under control and suffering if the hero put their sword down and did not play their role well. It will take more than the heroes to do the job, as strength is in numbers. Unity, loving-kindness, and defense (which in certain circumstances may appear as an attack) are the best tactics for beings moving in the positive polarity direction.

Contrariwise, the villain chose their role and should play it as well as possible. It is a hard role because the audience may dislike them, but someone has to play the part. As villains get better at their role of using deception, they can manipulate the roles of governmental and organizational structures more to their advantage. Clever villains use deception so effectively that they can make themselves appear as the heroes and the philanthropists in their civilization or planet. They can continue to put the majority of humanity under their control while being praised at the same time. The craftiest villains learn the ways of 4th density beings and remove themselves from being known in the public and rule and control from behind closed doors, ordering their underlings to instruct their minions to do their bidding. The more layers the villain places between the public's eye and themselves, the safer they are from being discovered and dethroned. There are such villains/clever negatively oriented human beings on planet Earth. Selfishness, deception, separation, and attack are the best tactics for beings moving in the negative polarity direction. When we say "separation", we mean to divide the majority in as many ways as possible so they do not act in unity and fight each other instead of the few negatively oriented human beings who desire to take control or further their control over the majority.

We feel at this time we should restate that every game has rules to make it fair and enjoyable for all players. The most important rule in the Cosmos is the universal law of balancing, which human beings have called karma. Since every being is part of the same whole, when one being does something negative to another, it is the same thing as doing that negative thing to oneself. One has to make up with themselves eventually by balancing karma. In order for those two parts of Source to fit back into the big jigsaw puzzle picture, the unique parts that connect the two beings' pieces need to be balanced, which means returned to their original state to fit back together. Only when all the jigsaw puzzle pieces are put back together is the experience completed. This is why choosing the villainous role, which some have to play in order for all to have an experience, is a hard role to play. Part of their role is balancing the negativity they create while playing their part. Even though there is no wrong and right from the highest perspective and the experience is similar to a game, there are set rules and consequences or duties for a being's actions. One cannot perform many negative actions within the game and walk away without karmic balances being made at some point for their actions. It does not matter in what incarnation(s) one's karma is balanced, but it must be balanced before graduating to 7th density. Positive polarity beings tend to balance their karma as they ascend the densities. Negative polarity beings tend to balance their bulk of karma after switching polarities to the positive side, which must be done at the latest in the middle 6th sub-density.

Some human beings are perplexed at how a negatively oriented human being can keep performing negative deeds and seemingly avoid karma. Karma does not operate how they perceive it does. Besides karma, a being who entertains and practices negative states of being is in disharmony and mental pain as long as they decide to create a negative state of being for themselves. Karma does not need to be balanced within the same incarnation it was created, but there is always the potential for it to be balanced out in any of a being's incarnations in the 3rd density experience. For negative beings, it can be partially put off for densities. When they switch polarities, they have heaps of karma to balance out. All must be balanced at some point. Another misunderstanding of karma is that those taking orders under a command structure—such as in the military, black operations, a basic job of any sort, or any other position where orders are given by a higher-ranking position or boss—the beings following orders think they are exempt from karma. This is not the case, as it is the responsibility for the 3rd density being, no matter what position or situation they are in, to use their discernment and free will to make their own choice. If their choice is to ignore using discernment and their free will, they still accrue karma for all the acts they perform. All are responsible for their choices. Every single thought, action, and all details to the smallest degree are recorded in the subconscious mind and is connected with Source. There are no free passes when pertaining to karma—no exceptions. Every being must balance out all their karma before merging back with Source.

In order for a being to finalize their choice in 3rd density and graduate to 4th density, a being has to work on particular chakras. To graduate on the positive path, a being has to work on and adequately balance out their red-ray, orange-ray, yellow-ray, and partially the green-ray energy center. Red-ray being the foundation, orange-ray dealing with personal and one-on-one interactions, yellow-ray dealing with group associations, and green-ray dealing with universal love. The green-ray chakra only needs to be partially balanced out to graduate to 4th density positive. We will expand upon chakras in 103 subjects that pertain to self-growth. Working on these particular chakras (red-ray through green-ray) adequately to graduate to 4th density positive equates to being at least 51% service to others at the end of a major cycle, which is every approximately 25,170 years for Earth.

To graduate on the negative path, a being has to work on their red-ray, orange-ray, and yellow-ray chakras. Red-ray being the foundation is worked on and balanced the same way as for the positive path, but the orange-ray and yellow-ray chakras are worked on in the opposite manner of that of the positively oriented being. Working on these particular chakras adequately in a self-serving way to graduate to 4th density negative equates to being at least 95% service to self at the end of a major cycle. The negative path requires much dedication.

If a 3rd density being, either moving toward positive or negative, manages to utilize their indigo-ray chakra and goes through their violet-ray chakra to open up a greater connection with Source energy and mind, they can graduate at any time and do not need to wait till the end of a major cycle. This action is the way of the adept and clearly conveys the being is more than advanced enough to move on to the next density, so there is no reason for them to wait till the end of a major cycle. If it is a positive being, they may decide to stay in 3rd density for the remaining major cycle or the whole grand cycle to aid and teach other beings, which may increase the positive harvest. If it is a negative being, they choose to graduate to 4th density negative after their current incarnation ends. Since they focus on being selfish, moving forward as soon as possible to increase their polarization and power suits the disposition of their role.

In order for a positive being to utilize their indigo-ray chakra and go through their violet-ray chakra to open up a greater connection with Source energy and mind, all their chakras need to be adequately balanced. For a negative being, they need to adequately balance their red-ray chakra and intensely work on their orange-ray and yellow-ray chakras to bypass the green-ray and blue-ray chakras and utilize their indigo-ray chakra. This requires great dedication and focus because it is very difficult to activate and utilize the indigo-ray chakra from the yellow-ray chakra.

Most beings choose the positive path due to an inherent bias of being part of Source, which is unity and all loving. It should be noted that a being cannot fake service to others; if their true intentions of assisting others is to simply look good in other's eyes or to simply graduate themselves—the latter being mentioned due to this educational course making the choice known—it does not count toward the 51% of being service to others. Even if they do the planet a great service, their true intentions are still self-serving. Such actions are not adequate for one to graduate to 4th density negative, but they certainly hinder one from graduating to 4th density positive. The weight of importance lies in one's intentions. Actions can be beneficial, but they are empty without the state of being to inspirit and empower those actions. First work on the state of being, and then one may do the actions honestly and more effectively. The intention in serving others is what matters, not how effective it is, because one can change and direct themselves, but they have no control over what others do, nor should they, as being forceful and controlling is a self-serving action even if it is seen to be acting for the benefit of the being. All must make their own choices for their free will to be honored. A being with positive intentions in serving others could perform positive actions but create no noticeable change in their civilization and still graduate to 4th density positive, as the change in others is out of their hands. Those advancing toward the positive path naturally want to aid and assist others, typically after they have aided themselves appropriately, but the lack of positive changes in others due to their efforts does not hinder their graduation to 4th density positive.

A 3rd density being moves towards a chosen path of positive or negative polarity throughout their 3rd density incarnations. At no time is a 3rd density being fully positive or negative; they are always positively oriented, negatively oriented, or neutrally oriented because they have not made the choice and graduated to 4th density yet. For some it may seem clear what path a particular human being is headed toward, but they could change polarity at any time. As a being gains more polarity in either direction, it is easier for them to switch polarities in the middle to later sub-densities when their polarity has a greater charge. Only when beings make the 3rd density choice and graduate to 4th density positive or negative do they finalize the choice and become fully service-to-others positive or service-to-self negative beings.

Of all the 3rd density planets in the Cosmos, the approximate graduation of planets to the 4th density positive and negative paths are as such: 62% of all planets have only beings who graduate toward the positive path. 10% of all planets have only beings who graduate toward the negative path. 28% of all planets have beings who graduate with a mixed amount toward positive and negative. In a mixed graduation the majority typically chooses the positive path. In all three of these cases, it does not mean that all beings graduated. In all three examples given, there are a percentage of beings on planets that do not graduate to either the negative or the positive because they did not polarize enough in either direction to make the choice, and so repeat at least another major cycle in 3rd density on a different planet.

Approximate percentages of all 3rd density beings in the Cosmos: 86% of all 3rd density beings choose the positive path and 14% choose the negative path. However, it is not mathematically accurate to assume that planet Earth or any singular planet has an average of 14% of beings who graduate to 4th density negative. Most of the 14% who choose the negative path come from the approximately 10% of planets where only beings graduate to 4th density negative. These planets have a heavy hand in raising the overall negative percentage. Typically mixed graduation planets, such as Earth, have far more positive than negative graduates, where the negative graduates are far below the Cosmos's overall 14% negative graduate figure.

——∞——

We will now speak of the influences higher-density beings have upon 3rd density beings, such as human beings. 4th density focuses on love—universal love or solely love of self—and understanding. Some of the 4th density positive experience will be restated here. 4th density is no longer subjected to the way of confusion since the veil of forgetfulness only applies to 3rd density. Those who choose to polarize positively and be a service-to-others being spend about their first half of 4th density forming a tightly knitted group experience, a united group where beings use their individual minds but also have access to a shared mind that is created due to a shared focus and intention. In 4th density, united groups are constructed for the first time, both for the positive and negative paths. Since all are service-to-others beings in 4th density positive, opposition that was had in 3rd density is no longer a detractor in forming this group unity. All ideas and concerns are heard and harmonized through the group. Since everything is transparent in 4th density from being to being—thoughts, feelings, emotions, aura, and vibration—this allows the group to harmonize more efficiently. Words and different languages are no longer a hindrance because telepathy is used. From a 3rd density being's perspective, this type of openness or transparency may sound scary and invasive, but since all in 4th density positive made the choice to be service to others and show loving-kindness and compassion, acts such as judgment, shame, alienation, or any other form of separation and negativity that a being experienced in 3rd density is removed on the 4th density positive path; because of this, such transparency only assists harmonization and is seen as beneficial. While the group is harmonizing, they are learning the lessons of universal love and understanding at the same time.

Forming a united group does not mean all beings become the same. It is quite the opposite, as all beings use their unique skills and abilities for the benefit of the united group. This collection of uniqueness with a shared intention affords great power and effectiveness that far surpasses that of a collection of beings who are all the same and have the same skills and abilities.

Once a unity of mind is established for the united group, the role of a 4th density influencer begins: assisting 3rd density beings who show positive intentions of seeking or striving, either mentally or vocally. Positive 4th density beings respect free will, and so do not give aid that has not been asked for in some way, either mentally or vocally. The more a 3rd density being strives for and focuses on something that has the potential of being positive for themselves and others, the more invisible assistance they are given by 4th density positive beings. 3rd density beings' positive intentions in their seeking and striving are what warrants the invisible 4th density assistance, and the mental asking for assistance is what strengthens the aid. More assistance is able to be provided to those who seek or focus on something with dedication. The saying, "God helps those who help themselves" is most accurate; in this case the part of God/Source helping is 4th density beings or your spirit guides. The more a being seeks and strives, both in states of being and through states of action, the more opportunity for aid arises.

When aid is provided, a thought or an idea may seemingly pop into a 3rd density being's mind: a simple decision to do or say something, an answer to a question they have been pondering over, or an illuminated light-bulb moment. The being typically thinks they came up with the idea, that the thought or idea originated from themselves, but it was actually gifted to them telepathically by 4th density beings or from their spirit guides. The 4th density positive being has already worked past the ego and does not need recognition, so it does not bother them that the 3rd density being thinks it was their own idea. Instead, it delights them that they got through and were able to aid; their service is their aim and recognition is not needed. One could say the positive polarity garnered by the positive being for such an action is a form of passive recognition. Being of service itself is their reward, and their actions assist their united group in polarizing more toward the positive, moving toward graduating to 5th density. When one serves and helps others, they are serving and helping themselves at the same time. All are One.

The best way for a 3rd density being to receive aid is to have daily periods of downtime. Daily meditation where the clearing of mind and the relaxing of the body allows not only healing and inner work to take place, but makes one open to the influence of their spirit guides and 4th density beings' ideas, solutions, and guidance to come through while the mind is not active and blocking such channels of communication. Quiet times of contemplation and reflection can also open up avenues for assistance. Typically the guidance is gifted to the 3rd density being during meditation and sprouts or becomes known sometime after the meditation. Possibly within the same day as the meditation, or possibly days, weeks, or even months later when synchronicities in life align or when the being triggers the coming forward of the information through states of being or reaching a certain level in one's spiritual progression. It all depends on the particular type of guidance or download gifted and the path of the being who receives it.

3rd density beings can channel 4th density beings in the traditional sense of the word "channel": to be in a relaxed meditative state and give consent to the 4th density being to talk through oneself as the receiver and be asked questions by at least one other present 3rd density being. The messages received are mainly focused on love, unity, and expressing how meditation is important. Typically the 3rd density being keeps asking questions instead of following through with the advice, and so they end up receiving a repeated message in different words over and over again. If the 3rd density being wants new information, they need to put the advice into action and show dedication. The 4th density being does not do the work for them, as that would be infringing upon one's free will. Only you can do the inner work for yourself to spiritually grow. Once the 3rd density being practices the advice and performs loving-kindness and daily meditation, even if for short periods of time, they will be able to grow, expand, and understand why both acts are very beneficial. Doing the inner work and practicing meditation also opens up doors for more assistance in everyday life without the need for traditional channeling, because one is open for telepathic pathways where one's spirit guides and 4th density beings can be more of assistance by offering aid in the moments of everyday life as they arise. One's preceding lessons learned and practiced in the classroom setting grants access to the next sub-density grade level's information and lessons.

The more aid a 4th density being gives, the more love and compassion they attain, and the more they polarize to the positive. The more experience obtained in service through trial and error garners more understanding of the minds and ways of a particular societal disposition, their dance so to speak, which makes the 4th density being more efficient at aiding. This growth of understanding not only strengthens love and compassion, but allows more positive polarization to occur for both the 4th density being doing the service and possibly for the receiving 3rd density being if they follow through and do the work themselves. Serving others increases understanding, universal love, compassion, and unity, all of which moves a 4th density united group toward graduation.

A rotating position of a very, very few 4th density beings take on the role of attacking or defending their united group from the opposite polarity in their density. 4th density negatives do the attacking and 4th density positives do the defending. 4th density battles typically end up being a stalemate, as both sides are well-skilled and equipped in their ways.

The 4th density negative experience starts out with intense fighting between the beings in this group in order to establish the hierarchy of power and authority. Beings use tactics that utilize the transparency of 4th density against each other in a mental battle of willpower, opposite of how the positives use transparency to harmonize. Once the pecking order is established it resembles something like a military ranking order. This military unit is the united group for those on the negative path. They are not a harmonized united group, but they are a united group in that they have a shared intention: to teach and spread their doctrine of the service-to-self path. They can mobilize like a military unit and set out to influence 3rd density beings just like the positives do, but the negatives use temptation, manipulation, and deception rather than honesty in their telepathic acts to assist 3rd density beings in polarizing toward the negative. 3rd density beings or groups who lust for power and control beam out such intentions, even if only done mentally. 4th density beings, who can read thoughts, feelings, and emotions, are drawn to such 3rd density beings like a magnet. This magnetic pull is the same for positive and negative beings; it is the mental intentions and the asking for assistance by 3rd density beings that initiates the process. Most 3rd density beings are not aware that their thoughts are real things and can affect the physical outer planes. Mind over matter is knowledge that few 3rd density beings consciously practice, but it is learned and practiced by every 4th density being, and in 5th density beings become adept at it, and it is close to perfected in 6th density.

A tried-and-true method used by 4th density negative united groups is to sniff out some type of group—nation, race, organization, secret society—that is already powerful, or has the ability to rise to power, and influence them into thinking or strengthening the idea that they are elite and superior to others. If the 4th density negatives are successful, the influenced 3rd density group uses their power to establish themselves as the few so-called elite and work toward controlling and enslaving the majority, which they perceive themselves to be superior to and therefore feel justified in controlling and ruling over them. This is typically done through war; a nation or race expands as much as possible through military might, thinking their cause is justified because they believe they are the superior, more civilized, more intelligent, and/or more spiritual 3rd density beings. Examples are not needed, as Earth's history is littered with such examples, even up to the present. When a certain level of technological advancement and/or cleverness is reached for the civilization or planet, wars can be waged clandestinely instead of through public conflict. This is the case with Earth, where clandestine acts happen on a daily basis without the general population being aware of what is transpiring and what is shaping their society.

Shaping a 3rd density civilization, or entire planet if possible, into such a hierarchy of power and control is mirroring the structure of the 4th density negative's united group. It is an effective method that has proven itself to work, so the negatives continue to use it. 4th density negative beings are not only drawn to beings who produce negative mental intentions, they are also drawn to individuals and groups who are or who potentially will create much positive polarity by aiding a large amount of beings. The negatives attempt to stop the aid from coming to fruition, and the more negative inroads the positively oriented being or group they are targeting produces, the more the negatives have to work with. Due to the illusion of time, 4th density negative beings can see 3rd density possibilities/probabilities in timelines approximately up to 3 months before they transpire in 3rd density, and 5th density negative beings can see up to 5 months in advance. It is the same for 4th and 5th density positive beings, with 6th density positive beings being able to do this with the same accuracy up to 10 months in advance. Higher-density beings, positive and negative, can see further than the specified periods, but only perceive possibilities where the probabilities become less clear the further out into the time/space continuum.

When 4th density negatives are attempting to separate and disassemble a positively oriented 3rd density group who is endeavoring to majorly aid their civilization or planet, the negatives use their telepathic tactics of temptation, manipulation, and deception on the weakest link(s) in the group, making them think they are not getting enough recognition, enough money, become jealous of other members, or any of the myriad of other ways—there are countless temptations and deceptions for any given case and any given being. 4th density negatives can take down even some of the most stable of organizations, movements, or causes. They do so by implementing a two-way attack: tempting the weakest link(s) in the positively oriented group while at the same time influencing other 3rd density individuals or groups who are already in or could be in some way in opposition to the positively oriented group. These human tools could be power-hungry and/or money-hungry and see their power and/or wealth being threatened by the positively oriented group's advancements, or they could be a religious or scientific group firmly set in their dogma or ways of thinking.

If a monetary system has been established in a civilization or the entire planet, 4th density negative beings lick their lips with glee, as such a tool is the most powerful weapon for causing separation and forming a minority of so-called elites who wield control over a majority that find themselves moving further and further into enslavement as time progresses. If these control-hungry negatively oriented human beings are good enough pupils to their 4th density chosen masters, they are successful at shaping a heavily controlled nation or entire planet where the majority do not even think they are enslaved. This can be accomplished with 4th density telepathic assistance and temptation alone, but if the 3rd density so-called elites have established a direct line of communication via so-called magical rituals with their 4th density negative chosen masters, it is much easier to shape the planet in their controlling image. If this shaping is done gradually enough over time, or even quickly if programming and social conditioning tactics are fully utilized, generations are born into a type of slavery they do not question or even realize, and think it is just how the world is and there is nothing to be done about it but get ahead by doing what you are told to do by the authority structure. If the civilization or planet has been captured by a monetary system, this tool is used by negatively oriented 3rd density beings as a dangerous weapon against the majority; it is fully utilized for temptation, compliance, submission, and control.

4th density negatives work on their tactics by increasing their understanding of the particular dance of a societal disposition and advance toward graduation by polarizing more to the negative through their influential deeds. Their service of offering 3rd density beings temptation, manipulation, and deception that leads toward the negative path is how they increase their negative polarity and power.

There is always a possibility for a technologically advanced negatively oriented later 3rd sub-density society/race to be used by their 4th density negative chosen masters to collude with a negatively oriented 3rd density group that invites them to openly attempt to take over their civilization or planet. But typically the two groups work together behind closed doors.

When interacting with positively oriented beings and the majority, a specific advanced later 3rd sub-density society/race is typically selected for this role because they are deemed physically pleasing to the particular civilization or planet they are attempting to bring under the negatives' rule. They use manipulation and deceptively come across as higher-density positive beings interested in aiding the civilization or planet, tempting them into agreeing to something that would unknowingly enslave them, either outright or through time. Technology augmentation is one of their typical tactics because through this method a type of possession or mind control is possible. If the deceptive method is rejected by the civilization, they leave and continue to work behind the scenes with the negatively oriented 3rd density group that invited them, assisting the 3rd density group at taking control of the planet for the negatives. If even a minority of the 3rd density civilization or planet accepts the method of deceitful aid, it offers inroads that alter the planet's possibility/timeline and may be majorly detrimental.

Unlike 4th to 6th density positive beings, 4th and 5th density negative beings do not need a calling or approval from a Council and set out to conquer on their own accord, but the polarity rules set up by the Logoi keep them in check so they do not spoil the game play or cosmic experience. A negative being does not gain negative polarity by simply doing negative and controlling actions. If they break cosmic rules while performing certain negative deeds, they lose negative polarity. Since gaining polarity in one's chosen direction is advancement, rules are followed by the negatives and positives.

If positively oriented 3rd density beings—a civilization, group, or individual—are contacted in any manner by higher-density beings offering assistance, the 3rd density being(s) have to use their discernment to assess if the contact is genuinely positive or not. Negative 4th and especially 5th density beings are skilled at deception and temptation and attempt to trick positively and neutrally oriented 3rd density beings into thinking they contacted and made deals with positive higher-density beings. Positive higher-density beings do not make deals; they offer their services freely and do not ask for anything in return. This negative deception has happened many times on Earth and is recorded in Earth's so-called holy religious documents and books. Commonplace positive material is given in order to deceive the 3rd density being into thinking they are in contact with a positive higher-density being or "God". Negative material is slipped in with mediocre positive material and the negatives gain inroads to the individual conversing with them and with the group the individual represents, and potentially even an entire civilization if the 3rd density group takes control of it with the aid of the negatives they think are the positives. If 3rd density beings use their discernment and recognize what is not positive instead of mindlessly obeying what they are told, such deception may be recognized and avoided. (This will be expanded upon in the subject about religions and their origins.)

There is always a decline of negative beings with each graduated density because some switch polarities to the positive. Approximate percentages of beings graduating from 4th to 5th density are: 92% graduate to the positive path and 8% graduate to the negative path. The negative decline can be seen when comparing the negative graduation approximate percentages from 3rd to 4th density (14%) to 4th to 5th density graduation (8%).

In at least the middle sub-densities of any density a being can choose to switch polarities, so a being is not stuck in the negatively or positively polarized path after they have made the choice in graduating 3rd density. A positive being does not feel the need to switch polarity, as one who lives harmoniously does not wish to switch to living disharmoniously. A negative being can choose to work at switching polarities and join the positive path in the middle to later sub-densities of the 4th or 5th density; we have already covered 6th density for this but will expand upon it during the 6th density section. Some 3rd density beings who end up graduating to 4th density negative did not know what they were signing up for, but they cannot simply switch polarities to positive at the beginning of 4th density. They have to see their choice through to at least the middle sub-densities of their current density before they are able to switch polarities, which is approximately 15 million years for 4th density and 27 million years for 5th density. Other 4th density negative beings, having experienced the adversity and spiritual entropy on the negative path, decide to switch polarities instead of continuing on the negative path to graduate to 5th density negative. These are the reasons why approximately 14% graduate to 4th density negative, but only 8% graduate to 5th density negative.

—∞—

5th density is where beings learn wisdom and the ways of light energy. This is a density where beings become masters of the art of thought creation, shaping and utilizing light so as to materialize in physical matter whatever they require. As with all higher densities, they focus on progression and influencing the density directly below them, the 4th density in this case. Sometimes 5th density beings directly influence the 3rd density instead of relying on the 4th density to do so, but this is rare.

Positive 5th density beings either choose to learn, work, and graduate in group unity or individually. They learn how to work with light and be empowered by universal love and light energy and then beam love and light energy to where it is needed in the 3rd and 4th densities. As with all higher densities, positive and negative beings in the early to middle sub-densities teach the later sub-densities of the density below them a partial amount of the ways of their density. In this case a partial amount of the ways of wisdom and light are taught to later 4th sub-density beings.

Negative 5th density beings learn wisdom that can be used for themselves in clever ways and how to work with light energy and use it for themselves and their self-serving interests. They only work individually within their density, the art of focused thought granting their needs. Some early to middle 5th sub-density negatives choose to teach and give commands to 4th density negatives because it benefits them in increasing their negative polarity. Very few 5th density negatives past the middle sub-densities see the value in working with 4th density negatives because it no longer benefits them enough in their polarity advancement. Most of them continue their negative path on their own in seclusion.

Positive and negative 5th density beings do not battle each other, as the wisdom they have learned in their density has shown the futility of warring with each other. This same futility of directly battling each other in 4th density exists but 4th density negative beings are not wise enough to cease the action.

Approximate percentages of beings graduating from 5th to 6th density are: 93.5% graduate to the positive path and 6.5% graduate to the negative path. The lighter decline of negative graduates into 6th density as compared to 5th density graduation is because the few remaining service-to-self beings are the extremely dedicated beings who adhere to their particular path against all odds.

——∞——

6th density is where beings learn to unite and harmonize universal love learned in the 4th density with the wisdom they learned in the 5th density. (Although, negative beings learned self-love in the 4th density.) Like snowflakes, no two beings' chakras are balanced and interact in the exact same way. Each being is an expression of uniqueness, serving Source in the knowing of itself. A being learning more about themselves is synonymous with Source knowing itself more fully, as the collection of sparks is Source. The All are the One and the One is the All. Paradoxes of the cosmic illusion end in the 6th density.

Early 6th sub-density negatives teach later 5th sub-density negatives because it aids the 6th density negatives' polarity. As the early 6th sub-density negatives polarize more to the negative and advance toward the middle sub-densities, they eventually face an insurmountable wall in their advancement. 6th density is where the dualism of polarities comes to a conclusion as the positive and negative polarities harmonize and only positive polarity remains. Somewhere up to the middle 6th sub-densities, the negative 6th density beings become fully aware that it is impossible to advance in polarity and power by continuing their path back to Source on the negative path because they have to unite and harmonize wisdom with universal love—not just love for themselves—in order to advance any further in the 6th density. These beings experience spiritual entropy from not working in harmony with 6th density positives, as 6th density is no longer separated into positive and negative and unlike in 5th density, beings must work together in a united group in order to advance past the middle 6th sub-density. These wise 6th density negatives come to fully realize that they have to switch to positive polarity and join the positive united group in order to advance any further.

A being can only get so close on the negative polarity path back to Source before the knowing and acceptance sets in that all are truly One, and to deceive and control other beings is to do so to oneself, which is neither a wise nor a loving thing to do. Like a negatively charged electron can never get close to entering the nucleus or center of an atom where positively charged protons and no-polarity-charged neutrons reside.

At this time, the negative-turned-positive beings set out to balance their built-up karma that had been put off, as when a being performs enough service-to-self acts to graduate from 3rd density and starts 4th density on the negative path, the act of balancing their karma is delayed. They had to face their karma for all the incarnations in 3rd density where they did not graduate, but once they graduated to 4th density negative, it is delayed. If you are playing a game, you do not penalize the player that accomplished their mission, their "success". In the 4th and 5th densities, these negative players may continue to play their negative roles, building up karma instead of having to face it. When negative beings switch to the positive path—at the latest in the middle 6th sub-density—they do not see balancing their accrued karma as a hassle or a judgment; instead, now on the positive path, they see it as a duty/honor to willingly perform the balancing, as a service-to-others being does, knowing that all are

One and to hurt another is to hurt oneself, and the balancing of harmful actions is not only helping other-selves but helping oneself since all are One/Source.

From a positive being's perspective, those playing the negative roles have to face a type of permanent karma situation that is separate from their delayed karma because to be in opposition with the true loving and united Source within every being is to live without peace. There is no peace when one lives in separation and is at odds with its teammates, which is the same thing as being at odds with oneself since all are One. To do so is to experience spiritual entropy. Having to constantly take orders and bow down in submission to those above you also takes its toll.

Hell is not a place, it is a state of being, and one might say that dwelling on the negative path is to be in a hellish state of being; whereas being on the positive path is to be in a heavenly state of being, experiencing universal love, joy, and peace. These are concepts brought forward by Yahushua/Jesus and other higher-density beings that were misunderstood.

Later 6th sub-density beings, whom are only positive as all negatives have switched polarities before this point, beam love and light energy out to where it is needed in all the densities below them. A later 6th sub-density united group eventually inhabits a Logos/star and adds to the intelligently conscious love and light energy that is constantly being provided by a Logos out to all the planets and all the beings on those planets within its orbit. At some point during a later 6th sub-density united group's experience, moving off their 6th density core planet and inhabiting a Logos/star is done so that the partial early lessons of the 7th density can be learned and graduation to 7th density made possible for their united group. Our later 6th sub-density united group is currently doing this while inhabiting your Sun. A large amount of wanderers on Earth are of our united group. (Wanderers will be covered in the next subject.)

If a 3rd density civilization creates a sufficient mass calling—beings seeking and striving through positive mental intentions for assistance—later 6th sub-density united groups can answer this mass calling with benevolent telepathy where the receiver usually believes it is their own thoughts. This is something spirit guides and 4th density beings do all the time, with 4th density negatives using malevolent telepathy, but later 6th sub-density united groups telepathically aid beings who have the greatest probability to be effective on their planet: ideas and solutions given to inventors who are on the cusp of a breakthrough that will advance their civilization, leaders trying to avert war or a major crisis of some sort, leaders working toward a major benefit for the beings they serve, those who give speeches or write material down that can potentially reach many (as we are doing with this awareness-expanding material), or any other circumstance where a being has the potential for positive change for many.

Another way later 6th sub-density united groups can answer a sufficient mass calling is to present their case or plan to the local Council. If their plan involves direct contact and is approved, a selected entity or a few entities from the later 6th sub-density united group appears before a 3rd density civilization and offers them teachings face-to-face in their own language. Beings from the 4th to 6th density can scan a planet and instantly know the 3rd density languages used, but are typically not effective at using the language due to not having lived among the civilization. Direct contact is only done if the later 6th sub-density united group thinks it would be effective for the particular civilization that the mass call originated from. If the later 6th sub-density united group can effectively aid through more subtle means other than direct contact, it is preferred, as the chances of infringing upon free will and developing karmic ties is greatly reduced without direct contact. Direct face-to-face aid from later 6th sub-density united groups has happened several times within the last 13,000 years of Earth's history due to such a low percentage of graduates from Earth, which prompted aid to be offered. (We will cover this in a future subject about Earth's history.)

——∞——

7th density is like the hallway back to Source, with the hallway becoming narrower with each sub-density reached. This density approaches timelessness where the present moment is lived and the self's totality is seen. The illusion of time that resides in the Cosmos is almost to an end because merging with Source is approaching. In the narrowing hallway that leads to Source, the illusion of time narrows along with all other aspects of the illusion in the Cosmos until the merging back with Source ceases the entire illusion; the dreamer truly awakens from the dream.

7th density beings do not interact with any density except later 6th sub-density united groups. When 7th density united groups reach the middle sub-density, they become the totality of themselves. At this point each being reaches a totality of all their selves throughout the possibilities/timelines. This totality of a being contains the infinite possibilities the self experienced in every timeline they resided in. It is the nexus at the end of all the infinite roads, the infinite possibilities/timelines throughout all densities leading up to the totality of a being in the middle 7th sub-density. Even at this nexus, one's totality of being does not know what roads its 3rd density self will end up taking in their future due to free will, but it does know the destination that all the possible roads lead to because it is at that nexus/destination.

Your 7th density totality of being is your future self that exists right now in the same timeless instance as your focal point of awareness in 3rd density because time is an illusion. This is also why your later 6th sub-density higher self can assist you while you are discarnate in the inner planes while preparing for your next incarnation.

After the totality of a being is reached in the middle sub-density, the totality of the united group is reached in the later 7th sub-density. In the middle sub-density, the 7th density united group leaves behind a living memory bank of itself for later 6th sub-density united groups to interact with and learn from as they advance toward their graduation. This is the last action of 7th density united groups before ceasing all interaction with densities below them and setting their entire focus on continuing down the ever narrowing hallway, increasing spiritual mass and losing physical mass on their way back to merging with Source.

101.8 – Wanderers

We will speak of wanderers, also known as star seeds. Later 4th sub-density to later 6th sub-density beings can choose to re-experience an incarnation or more in the 3rd density to offer aid and teach universal love, knowledge, wisdom, and assist in raising the collective's consciousness simply by adding their potentially high vibration to the planetary collective. This also gives the higher-density being the opportunity to further their or their united group's advancement toward graduation in their true density more quickly than they could by staying in their true density doing service-to-others work because there are more opportunities in the intense 3rd density; the greater the challenges, the greater the possibilities of gaining polarity.

Beings who perform this action have been called wanderers or star seeds on Earth. We will refer to all of them—4th through 6th—as wanderers because only 6th density wanderers' united groups may inhabit a star, and so be in line with the label star seeds. Typically wanderers offer their services to a civilization or planet at pivotal times during a 3rd density experience. The time period close to the end of a grand cycle where all are harvested is the most pivotal time period, so this is when there is the greatest influx of wanderers incarnating onto 3rd density planets.

Beings on the negative path seldom become wanderers because there is a large risk they will not remember their mission and get stuck in 3rd density by way of karmic ties. Since they are service-to-self beings, typically the best way to serve oneself is to continue to focus on oneself in the current density and not risk being a wanderer in a lower density. It is seen as a risky and brave action to be a wanderer because they have to go through the veil of forgetfulness like all other 3rd density beings and so forget who they are and their pre-incarnate planned mission. It is also risky because if the wanderer does not remember their mission, they run the risk of creating karma and getting entangled in the 3rd density experience. If this happens, they have to keep reincarnating onto the 3rd density planet till they balance the created karma instead of incarnating back into their true density after the 3rd density incarnation is over. After they have balanced the karma created on the 3rd density planet, or when harvest-time begins, they return to their true density.

Karmic ties being created in 3rd density by a wanderer is akin to trying to help others out of the mud pit and instead ending up in the mud with them. The challenging dance of a wanderer is one of balance and fortitude, being in the world to directly assist as much as possible but not being of the world and getting caught up in low vibratory mentality and actions. Most wanderers incarnate onto 3rd density planets near the end of a grand cycle, living only one incarnation before the harvest-time so they do not get stuck in karma and have to keep reincarnating onto the planet. They can still accumulate karma that lowers their positive polarization, prompting them to serve and aid more in order to recoup polarity and continue working toward graduating from their true density, but they will not be tied to reincarnating onto the 3rd density planet due to karmic ties since that particular 3rd density experience ended. This, along with the fact that the challenges in the time period before harvest-time offer numerous polarization opportunities, is why most wanderers choose to incarnate near the end of a 3rd density planet's grand cycle.

Due to the veil of forgetfulness of incarnating into 3rd density, most wanderers do not end up remembering their mission. The path to a wanderer's remembering comes through in stages of awareness, just like any 3rd density being's path of awareness expansion, but since the wanderer has already experienced at least a 3rd and 4th density, they have the ability to remember much quicker, unconsciously tapping into their subconscious mind and accessing the trunk or roots of the tree of mind. First the wanderer notices there is something different about them compared to other beings, which then could grow into a feeling of alienation as the feeling strengthens through observation of the low vibratory planetary ways. This may grow to the point where the wanderer recognizes to an increased degree that the planetary ways of insanity are not their personal ways, and the planet does not feel like their true home. Pre-incarnate agreements with other beings are carried out as they grow older, offering the wanderer more and more opportunities to gravitate toward a field or fields of work where they may carry out their mission or where they get equipped with knowledge, wisdom, skills, and abilities to perform their mission elsewhere. Often the mission is carried out with the wanderer not even remembering they are a wanderer or that they had planned a certain pre-incarnate mission, but they know their work will aid their fellow planetary beings in some way, perhaps greatly. Accomplishing the mission is their goal. Remembering one is a wanderer is not the goal, although remembering may assist in accomplishing their mission, depending on their particular mission.

Even if a wanderer does remember and/or is gravitated toward their mission, they still need to overcome the many obstacles that have been created in the civilization or planet they wish to aid. The more negative polarity actions that have taken root in a civilization or planet, the greater the obstacles for the wanderer. In addition to those obstacles, when/if a wanderer remembers who they are and/or their mission and starts to put it into action, 4th density negative beings are drawn to them like moths to a light and target them heavily. Light attracts the light, and dark attracts the dark, but the opposite is also the case: light attracts the dark, and the dark attracts the light. One attracts the aid of their own polarity because of a shared intention, which is similar to those hearing and communicating with each other due to using the same radio frequency. One attracts hindrances from the opposite polarity when a significant amount of polarity is attempting to be created or being created that signals the opposite polarity beings who attempt to limit or stop the polarity from being created for energy balancing purposes and to assist their chosen polarity, positive or negative.

The wanderer has to rely on the limitations of being in 3rd density and does not have the abilities of their true density they came from, even if they remember their true density and that they are a wanderer. But if a wanderer adequately balances their chakras, small aspects of their higher-density abilities are recovered when they bleed through from the subconscious mind. When a wanderer incarnates into 3rd density, they must play by the ways/rules of that density; at no time can they fully recoup their true density's abilities and be an unstoppable force in 3rd density. Even though it is very difficult for a wanderer to remember who they are, fully recouping their true density's abilities would be considered unfair on the 3rd density game board. Although, a wanderer is able to relearn things very quickly since they have already learned them and intuitively tap into their subconscious mind where all their incarnations reside and all they have learned. Since a wanderer has recently experienced a higher density, what they have experienced and learned in that higher density resides at the top layer of their subconscious mind, so it is easier to intuitively access instead of it being buried at the bottom layer of the subconscious mind like it is for true 3rd density beings. If this were not the case, there would not be much of a reason in signing up to be a wanderer, as the percentages would be very extremely high for one to not remember their mission, not provide aid, and get caught up in 3rd density karma. As it is, it is already very difficult for a wanderer to remember their mission and accomplish it.

Wanderers, especially from the 6th density, might feel at a young age that their Earth family is not their real family, as they subconsciously have a link to their united group in their true higher density, which is their true family. The feeling may be similar to that of an orphan taking up residency with a new family.

It is rare, but if the wanderer remembers their mission and is making great advances toward fulfilling it and does not give into temptation nor allows major hindrances from 4th density negatives, a 5th density negative being might reluctantly take up the task their 4th density underlings could not handle and target the wanderer themselves with psychic attacks. They cannot attack directly and create that which is not already established; they have to work within negative inroads the wanderer allows to exist—such as negative thoughts and emotions created and/or entertained—and pre-existing flaws in a wanderer's body and mind from a pre-incarnate planned genetic disposition and other pre-incarnate set ways that present limitations the negative being can utilize and take advantage of. They also have a greater ability than their 4th density underlings at using telepathy to potentially manipulate and tempt the 3rd density beings around and close to the wanderer, specifically utilizing anyone who is working with the wanderer to fulfill the mission or who spends a lot of time with the wanderer. They also may target the wanderer's family and friends in an attempt to create discord with the wanderer. Even strangers the wanderer comes in contact with may be utilized as tools. Everything that can be done to unbalance and stop the aiding work of the wanderer is done if fulfilling their particular mission has the probability of causing great advances toward positive polarity for the civilization or planet. Even charging a situation to end the wanderer's incarnation, causing them to transition is possible. 3rd density weak links are targeted and used as tools against the wanderer. If the wanderer has to work within a group to fulfill their mission, it would behoove them to make sure it is a tight and faithful group to the cause.

All the opposition a wanderer faces is an indirect message from the negatives that the wanderer is doing a great job performing their role, an indirect compliment or praise so to speak. The same goes for any positively oriented 3rd density being who is attempting to or is currently creating large amounts of positive polarity. The negatives would not be attacking if the being was not doing something of importance. If the wanderer is wise enough to comprehend this, they may deal with the attacks more gracefully. If the wanderer is also wise enough to know that it is nothing personal, but rather is simply the role of the negatives to stop positive polarity, then it is easier for the wanderer to shrug off the attacks. A 3rd density being, wanderer or not, cannot create great amounts of positive polarity and not be attacked by the negatives. Just as a sports player is much more intensively guarded and attacked by the opposite team the closer they get to scoring a goal. It is simply the way of the game board and when the pieces are familiar with game play, they do not take other player's actions so seriously or personally.

Feeling like a victim, being angry, fearful, or creating and/or charging any other self-sabotaging thoughts or emotions due to the negatives' attacks is falling right into the tactics of the negatives, as doing so lowers the wanderer's vibration, which affects their mission if not ceasing it entirely. If the negatives can manipulate the wanderer into ceasing their loving-kindness nature with the attacks, this is a win for them in itself because as we have said, the state of being is more important and has a major impact on the actions done in the physical.

One of the tactics of the negatives is to get wanderers or 3rd density positively oriented beings to sabotage themselves with self-defeating thoughts, emotions, and feelings toward themselves and/or others around them. Doing such not only lowers one's vibration, but charges possibilities that fuel even more tension with oneself and others. If this is accomplished in a major way, the negatives can step away because the positive being is now actively destroying themselves, doing the negatives' job for them. With no more light being produced, moths would no longer be drawn to the light to blot it out.

Due to the attacks and friction from so many 3rd density beings who are used as tools against the wanderer, the wanderer, if not dedicated and wise enough, might cast their mission aside, no longer willing to help their fellow planetary beings that seem to be against them at every step of the way. Or a wanderer, from merely observing low vibratory planetary ways, may develop a mental stance of apathy towards assisting the planetary beings they had pre-incarnate planned to assist. If such mental states arise, 4th or 5th density negatives read this mental state of the wanderer and utilize these inroads by attempting to charge/bolster the negative thoughts in order to stop the wanderer from fulfilling their mission. The negatives use telepathy to do this, offering temptation to the ways of negativity, selfishness, and separation. Their service-to-self doctrine offers telepathic thoughts or charges similar pre-existing thoughts like: "They do not deserve to be helped. Just focus on yourself." Or "Why continue to help humanity when they do so many negative things to you? Just focus on yourself."

All these tactics of the negatives against the wanderer we have listed are also used for any 3rd density being who is positively oriented enough in nature to be performing work that could affect the dualism of polarity in their civilization or planet. The most effective defense against the negatives is to stay positive and keep a loving-kindness nature no matter how great the opposition. The positively oriented 3rd density being known as Martin Luther King Jr. is a fine example for having done such.

Showing loving-kindness does not mean being a doormat or blindly trusting every 3rd density being one comes in contact with, especially since 3rd density beings will continue to be sent to their specified target, consciously or unconsciously, both being tools for the negatives—the target being a wanderer or a positively oriented 3rd density being whose acts have the probability to positively polarize many other beings. Keeping a balanced level of analytical intelligence and intuition for one's discernments is of much benefit. Notice the opposition for what it is and deal with it accordingly without losing positivity and producing negativity. This is a hard task and one will find themselves automatically reacting with negativity in the beginning, but if they continue to observe themselves and notice when they have slipped, they will become more unwavering through practice. The negatives want you to produce negativity from their attacks, as producing negativity poisons oneself and lowers their vibration, which is the negatives aim. By producing negativity, you are helping the negatives to destroy yourself.

During attacks or in between, bathe yourself in universal love and even send it to the negatives who attack you. This is like poison to them. If you react to them with their same fiery negativity, it fuels them and the fire, but if you love them, they shrink away like fire coming in contact with water. During attacks, you can call on your higher self and/or other positive higher-density beings you have an affinity towards and ask for love energy and protection, doing so with confident power instead of with fear strengthens the call for assistance and the aid that can be offered.

A later 4th sub-density wanderer teaches what they have learned in 4th density—universal love, loving-kindness, and compassion. A later 5th sub-density wanderer teaches what they have learned in 5th density—wisdom, knowledge, and effectiveness. A later 6th sub-density wanderer, having learned how to balance universal love with wisdom, has the greatest chance of being effective at their mission and teaching the ways of both the 4th and 5th density as well as 6th density concepts and a higher viewpoint that ascends duality.

The later 6th sub-density wanderers who graduated up to 6th density on the negative path and switched to positive polarity are very familiar with the ways and tactics of the negatives. The veil of forgetfulness is somewhat offset by their intuition, and the more practice they get from each attack, the more those tactics are recognized and how to overcome them rises from their subconscious mind to their conscious mind. Given this, and that they are very eager to aid 3rd density to balance their large amounts of delayed karma, they could be seen as a force to be reckoned with, as long as they do not fall into old patterns before they grow aware enough of their pre-incarnate mission. They, as with all positive higher-density beings, see their duty as an honor and are honored to perform the duty instead of seeing it as assigned from judgment. Judgment is abandoned by 4th density positive beings, or in the density that a negative being switches polarities.

Since later 6th sub-density beings are most equipped for the job, they are by far the largest percentage of wanderers who incarnate into 3rd density to assist and teach near the end of a planet's grand cycle. At the end of a grand cycle, 3rd density beings are all harvested whether they are ready to graduate to the next density or not. Those that are not ready to graduate incarnate onto a different planet, one where the 3rd density experience can be continued for them. (We will expand upon this in a future subject about the harvest.)

One of the cases where 6th density beings influence and assist 3rd density beings with teachings is when the contacted—in some manner—3rd density being is a wanderer from the same later 6th sub-density united group that is assisting them, thus the wanderer's true density is of 6th density, which is precisely how and why this awareness-expanding course is being made available to all 3rd density human beings; the wanderer conveying and bringing this awareness-expanding course forward is of our later 6th sub-density united group. Since he has done the inner work to adequately balance his energy centers and expanded his knowledge and wisdom on his own accord during his incarnation, he is able to receive this information with no free will being abridged, then, since he has wandered and incarnated back as a 3rd density being, he is able to relay this wide scope of information with other 3rd density beings without abridging their free will because he is of the same density—even though temporarily—as those being offered the information. And he is not forcing the information onto any human being, but rather offering cosmic reality that human beings can choose to align with or not. In this way, free will is not abridged anywhere within the links.

Typically, a wanderer is responsible for adequately balancing their energy centers/chakras in order to pierce the veil in some way before some type of nonphysical contact can be made by their united group, otherwise this nonphysical contact is typically not established. A later 6th sub-density united group could offer a certain level of information to a positively oriented 3rd density being if their civilization produced a sufficient mass calling, or the united group could do the same through a 4th or 5th density wanderer who has adequately balanced their chakras or is part of the civilization that has produced a sufficient mass calling. But when pertaining to bringing forward the wide scope of information and reality within this awareness-expanding course, the pathway would have to be through a later 6th sub-density wanderer who already knows this information in the top layers of their subconscious mind and can remember it after they have done the inner work to adequately balance their chakras and put much focus on seeking and striving because such a pathway is necessary for the wide scope of information to be understood and accurately brought through.

There are two exceptions for beings who have chosen the positive path in the 4th to later 6th sub-densities where switching to the negative path may occur. A positive wanderer might not remember their mission and feel animosity toward the less-advanced civilization they incarnated into, going on to perform at least 95% service-to-self actions and graduating to 4th density negative after the end of their 3rd density wanderer incarnation. They would become aware of their actions when they transition and the veil of forgetfulness is lifted. They would be dismayed with the actions they performed in their wandering incarnation and transition to the negative inner planes where they would have to learn and prepare for incarnating onto a 4th density negative planet. This is difficult for them since they are not used to the negative ways. Even though they performed selfish actions in the last singular incarnation, they have many incarnations spanning more than one density stored in their subconscious mind of performing service-to-others acts that aligns them with the mentality that is of positive polarity. They will have to advance through the sub-densities as a 4th density negative being until they reach at least the middle sub-densities and are able to switch their polarity back to positive and return to the positive path and their true density.

The second exception is even rarer of an occurrence. If a 3rd density being, typically a wanderer, is etheric projecting or in a trance while allowing a positive higher-density being to temporarily use their body for traditional channeling with service-to-others intentions which produces enough light energy for a 5th density negative being to detect and take notice of, the 5th density negative being could use deception to try to get the 3rd density being to follow them in their out-of-yellow-ray-body state to a negative inner planes area of time in space. If this happens to a true 3rd density being, they may fall into a coma and/or transition/die and reincarnate into 3rd density again. If this happens to a wanderer, they may fall into a coma and/or transition/die and be forced to incarnate into 4th density negative. What happens next for them to solve this issue we have already explained in the first exception.

Some recognizable wanderers in Earth's history are known as: Socrates, Benjamin Franklin, Thomas Jefferson, Nikola Tesla, and Albert Einstein. Other Earth wanderers who taught universal love and wisdom that was later after their departures turned into heavily distorted religions will be covered later in the subject focusing on religions and their origins. Many wanderers who were just as effective or semi-effective as those listed are not known figures recorded in your history books.

Since the end of a grand cycle on Earth is approaching very soon, an influx of wanderers have been incarnating onto Earth for decades, some even centuries ago, but most have incarnated close enough to the end of Earth's grand cycle for them to still be incarnated when harvest-time begins. There are approximately 385 million wanderers incarnate on planet Earth now, most of them being 6th density wanderers. They are having an extremely difficult time remembering and fulfilling their missions due to the amount of programming and major control implemented on societal systems on Earth that were consciously or unconsciously engineered by negatively oriented 3rd density beings with the influence and/or greater assistance from their negative 4th density outer planes beings and 4th and 5th density inner planes negative beings, their chosen masters. Highly negatively oriented 3rd density human beings have been called psychopaths, elites, or globalists by their fellow human beings. These are the human beings we speak of when we say highly negatively oriented 3rd density beings, and also possibly when we say negatively oriented 3rd density beings or simply the negatively oriented. The latter two being for brevity's sake.

——∞——

A similar circumstance to wanderers, although much rarer, are what have been called walk-ins by some human beings, so we will use this term to refer to them. When a 3rd density being becomes overwhelmed with life situations and intensely feels they can no longer accomplish their pre-incarnate plans, often contemplating suicide, a dream state contact might be made with a positive higher-density being offering a solution. We will use a walk-in example of a known entity in your history that is a good example and has been used before on Earth to explain walk-ins: Abraham Lincoln. At the age of 44, Abraham had grown exhausted and overwhelmed with life. He did not wish to continue his life but had a strong enough character to avoid suicide. It was seen that he would not follow through with his pre-incarnate plans, so a positive 4th density being contacted him during dream state and a walk-in agreement was made because the 4th density being saw Abraham's pre-incarnate goal to be pivotal in the duality of polarity. The walk-in would use Abraham's 3rd density body to fulfill the pre-incarnate agreements with other beings in his life and attempt to accomplish the goal Abraham had pre-incarnate planned that he felt he no longer could accomplish. In this way, the mission would still be pursued. Abraham's etheric body would reside in a plane of suspension until the transition/death of his 3rd density body, the yellow-ray body. The walk-in then went on to become president of the United States of America nation and used this position to legally end the service-to-self action of owning other human beings as property. This was the main pre-incarnate goal set by Abraham and it was accomplished by his walk-in who saw it as an important enough goal to warrant walk-in assistance.

As with wanderers, walk-ins pass through the veil of forgetfulness when they move into the 3rd density body they will utilize, so they are not aware they are a walk-in and that the exchange has occurred and still think they are the same being until they transition/die, or visit a quality regression hypnotherapist. They hold the same memories of the current incarnation from the original being. They still hold their own past incarnations in their subconscious mind, so they will relearn things quicker like a wanderer does. Due to their subconscious influences, they may do things a little differently than the original being, which may be noticed by those in close relationships with them, but ultimately disregarded and seen as usual change and shifting traits of a personality.

101.9 – Higher-Density Organizations

We will cover the higher-density organizations and affiliations of the positive and negative paths and their influences upon 3rd density. If a being graduates to 4th density negative, they join the Orion Empire, which is the name this group has been called on Earth due to human beings' labeling and applying names to what they call constellations, so we will refer to this group as such. Since those at the top of this power and control structure reside in what has been labeled the Orion constellation on Earth, the empire is named after these top players, but their empire contains negative beings from anywhere in the universe. The same negative group exists in the infinite universes within the Cosmos, but may go by different names, some according to where the negative top players originate that is not within the Orion constellation for the particular universe.

The Orion Empire consists of 3rd to 5th density beings. At the bottom of this negative polarizing control structure are a very small amount of highly negatively oriented 3rd density beings who have chosen to make a deal with 4th density negative beings or technologically advanced negatively oriented later 3rd sub-density beings who are part of the Orion Empire. The Orion Empire is mostly made up of 4th density negatives. A very small amount of 5th density negatives are in the Orion Empire and they are the top players of the Empire's power structure.

3rd to 5th density negative inner planes beings are also in or assist the Orion Empire. 5th density negatives order, manipulate, and teach later 4th sub-density negatives the ways of love for self and understanding oneself in regards to wisdom and the ways of utilizing light energy. In turn, the 4th density negatives order and manipulate the very few 3rd density negatively oriented underlings they have acquired and attempt to influence all 3rd density beings more indirectly with telepathic temptations, attempting to teach their doctrine of service-to-self via telepathy, where the receiver does not differentiate their thoughts from the negatives, or direct communication to those with very similar dispositions who have called and invited them. 4th density negatives, by order from their 5th density negative masters, also attempt to manipulate positively oriented 3rd density beings via telepathy and other means who are threatening negative polarity by attempting to aid or being too effective at service-to-others actions that have the potential to produce much positive polarization in a 3rd density civilization or planet.

5th density negatives look at the Cosmos as something that needs to be specifically organized and ordered under the power and control structure of service to self. They feel they are doing all in the Cosmos a service in doing this because they perceive themselves to be at the top of superiority and the wisest beings, and therefore the most suited in making decisions and ordering others in the universe. This is similar to how human beings who are so-called royals conduct themselves on Earth. A large portion of 5th density negatives, especially middle to later 5th sub-density negatives, no longer see much benefit for themselves in remaining in the Orion Empire and work individually toward advancement and graduation to 6th density. Since they are service-to-self beings, they do what they consider to be the most efficient way for themselves to advance, which is not working with others. 6th density negatives are thrown into confusion when they enter the 6th density and find it very difficult to advance, confronting obstacles they have not experienced before. Before they become too confounded, they teach and manipulate later 5th sub-density negatives only because it adds to their negative polarity. Even while 6th density negatives are teaching later 5th sub-density negative beings, they are not part of the Orion Empire because they do not see any benefit in working within a group any longer for their advancement. Somewhere up to the middle 6th sub-densities, they switch to the positive path because it is the only path forward and they become fully aware of the negative path's folly. Since 6th density negative beings do not work with others until they switch to positive polarity, the very few 5th density negative beings who still work within the power structure are the top players in the Orion Empire.

4th density negatives' power in their united groups is diminished by their constant power struggles with each other, as the service-to-self being never passes up an opportunity to advance in the rankings, always practicing self over unity. This spiritual entropy causes much disintegration and lessens the amount of power wielded by the Orion Empire. Unity is always stronger than separation. Due to this constant disintegration and less beings choosing the negative path, the Orion Empire's numbers stay approximately at only 10% of that of the positive organizations' numbers.

This may appear to be an unfair balance for the service-to-self negative polarity path in regards to game play, but the cosmic experience is balanced out by the negative beings performing forceful and manipulative actions that the positive beings do not. Negative beings disregard beings' free will every chance they get as long as it does not jeopardize the strengthening of their negative polarity. Whereas positive beings attempt to honor beings' free will as much as possible. The ways of One and the cosmic game board rules are what keeps all of the players, including the negative beings, in check. Every being, positive and negative, serves Source in their own way. That service is measured with polarity. Polarity could be seen as a type of point system where one can only advance on the multilayered game board (the Cosmos) toward the finish line (merging back with Source) by collecting points (gaining positive or negative polarity). Therefore, players' actions are rewarded by staying in check and following the set rules, not wanting to be penalized and losing points if they break the rules of game play, so they perform actions to gain more points and avoid actions that take away points. As with any rules set up for a game, the rules ensure the game is played fairly so it can be enjoyed and provide learning experiences for all players.

The negative beings' desire to gain or not lose polarity is the only reason why they honor free will at certain times. If an action does not lose polarity by infringing upon free will, they always abridge free will. If a certain action of breaking free will would result in a loss of polarity, negative beings typically do not do it because they want to move forward on the game board, which is synonymous with gaining power. Being controlling is always negative, but power is not negative or positive. Power is not a negative thing, it is a tool, and like any other tool can be used to perform positively or negatively polarized actions. If positives deemed power a bad thing and did not use it, they would be instantly crushed by the negatives. The polarity, or point system, is why 4th density negative united groups do not simply take over by direct brute force an entire 3rd density planet. This type of action that infringes upon free will is against the cosmic rules and so would result in much loss of polarity for the 4th density negative beings. The very few 3rd density negatively oriented beings in the Orion Empire are ordered to do their 4th density master's bidding against other 3rd density beings so the 4th density negative beings do not lose polarity by doing it directly. The set cosmic game rules are followed so polarity/points can be acquired. When a negatively oriented 3rd density being gravitating toward 4th density negative graduation abridges another 3rd density being's free will, there is no loss of negative polarity because they reside in the same density; instead, they gain negative polarity, and if the manipulated being(s) willingly give up their free will by being deceived, the manipulator gains even more negative polarity. This latter situation is the case on Earth; since a large portion of the majority of Earthlings have been deceived and have willingly given up their free will under the engineered control system that directs the societies on Earth, the highly negatively oriented human beings have gained much negative polarity. They would lose this negative polarity if the majority of human beings realized their folly and stopped willingly giving away their free will.

If a positively oriented 3rd density being does a negative action, they lose positive polarity due to the gain of negative polarity for having done the negatively polarizing action. Similarly, a negatively oriented being would lose negative polarity if they performed a positive action, which would only benefit them if they have decided to switch polarities. It is never too late in 3rd density to switch polarities before making the final choice to graduate to 4th density positive or negative.

Here is an example of negative beings taking over a planet directly without losing polarity (4th density beings are already aware of this, so we are not assisting 4th density negatives by sharing this example): If a 4th density negative united group directly conquered a 3rd density planet and managed to make the 3rd density beings hand over their free will willingly, then the loss of polarity from the initial abridging of free will would be recovered. It is a gamble that 4th density negative united groups typically do not take because most 3rd density planets do not willingly relinquish their free will and assimilate into the power and control structure of the Orion Empire. Transitioning/dying or being forced into slavery is not considered willingly relinquishing one's free will. The rare occasions where 4th density negatives did make this gamble was due to them knowing there was a very high probability that the 3rd density planet's beings would willingly give up their free will. Therefore, it was not considered a gamble because the dealer was almost assured victory.

Instead, 4th density negative united groups choose to gain polarity as they clandestinely and indirectly conquer a 3rd density planet by manipulating negatively oriented 3rd density beings on the planet to do it for them, which also increases the possibilities for the negatively oriented 3rd density beings to fully join and strengthen the negative power structure by graduating to 4th density negative. Enormous advances have been made by the negatives on planet Earth in the last several decades. This information may be shocking to human beings who do not know how the Cosmos functions, but that is simply the game board role of 4th density negatives, who are ordered by 5th density negatives. It is what they attempt to do to every 3rd density planet and is not personal; it is simply how the negative players function on the game board. Giving into fear or anger in the case of such a matter only strips one of their power that could be used to avoid or solve any matter; being fearful or angry offers no benefits, only disadvantages. Anger may galvanize a being to do something rather than continuing to do nothing, but until anger is relinquished, the being will not have access to their higher mental faculties that are required to get the job done properly due to anger creating blockages in the red-ray chakra.

The majority of a 3rd density planet may disbelieve the reality we have provided, as is their free will to do so, but one who willingly wears a blindfold over their eyes is a very easy target for an attacker they wish to not believe in. Whether the 4th density negatives' attempts are fruitful or not is the question. The current state of planet Earth clearly shows that their temptations and deceptions have bore fruit. If human beings continue to follow the negatively oriented beings' programming that states there are no highly negatively oriented 3rd density human beings who are devoid of morality and who are attempting to clandestinely conquer the planet by any means necessary, then the negatives' probabilities of success are greatly increased, as human beings do not attempt to stop that which they do not believe exists. This is why the highly negatively oriented human beings implement strong and numerous programming methods to keep the majority disbelieving that they exist, or that there is a rather small minority who control a weighty portion of the planet and are actively conspiring to control the entire planet. It is not a theory that they are conspiring, as that is what they are doing. The majority of human beings are aware of the many corrupt beings and groups that are powerful on their planet, and they often witness how the corrupt rise in the power structure and typically get away with high crimes, so why do the majority of human beings disbelieve there is a highly negatively oriented group of human beings who are attempting to take control of as much of the planet as possible when all signs of activity point to such a conclusion? It is because of the negatively oriented beings' programming and the social conditioning that is shaped by the programming.

We understand that making these highly nefarious actions known may cause great anger and/or fear, so we inform you that anger and fear are the two leading causes of cancer. It would not serve one to add additional emotional poison to themselves on top of the poisons they have unknowingly been putting into their body via foodstuffs and everyday products, effectively assisting the negatively oriented human beings further in their aims of poisoning and weakening the majority, which allows easier manipulation and control. Instead of producing anger or fear, which does nothing to solve the issue and only makes it worse, take positive action to solve the problem. (We will expand upon this in a later subject.)

4th and 5th density negatives manipulate, deceive, teach, and order the very, very few 3rd density beings on Earth who have either shown great intentions toward service-to-self actions, which is an unconscious negative calling, or who have consciously invited the negatives via certain actions or so-called magical rituals. Other 3rd density beings are unknowingly used as tools via telepathic temptation and manipulation to fulfill the negatives' plans. The negatives' tried-and-true method of tempting the few negatively oriented 3rd density beings into believing they are superior and enslaving the majority is a prime tactic in the negatives' playbook. The group known as the Nazis were a public example of a tempted "elite" few. The so-called elite factions that are composed of very few human beings that came before the Nazis and hold much more power on planet Earth currently are not all public figures, as the top players know not being public serves them well. Clever top players use trusted tools/puppets they can control to appear as if they are the top players so the real top players can stay hidden. As long as their puppets play by their rules, they can keep enjoying financial wealth, controlling power, and/or fame, which are prominent temptations on planet Earth and on most planets that develop a monetary system. These clever negatively oriented human beings have learned from their chosen 4th density negative masters—who are literally able to be invisible—that staying hidden and invisible means protection from being dethroned and losing control. A saying known on Earth conveys this clever method: "The greatest trick the Devil ever pulled was convincing the world he didn't exist." The religious term "Devil" can be replaced with either highly negatively oriented 3rd density human beings or with 4th density negatives. The controlling service-to-self hierarchy structure of a 3rd density planet mimics the structure of a 4th density negative planet and the Orion Empire itself. Planetary domination by utilizing the planet's own beings is the method and goal of the 4th density negatives in regards to 3rd density planets.

The greatest victory for the Orion Empire is to add another planet to its power and control structure. If they can cause enough separation and service-to-self actions on a 3rd density planet in order to get more negative graduates than positive graduates at the end of a grand cycle, the 3rd density core planet begins its transition into a 4th density core negative planet and joins the Orion Empire after harvest-time. If this occurs, the 3rd density beings who graduated toward 4th density negative reincarnate on the same planet and the fewer, if any, 3rd density beings who graduated toward the positive would incarnate on a different 4th density positive planet. The 3rd density beings who did not polarize enough toward negative or positive to graduate would incarnate on a different planet that offers them a continuation of the 3rd density experience. There they can continue their 3rd density experience until they have polarized enough to graduate at the end of a major cycle or another grand cycle.

The negatives' planetary domination on Earth was not secured through public military might with the Nazis and the many that came before them, so planetary domination plans were altered to proceed clandestinely, utilizing the very, very few highly negatively oriented 3rd density human beings to act as their tools in using their controlling powers to create or shape existing organizations, corporations, and nations via governmental positions. On planet Earth, a large portion of these functioning bodies have already been clandestinely taken over, or established from the start by negatively oriented human beings. These structures work against humanity instead of for humanity, showing the planet a fake positive face while the real negative face works behind the scenes. The United States of America nation is their prime target because of its position on the planet. Infiltrate and topple from within the biggest domino and it has a good chance at knocking down the rest of the dominoes. Although, a comprehensive military plan does not focus solely on the prime target; the most effective and calculated move is to infiltrate as many nations as possible, striking them all at once, shaping the planet while concentrating the largest efforts on the biggest players. Rights and freedoms of the planetary majority are slowly or quickly stripped away in the guise of whatever is the most effective means for the given planet. On Earth, which is also the case on most 3rd density core planets, the guise is protection, cultural progression, health safety, and technological advancement.

With influence and/or direct orders from higher-density negatives, negatively oriented 3rd density beings create and inspire as much separation and confusion as possible, some of which are transient diversions that aid their cause, others are major agendas that have the most likelihood of fulfilling their planetary domination. Do you notice your rights and freedoms being taken away? Rights and freedoms your grandparents still possessed. Do you notice the diversions? Do you notice the increasing divisions and intensifying fighting? Do you notice the programming and how it is shaping social conditioning? Are you aware of the major agendas? All these tactical cards have already been shown on planet Earth and noticed by those who are observant. These tactics have majorly increased since approximately 2020 CE, with the conclusion of planet Earth's grand cycle being just around the corner. Part of the programming that shapes social conditioning is used to make the majority disbelieve and mock the observant, freethinking human beings who point out the reality we speak of. Since there is too much evidence to support the reality expressed by the observant human beings, the programming that shapes social conditioning is used to turn off the open-mindedness of the majority so they do not even bother to look at or consider the evidence that is right in front of their faces on a daily bases.

——∞——

The positive path organizations and affiliations consist of 3rd to 6th density beings, as well as beings who have already merged back with Source and chose to take on an overseeing or caretaker role in this Cosmos while being in the 7th density inner planes. Positive beings may work in the Confederations of Planets, which alleviates sorrow and aids all solar systems. The local Confederation of Planets aids and cares for 7 solar systems, which includes the solar system Earth resides in. 3rd to 7th density beings make up each Confederation of Planets. Positive beings from the inner planes are also in or assist the Confederations of Planets. The 3rd density beings in the Confederations of Planets are wanderers and walk-ins, so their true densities are later 4th sub-density to later 6th sub-density. Besides these beings, a Confederation of Planets truly consists of 4th to 7th density beings. One density assisting and teaching the one below it right down to 4th density positives, who aid 3rd density beings who mentally project positive intentions into the ether and mentally ask for assistance. We have already covered how they influence each other down to 3rd density and their way of unity in love and light. It is a clear message offered without deception, so unlike unveiling the negatives' deceptions, there is no lengthy description needed to convey the positives' loving agendas, which have already been covered and will continue to be covered along with more exposing of the negatives' tactics in later subjects. (The local Confederation of Planets' face-to-face encounters and major influential occurrences with 3rd density human beings on Earth will be covered in later subjects.)

The highest position that guides and governs the Confederations of Planets, and are technically part of it as well since they are also of positive polarity, are Council positions. The Council positions consist of beings who have already experienced this Cosmos and merged back with Source and then chose to take on an overseer and caretaker role in this Cosmos instead of directly moving on to the next Cosmos. Council position beings' true density is that of Oneness with Source, and they wander back into the illusion to the 7th density inner planes to perform overseer and caretaker roles. 7th density inner planes beings have the largest viewpoint of any beings in the Cosmos. There is a Council for every solar system and every galaxy. Each Council position consists of 9 beings who eventually move on to other experiences and are replaced by similar beings so that the 9 positions are filled and always on duty. The only exception is when there is 8 or 10 Council positions filled during transitional times.

The second highest position in the Confederations of Planets is held by the Guardians who back up and assist the Council members. Guardian positions are filled by later 6th sub-density outer planes beings from united groups. There are 24 rotating Guardian positions who assist each Council. One of the ways Guardians care for a solar system is to partially protect the beings on 3rd density planets from 4th and 5th density negatives and technologically advanced 3rd density beings from different planets acting in service to self by way of planetary manipulation and conquest. We say the Guardians partially protect instead of fully protect because there are ways the negatives can slip onto a planet undetected, and when the negatives are called and invited by negatively oriented or confused 3rd density beings from a planet, the positives must allow the invitation to occur in order to not infringe upon free will.

The Councils oversee the admission of beings into each Confederation of Planets. If a mass calling is adequate in percentages from a 3rd density civilization, the local Confederation of Planets is able to assist in some manner pertaining to the specific conditions of each mass calling: telepathically where the receivers think it is their own thoughts and ideas, sending love and light energy, offering dream visions, working through those who channel information, and direct contact are the main methods. For a later 6th sub-density united group's aid to be direct face-to-face contact, they have to bring their case before the local Council, which either approves or declines the request. If the united group is not sure how to assist the mass calling, the local Council gives advice on the matter according to the specifics of each case. If the request is approved, the later 6th sub-density united group may send one or some of its beings to aid a civilization in the manner they believe to be the most effective without infringing upon the free will of the 3rd density beings they are assisting.

Pertaining to a mass calling, when we say "calling" we do not mean verbal communication; we mean a sincere mental intention that asks for assistance. The calling needs to be in mass—an adequate percentage of positive seekers—from a specific civilization over a period of time; the mass calling does not need to be done all at once. If these requirements are met, all forms of aid we listed may be given except for direct face-to-face contact.

For direct contact to occur, all these requirements must be met and the civilization needs to have an adequate amount of beings whose belief system—you may call this religion or way of life—is adequately unified and not of a hostile nature.

Since there is no more isolation of civilizations on Earth due to the population growth and technological advancement, the present requirements would need to be met by the entire planet instead of by one civilization. Due to the major diversity of religions or ways of life on planet Earth, such unity needed would not be met unless a major planetary issue arose to invoke unity and for Earthlings to set aside their divisions and trivialities and unite under one cause.

Given the current state on planet Earth, some human beings feel there are more leaning toward service to self than service to others on Earth and that more would graduate toward the negative, but this is not the reality. The majority of beings, who are mostly leaning toward positive polarity, have allowed the self-serving few to rise to the top of the power and control structure, as they always hunger to do. From such top positions, these negatively oriented beings have disseminated their self-serving mentality and ways like a contagious disease released upon the majority of the population.

There have been substantially more human beings during Earth's grand cycle who have graduated to 4th density positive than 4th density negative. All possibilities/timelines show a higher percentage of graduates to 4th density positive instead of negative at the end of Earth's grand cycle. Therefore, Earth is already locked-in to become a 4th density core positive planet. Human beings who have and will graduate to 4th density positive will reincarnate back onto Earth in 4th density physical bodies, also known as astral bodies. The few who have and will graduate to 4th density negative have or will incarnate onto a 4th density negative planet in a different solar system. The majority of human beings, not having polarized enough in either direction, will incarnate onto a different planet in a different solar system that offers 3rd density lessons so they can continue their 3rd density experience until they make the choice to graduate in either direction. Planet Earth is locked-in to become a 4th density core positive planet, but the possibilities/timelines for how long the transition takes and how smoothly planet Earth transitions into a 4th density core positive planet is still up to 3rd density human beings to decide.

102.1 – History of Earth Cycles

We will summarize planet Earth's three major cycles which make up a grand cycle. A major cycle for Earth is approximately 25,170 years. Three major cycles make up a grand cycle, which for Earth is approximately 75,510 years. At the end of a grand cycle there is the harvest-time. When Earth transitioned into a 3rd density core planet approximately in 73,498 BCE, the advanced enough beings of the later 2nd sub-density species of apes were selected by the Logos/star to rapidly evolve and transition into 3rd density beings, the primitive beginnings of the human being. We have already spoken of this transition and rapid evolution.

These transitioning later 2nd sub-density apes into early 3rd sub-density primitive human beings made up approximately 20% of Earth's 3rd density population when Earth became a 3rd density core planet at the beginning of the grand cycle. Approximately 31% of Earth's 3rd density population came from other planets and incarnated onto Earth through the typical birthing process from the transitioning apes to primitive human beings. These beings were ready to start the 3rd density experience but their 2nd density core planet was not ready or not able to transition to 3rd density, so they started their 3rd density experience on Earth. Approximately 49% of Earth's 3rd density population did not incarnate onto Earth in the usual manner. These beings were originally from Mars. After their planet became inhospitable by ways of war during their 3rd density experience and transitioning/dying, they spent much time healing in the deep resting place in the inner planes before viewing their last incarnation and preparing for their next incarnation. The local Guardians at the time decided to genetically adjust/assist what was the Mars beings' physical bodies with a Guardian's genetics and genetics from apes on Earth so the post-Mars beings could continue their 3rd density experience on planet Earth. This mixing of genetic stock is common, but it is rare for a Confederation of Planets to utilize this method to alter the physical body of a species of 3rd density beings so they can function properly on a different planet. Rare measures were decided upon because the situation that needed a solution was itself rare.

The first major cycle on Earth was approximately from 73,498 BCE to 48,328 BCE. The different groups of beings mentioned lived isolated from each other in different locations on the planet. Since there were far fewer 3rd density beings on Earth at the time and advanced ways of traveling had not been invented yet, the isolation of civilizations was typical for that time. The average planetary lifespan was 900 years, which is typical for beings starting the 3rd density experience. The lifespan starts at an average of 900 years and then decreases if the mantle of responsibility attained from growth is abandoned or ignored, which it typically is to some degree for 3rd density planets. This abandoning or ignoring creates a level of stress for the 3rd density beings, so breaks from the 3rd density experience are needed more frequently in the inner planes. The alleviation of stress is achieved by decreasing the duration of the lifespan. A being is not given an experience beyond what they can handle, so as more disharmony arises, such as warring, violence, dysfunctional ways of living, and strained interactions between beings, the average lifespan for incarnations reduces.

As is usual, the seeds are planted and given time and experiences for free will to naturally grow and evolve the mind, body, and spirit of each being. The local Confederation of Planets did not assist beyond general caretaking as there was no call for assistance (with an exception we will cover later), which is typical in the infancy of a 3rd density experience starting out at the baseline of self-awareness. Beings at this early stage, having recently come from the 2nd density experience, are still animalistic in their ways and their tribes focus on survival. Beings gradually become aware of other needs and wants beyond survival, such as companionship, cleanliness, beauty, humor, and exploration. As more 3rd density incarnations are experienced by the beings, their needs and wants continue to expand beyond the animalistic: refining mannerisms, creating more efficiently functioning civilizations, striving to know and understand their particular landmass, and giving and receiving universal love. Sometimes an entire grand cycle of the 3rd density experience can run its own course without any direct contact aid from their local Confederation of Planets.

In approximately 58,280 BCE, Orion Empire 4th density negatives attempted to offer the ways of service to self to some of these tribes and civilizations after scanning their societal minds from off planet to find effective temptations to utilize. Then they attempted to inspire separation by way of power infused in thought-created structures and rock formations in different areas of the planet where tribes lived, but they were unsuccessful because the temptations offered were not received.

The only great civilization established in the first major cycle was Lemuria, also known as Mu, as they called the landmass/continent they resided on Mu, and it was situated in your present-day Pacific Ocean. The beings in this civilization originated from the same planet and were part of the approximately 31% that came from different planets. Their original 2nd density core planet that orbits what Earthlings call the Deneb star found in the Cygnus constellation could not transition to a 3rd density core planet due to the age of the Deneb Logos/star, so they began their 3rd density experience on planet Earth.

Lemuria was not technologically advanced and would be considered primitive by present-day Earthlings' standards. Lemuria, like the other civilizations around the planet at the time, used simple tools they made out of wood and rock. It was not a warlike or hostile civilization, but rather a friendly and harmonious civilization that became very spiritually advanced. The harmonious nature and positive intentions of these beings prompted telepathic assistance from the local Confederation of Planets when they established an adequate mass calling for assistance in their spiritual seeking—the exception we noted earlier. The mass calling was answered with telepathic assistance. The beings mostly did not know the beneficial thoughts came from outside of their own minds. This indirect assistance carried on from Lemuria's humble beginnings in approximately 57,960 BCE, where their spirituality advanced steadily, to the end of their civilization when the Mu continent sank underwater due to geological changes at the end of the first major cycle in approximately 48,328 BCE. The Mu continent started shifting geologically due to tectonic plate movements about 3,080 years before the end of the first major cycle, and the influx of energy from the Logos/Sun that happens at the end of every major cycle naturally quickened the geological adjustment, causing the Mu continent to rapidly finalize its adjustment and sink deep underwater.

Due to their unity, teamwork, and intuition that made them aware of the coming major changes, most of the Lemurians survived. They used simple boats, which they had constructed in mass due to their intuition, and reached what is today the continents of North and South America. The beings you call Native Americans are the descendants of Lemuria. Some of these beings continued migrating across a land bridge, which used to connect the continents of North America and Asia, where they traveled to what is presently called Russia and then China. They, along with other groups that migrated, gradually evolved physically to suit the climate and area of the planet they resided in, altering the color of their skin as well as other minor physical changes. The Oriental/Asian races of present-day China, Japan, Korea, and Taiwan are all descendants of Lemuria.

By the end of the first major cycle, the average planetary lifespan had decreased to 680 years due to some inharmonious relations between beings on the planet that were not of the Lemurian civilization. Some later 2nd sub-density beings on Earth advanced enough to graduate and incarnate as 3rd density beings throughout the first major cycle, increasing Earth's 3rd density population by the end of the first major cycle. Since the beginnings of the first major cycle are the early stages of the 3rd density experience, beings reincarnated automatically, still focusing on baseline lessons and so not needing time to review and plan for their next incarnation. By the end of the first major cycle on Earth, a little over half of the 3rd density beings had at some point activated their green-ray heart chakra, which prompted time in the inner planes for reviewing their last incarnation and learning and preparing for the next incarnation. When reincarnation is no longer automatic, the beings prepare and make life agreements with other beings for their next incarnation with the assistance of their higher self and other guides in the inner planes.

0 3rd density beings graduated to 4th density at the end of the first major cycle.

——∞——

The second major cycle on Earth was approximately from 48,328 BCE to 23,158 BCE. During this major cycle there were no great civilizations established like that of Lemuria, but some of the Lemurian descendants who migrated to what is present-day China made some notable advances in their civilization.

In this major cycle most civilizations transitioned from a barter and trade system to a type of monetary system, which offered major temptation for separation—the few who saw themselves as superior started manipulating the majority with this new dysfunctional tool. Most groups remained isolated from each other, but some tribes and civilizations started exploring further, which led to some warfare. Warfare between tribes and civilizations and monetary systems were responsible for the emerging idea of ownership of human beings, both individuals and conquered groups becoming slaves.

Despite these issues, a good percentage more of beings throughout the planet began activating their green-ray heart chakra at some point in their incarnations, and some engaged it more fully and balanced this energy center partially or adequately. The most notable of which was the spiritual advancement of a group in present-day South America who practiced high levels of universal love and service to others to the point that some of them were ready to graduate to 4th density positive.

Approximately in 43,720 BCE, a great influx of incarnations on Earth occurred by way of genetic preparation assistance by the local Guardians. 3rd density beings from a planet called Maldek, also known as Tiamat, which no longer exists due to warfare, started incarnating within Earth in a physical body similar to later 2nd sub-density animals so that these 3rd density beings could have the opportunity to balance out their heavy karma for destroying their planet. In your current time they are known as beings called Bigfoot. They live deep below the surface in pathways and open spaces and rarely come onto the surface of the planet. We will expand upon them and planet Maldek in a subject about your solar system's history.

After having incarnated within Earth as the entities known as Bigfoot, the post-Maldek beings produced a mass calling for help in their confused state. Love and light energy was sent to them by beings in the local Confederation of Planets whose roles include the sending of love and light energy to beings who make the mental calling for aid. Despite not recognizing this aid, the post-Maldek beings gradually made progress at balancing their karma throughout the tens of thousands of years.

By the end of the second major cycle, the average planetary lifespan had decreased to being approximately the same as in your current time due to continuous and major inharmonious relations between beings: red-ray chakra lessons of anger and fear that led to violence and war, orange-ray chakra lessons of dysfunctional relationships between individuals, and yellow-ray chakra lessons of aggressive and controlling relationships between tribes and groups within tribes. When beings activate their green-ray heart chakra, they take on the mantel of responsibility. Like a child who has grown old enough to know better than to perform negative actions against others but does it anyway, they are corrected by their parents. This is not a punishment or judgment; it assists the beings in their present and in their future incarnations. A being is not given more than they can handle for an incarnation. The recognition of hostile actions by beings, no longer being innocent like a child who does not know better, causing suffering in many ways—hostile acts, warlike acts, slavery, superior acts through ways of a monetary system or otherwise, selfish acts—creates more than a being can handle in a long lifespan.

Since there was still isolation between most tribes and civilizations, beings in harmonious and less-hostile tribes and civilizations lived a longer lifespan than others. Some of the beings in the South American group with those who graduated were still living a lifespan up to 900 years. The determination of the lifespan is not an entire planetary circumstance, but a being by being case, but even healthy positively oriented beings living under the conditions of an inharmonious society are exposed to suffering and therefore have a shorter lifespan. In this way, the average lifespan largely depends on the ways of each society/civilization.

If there was an isolated group on planet Earth in your present time that lived very harmoniously and healthily, they could have a lifespan from 200–500 years. They still would not come close to living a 900 year lifespan because even with complete physical isolation the group would still be subjected to contaminated air and water that has become a planetary issue. The contamination of your oceans is no mystery to Earthlings, but some of the ways of contaminating the air, which also results in the contamination of the lands and oceans and all that live on and in them is not known or believed by most Earthlings. Besides the burning of fossil fuels, which is known to be a problem on your planet, the Orion Empire uses the highly negatively oriented 3rd density human beings as tools and manipulated them into constantly releasing by plane what has been called chemtrails by human beings. The reasons for this poisonous action the Orion Empire gave to these so-called elites and the reasons the so-called elites gave to all that carry out their orders in making it happen are varied deceptions and lies. The main reason is to poison and make weaker human beings so they are easier to manipulate and control, as a healthy being is harder to control.

Another planetary issue impacting the theoretical isolated, harmonious group in your present time that would lessen their lifespan would be the mental pollution created by billions of beings that affects the planetary vibration and is similar to an ailment upon the Earth and the beings inhabiting the Earth. This effect is quite significant since it involves billions of human beings instead of the far fewer population during the second major cycle. Thoughts are creations just as actions are, and they have a great effect on physical matter and other minds. Most human beings do not know this. All 4th density beings know this very well and can create physical matter out of thin air with group-focused thought.

More later 2nd sub-density beings on Earth advanced enough to graduate and incarnate as 3rd density beings throughout the second major cycle, increasing Earth's 3rd density population up to the end of the second major cycle.

148 3rd density beings graduated to 4th density positive at the end of the second major cycle, but they all chose to keep reincarnating onto 3rd density Earth in order to assist others in doing the same for the next and last major cycle. The 148 were all beings from the South American group we spoke of.

—∞—

The third major cycle on Earth, which completes the grand cycle, was approximately from 23,158 BCE to 2012 CE. The harmonious and spiritually advanced civilization known as the Mayans were accurate with their calendar's end date, as the grand cycle's end was originally set for approximately 2012/2013 CE, but the Logos/Sun's activities have been delayed two solar cycles (approximately 22 years) due to very rare circumstances. This holding back by the Logos/Sun delays its major influx of energy activities that happen at the end of every major cycle, which have been delayed to approximately 2034 CE, the delayed end of Earth's 3rd density grand cycle.

This delay of a Logos/star's influx of energy is an extremely rare occurrence, as when a cycle or gear in the cosmic clock hits upon the hour with precision, the corresponding Logos/star is energetically activated and produces an activity that some on Earth call a micro-nova or a solar sneeze, which occurs at the end of every major cycle. The local Council and Guardians decided that the delay would greatly assist Earthlings and the Earth's transitional period into 4th density, so they confided with the Logos/Sun, who agreed and the delay was approved. Since Earth is the only planet with natural 3rd density life origins in your solar system at present, this delay was an option because there are no other 3rd density beings originating from other planets who would be effected by the delay. There is also the matter of 3 planets' worth of beings in your solar system—Maldek, Mars, and Earth—as well as beings from many other planetary origins, experiencing planet Earth at the same time that adds focus and consideration to Earth's transition to 4th density positive.

The great civilization of Atlantis occurred in this major cycle, the third and last major cycle. Other than your current civilizations, it was the most technologically advanced. It was more spiritually advanced than your current civilizations and also more technologically advanced in some ways. Atlantis's humble beginnings started in the second major cycle in approximately 32,500 BCE. It was a civilization diverse in races that worked together harmoniously. By approximately 13,750 BCE, Atlantis had grown to be quite technologically and spiritually advanced. It was around this time that an Atlantean mass calling of positive intentions was received by the local Confederation of Planets. The decided action to respond to this mass calling was through traditional channeling of information, which offered the Atlanteans information that aided them further in their technological and spiritual advancement because they had demonstrated responsibility over their technological advancements.

In approximately 10,740 BCE, Atlanteans had advanced even further as a harmonious civilization due to the channeled information. At this time another mass calling prompted a later 6th sub-density united group to offer aid. Their case was presented and approved by the Council, so they sent a few of their beings to walk among them and made their physical bodies visible to further assist in the Atlanteans's advancement by guiding the construction of pyramid structures and utilizing crystal technology. Like the Great Pyramid in Giza, Egypt, which was constructed by a different later 6th sub-density united group assisting the Egyptians, the Atlantean pyramids were of a certain height, shape, ratio, and orientation so their harnessed energetic powers could be used for healing and learning. Those who were fit for the role of healing by opening up a pathway from Source energy and activating crystals, due to having done the inner work to adequately balance their chakras more than others, were taught how to adequately balance their remaining chakras so they could activate crystals within the pyramids and channel healing energy from Source to members of their civilization and provide them with learning opportunities by ways of accessing aspects of the tree of mind in the pyramids.

These healers, and all who have been healers throughout time, do not heal by themselves; they have adequately balanced chakras and have learned how to open up a pathway to and from Source so that Source energy may work through them and heal the one who is the willing receiver. If the defect wanting to be healed is a pre-incarnate planned defect, it will not be healed for the benefit of the being.

The later 6th sub-density united group aiding the Atlanteans had been assisted in the same way by a later 6th sub-density united group when they were 3rd density beings. It had been effective for them, so they were using the same method to aid the Atlanteans. After the pyramids had been constructed, pyramid healers taught, and all was running effectively and harmoniously, the later 6th sub-density beings departed.

The Atlantis civilization advanced greatly from the aid of the pyramid structures and crystal knowledge. Nuclear power was invented and later replaced by cleaner crystal technology to power their civilization. Slowly, the pyramid and crystal technology started to be used unwisely by some in ways that were more leaning toward service to self. The pyramid healers, having learned how to tap into Source energy from the indigo-ray chakra through the violet-ray chakra, learned how to create beings by way of genetics and cloning. Curious to see how far their experimentation could take them, they created a servant caste of half-human, half-animal beings to do their civilization's daily chores. These beings are spoken of in your Greek myths. Some questioned the ethical nature of their creation, but the majority ignored the ethical concerns. The caste beings were treated with enough kindness so they would perform their duties. The civilization started focusing on creating these beings and using their knowledge in other less-harmonious ways, shifting their attention away from the original reasons the pyramid structures and crystal technology had been provided: advancing the individuals of their civilization in service-to-others ways of healing and learning that would further expand the awareness and spirituality of the civilization's collective.

A faction of the Atlanteans were further telepathically tempted by the Orion Empire over time and grew heavily toward service-to-self ways, thus a separation in the intentions and unity of Atlanteans became great. Many of the corrupted Atlanteans acquired positions within the Atlantean government, which had grown in size and power and turned toward gaining more power and control over the majority instead of serving them, which also stemmed from telepathic temptations by negative 4th density beings. The government officials had developed opposing factions, as separation is a common development when service-to-self intentions and actions arise. These occurrences could be seen as the beginning of Atlantis's downfall.

When opportunities given by positive higher-density beings create the advancement of 3rd density beings, negative higher-density beings have the opportunity to offer their services in return, and vice versa. When a chess piece from the white or black team is moved by a player within a team, a corresponding move is made by a chess player in the opposite team. This does not mean either side's offer will be received, but the opportunity is always given.

In approximately 9,330 BCE, the Atlantean factions' tension had grown considerably and started warring with each other, resulting in the transition/death of 37% of Atlantis's population. This caused some of the positively oriented Atlanteans to flee their continent and migrate to high-altitude locations of what is known today as Tibet, Turkey, and Peru. Some neutrally oriented Atlanteans migrated off the Atlantic continent and established a colony civilization in what today is in the North African Sahara Desert. The land formation that has been called the Richat Structure, also known as the Eye of the Sahara, is where this Atlantean colony once resided.

In approximately 8,840 BCE, the Atlantean factions started warring again, carelessly using nuclear bombs and crystal weapons against each other. They used crystal technology to penetrate deep into the earth and produced earthquakes of immense intensity and destruction as weapons against each other. This caused immense geologic tension that resulted in most of the Atlantic continent sinking below the ocean.

In approximately 7,717 BCE, the Atlantean factions started battling each other again. The North African colony and the area around it was destroyed by several powerful nuclear bombs and other advanced technology, and the remaining Atlantic landmass sank far below the ocean due to earthquake-producing weaponry. Atlantis and its colonies were no more. Almost all of their technology and knowledge gone by way of advanced weaponry misuse and sinking to the depths of the ocean. Survivors migrated east and joined more primitive civilizations in what is known today as Egypt, Italy, Greece, and other locations. The Atlantic Ocean, which was named such by Atlanteans, had now considerably grown in size due to the sinking of the continent where Atlantis resided. The once harmonious and peaceful civilization had slowly grown sour and then very hostile by not honoring the responsibility of their technological might. Similar types of technology that Atlantis had access to, if used even more carelessly, could blow up an entire planet instead of only sinking a continent, and there is an example of this happening in your solar system, which we will cover in a later subject.

This is a fine warning for present-day civilizations on Earth, which have many factions, secret organizations, and secret societies operating separately from nations and their governments and that have followed in the footsteps of Atlantis's technology and have clandestinely—knowing the public would be against their actions and to keep it secret from their enemies—created their own genetic half-breed experiments underground, cloning technology that has advanced to considerable levels, earthquake-producing technology, particle beam weaponry, psychotronic weaponry, weather-pattern-altering weaponry that is mistaken for natural disasters and can be used in an ongoing manner for crop failure or scarcity, and virus-creating labs all over the planet that are operated and controlled by international organizations that profess to stop the spread of the same viruses they have created and released intentionally. This is only naming a small amount of hidden capabilities and technology on Earth that is potentially very dangerous and heavily service-to-self oriented. There is also a large amount of hidden potentially positive technology. This suppressed technology from even many decades ago could solve all major and minor problems on the planet and quickly advance the planet toward a utopian-like existence if hostile ways are abandoned and some degree of unity is established. Here we have yet another case of separation—in this case major—working against planetary beings instead of practicing unity and transparency that would advance the planetary collective both technologically and spiritually. This suppression of technology and knowledge acts as a major hindrance in holding back the majority from working towards graduating to 4th density.

Many of the half-human, half-animal Atlantean-created beings survived the sinking of the Atlantic continent and migrated east along with the surviving Atlanteans. These centaurs, minotaurs, harpies, mermaids, gorgons, sirens, and others are spoken of in your Greek, Roman, and other civilizations' myths. There are almost always some facts in your myths. As represented in the myths, these beings were hostile toward human beings due to being abused and killed by the less-civil human beings in the civilizations they had migrated to, so they sought isolation from human beings. Atlas and the Titans were invented Greek myths about Atlanteans and their so-called mighty gods. It is no surprise that the ancient Greek accounts have all been labeled myths, as the tall tales of the one known as Heracles/Hercules and other Greek heroes whose legends were used to bolster a civilization's standing and morale, as well as make their enemies tremble, are purely fictional or grossly misinterpreted. These half-human, half-animal beings were hunted down and exterminated off the surface of the planet throughout the centuries, but some mermaids are still in existence, keeping to themselves.

——∞——

From approximately 10,000 BCE to 1,000 BCE, different positive higher-density united groups assisted many civilizations around the planet, resulting in a total of 58 pyramids for healing and learning aid to human beings. 6 of these pyramids, having been placed on planetary ley lines, were also for balancing the planetary body, Earth, so the in-pouring of potentially unbalanced energy could be transmuted to a degree. Some civilizations kept building their own pyramids long after higher-density aid departed, but they are mostly less effective pyramids due to design flaws. This happened extensively in locations known as South America and Central America.

Since the end of the grand cycle was approaching and there were extremely few beings who had been able to graduate to 4th density, the local Confederation of Planets became concerned and decided to use the pyramid structures in an attempt to offer more opportunities for advancement, which could lead to graduation. One of the benefits of the pyramids is a longer lifespan, which human beings could have used for more opportunities to grow and advance toward graduation instead of being stuck in a short lifespan, transitioning and reincarnating over and over again while being perpetually stuck in a spiritual infancy due to the veil of forgetfulness of 3rd density. The aid of the pyramids had worked on other planets before and the Atlanteans had shown in their beginnings that it was potentially beneficial for human beings. Now there is no need for a longer average lifespan because the harvest-time is just around the corner.

We will speak of two of the civilizations besides Atlantis where positive higher-density united groups assisted with pyramid structures and crystal activation to be used within the pyramids.

The Egyptians were one of the civilizations. In approximately 8,600 BCE, the Egyptians had adequately turned toward being less hostile to a degree that warranted assistance when they produced an adequate mass calling for assistance. A later 6th sub-density united group thought it would be appropriate to aid with face-to-face direct contact. The local Council approved their request for direct contact and the united group sent a few of its beings to walk among the Egyptians and phased their etheric bodies to be visible by 3rd density beings. While trying to understand the teachings of the higher-density beings, even though the Egyptian language was used, the Egyptians were highly confused and were making no progress in understanding, so the higher-density beings departed after a short period of time. The difficulties of attempting to teach in this disparity of densities was covered by the wanderer in this awareness-expanding course's introduction. That was the only time this united group made direct face-to-face contact on Earth, as they decided to assist by thought-form alone from there on. The united group spent much time thinking about how to proceed with effective service to the Egyptians and how best to construct the pyramids that would aid the Egyptians.

In approximately 2,679 BCE, coinciding with Imhotep's birth, who would later become a great architect, the structure known as the Great Pyramid of Giza was created in an instant by thought creation alone from afar by the later 6th sub-density united group. This may sound baffling to a 3rd density being, but we have stated that even 4th density beings are able to create physical objects and formations from group-focused thought alone. Therefore, one could imagine that 6th density beings could do such with ease. The Egyptians were shocked to wake up and find a towering formation—a pyramid—that had not been there the day before. The united group then used their mind to project thought-form beings upon the planet who worked with the Egyptians in building the other pyramids of Giza. It took approximately 1,655 years to complete the other pyramids, but the thought-forms did not need to stay till completion because the Egyptians had been taught how to finish the pyramids. While these other pyramids were being built, the thought-forms were also teaching how to use crystals to heal and to adequately balance out the chakras of the Egyptian priests who would act as healers in the pyramids.

The pyramids that were completed were only being used by the Egyptian royalty at the time, even though the pyramids were meant for all to utilize. It was not until approximately 1,351 BCE when Akhenaten became ruler at a young age that things would start to change. Akhenaten was a wanderer and was able to telepathically communicate with the later 6th sub-density united group, which would result in him making major changes during his rule. He decreed the Egyptian's religion be changed to focus on one god instead of the many gods Egyptians had been worshipping. Most Egyptians kept to their old ways and continued to worship many gods. The priests reluctantly followed the will of

Akhenaten but not behind closed doors, where they also continued worshiping many gods. Akhenaten made the pyramids available for all and not just Egyptian royalty, and corrected the priests who acted as healers in the pyramids in doing their role more in line with Akhenaten's information he received from telepathy.

The geometric shape of a pyramid is used to collect and intensify the life-force energy/prana flowing outward from a planet. Like a funnel is used to direct and concentrate liquid in a downward direction using gravity, the pyramid acts similarly with upward flowing prana. Since prana recognizes geometric shapes and flows accordingly, it may be concentrated with a pyramid and other shapes that possess the mere necessary framework. The intensification of prana is equal in an open or enclosed structure because prana is not physical and so does not adhere to the laws of physicality. Meaning, putting four straight pieces of wood down so they meet at an apex concentrates prana equally to that of four pieces of wood that are enclosed with material. When prana meets the geometry/framework of a pyramid shape, it spirals around the structure in a coiling fashion until flowing outward through the apex. Any material can be used but metals that are not silver, copper, or gold should be avoided to ensure effectiveness. Wood and PVC pipes work just fine. Geometric shapes other than the pyramid also work: domes, circular shapes like the silo, and cone shapes like the teepee. Any structure that is peaked, circular, or rounded, spirals the upward flow of prana into a concentrated coil. Within one of these structures, since the energy is concentrated, it intensifies the effect upon the mind, body, spirit complex, which makes these structures potentially beneficial and dangerous if not used correctly, especially the top half of the pyramid or cone structure where prana is even more concentrated. The reason for having very large pyramid structures like those at Giza in Egypt are so the being inside may completely be within the most beneficial areas of the pyramid, making it much more effective than smaller structures.

The purpose of the air shafts in the Great Pyramid leading to the so-called Queen's and King's chamber are meant to provide a flow of fresh atmosphere into these chambers without producing drafts that would disturb the healing and learning practices held within these chambers. They also assist at setting the chambers to an effective temperature and barometric pressure. King's and

Queen's Chamber were the names the Egyptian royals gave these chambers, but since the chambers were meant for all, these labels are misnomers. The Queen's Chamber is more accurately called the Initiation Chamber, and the King's Chamber the Healing Chamber. The chamber below the ground floor of the pyramid provides an effective resonation so a certain vibration assists in the healing process within the Healing Chamber. First a being starts out in the Initiation Chamber where their mind, body, spirit complex are initiated. First the mind is initiated by knowing its true self, then the spirit is able to flow through the mind more effectively to work on the body and initiate it. This initiation of purification allows the love and light energy of Source to flow through the energy chakras in a more dedicated fashion. This process could be seen as being reborn in that the birth of a balanced and more aware being is now entering the world for the first time. Then the being is ready for the Healing Chamber. In the Healing Chamber, the crystal is activated by the priest acting as the healer and the charged atmosphere in the chamber offer the one being healed, with the will to do so, the needed adjustments and alleviations to their mind, body, spirit complex. In this state the being faces itself so their traumas and distortions come to light to be dealt with, offering the possibility of clearing and transmuting such distortions. This provides an amplification while doing the inner work, offering a potentially quickened transformation.

After Akhenaten's transition/death a little under twenty years into his rein, things reverted back to before: the Egyptians worshipped many gods and only the Egyptian royalty used the pyramids, which they used incorrectly and so ineffectively. Pyramids are not meant to be tombs, as it serves no purpose.

The original capstone of the Great Pyramid was made out of granite to ensure effectiveness. The Egyptian royalty later removed this capstone and replaced it with a somewhat larger capstone plated with material they thought to be more precious and valuable, which wore away and was pilfered over time. The replacing of the original capstone decreased the effectiveness of this pyramid slightly.

Around the same time the Egyptian pyramids were being constructed, other positive higher-density beings were assisting different civilizations around the Earth in their construction of pyramids. One of these cases was in South America near the

Amazon River where a later 6th sub-density united group sent one of its beings to walk among the civilization visibly and assist in the construction plans for underground cities and surface cities with pyramids. When construction plans were seen to be understood and underway, the higher-density being departed. It took approximately 3,470 years for this civilization to complete these construction plans. At the time of their completion, the instructions on how to utilize the pyramids had become slightly inaccurate, so the same later 6th sub-density united group sent one of its beings to directly walk among them visibly and fix the instructions. These instructions were received by the civilization and the higher-density being departed. As time passed, the use of the pyramids altered, eventually leading to such a perverted manner as being used for human sacrifice, which was quite the opposite of the healing purposes of the pyramids.

In the present time period, due to the shifting of the electromagnetic field of planet Earth and geological shifts, the Great Pyramid, as well as the other 57 pyramids build by or instructed to be built by the positive higher-density beings, are not in alignment. They are still useful for their original purposes, but their effectiveness has decreased considerably. Due to the powerful in-pouring of love and light energy coming into planet Earth because of the current space in time of your solar system, a 3rd density being can do everything the pyramids aided with without the need for such structures.

None of the civilizations given the pyramid structures reached the potential that the Atlantis civilization had, and even they eventually abused it and created much destruction and suffering in the end. Since suffering and the lack of ongoing spiritual advancement occurred for all civilizations, it was agreed upon by the local Confederation of Planets that the aiding pyramid structure was not suited for Earthlings, and so such aid would not be repeated on Earth. The higher-density united groups continue to work with the civilizations' descendants in balancing out the karmic ties they had a part in creating. It is their duty/honor to assist—duty and honor being the same thing for positive higher-density beings. Attempting to alleviate suffering is a major role for later 6th sub-density united groups. After the pyramid structures were seen as ineffective for aiding Earthlings, entities of the local Confederation of Planets decided to incarnate as wanderers and attempt to aid civilizations in their spiritual advancement. This could be considered the next part of Earth's history in regards to receiving aid and will be covered in the subject about religions and their origins.

Aspects of the religions of civilizations that come next for Earth's history—ancient Greeks, Romans, the Vikings, and others—will also be covered in the subject about religions, but there is no need to cover these civilizations' histories, as Earthlings' current knowledge on their histories already provides a good picture of what happened in those times. With so much separation and secrecy currently happening with many factions on Earth in your present time period, Earthlings have a better idea of what transpired in ancient Rome than they do of the last 100 years on Earth. The Earthly factions that see themselves as superior/elite hide as much knowledge and information as possible in order to more effectively wield power and control over the majority of human beings they have been slowly attempting to bring toward complete control. This is precisely why the wanderer from our united group who is bringing this awareness-expanding course through has already published a book that offers the unveiling and understanding of the highly negatively oriented human beings' mindset and agendas and the constructed detrimental societal system that influences and molds human beings' mindsets and actions in your present time. It is considered 104 information that focuses on the current Earth situation that is best reflected on and analyzed after absorbing this essential awareness-expanding course, which provides a spiritual and knowledgeable foundation so that human beings have an increased possibility of absorbing 104 information, and doing so with a spiritual foundation that limits the possibility of a human being becoming angry, fearful, or hysterical after being exposed to dark 104 information, which focuses on the dualistic nature of positive and negative polarity that is played out on planet Earth, but mostly focuses on exposing and explaining aspects of negative polarity for the majority's benefit.

After so very few 3rd density beings graduated at the end of the second major cycle on Earth, the local Council decided to allow beings from other planets to incarnate onto 3rd density Earth for the third and final major cycle in hopes that it might change the dynamic on Earth and create opportunities for the advancement of the whole. Throughout the third major cycle on Earth, an influx of later 2nd sub-density beings who graduated on their planet started their 3rd density experiences on Earth, and 3rd density beings who did not graduate at the end of their grand cycle on their planet continued the 3rd density experience on Earth. The origin diversity of beings experiencing 3rd density on Earth increased greatly during the third major cycle due to this major influx.

The current 3rd density beings on Earth consist of: post-Maldek beings who have balanced their karma while residing in later 2nd density-like bodies (Bigfoot) and incarnated into typical 3rd density human bodies to continue their 3rd density experience, post-Mars beings continuing their 3rd density experience, later 2nd sub-density beings on Earth who have graduated and incarnated into 3rd density as human beings, beings from many different planet origins starting or continuing their 3rd density experience on Earth, and the wanderers who have incarnated to aid the advancement of all 3rd density beings on Earth regardless of their origins. Such origin diversity is somewhat unique for a planet.

102.2 – The Harvest

We will speak of the harvest-time. The Cosmos could be seen as a cosmic clock with infinite gears or cycles. The gears or cycles within each universal clock of the cosmic clock range from tiny to extremely large. Patterns in each universe are cyclical. The larger the cycle, the more changes that take place at the end of that cycle. A grand cycle for Earth is a tiny cycle in a universal clock, comparatively speaking. Since the ending of a 3rd density grand cycle is the largest cycle pertaining to the 3rd density experience, the biggest changes happen at that time on the planet as it transitions into a 4th density core planet.

Even though we have already stated that transitioning/dying is something that beings do countless times and is nothing to fear, we realize that the programming on your planet of the fear of death is strong, so we will reiterate before proceeding with this topic. There is nothing to fear about the influx of energy from the Logos/Sun and major geological changes on Earth that assist in transforming the planet and assist beings in transitioning. Every being's existence is infinite and change is a primary aspect of the cosmic experience, as well as beyond. Not changing is what presents a problem. One who holds tightly to what they know and do because they do not understand, and so possibly fear, what there is to learn and what is to come, limits themselves greatly.

While journeying down the river, if one holds tightly to the shore instead of letting go with the flow of the river, stagnation occurs that may make the area of collecting water contaminated. One may not know what lies around each bend, but if they know all rivers eventually flow to the ocean and possess spiritual faith in the process, strength and fortitude is mustered and flowing down the long river can be a joyful and enlightening experience. One is not floating down the river as something separate from the water; they are parts of the water flowing among other parts of the water within the water system toward the total uniting of themselves in the ocean. From within the ocean and of the ocean, they then relax in the calming deep waters for as many seasons as seen fit before choosing to evaporate into the air and prepare themselves while in a cloud that guides them to the specific location on land where they rain down from the etheric cloud and begin a new and different journey toward the ocean. The more river paths experienced, the greater understanding of the whole water system. Water that knows it is always a part of the ocean and connected to the ocean does not fear change or the journeys, no matter how rough the currents become. Instead, the water enjoys and is entertained by the journeys, knowing it is their choice to venture far and learn from their experiences along the journeys. The experiences are collected like gifts that are opened and enjoyed by both the water and the ocean and forever held dear by the deep loving, joyful, and peaceful ocean.

There are smaller cycles within a grand cycle (a grand cycle for Earth is approximately 75,510 years), such as a major cycle (a major cycle for Earth is approximately 25,170 years) that always ends with what some human beings have called a micro-nova. A Logos/star keeps working after a micro-nova, unlike what humans have called novas or supernovas where the Logos/star is done with its work of nurturing the spheres and all the beings on those spheres that cycle/orbit it. A micro-nova could be seen as an extremely intense coronal mass ejection (CME) that ejects off of the whole surface around the Logos/star at the same instance, like a solar sneeze, greatly affecting the entire solar system. When this influx of intense energy meets a planet, there are major geological changes. Then there is a minor cycle on Earth (approximately every 12,585 years) where geological changes also happen to a smaller extent, but may still be perceived as major to the beings on the planet. Then there is a more minor cycle on Earth (approximately every 6,293 years) where geological changes still occur. The cycles continue in this halving manner for a mathematical infinity; the smaller the cycles get, the less noticeable the geological changes are until they are too slight to notice.

A grand cycle for 4th density beings and in higher densities is set to a much larger cycle within each universal clock. The higher the density, the larger the cycle. Just as every being has 7 potential physical bodies (red-ray to violet-ray body) to utilize throughout the densities—with only one of these bodies typically being activated at a given time—the 7 physical densities are in potentiality for every planet along its respected journey. The higher the density, the denser with intelligently conscious love and light energy. The denser with this life-force energy, the less sway physical matter changes, such as geological changes, have on the beings in their respected densities, as spiritual mass increases and physical mass decreases as the densities are ascended.

The major cyclical changes of a planet pertaining to 3rd density beings could be seen as the endings of rounds on a game board, where there are three rounds or acts. Each round in the board game starts with geological shifts that shake up the play of the experience on the board and offers a new round where new possibilities and opportunities are available instead of an experience getting locked into the same type of play for the whole duration of the grand cycle. There are always 3rd density players to continue the experience on the board; a major cycle does not end with extinction across the board, even at the end of a grand cycle. All extinction occurrences that may happen sometime within the grand cycle are due to players' actions and are not pre-determined occurrences, not standard game play incidents. Some players get so caught up in game play that when they become infuriated with actions that have transpired on the game board, they selfishly attempt to smash their fists down on the board game and destroy the board, ruining the experience for all players, all players who naturally try to prevent the selfish player(s) from destroying the board. This equates to highly negatively oriented 3rd density beings making their planet inhospitable or even blowing it up into pieces.

From a higher-density being's viewpoint on top of a tall mountain, the natural cyclical changes are seen to make sense and serve a purpose for the 3rd density players below in the valleys and plains. The 3rd density being's viewpoint on top of a hill does not provide a large enough viewpoint to understand the purpose. Everything serves a purpose.

The Earth's 3rd density experience has been far below the average for beings graduating to 4th density. The end of the grand cycle is just around the corner and only a small amount of beings have graduated so far. This is precisely why there has been so much higher-density assistance in the last major cycle on Earth. First the offering of pyramid structures and then the offering of wisdom and knowledge from wanderers or channeled material to positively oriented 3rd density beings, which unfortunately turned into religions filled with distortions where the material received was thought to be different and in opposition with another's received material. However, from Source's viewpoint, what transpired during each possibility/timeline of Earth's 3rd density experience is exactly as it should be. All roads long and short serve a purpose and lead back to Source.

When it is close to the end of a grand cycle on a 3rd density planet, beings who are the closest to graduating to 4th density positive or negative have precedence for incarnation openings. It is a seniority by vibration, letting those beings of later 3rd sub-densities who have the best chance of graduating to incarnate. This short period of time could be seen as the final and most intense part at the end of the third round on the game board. Such intense and challenging experiences offer opportunities for a major increase in polarity toward the positive or negative for each being. All the most advanced and skilled players in a 3rd density experience mingle or go head-to-head on a mixed graduation scenario during this short time period. Lower vibratory beings are going to have to transition to a different 3rd density planet anyway to continue their 3rd density experience, so having them incarnate and take a spot that another being could have used to graduate would not be ideal. This priority or seniority of a being's vibration offers later 3rd sub-density beings increased chances at graduating after their last incarnation of the grand cycle because the influx of in-pouring energy raises the vibration of the planet and the collective, which provides increased challenges that coincide with opportunities that offer major advancement and possible graduation, if not already eclipsed. Seniority of vibration also occurs because each being is not given an incarnation experience that is seen as too difficult for them. Since the Earth is a mixed-graduation planet with both positive and negative graduates, the end of a grand cycle and the transitional period from late 3rd to early 4th density can be intense since the most advanced later 3rd sub-density beings on opposite sides of polarity, positive and negative, are incarnated during the same time period.

There are many variables that go into gauging whether a being is ready to graduate to 4th density, as all beings are unique, but for simplification it could be stated that a being needs to have performed at least 51% service-to-others actions to graduate to 4th density positive, and a being needs to have performed at least 95% service-to-self actions to graduate to 4th density negative.

We reiterate that there have been far more positive graduates on Earth than negative graduates. Even the one known as Adolf Hitler did not graduate to 4th density negative, as he actually thought he was doing a good thing for the planet. Displaying this kind of violent confusion accrues much unbalanced karma, but intention is key for graduation. Two well-known beings in your known history that have graduated to 4th density negative are known as Genghis Khan and Rasputin. Their intentions were purely selfish and they intentionally performed service-to-self actions. Both of these beings are currently working for the Orion Empire in the 4th density. They did not have to wait till the end of their major cycle to graduate because they worked through the indigo-ray chakra and penetrated the violet-ray chakra to connect with Source energy, which allowed their graduations to 4th density negative after they transitioned/died. Rasputin was a negative adept. Genghis Khan unintentionally connected with Source energy purely through his laser-focused intentions of self-serving actions.

We reiterate that there is no possibility/timeline/dimension where Earth becomes a negative 4th density planet after harvest-time because far more beings have and will graduate to 4th density positive instead of negative. The possibilities/timelines/dimensions for the smoothest transition into a 4th density core positive planet are still in fluctuation and in the hands of incarnate 3rd density beings, such as yourself, to decide. Due to this fluctuation, there is a very wide range of possible space-in-time scenarios to unfold while planet Earth fully transitions into its 4th density experience. The range is wide due to the amount of variables factored into planet Earth's atypical transition. The majority of human beings who have and will graduate to 4th density positive and will keep experiencing planet Earth will transition/die in order to relinquish their 3rd density bodies and incarnate on Earth again through the typical manner of sexual reproduction in 4th density astral bodies, which are completely visible to 3rd density beings until much time passes and they learn how to be invisible to 3rd density beings and their technology so the two densities can experience different collective experiences when the second wave of 3rd density beings start incarnating onto Earth again millions of years later. A transition/death is necessary for advancement, which is one of many reasons why a being should not fear transitioning. All beings must transition countless times in order to advance on their journey back to Source. Even if one could cheat death/a transition, they would only be cheating themselves by holding themselves back.

At the end of a grand cycle, all are eventually harvested whether they are ready to graduate to 4th density or not. The harvest does not happen in one grand moment as depicted in your distorted religious material. The harvest may happen in a short period of time for the many that transition/die during the micro-nova and major geological changes at the end of the grand cycle, but for others it takes longer to be collected during harvest-time. If a farmer's field is as large as a whole planet, it takes a period of time even if the farmer has a great amount of assisting farmhands during harvest-time to get to and sort out all the wheat and chaff. All will be harvested, the when is of little importance. The end of a grand cycle never naturally ends with extinction, so all are not harvested at once. Removing all the beings or players from the board at once would not be a wise approach for continuing the experience. The human beings who survive the Earth changes are harvested at the end of their incarnations. All 3rd density beings who took part in the 3rd density Earth experience are harvested whether they are currently incarnate or disincarnate during the duration of harvest-time.

To be harvested is for a being's violet-ray chakra to be analyzed in the inner planes while transitioning—after so-called death—and found ready for graduation to 4th density or to continue the 3rd density experience. There is no judgment or punishment; all beings' journeys are as they should be from a perspective held by middle 6th sub-density beings up to Source. During a harvest-time transition, there is one step that is added to the transition while entering the inner planes: during the tunnel of light (or however the being is making the transition to the inner planes), the being temporarily moves from their indigo-ray etheric body to their violet-ray body so they may be analyzed before moving back into their etheric body and continuing to the specific inner plane their level of spiritual advancement is aligned with. The violet-ray body is the whole/complete body that the 7 red-ray to indigo-ray bodies operate within. The violet-ray body is the totality of experiences for a being and so is used to gauge if the unique being is ready to graduate to 4th density.

We reiterate, since Earth is locked-in to being a 4th density core positive planet, beings who graduate to 4th density positive will continue to incarnate onto Earth in its higher vibratory state and have their 4th density positive experience on Earth. Beings who graduate to 4th density negative will incarnate on a different planet that is a 4th density negative planet, in a different solar system, where they will have their 4th density negative experience. A grand cycle for 4th density, positive or negative, is approximately 30 million years, but united groups could graduate to 5th density sooner or much later. If a 4th density negative being wants to switch polarities to the positive path, they cannot perform this action until at least the middle 4th sub-density, which is reached in approximately 15 million years. Beings are responsible for their choices, so one cannot simply switch polarities in the early stages of the next density. Human beings who are not ready to graduate to 4th density, which will be the majority on planet Earth, will incarnate on a different planet that offers a continuation of the 3rd density experience in a different solar system. They will graduate to 4th density when they are ready and have made the choice.

After the transitional period from the later 3rd to full 4th density experience, planet Earth will no longer offer a 3rd density experience until millions of years later after the 4th density positive beings on Earth have learned to be invisible to 3rd density beings and their potential technology and when the 3rd density cycle hits the precise position in the cosmic clock. This is typical for all planets that have shifted into 4th density core planets. When the cosmic clock's gears align, the Earth will again offer an experience for 3rd density beings, the second wave, while at the same time accommodating the 4th density positive beings who will have formed a united group at that time. Both the 3rd and 4th density beings on a planet exist in the same dimension, with the 4th density beings' physical bodies only being invisible to 3rd density beings because they have learned how to do so and do so in order to play their role in the cosmic experience and not infringe upon 3rd density beings' free will.

This higher-density single and multiple-density experience on a planet continues throughout a planet's density ascension. After a planet fully transitions to a 5th density core planet, 4th density beings cease incarnating onto the planet until millions of years have passed and the 5th density beings have formed a united group and have learned to make their physical bodies invisible to 4th density beings. Then the second wave of 4th density beings may start incarnating onto the planet and the planet hosts 4th and 5th density beings at the same time. After a planet fully transitions to a 6th density core planet, 5th density beings cease incarnating onto the planet until millions of years have passed and the 6th density beings have formed a united group and have learned to make their physical bodies invisible to 5th density beings. Then the second wave of 5th density beings may start incarnating onto the planet and the planet hosts 5th and 6th density beings at the same time. At some point the later 6th sub-density united group is ready and chooses to depart the planet and inhabit a Logos/star where they start learning the early 7th density material they need to adequately learn before graduating to 7th density. At this point only 5th density beings reside on the 6th density core planet. At the end of their grand cycle, the 5th density beings who are ready to graduate to 6th density then make the quick evolutionary shift on the planet as it still resides in 6th density. The 5th density beings who are not ready to graduate yet incarnate onto a different planet. When the 6th density beings reach a point during the later 6th sub-density and are ready and choose to depart the 6th density planet, their united group inhabits a Logos/star so they may begin learning the early 7th density material they need to adequately learn before graduating to 7th density. Later 6th sub-density united groups remain on a Logos and continue in service to the One until all the beings they experienced the 3rd density with that were not ready to graduate at different times during density shifts have all advanced and met back up on the Logos. This may take millions to billions of years, but time is of no consequence for the later 6th sub-density united group as they continue in honor/duty to be in service to the One, and there is no location more blissful and loving in the Cosmos than inhabiting a Logos. When all these beings have joined the later 6th sub-density united group and are ready to graduate, the united group transitions to the 7th density experience and remains on the Logos. Only later 6th sub-density and 7th density beings may inhabit Logoi.

The 7th density experience is only experienced while inhabiting a Logos/star and not on a planet. When the 7th density united group on a Logos/star is ready to merge back with Source, and the cyclical timing is right within the cosmic clock, the Logos/star phases into a black hole and the 7th density united group merges back with Source. The beings reside in their totality as Source, experiencing pure love, joy, and peace for as long as they please. Then they decide to either move onto the next Cosmos or wander back to the Cosmos they already experienced to take up a caretaker or overseer position on a Council or elsewhere for a period of time before merging back with Source again and eventually moving onto the next Cosmos.

Let us focus back on planet Earth. Planet Earth's vibration continues to rise until full 4th density is reached. Planet Earth's vibration started slowly rising in approximately 1935 CE and will exponentially increase until the micro-nova sends an intense wave of love energy and photons that will saturate Earth from the molten core center to the surface, greatly accelerating the process of vibratory ascension. Every atom on and in planet Earth will be affected. After the micro-nova, planet Earth's vibration will continue to rise until the 4th density experience in full is offered and 3rd density beings naturally cease their experience on Earth when each being transitions/dies in their own time. The second wave of 3rd density beings will begin to incarnate millions of years later when the cyclical timing is right within the cosmic clock. At that time, Earth will host 3rd and 4th density beings at the same time and will not share a societal experience because the 4th density positive united group will have learned how to be invisible to 3rd density beings and inhabit an area of the planet where the 3rd density beings are not living. Typically the 4th density united group lives underground so they do not infringe upon the 3rd density beings on the surface of the planet and are more protected from influxes of energy from the Logos/star throughout the cycles. The underground structure of planets, including Earth, is not what human beings perceive; this will be expanded upon in a later subject.

Since the Earth has already rose in vibration considerably, current 3rd density beings on Earth have been exposed to this rising vibration that has already crossed into the beginnings of the 4th density vibration. All human beings are in the bathtub and the water's temperature has been rising. Those who are not able to deal with the rising vibration exhibit inharmonious mental states and actions, or even insanity. Typically these are early to middle 3rd sub-density beings, but later 3rd sub-density beings and wanderers who are not adequately balanced may equally be affected. This will only increase as the vibration continues to rise. Due to your solar system moving into a highly charged area of the Milky Way galaxy, and due to the Logos/Sun delaying the micro-nova that initiates the later stages of the transition to full 4th density, higher-density beings have buffered the incoming intense energy in order to lessen the adverse effects on Earthlings during the time period of the delay. The highly charged energy is lessened by this buffering, but not completely stopped. There would be not much of a reason to grant Earthlings a couple more decades that offer opportunities for them to expand their awareness and spiritually progress before the micro-nova if the incoming intense energy made all beings unstable and therefore unable to do so.

This awareness-expanding course we offer you is one of those opportunities for spiritual progression during this time period of delay. With the wide scope of information presented in this course, this course is considered one of the major opportunities for progression during this time period of delay. By simply absorbing this course, a human being expands their awareness to some degree. If the human being practices the knowledge and wisdom presented in this course and does the inner work, they may spiritually progress majorly. This is best done when this awareness-expanding course in book form is read at least two times to process and integrate more of the material. A better idea of what the inner work is and how to do it will be known by the end of this course. Some human beings who would not have graduated during harvest-time will be ready to graduate due to having absorbed this course and doing the inner work. If this course's information is not practiced, it is just that—information. This course provides the catalyst for change and spiritual advancement, but it is up to the individual to use this guiding information in practice for growth to occur.

There are human beings fearful of death/transitioning who think surviving the micro-nova, geological changes, and repositioning of water on the planet will be the only obstacles they need to overcome, but as long as they avoid the self-work/inner work and do not strive to raise their vibration to adapt to the new planetary vibration, they will survive and live out the rest of their incarnation disharmoniously with mental and bodily suffering. But all beings have the free will to choose what they want to experience, and there are no judgments put upon their choices.

At the end of a 3rd density grand cycle, planets with a mixed and negative graduation have more geological changes. This is because mental thoughts and emotions are real things that charge and create changes in physical matter. The physical impact from mental creations happens slowly in 3rd density, but it happens quicker at the end of a grand cycle when the vibration of the planet has started moving into 4th density vibration. Just as inharmonious thoughts and emotions embed tension in the human being's physical body till the inner work is done to transmute and release such energy, human beings' inharmonious thoughts and emotions also embed tension in geographical areas of the planetary body of Earth where they transpire. When an influx of energy is applied to the planet at the end of major cycles, and even minor cycles where micro-novas do not occur, the energy reacts with the stored tension in the planetary body and transmutes, releases, and balances out the tension. Geological shifts and repositioning of water on the planetary body are what occur while this process of transmutation is transpiring. Due to more negativity being produced, mixed and negative graduations create more tension in the human body and the planetary body than positive graduations, so more geological shifts need to occur to cleanse the planetary body of built-up inharmonious energy. During the end of major cycles, and especially a grand cycle, landmasses or continents can sink and rise out of the oceans in a matter of minutes or hours. Grand Canyons and other major geologic formations are made and unmade quickly.

If one wants to respect the entity that is planet Earth, one needs to respect their own mind, body, spirit complex, for to not respect one's mind while producing negative thoughts and emotions is similar to not respecting the entity of planet Earth, who is known as Gaia, because those negative thoughts and emotions not only affect oneself and other beings in the collective, but they also affect Gaia. All are connected. All are One. What one does affects all.

Just as it is appropriate to respect and honor the planetary body, it is appropriate to respect and honor one's own human body, which is their temple. Just as it would benefit a human being to care for and give maintenance to their transportation vehicle (cars, trucks, etc.) so that it runs properly and does not break down before it gets them to where they need to go, the same is appropriately done to a human being's body so experiences can be had and goals that were pre-incarnate planned can be accomplished before transitioning. At some point a human being discards their transportation vehicle and their 3rd density body, and so the chemicals they derive from return to the planetary body where they came from, where they were borrowed from. Until that time comes, keeping them running smoothly and in top condition aids the human being in their incarnation endeavors.

A being's inharmonious mental thoughts and emotions and chosen foodstuffs to consume affect their physical body—as well as their mind and spirit complexes—and eventually the body signals this to the being with aches and pains, eventually leading to more serious ailments such as cancer if the body's signals are ignored. The last result of continuing to ignore such signals is to transition/die. These inharmonious thoughts, emotions, and foodstuffs poison the being's own body, other bodies it shares spaces with, affects the mass consciousness of the collective, and harms the body of the Earth. All is connected because all is One being in reality.

Inharmonious mental thoughts and emotions embedded in the human body are like stains on a shirt. If not cleaned in the wash machine in time, the structure of the fabric of the shirt becomes compromised and deteriorates. The increase in ailments and cancer cases on Earth is partially due to inharmonious mental thoughts from not harmonizing with the higher vibrations. When exposed to vibrations that are higher than one is used to, which is currently the situation on Earth in this time period as Earth moves further toward full 4th density vibration, everything is expedited: positive thoughts and emotions cause one's vibration to raise quickly and more intensely, and negative thoughts and emotions cause one's vibration to lower quickly and more intensely. The quickening and intensity of raising vibrations assists in the separation of the wheat from the chaff during harvest-time.

It should be noted that other main culprits for rising cancer cases and other life-threatening diseases are due to chemical polluting and engineering of your foodstuffs, pollution via chemtrails, 5G wireless frequencies, and harmful and potentially fatal genetically altering formulas being passed off as beneficial vaccines. All of which—except for a portion of foodstuff altering—have been purposefully done to reduce and weaken the majority of human beings so the highly negatively oriented 3rd density human beings may fulfill their agendas more easily. We restate, highly negatively oriented 3rd density human beings—whom humans have labeled elites, globalists, or simply "they"—use programming methods to shape social conditioning for the majority so there is a probability increase in disbelieving and mocking freethinking, observant human beings who raise important issues, exposing the highly negatively oriented human beings' agendas, such as those we just mentioned. A highly charged term in the negatively oriented 3rd density human beings' programming package, "conspiracy theory" and "conspiracy theorist", has been utilized to dismiss and ridicule the freethinking, observant human beings who expose the highly negatively oriented human beings' agendas. Most of the ideas that have been labeled with this programming term are accurate. Many of the inaccurate ideas that this programming term has been applied to were ideas created by the clever negatively oriented human beings themselves who made it appear as if the freethinking human beings came up with the inaccurate ideas, which then jeopardizes the freethinkers' entire body of information through association, damaging their credibility and making others less likely to consider any of their ideas. A prime example of one of these ideas originally created by the negatively oriented beings and passed off as a freethinker's idea was the so-called flat Earth theory. Since this theory is inaccurate to the degree of humorous amusement being displayed by those who come across it, it was an accomplishment by the clever negatively oriented beings in poisoning the whole well of the freethinkers' body of information. Paid human tools are ordered to spread the so-called flat Earth theory throughout the Internet in order to associate the foolish idea with the freethinkers' body of information in order to drive human beings entirely away from the actual freethinkers' body of information, the accurate ideas. This tactic of applying false information to targeted individuals, groups, or movements in order to discredit them has been widely used in many areas and forms because it has been proven to be effective.

The coming micro-nova at the end of Earth's 3rd density grand cycle has been known for decades by some human factions on Earth, but they have kept it secret, along with so much else different factions have kept secret from each other and the vast majority, using human tools through social conditioning to verbally or even physically attack those who try to expose such secrets, or those who simply do not follow the basic programming. Many human beings have been force-transitioned/killed while attempting to expose such secrets held by those human beings who practice service-to-self actions that cause separation and major disharmony.

——∞——

Beings who have already graduated to 4th density positive have been incarnating on Earth with dual-activated 3rd and 4th density bodies for some decades in order to assist with the transitional physical body for the coming 4th density experience. Like apes to humans, this takes a transitional period where the offspring's physical body becomes closer and closer through rapid evolution in reaching the new baseline physical body to be used in the next density. These beings with dual-activated bodies are not of any particular race and should not be seen as more special than 3rd density beings with only one activated body, the yellow-ray body. They have simply graduated already and are aiding in the transition. As with wanderers, this reality is unknown to their conscious mind, but they may feel they are different in some way than those in their society.

Beings with dual-activated bodies (true early 4th sub-density beings), wanderers, walk-ins, and all higher-density beings are part of Oneness like all beings. They are currently more advanced, further along the journey than true 3rd density beings, but they are not superior. No being, no matter their advancement or density, is superior to another. All are One. All are of Source and are Source collectively. A 3rd density being is experiencing a focal point of awareness in a long line of their incarnations that lead up to their higher self in later 6th sub-density and their totality of selves in 7th density. To think of oneself as superior than another is a falsity and a confusion trap that negatively oriented and negative beings fall into.

The exact time of the coming micro-nova is known by no being who is an active player in the illusion. We have stated that it will occur approximately in 2034 CE. This is approximate. It could potentially occur a year or two sooner or later. It will transpire when the time is right and the Logos sees fit. There will also be powerful coronal mass ejections (CMEs) leading up to the micro-nova; more than one powerful act of energy by the Logos will occur.

A portion of 3rd density beings, including some wanderers, have pre-incarnate planned on surviving the micro-nova and geological changes to aid with rebuilding communities and assist with the transition to full 4th density. We restate due to Earthlings strong programming of fear of death, transitioning is as natural as breathing. You have done it many times before and you will do it countless more times. Transitioning quickly during the end of a major cycle is a much smoother and less painful experience than slowly dying of a disease over months or years while continually suffering in the 3rd density body. Whether a being transitions/dies during the micro-nova and geological changes or decades after is as it should be, as all beings have already planned the timing of their transition before they incarnated. There is no reason to fear transitioning during the end of a major cycle, or at any time. If one pre-incarnate planned to transition during the end of a major cycle, then they will; they fulfill their plans and continue on their journey back to Source by preparing for their next incarnation on planet Earth or on a different planet.

Some human beings may label this topic as what they call "doom and gloom". We do not see any doom or gloom in this topic. Change is inevitable, welcomed, and necessary for the flow of the cosmic experience. If one still perceives this topic as being of doom and gloom or experienced fear while absorbing it, it means they have not understood nor removed their fear of transitioning. A lesson that was first offered to be absorbed in the introduction subject 101.4. We suggest returning to subject 101.4 and this subject again and then ruminating and meditating on the material if you felt fear while covering this harvest-time topic. If you are triggered—strong inharmonious emotions or thoughts arising from stimuli—by this topic or any other topic, it is a sign that inner work needs to be done to resolve and transmute the tension embedded in your mind, body, spirit complex. Avoiding heavy issues leaves the tension in one's mind and body complexes and acts like a poison where the negative programming remains and perhaps strengthens. These deep-seeded traumas or other distortions not only affect the mind, they collect in the body and may result in ailments, or even cancer. Even the baby does not forgo trying to walk if they fall down several times and hit their head in their attempts and resign to crawling everywhere for the rest of their incarnation, so why should a so-called adult. We restate, the mind, body, and spirit are all connected; when one is unbalanced, all are unbalanced to a certain degree. To ignore the signs of an imbalance is to ignore growth and spiritual progression.

102.3 – Solar System History

We will summarize your solar system's history by listing in order the planets in your solar system that have and will host the 3rd density experience. First we will make known that all spheres/planets and most moons are sentient entities/life-forms. Thus, it is appropriate to honor and treat them with respect.

The first planet in your solar system to naturally develop 2nd density and then 3rd density life-forms is the entity known as Venus. The 3rd density experience on Venus started approximately 2.6 billion years ago. (All preceding and proceeding "years ago" and "years" in this awareness-expanding course are calculated by what is considered years on Earth by Earthlings.) As with most of the 3rd density beings in your solar system, the Venus beings had what Earthlings call a humanoid structure of two legs, two arms, and a head. They evolved from 2nd density beings similar to birds on Earth, so had birdlike features, including feathers. The living conditions regarding climate were more difficult than they are on Earth due to Venus being closer to the Logos/Sun, but the planetary temperature was a lot cooler than what it is on Venus at your present time due to natural changes in atmospheric conditions.

These beings progressed quickly due to mostly harmonious interactions between beings. Their society focused on what you would call philosophy and upholding to ethics. Wars did not take place on Venus. The Golden Rule of treating others how one wishes to be treated themselves was not only common knowledge, but common knowledge they put into practice. For these reasons, they never implemented a monetary system, nor did they construct a powerful and controlling governmental body like Earth possesses. When beings are mostly harmonious and follow the Golden Rule, powerful governmental bodies are not needed to oversee the population. Beings recognized their unique skills and abilities as they grew older and utilized them to serve themselves and their communities. They spend large amounts of time in solitude.

As with all 3rd density experiences, their average lifespan started out at 900 years and declined appropriately as their 3rd density experience transpired. At the apex of their population, there was approximately 39 million beings.

They produced an adequate mass calling during their second major cycle within the 3rd density experience and later 6th sub-density beings aided them with pyramid structures and how to activate crystals within these structures for their spiritual growth. Due to the harmonious society of the Venus beings, the pyramid structures were of much assistance with their healing, consciousness expansion, and spiritual advancement. At no time were they misused.

Out of all the planets in your solar system that have developed 3rd density life-forms, including Earth, Venus was the most spiritually advanced.

At the end of their grand cycle and harvest-time, approximately 6.4 million beings graduated to 4th density positive and the remaining beings continued 3rd density on a different planet in a different solar system that offered a 3rd density experience. None of the Venus beings graduated to 4th density negative, so Venus had what is considered a positive graduation as opposed to a mixed or negative graduation.

As with all planetary cases, the Venus beings who incarnated on a different planet, due to not being ready to graduate, incarnated back onto Venus's 4th density core planet if they were able to graduate to 4th density positive before Venus transitioned to a 5th density core planet. Whatever the different paths taken by beings after a 3rd density core planet experience—long road or short road, positive path or negative path—they all eventually join back together in the later 6th sub-density on the Logos they inhabit.

After the 3rd density experience ended, planet Venus transitioned into a 4th density core positive planet and due to the harmonious and compassionate nature during their 3rd density experience, they graduated from their 4th density experience faster than the average united group. A second wave of 3rd density beings evolved and developed while the first wave of beings on Venus were well into their 4th density experience. The first wave of beings on Venus spent much more time graduating from 5th density than what is average due to having to balance their high levels of compassion learned in 4th density with wisdom.

Compassion is a needed trait for the positive path, but from wisdom's point of view, which is learned in the 5th density, it is not wise to be overly compassionate. All must be balanced to function to the upmost effectiveness in the ways of love and light. For example, a later 4th sub-density positive being may become a wanderer on a 3rd density planet and take on the pre-incarnate plan of transitioning/dying by being a martyr due to their high level of compassion. This plan is fine for a 4th density being, but most 5th density wanderers would not pre-incarnate to be a martyr because they see it as wise to stay longer in 3rd density so that more aid may be offered.

The first wave of Venus beings graduated to 6th density and at this time in space are a united group in later 6th sub-density. During their later 6th sub-density experience, they departed planet Venus to practice more service-to-others acts and learn early 7th density material and inhabited the Logos/Sun, where they currently reside. The closest translation for Logos is love. When 6th density beings practice the act of sex, it is a blending of two beings' energy that produces what is similar to fusion energy. It is a temporary combining of the two mind, body, spirit complexes that results in a constant orgasmic feeling as the two beings enjoy each other's beingness during the sexual act. When inhabiting a Logos, their sexual acts add to the nurturing and life-force energy—intelligently conscious love and light energy—that is produced by the Logos/Sun, which is a service to all in your solar system.

They are the united group that assisted the Egyptians with the pyramid structures and are known as Ra. A name they gave themselves for the benefit of 3rd density beings since 3rd density beings are not naturally telepathic and desire vocal naming.

In your present time, planet Venus is a 6th density core planet that can support 5th and 6th density life-forms. There are no 6th density beings on planet Venus because, as we stated, they now inhabit your Sun. As we stated, later 6th sub-density united groups may inhabit a Logos/star. There are 5th density positive beings on planet Venus at this time. The vibration of a 5th density being and higher-density beings makes their physical body automatically invisible to 3rd density beings. When we say "automatically" we mean they do not need to learn how to become invisible to 3rd density beings because they already did that when they were 4th

density beings. The same case applies to early 6th density beings being automatically invisible to 4th density beings.

——∞——

The next planet in your solar system to develop 2nd and then 3rd density life-forms was the entity known as Maldek, also known as Tiamat, which now comprises what Earthlings call the Asteroid Belt. This planet was substantially larger than Earth and was situated in orbit between Earth and Jupiter. Mars was not a planet at the time, but rather a moon that orbited Maldek, which conveys how large of a planet Maldek was. On Maldek, the 3rd density experience started approximately 580,700 years ago. The Maldek beings had what Earthlings call a humanoid structure of two legs, two arms, and a head. They were very tall. At the apex of their population, there was approximately 4.3 billion beings.

During their first major cycle they were influenced by 4th density negative beings and later assisted by technologically advanced negatively oriented 3rd density beings from a different solar system, which advanced their technology greatly. Due to not advancing enough spiritually and being advanced technologically, an unbalancing energy warped their mentality into believing their viewpoints and actions were service to others, but were actually service to self. At the time, Mars was a moon that orbited Maldek, and it was inhabited by the Maldek beings because it was hospitable. The so-called royals of the Maldek society moved to this moon and utilized it as their royal area. They, and the other Maldek beings that accompanied them, evolved over tens of thousands of years due to the much different conditions on Mars, becoming much shorter than the very tall beings who stayed on Maldek. The Maldek beings were aggressive and warlike. Their technological advancement allowed them to construct a fleet of spacecraft and they traveled into other solar systems, creating many enemies with their warlike nature. Similar to the Atlantis civilization, they carelessly used their technological might for warfare and it was their unmaking in the end. Maldek beings were more technologically advanced than Atlanteans at their apex of advancement, but Maldek beings were far less spiritually advanced. Due to their spirituality being far behind their technological advancement, and not fully understanding what they were doing, their attempts to weaponize highly advanced technology they had found outside their solar system backfired and resulted with planet Maldek exploding into pieces approximately 549,800 years ago. When Maldek exploded, Mars took much damage from projected debris, which can still be seen on the half side of Mars that was facing Maldek at the time of the explosion. No beings on Maldek survived and no beings on the surface of Mars survived, but a small amount of beings situated in underground facilities in Mars did survive, which included some of the so-called royals.

Out of all the planets in your solar system that have developed 3rd density life-forms, including Earth, Maldek was the most technologically advanced and the least spiritually advanced. Such unbalance creates disharmony and tends to lead to disaster.

The damage inflicted upon Mars caused its electromagnetic field to become majorly out of balance, thinning the atmosphere. Mars, the moon at the time, was thrown into an orbit where it became its own planet, situated in its current orbit between Earth and Jupiter. The Asteroid Belt between what is now planet Mars and Jupiter is the remains of planet Maldek. The atmosphere of Mars was largely affected due to the Maldek incident, and the unbalanced electromagnetic field of Mars caused it to further lose its atmosphere as the years progressed, causing breathable oxygen levels to become thin.

The beings on Mars received communication from some Maldek beings who had been inhabiting one of their artificially created satellite/moon bases when Maldek exploded. They took heavy damage from exploding debris and were flung through space, but they regained control of their spherical base and traveled to a close planet where they locked their base into orbit around this planet. They had started a colony on this planet and used communications to attempt to contact any other survivors and for the survivors to join them on this new planet. Due to Mars being inhospitable and due to the beings situated underground knowing that the atmosphere might continue to thin, when they picked up the communication, the so-called royals and their selected crew left the rest of their small population to fend for themselves and departed Mars in their remaining fleet, a few spacecraft.

The sudden and intense explosion of Maldek caused such confusion and trauma in the mass consciousness of the Maldek beings that a group ghost-like scenario arose. None of the beings on Maldek escaped the destruction of their planet and were melded together in ghost form, living out the terror and trauma of the explosion for hundreds of thousands of years because the local Confederation of Planets was not able to mentally reach them. Approximately 199,500 years ago, members of the local Confederation of Planets at the time were able to slowly break through to the Maldek beings and make them conscious of their situation. They then made their way to the inner planes and spent much time in the deep resting place where traumas are distilled and transmuted and the being is healed.

After having fully realized their actions and making plans in the inner planes to balance out their karma, approximately 46,650 years ago Maldek beings were genetically assisted by entities in the local Confederation of Planets and incarnated within planet Earth (not on the surface) with later 2nd sub-density-like bodies (Bigfoot) while still being self-aware in 3rd density. Such an occurrence like this is rare. Unlike what is taught in Buddhist sects, once a being reaches a density, they never reincarnate below that density no matter how much negatively polarizing actions they perform. As we have stated, if a 3rd density being performs enough service-to-self (negatively polarizing) acts, they graduate to 4th density negative instead of reverting to the 2nd density. Post-Maldek beings stayed in 3rd density and agreed to inhabit the Bigfoot bodies for karmic balancing, but they did not revert to 2nd density consciousness, they stayed self-aware in 3rd density.

The post-Maldek Bigfoot beings lived not on the surface of planet Earth, but rather deep underground in open honeycomb-like spaces and passageways. Existing separately from surface-dwelling beings on Earth provided a good setting for them to balance their karma in an unimpeded manner. A very small amount of outcasts have made their way to the surface and live in caves and shallower passageways underground. These are the Bigfoot that human beings have encountered. The so-called Hollow Earth theory is not completely accurate in that the Earth is not hollow and has a molten core. However, throughout the planet, deep underground is littered with large pockets—some quite enormous—of space where underground cities can be built and house millions. The area between the surface of the planet and the molten core of the planet is highly misunderstood by the surface population due to disinformation. Deep under the surface, the Earth adheres to the invisible geometric honeycomb structure where some honeycomb areas are filled with earth, water, or open spaces. Larger open areas consist of more geometric honeycomb-like areas combined, where there is no physical framework separating the combined honeycomb areas and is all open space. Other beings reside deep underground besides the post-Maldek Bigfoot beings. Some are from this planet and some from other planets, some ranging from positively oriented, negatively oriented, and neutrally oriented. Due to this, exploring deep underground is not advisable to the average human being.

A good amount of the post-Maldek Bigfoot beings have adequately balanced their karma for being warlike and destroying their planet and have incarnated into typical 3rd density human bodies on the surface of the planet through the typical birthing process. Over 2.3 billion of them did this and incarnated throughout the third major cycle you currently reside in. Of all the diverse 3rd density beings on Earth, the largest piece of the origin pie is from human beings who in past incarnations were Maldek beings and then used to be post-Maldek Bigfoot beings.

The next planet in your solar system to host 3rd density life-forms was the entity known as Mars. Rather, it was not a planet but a moon orbiting Maldek, which some Maldek beings had moved to during their first major cycle, as we covered already. On Mars their offspring over tens of thousands of years evolved into a much shorter being than that of the very tall beings who stayed on Maldek, and they also developed elongated skulls. Beings did not naturally start evolving from 2nd density beings into 3rd density beings on Mars due to natural cycles, but we will cover this sphere in this subject regardless. At the apex of the Mars population, there was approximately 380 million beings.

Returning to where we left off when covering Maldek: The so-called royals and their selected crew had left the rest of their small population to fend for themselves and departed Mars in their remaining few spacecraft. They traveled to the planet where the communication came from, planet Earth. When they arrived in Earth's orbit, they noticed a familiar satellite orbiting Earth. This artificial satellite had been constructed by Maldek beings and was orbiting Maldek like Mars had been before Maldek exploded.

It is a spherical base that was built with an intricate internally layered structure that could hold and house a lot of living quarters for beings and their goods. The side of the spherical satellite facing Maldek had been struck by much debris when Maldek exploded and sent it traveling through space, similar to what happened to Mars, leaving half of its sphere visibly damaged with indentations/craters. Most of the Maldek personnel inside the base had died during the debris impact, but those remaining traveled into planet Earth's orbit. Using the technology that was still operational after the debris impact, they positioned the spherical base in a precise orbit and manner around planet Earth.

This artificially constructed spherical satellite is what Earthlings call the Moon. Current scientists on Earth are already aware of the many unnatural and highly abnormal aspects of the Moon when compared to natural satellites/moons that orbit other planets: the Moon's degreed tilt, distance from the planet it orbits, gravitational abnormalities, lack of adequate atmosphere, and its inner complex configuration. This evidence that scientists are already aware of, and is information freely available to Earth's population, should warrant no surprise that the Moon is artificial and was constructed rather than being a naturally formed moon. This artificially built moon base that originally orbited Maldek started orbiting planet Earth approximately 549,800 years ago.

Before the Mars beings arrived in Earth's orbit with their spacecraft, the Maldek beings in their satellite base had taken craft and landed on what is present-day Antarctica because they noticed the remnants of an old abandoned civilization and thought the materials could be of use. They found the old and dilapidated structures had been built by beings even more technologically advanced than themselves billions of years ago. At that time the continent of Antarctica was not situated at the South Pole and was not covered in ice and had a tropical climate.

They had built some structures, but when the Mars beings arrived in their spacecraft and joined them, they were able to build more structures for their settlement. They used their advanced technology to genetically create a worker caste to serve and work for them. Their civilization grew and functioned for tens of thousands of years and ended during one of Earth's cycles where major geological shifts and the displacement of bodies of water occurred that placed Antarctica at the South Pole and under ice and snow. Some of the so-called royals and others managed to take cover in one of their spacecraft and used the advanced technology they had found to put themselves into a sleeping stasis in the hopes of waking up at a more opportune time.

Over the tens of thousands of years that followed, there were battles between different 3rd density races in the area of Earth and over the possession of the satellite humans call the Moon. Eventually a treaty was signed and many different 3rd density races were assigned areas on the Moon, most being on the side that perpetually faces away from Earth—the dark side of the Moon—so they and their arriving and departing craft would not be visible to beings who would later naturally evolve and advance on Earth. Regardless, they use a masking technology to hide their bases and structures so they blend in with the rest of the Moon's surface. They still hold to this treaty in the present time and there are many bases and activity on the dark side of the Moon.

Around the same time as the battles around Earth and on the Moon, a reptilian group known as the Draco who were part of the battles constructed bases on Earth in what is present-day Antarctica approximately 360,000 years ago when Antarctica had a tropical climate. The bases are still there in your present time under the ice and used by these highly negatively oriented 3rd density reptilians who are heavily influenced and controlled via technology by their chosen 4th density negative masters. Within the last approximately 85 years, the Draco have made alliances and deals with negatively oriented human factions, such as the Nazis, and have allowed them to build bases in Antarctica under the ice as well.

Adhering to the template that is typically used throughout the universe, these reptilians evolved into being bipedal with a head and two arms. This is the typical template that beings naturally evolve into when starting the 3rd density experience—except for water-based 3rd density beings—because it allows a being to function and have experiences in 3rd density and 4th density. Since the 3rd density beings in this group evolved from 2nd density reptiles, they have scales instead of skin and reptilian-looking faces. There is a slight possibility for 3rd density beings to adhere to the nature of the 2nd density beings they evolved from. For the reptilians that make up the Draco group, they adhere to the cold and vicious nature of a 2nd density reptile.

The Mars beings who transitioned/died due to the heavy impact of debris impacting Mars when Maldek exploded approximately 549,800 years ago spent much time in the inner planes healing from the trauma in the deep resting place and afterwards reviewed their past incarnation and prepared for their next incarnation that would be on planet Earth when Earth started naturally hosting 3rd density beings, which was approximately 75,525 years ago. These Mars beings were not of the so-called royals on Mars who went underground and survived when Maldek exploded. Unlike the beings on Maldek and the so-called royals on Mars, they were not responsible for destroying Maldek. Since the Mars beings, who transitioned/died during the Maldek explosion, had already experienced close to half of the 3rd density experience and were not responsible for Maldek exploding, it was decided by the local Guardians at the time to have them incarnate onto Earth through a different means other than the typical incarnating from birth by the same density beings who resided on the planet, which at the time was the transitioning apes from later 2nd sub-density to early 3rd sub-density. Birthing through these transitioning ape beings would be retracing ground the Mars beings had already covered, so instead, like the post-Maldek Bigfoot beings, the Mars beings were genetically assisted and prepared from genetic stock from the Mars beings, the transitioning apes, and from a local Guardian who was part of the group known as Yahweh, which we will speak further about in a later subject regarding religions and their origins. This mix of genetic stock allowed the post-Mars beings' physical bodies to suitably function in Earth's atmosphere and conditions. The post-Mars beings' physical bodies would be at about the same level of advancement as they were on Mars instead of the post-Maldek beings who agreed to inhabit later 2nd sub-density Bigfoot bodies while still being 3rd density self-aware beings in order to balance their karma for destroying Maldek along with the so-called royals that lived on Mars and survived the explosion of Maldek by going underground.

At the beginning of the natural 3rd density experience on Earth approximately in 73,498 BCE, through genetic assistance/preparation and a cloning process, the post-Mars beings were directly placed on Earth rather than incarnating through the typical birthing process. Like all 3rd density beings, the veil of forgetfulness was applied so they would forget all their past incarnations and not know who they were or where they came from. They were placed on the Mu continent in a different location from where the post-Deneb beings who would be called Lemurians later on would reside. Due to the genetic preparation and cloning process that directly deposited the post-Mars beings on Earth, their 3rd density physical bodies were much more advanced than the transitioning ape bodies and the primitive human being bodies that rapidly evolved from the transitioning apes. The post-Mars beings having advanced 3rd density bodies at the time compared to other physical bodies on Earth eventually led many of them to their weakness of thinking they were superior than other 3rd density beings on Earth.

After the sinking of the Mu continent at the end of the first major cycle on Earth in approximately 48,328 BCE, the post-Mars beings who survived migrated to many different places on Earth. Some of them would be a part of the Atlantis civilization and later on the Egyptian civilization, both civilizations that were assisted with the pyramid structures from different later 6th sub-density united groups.

The temptation of superiority by the post-Mars beings often led to them becoming so-called royals who controlled different civilizations as Earth progressed through its major cycles. This was a mental stance that aligned with negative polarity and made them easily influenced by 4th density negative beings. Well into the third major cycle, a 5th density inner planes negative being deceived and manipulated some of the positively oriented post-Mars beings, which led to them considering themselves superior in a spiritual way and twisted their mentality into them thinking they were "God's chosen people". This will be covered in the subject about religions and their origins.

A treaty was eventually made with some of the negatively oriented post-Mars beings and the highly negatively oriented reptilian group known as the Draco, both 3rd density groups who consider themselves superior and therefore hold the mental belief that they are fit to rule the rest of the 3rd density beings on Earth. The post-Mars beings originally had elongated skulls, and were still partially so during their time in the Egyptian civilization, which is depicted in your ancient Egyptian records, but after breeding with different races on Earth throughout the tens of thousands of years since they were placed on Earth, they now appear like most human beings and are considered human beings due to genetic similarity. The genetic makeup of a 3rd density body is what makes a being during a specific incarnation fall into a classification of being a human being, but the term "human being" from the point of spirit and mind means close to nothing because so many beings' 3rd density bodies who fall into this classification originally came from other planets at the start or sometime during their 3rd density experience. This is why the term "alien" means close to nothing. All beings have experiences on more than one planet through their density ascension, so all beings would be considered aliens. Some human being descendants of the post-Mars beings are positively oriented, so we note that it is not wise to lump them all together. Since 3rd density groups/races typically consist of positively and negatively oriented beings, group generalization in regards to polarity is inappropriate for all races on Earth and throughout the universe.

The Mars beings' spacecraft buried under the ice in Antarctica have recently been discovered and some of the negatively oriented human beings who are the descendants from the post-Mars beings traveled there to visit the findings. They found the Mars beings in sleeping stasis and decided to wake them up in order to be led by them, but when they were brought out of stasis, the Mars beings who were the so-called royals of their race were apprehended by positive higher-density beings and relocated off planet to stand trial for being responsible for destroying planet Maldek, which also consequently altered the timeline probabilities toward negative polarity for the local Logos/star cluster.

Besides the 3rd density activity on Mars that we cover in a future subject, there is currently 2nd density plant and animal life on Mars. Mars has a thin atmosphere where human beings can utilize a breathing apparatus that supplies adequate oxygen to function on the surface of the planet.

——∞——

The next planet in your solar system to develop 2nd and then 3rd density life-forms is the entity known as Earth, which we have already covered in the subject regarding the history of Earth's 3 major cycles. Pertaining to the dinosaurs on Earth: Approximately 230 million years ago, a 3rd density reptilian race started a genetic experiment on Earth that produced 2nd density beings known as the dinosaurs. Approximately 75 million years ago, large asteroids impacted Earth and ended the reptilian's experiment. This reptilian race was disappointed and left the planet. Most of the dinosaurs, except for some water- and air-based dinosaurs, went extinct over a period of time due to the temporary hostile environment on the planet that the impact of the asteroids had created. More aspects of your current and final major cycle on Earth will be covered in future subjects.

—∞—

The next planet in your solar system to potentially develop through all the densities is the entity known as Uranus. It is currently progressing through the 1st density.

—∞—

Although the entity known as Saturn will not progress through the densities and host 3rd density beings, the area around the rings of Saturn is where the local Council resides. They reside in the outer planes but within a constructed magnetic field that places them in time in space, as is a conducive situation for their experience in protecting and serving your solar system.

—∞—

We will end this subject by making known that the universe is teeming with 3rd density beings and life-forms of all densities, which is the opposite of the programming or disinformation being fed to the majority by the negatively oriented 3rd density human beings. There have been countless different species/races of 3rd density beings who have visited and lived on Earth and in your solar system before 2nd density beings on Earth naturally started evolving into 3rd density beings approximately 75,525 years ago. In this subject, we covered the natural process of 2nd density beings that evolved into 3rd density beings when the density cycles allowed originating life to be naturally hosted on planets, but there has been countless different 3rd density species/races who have visited and lived in your solar system. Currently, there is 3rd density activity on every planet and their moons in your solar system that is not off limits due to higher-density beings residing there who deny lower-density activity in their areas. We will expand upon this 3rd density activity in a later subject.

102.4 – Spirit Guides & Everything has a Purpose

Every 3rd density being has at least three spirit guides assisting them at any given moment. You are never alone on your journey. As with other positive beings, they place no judgment upon your thoughts and actions. Their love and compassion always strives to assist you. Some spirit guides are with you for an entire incarnation, others for certain stages of your incarnation. The spirit guides who stay with you for the whole duration were specifically pre-incarnate planned. Other spirit guides are temporarily there for you if you choose certain paths and find yourself in an area of their expertise. A parent who transitioned/died before their pre-incarnate planned time may fulfill their aiding agreement with their child by being one of their spirit guides since they cannot be there in the physical to guide or protect them up to a certain age.

The little angel and devil depicted in Earth cartoons that stand upon one's shoulders and whispers in their ear is channeled creativity, for such actions are reality and not fiction. The "angels" are positive 4th density beings or one's spirit guides who whisper into one's right ear, offering guidance and thoughts that most think are their own thoughts. The "devils" are the 4th density negative beings who whisper into one's left ear, offering thoughts of temptation and manipulation that most think are their own thoughts. The left side of one's head is typically within the negative polarity of their electromagnetic field, and the right side of one's head is typically within the positive polarity of their electromagnetic field. This does not mean the left side of one's head is negatively oriented; it is simply part of the area where one's electromagnetic field is negatively polarized, just as magnets have a positively and negatively polarized side. In order to function, all electromagnetic fields must have positively and negatively polarized areas. This is the case for all apple-shaped electromagnetic fields which protect and nurture beings, planets, solar systems, galaxies, and universes. Sometimes an individual may hear a tone in their right or left ear. Each is a message of some sort. A whisper offering advice, giving recognition, or heeding you to pay attention is a tone in one's right ear from their spirit guides or positive higher-density beings (typically 4th density beings) offering assistance. A whisper offering temptation, deception, self-doubt, anger, or other forms of negativity is a tone in one's left ear from 4th density negative beings.

Your mind is a building complex that can be utilized by yourself and others who have remote access. Your thoughts are not always your own. This goes for all 3rd density beings—no exceptions. As a being needs to use discernment when they hear or read information, a being also needs to use discernment when hearing the thoughts in their mind. You sit in the main building of the mind's building complex with your own thoughts echoing around the main building. Positive beings—spirit guides or positive higher-density beings—reside in the attached building to the right of your main building within the building complex. They whisper thoughts into a vent that travels through an air duct that leads into your main building and then echoes around your main building like your own thoughts, inseparable from your own thoughts. The positives hope you will hear and heed their advice and guidance. They typically wait for your main building to cease all the useless, cluttering mental noise that keeps echoing around your main building, some of which are like bad songs that repeat over and over again. When there is a silence or a focused seeking, this is when the "angels" whisper into the air duct, for they know you have a chance at hearing them at those moments, or for information to be downloaded and potentially accessed in a future moment. If the mental noise in the main building never ceases, spirit guides have to resort to other ways of assistance to get through to you, other ways that may appear to be the opposite of assistance by you when they transpire in life situations.

When the main building is filled with useless, cluttering thoughts or with negativity, the "devils", who reside in the attached building to the left of your main building in the building complex, whisper into their air duct that leads to your main building, charging your confusion, assisting to twist reality during unbalanced states, and charging/bolstering the negative thoughts and emotions you are producing. The more the mental hamster wheel turns with negativity, fueling thoughts and emotions, the harder it is to stop the wheel. Even when the thinker tries to focus somewhere else and stops turning the wheel, they may get caught back into the wheel that is still spinning from its built-up charge/inertia. Better to jump out of a negatively spinning wheel and ignore it while starting and charging up a positive spinning wheel with all your focus. Or even better, recognize you are spinning a negative wheel and stop before it builds enough charge to sweep you away with it. Be the silent observer of your mind complex and oversee its activity. This is part of doing the inner work that offers a way to spiritual advancement.

If you are a being attempting to greatly raise the vibratory collective by performing great positively polarized acts of service for the planet in some way, 4th density negatives—and in rare cases a 5th density negative—may do more than merely whisper their thoughts into your mind that appear like your own thoughts; they can focus a powerful negative emotion into your field. Sometimes this emotion is not even connected with anything going on in your life or what you are presently feeling or doing and seems to come from nowhere. This is a sign that it is not your negative emotion and it can be dissolved if you disassociate with it and do not charge/entertain it. This is similar to empathic beings walking in crowded places and picking up emotions from other beings, but the attacking emotion from negative beings is far more intense because it is focused and directed at you. Recognize that it is not your emotion and it will dissipate. For quicker dissipation, whether the emotion originates from you or not, focus on your heart chakra filling your whole body and mind with love energy. The focused thinking is useful, but the feelings or emotions generated are much more beneficial as emotions are activators in mental consciousness. When bathing oneself in love energy, all negativity washes away like the dirt on a rock washes away when the powerful force of water from a waterfall hits it.

Spirit guides and 4th density positive beings can only assist you so much automatically. If you desire more assistance from them, especially 4th density positive beings, you must ask for it. Some human beings have called this act prayer, but no matter what label is applied to the mental action, it is mental communication. When the intention to communicate with spirit guides and higher-density beings is mentally made, the message is left on their answering machine real-time. You may ask for assistance and find your life taking a turn for what seems to be the worse: a relationship and/or job ending, or something else falling through or ending. This is the help you asked for. To be led to one path, you must depart from the path you are currently on. The path you are being led away from might have been what you thought you wanted or it may be a comfortable situation that offers relaxation without forward movement. It does not always mean you were on the wrong path; maybe you merely stayed on a particular right path for too long, so then it became the wrong path, according to your pre-incarnate plans, as there is no wrong or right path from Source's viewpoint. You may have dwelled in a comfortable place for too long due to its ease and convenience, not wanting to deal with harder aspects of life. Or you could have stayed in a situation longer than it was useful because you fear change. It is common for human beings to stay in a relationship or at a job for too long because of their fear of not finding another particular job or human being to connect with.

In order to learn different lessons and continue growing and moving toward Source, change is inevitable and at the heart of the cosmic curriculum. Since the planetary vibrations have already entered early 4th density conditions, thoughts manifest faster than they used to and asked-for assistance from your spirit guides and higher-density beings transpires a lot faster than it used to, as does the balancing and unbalancing act of karma.

If you stay mindful and balanced while flowing down the river on your way back to the ocean, you recognize currents or areas of turbulence and rocks in your path to avoid, whether from your own vigilance or from spirit guidance, although the former is typically needed for the latter to be effective. If while not reading the signs and not being mindful and observant you end up hitting a protruding rock that brings temporary pain and suffering but ends up sending you in the right direction at a separation in the fork of the river, thank the rock or current and continue onward. The more you stay observant, mindful, balanced, and embracing change and opportunities, the easier you flow in the right direction, not needing or lessening the potentially helpful yet painful rocks that lay before you. Adversity offers growth and needed realignments. Adversity is always there to assist, but it is rarely welcomed.

An analytical mind may look into the past and recognize how each setback and major difficulty—protruding rocks in the river—brought them to where they are now, and so gives thanks to the rocks for their assistance. If the rocks were 4th density negatives, they ended up being a tool for you instead of the other way around. Utilizing the analytical mind and intuition is to make use of the valuable tools you have been given. There is a place and time for either to be utilized.

Everything has a purpose in the end. Those who bring you hardship could be beings you pre-incarnate planned an agreement with to help you in a certain way: to balance karma from a past incarnation or another reason that may not seem clear to you in your limited viewpoint. 4th density negative beings and the 3rd density human tools they may manipulate against you may be allowed to bring adversity in your life to force you to make a particular choice that you have been putting off. This is when you have hit a brick wall on your path and are forced to either move toward a more positive or negative path and get off the lazy neutral fence. If you wallow in victimhood, anger, or another negativity due to the wall, you will navigate in the direction of a negative path, potentially finding that path. At some point you may recognize the error and navigate toward a positive path you initially did not take after the wall, which is more typical than one staying on the negative path. Spirit guides can even engineer these walls for you if all their asked-for whispered advice or signs have been ignored and the opportunities that reside on the pre-incarnate planned path you are not currently on are dwindling. If you do not change paths, your pre-incarnate plans will not be fulfilled, as well as the pre-incarnate plans with others you had intended to interact with, making your incarnation a missed opportunity in some regards. In this way, you can understand why spirit guides are acting in your best interest by engineering such a wall or allowing negatively oriented or negative beings to create the wall for you.

A 3rd density being's spirit guides often work with other beings' spirit guides to increase the potential for an opportunity to arise. They also indirectly work with 4th density positive beings, as they have the same role: performing service-to-others actions. We say "indirectly" because spirit guides are only in the inner planes and 4th density beings may be of the inner planes or outer planes. (When we speak of 4th density beings or any density beings without specifying, it is always physical outer planes beings we are speaking of and not metaphysical inner planes beings.) If you notice a string of perceived coincidences that led you up to a certain point, it is your spirit guides at work using synchronicities, working with other beings' spirit guides, especially if the opportunity involves more than one being. Spirit guides can work in a moment by moment bases to increase the potential of an opportunity for you. All self-aware beings have free will, and spirit guides are no different; they rely on their experience and instincts to guide you and other beings to interact with you in a certain way that they believe is effective and beneficial for you.

The web of interactions and correlations make up the infinite possibilities/timelines, so the purpose of anything can come from countless origins. One reason patterns happen to the same being repeatedly is because the energy a being puts out into the ether in the form of thoughts and emotions is what is returned to that being because that is what is being created and charged in their torsion field, which works like a magnet that attracts and pulls experiences toward the being. Since most human beings are not aware that their thoughts and emotions create, and do not observe their minds, they tend to create experiences and situations they do not want. Such a being is co-creating the same pattern for their experiences, typically doing so unconsciously. We restate this very important point: thoughts and emotions exist and they co-create your reality, as well as add to the collective consciousness, aiding it or doing the opposite. Every being, no matter how insignificant they think they are, has an effect on the collective consciousness that shapes the potentials for all civilizations on a planet or the entire planet. There is no being that does not matter. Every being is potentially powerful and valuable. If a being believes they are powerless, that is what they seemingly are because that is what they create for themselves. A being is only as powerful as they believe they are.

Many reasons for circumstances are pre-incarnate planned to best serve the being during their incarnation to fulfill their goals, which includes balancing their karma. Once a 3rd density being activates their green-ray heart chakra, which is typically all 3rd density beings in the third major cycle, they have a part in planning all the details in their next incarnation. They choose their parents, who also choose them, which leads to genetic dispositions. Genetic dispositions are starting blocks and most are not prisons one cannot escape, as a being can work past and overcome most dispositions with the same motivation and dedication it takes for all self-growth. Overcoming some dispositions may be a big part in a being's self-growth, which was pre-incarnate planned.

Being born with a disability of some kind is a pre-incarnate plan to balance karma. Even a healer is not able to work through the energy of Source to offer healing for such a disability because the subconscious mind does not allow the healing, knowing that it is what the being pre-incarnate planned to balance their karma. If it were healed, the being would not be able to balance their karma. Accepting limitations that cannot be overcome in a certain incarnation is part of self-growth. If you cannot change something, accept it and work with it. If this is done, your limitations offer benefits in your incarnation and future incarnations. If you can do this, you will have turned your limitations into gifts that keep on giving after the incarnation is done.

A being who has activated their green-ray heart chakra chooses precisely when they are born because the position of the spheres adds another layer of dispositions to a being's traits and abilities. This is known by some on Earth and they call it a birth chart. Unlike general astrological readings that lump so many factors together that they become almost meaningless or even self-destructive, a birth chart takes into account the moment of a being's birth, so it is calculated for a particular being. Although, even a comprehensive birth chart does not convey the entire disposition for a being, as the position of the spheres is only one layer of several set dispositions for a being. The moment of conception is another set layer for a being's disposition. The placement of the spheres gives a potential for traits and abilities that points to some of the self-growth needed for a being. If a being practices self-growth—does the inner work—in a certain area within their birth chart, the traits and abilities serve the being and act as strengths. If the being neglects to do so, the area acts as one of their weaknesses instead of their strengths. A birth chart is a good map to start the journey of self-growth. A being chooses their time of birth to have certain traits and abilities that—if one's inner work allows them to become strengths instead of weaknesses—will assist them with their goals and mission. Depending on the level of advancement of a being, the mere inner work of turning potential weaknesses to strengths listed on a birth chart could be a major part of their spiritual growth and/or balancing karma.

Even when more than one being is birthed at the exact same moment, the beings are not the same, and could be even quite different because the position of the spheres for one's birth is only one layer of several that dictates the outcome of traits, tendencies, and abilities. Some other layers besides the position of the spheres for one's conception and birth are the genetic disposition of parents, the long line of handed-down genetics of the particular 3rd density physical body you utilize for an incarnation, the social conditioning of a particular society one is raised in, and above all, the entirety of experiences of all your past incarnations that goes back even before the 3rd density experience that makes each being unique whether they are incarnate or disincarnate. Every unique being is valued and loved by Source, as every being is a part of Source, and is Source in their totality of Beingness. As is appropriate for a human being to love and look after every part of their physical body, their temple, Source loves and cares for all its parts that make up the Oneness that is Source. Separation is an illusion; all beings are One being.

Aspects of these layers of disposition and pre-incarnate plans are what humans call destiny, but destiny can only be fulfilled with a being's free will. A being's incarnation is a dance between destiny and free will. Free will is a primary universal law for all densities, as Source would not know itself better if free will did not exist in the Cosmos. Free will has upmost importance and purpose in the cosmic experience. Thus, the adversity a being creates for other beings out of their free will and not through destiny has purpose as well. It may not be destiny's purpose, but it has purpose for each being, as well as for the whole of the cosmic experience. All adversity offers growth whether it is planned for or not.

102.5 – Religions & their Origins

We will start at the major adaptation of the cosmic experience where being a negative being and the service-to-self path was first granted to be paved and experienced. We will restate and expand upon this topic, as we have already spoken of this topic in subject 101.5.

Source took what It had learned of itself in prior mental projections of creation—Cosmoses—to further its exploration in your current mental projection of creation—your current Cosmos. Each Logos/star, being directly connected to Source but operating with free will, made adaptations/upgrades of progression to their influential area of the cosmic experience. In the beginnings of your Cosmos, there was only the infinite positive paths leading back to Source and no negative beings existed. This is the state of the solar systems toward the center of the Milky Way galaxy.

It was not until a Logos made an adaptation that would prove to be very effective for Source's exploration of continuing to know itself: the creation of the negative paths that lead up to the middle 6th sub-density in the outer planes, and up to the end of the 5th density in the inner planes. During the early to middle 6th sub-densities in the physical outer planes, these infinite negative paths all cease when they harmonize with and join the infinite positive paths leading back to Source. This occurred by the Logos creating another partition in the mind complex, or tree of mind, to greatly empower the free will of beings. The choice of acting in unity or separately in the self-awareness of 3rd density was born; the inroads of service to self became available alongside service to others where the being eventually makes the choice in 3rd density and graduates to 4th density positive or negative. In the middle to later sub-densities of 4th and 5th density, negative beings are given the opportunity to switch polarities and continue their progression on the positive path.

When the idea of the Garden of Eden was channeled to a positively oriented 3rd density being, it was grossly simplified in story form, as the 3rd density beings on Earth at that time were not advanced enough to grasp the larger viewpoint of the higher densities. The "fall of Eden", as seen from a shallow viewpoint, was recorded as an "evil" event. Instead, it is when a Logos created the negative path in its adaptation/upgrade to the Cosmos and it came into existence. The Garden of Eden was not a place on Earth. Eden is the state of mind within the tree of mind where beings are always self-aware of their connection to Source as parts of Source, and so only positive polarity is practiced. Eden still exists and is the state of mind for the beings residing in the solar systems near the center of the Milky Way galaxy that were created before the negative path was established by a Logos's adaptation.

The inner planes beings, only being positive before the adaptation of choice was created, became split with inner planes beings choosing to play the role of negatives or staying positive in the inner planes densities of 3rd to 5th. This was depicted as being a "war in the heavens" by the positively oriented 3rd density being who channeled this information. Lucifer was the top negative being in the 5th density inner planes at the beginning of the negative path. Lucifer has since switched polarities and merged back with Source. Thus, the entity known as Lucifer is no more. The top negative polarity position is a rotating position and so is commanded by a different entity at this time in space. It is the same for the positive inner planes, as well as outer planes, each position/role is rotating, as playing a role for too long would become boring for the being/player. The top positions for positive polarity are held by beings in the 7th density inner planes.

From the beginning of a 3rd density experience on a planet, 3rd, 4th, and 5th positive and negative inner planes beings attempt to influence 3rd density outer planes beings, such as human beings, toward the service-to-others path or the service-to-self path. 3rd density outer planes beings are also influenced by positive and negative 4th density outer planes beings, and are rarely influenced by positive and negative 5th density outer planes beings and positive 6th density outer planes beings. A portion of inner planes beings focus on influencing 3rd density beings' belief systems and ways of living. Negative 4th density inner planes beings frequently order the 3rd density outer planes beings who have contacted them to address them by titles such as lord or master instead of giving their names. Negative 5th density inner planes beings attempt to deceive 3rd density outer planes beings into thinking they are "God" and therefore should be worshipped and shown complete submission with unquestionable loyalty. These negative inner planes beings show absolute authority, give commands, and offer deals for their services to 3rd density outer planes beings. Positive inner planes beings never attempt to come across as "God". When interacting with 3rd density beings, they are merciful, show loving-kindness, do not give commands but offer guidance, and do not make deals for their services but give freely in performing service-to-others actions.

Negative inner planes beings demand sacrifices for their services. If a 3rd density being can show they have the inclination to potentially advance toward 4th density negative graduation by sacrificing a 2nd density being or another 3rd density being in order to get what they want, then inroads are given to the negative inner planes being and they will honor the set deal, for as long as it suits them. Negative inner planes beings demand to be called lord or king in the language of the 3rd density being in communion with them. Negative inner planes beings love the smell of burning flesh and so make as part of their deals the roasting or complete burning of the sacrificial meat. At no time ever does a positive inner planes being, or positive outer planes being, ask to be called lord, king, God, or ask for a sacrifice. Why would a positive being ask another being to force-transition/kill on their behalf another part of Source? One should always use discernment when communicating with a higher-density being, inner or outer planes.

Negative inner planes beings found inroads in the first major cycle of the 3rd density experience on Earth with beings who either justified their actions in deals or simply did whatever was necessary for deals that would further their gain of power and control over others. Inroads by negative inner planes beings were expanded upon in the second major cycle and further expanded upon in the third major cycle. Positive inner planes beings also gained inroads throughout the cycles. Their information came across to 3rd density beings as honoring the many aspects of God/Source, or the many gods/entities that have a powerful influence over the 3rd density beings. The beings who followed their direction were never asked to make sacrifices or to perform certain tasks made in a deal or contract.

During the third major cycle when more advanced information could be offered, some positive advances were made when later 6th sub-density outer planes united groups offered pyramid structures along with the knowledge of Oneness of Source, but Earthlings largely continued to practice Pantheism and Paganism or whatever label was given to the honoring and worshipping of many selected "gods" instead of honoring the way of One/Source, where it would be appropriate to honor all positive parts of Source if one is positively oriented. Worshipping and honoring are two distinct differences. To worship is to declare or display oneself as inferior or worth less than another self of Source, which is a falsity. Sometimes the word "worship" is used by Earthlings to show very high regard or respect to another without thinking of oneself as inferior to them, and in this case there is no folly. To honor is to give respect to another, especially one who is currently more advanced in the ways of knowledge and wisdom in one's own density or of a higher positive density. Since Source has projected countless parts of itself into the cosmic experience, honoring (not worshipping) more than one part of Source is understandable and gives due respect, but knowing all parts stem from one Source is the ultimate truth. Therefore, to honor (not worship) many gods/entities or higher-density aspects of Source while recognizing that all, including oneself, are part of Source is a respectful and knowledgeable stance. Many Native American tribes did precisely this. We do not mean to cover your terminology of "honor" and "worship", as they are merely labels; what is important is the mentality and actions that are followed when labels such as these are applied. The actual words used are of no consequence.

The falsity would be in not recognizing that all stems from one Source, or to worship any part of Source, as to do so would be declaring oneself as inferior to another part of Source. You are a part of Source, and to worship another self and place them above you is to not know that you are a part of Source and Source itself on a level of totality. To know that every part of the Cosmos comes from Source and is a part of Source in Oneness is the primary way of One.

Before wanderers and positively oriented 3rd density beings, who channeled information in some manner, started making positive advances on Earth after 900 BCE in regards to the realization of all stemming from one God/Source, a great portion of beings on Earth performed sacrifices to negative inner planes beings, most of them unaware that they were worshiping negative beings, or that a difference between negative and positive higher-density beings even existed. Due to ignorance and many serving negative inner planes beings throughout a great period of time, human beings assumed God/Source was authoritative, commanding, and demanded sacrifices in order for worship, repentance, or blind obedience to be shown, and that God's commands should be obeyed unquestionably no matter what they were. In reality, Source does not want any of these things—nor does any positive higher-density being—and God/Source does not interact directly within the Cosmos.

When the deceitful action of negative inner planes beings pretending to be lords, kings, or God is believed by 3rd density beings and sacrifices are made, the negatives are invited into one's house. This allows inroads to be made and more power given to the negatives as to what they can perform and accomplish in the 3rd density physical outer planes due to the invitation and power being bestowed upon them by the 3rd density beings. The negatives then use this acquired power to bring hardship or destruction to those who do not continue to worship them and give sacrifices, or hardship and destruction is delivered to them regardless if the negatives see fit. Destruction may come soon anyway if another 3rd density being who is in opposition to them has sacrificed more to a negative inner planes being, either the same or a different negative being. There is no loyalty to agreements or deals with negative beings. Even if destruction by the negatives does not find itself coming back to the one who sacrifices for the negatives, the karmic wheel starts to spin and hardship and/or destruction for sacrificing and following the commands of negatives finds its way back to the human being in their incarnation and/or possibly in their future incarnations, depending on how much harm was inflicted, unless the human being graduates to 4th density negative. In this case they still have to balance their karma, but not until they have switched to positive polarity, which has to be done no later than the middle 6th sub-density.

Examples are shown in your Greek myths. The kings and war heroes depicted in Greek history were able to perform great deeds due to worshipping and sacrificing to negative beings, yet almost all their stories end with utter hardship and/or destruction. The Greeks and other civilizations at the time and older in Earth's history were not only deceived and tempted by negative 4th density outer planes beings and negative inner planes beings of densities 3rd through 5th, but also interacted with advanced 3rd density beings who were from negatively and positively oriented societies who had taken their civilizations underground tens of thousands of years ago for protection from major geological shifts during major and minor cycles. They advanced technologically, and some spiritually, and used their advanced technology and craft to convince the surface dwellers that they were gods. (These underground civilizations will be expanded upon in the next subject.)

Another prime example in history of human beings being deceived into thinking they were interacting with positive higher-density beings, and in this case "God", are the books that make up the *Old Testament*, as well as similar books. Those depicted in these books thought they were making sacrifices and worshipping a positive being, usually what they thought was God, who, to human beings in that time period, did not need to come across as positive or negative in their minds because "He" created all on Earth and "the heavens". The positively oriented 3rd density beings depicted in the *Old Testament* were influenced by both positive and negative higher-density beings. Their honest intentions of seeking to communicate with God/Source allowed positive beings to influence them, but their sacrifices, which were thought by most at the time as positive actions towards God/Source, allowed inroads for negative inner planes beings to influence them, especially if they were human sacrifices.

We will give an example of the dual influences recorded in the *Old Testament*, and other books and documents that speak of the same stories and occurrences, by speaking of the one known as Moshe/Moses. Moshe was a positively oriented 3rd density being who, after mentally seeking and asking for God's assistance in freeing his tribe from their slavery and harsh treatment in Egypt, was contacted by a positive higher-density being known as Yahweh, who was a local Guardian at the time. This local Guardian's later 6th sub-density united group was known as Yahweh and the entity of this group that was a local Guardian at the time also simply went by the name Yahweh. When a single entity from a united group is interacting with 3rd density, it is basically the same thing as interacting with the whole united group, as all entities in the united group may participate in the interaction through the group mind that is utilized by the united group. Typically Guardians do not directly influence 3rd density beings after a 3rd density experience is started and underway, but Yahweh's assisting actions of genetically altering what would become the post-Mars beings was seen by other Guardians, although done with positive intentions, as infringement upon the Mars beings' free will. Therefore, the one known as Yahweh felt inclined under duty and honor to further assist the post-Mars beings in order to balance out the karmic ties from the assisted genetic alterations. A portion of the post-Mars beings are known as the Israelite tribe depicted in the *Old Testament* and other books of recorded history that speak of the same stories and occurrences.

Yahweh contacted Moshe on Mount Sinai/Horeb, freely offering his assistance without asking for sacrifices or deals, as only negative beings demand such actions. Yahweh explained to Moshe how they would use prophesy in order to influence the pharaoh at the time, Ramesses II, to release Moshe's people from slavery and let them leave Egypt.

The average lifespan of the Egyptians at the time was approximately only 42 years because they were not knowledgeable about water conditions. The Nile was allowed to flood and recede, which made the soil ripe for the breeding of diseases that made their way into the water at the Nile and other sources of water the Egyptians used, and these harmful organisms would be drank by the Egyptians. Also, insects would carry this disease to the Egyptians and contaminate their foodstuffs.

Yahweh, observing the probabilities/timelines, knew that a greater than typical flooding of the Nile was about to occur and it would bring much hardship, suffering, and death to the Egyptians. The Nile's source that ran to the Egyptians would flood more than usual and cause red algae along with its bacteria to get into the Nile and flow all the way to the Mediterranean. This caused the Nile to appear like blood, which was the first plague, and the algae's bacteria would breed more disease than a typical flooding and receding of the Nile and consequently cause the proceeding plagues that actually happened. Knowing that certain foodstuffs would contain diseases due to the flooding and receding of the Nile and the pestilence created afterwards, Yahweh advised Moshe and his people not to eat bread with leavening agents because these ingredients would be contaminated. Yahweh told Moshe these prophesies and their timing and advised him what to tell the pharaoh before each one. Moshe reluctantly agreed as long as his brother Aharon/Aaron would assist as his orator since Moshe believed he was not the best of speakers.

The depicted plagues regarding days of darkness and death of the firstborn in the *Old Testament* did not happen and were inserted into the story later to make "God" sound more powerful, and so future readers would believe Ramesses II had no other option but to let Moshe's people leave. The reality of the situation was that Ramesses II did not let Moshe's people leave after the plagues that actually happened, so Yahweh, knowing there were no more plagues coming and that Ramesses II was not going to let the Israelites leave, told Moshe to secretly flee with his people during the night and that Ramesses II and his army would pursue them at daybreak but Yahweh would protect and provide for them on their journey to Mount Sinai. Ramesses II and his military pursued them the next day after finding out they had fled during the night, but Yahweh kept the promise by protecting and nurturing the Israelites until they reached Mount Sinai.

The false account of the tenth plague, the death of the firstborn, is an action a positive higher-density being would not do. Allowing hardship and death to occur that was already going to happen due to the great flooding and receding of the Nile was simply letting events unfold as they were intended, but creating the death of 3rd density beings is not the way of a positive higher-density being, nor is having lambs, or any 2nd density being, sacrificed to mark doorframes. Again, positive higher-density beings never ask for the killing of 2nd or 3rd density beings for sacrificial worshiping rituals. This should not be confused with 3rd density human beings preparing, possibly cooking, and eating 2nd density beings whether they are plants or animals, which is a natural part of the dietary system. We are simply speaking of ending 2nd or 3rd density beings' incarnations by way of sacrifice. To sacrifice is to end a being's incarnation simply to please a negative being, which is typically done by way of ritual.

When Moshe and his tribe finally reached the base of Mount Sinai, the tribe became unmanageable and was skeptical and demanded miracles as proof that Yahweh existed and was powerful. Positive higher-density beings do not give proof in this direct manner because it would be infringement upon free will, but negative beings infringe upon free will whenever they can as long as there is minimal or no loss of polarity in the act, so a negative 5th density inner planes being gave them proof instead, which the tribe assumed was Yahweh's proof, and Moshe's tribe was satisfied and bowed down and worshipped the negative 5th density being they assumed was Yahweh. This created inroads for the negatives and set the stage for the confusion that was to follow.

When Moshe went to the top of Mount Sinai to seek communion with Yahweh, it was the same negative 5th density inner planes being who had provided proof that Moshe communicated with instead, since the negatives still had a hold on the situation due to being worshipped for the provided proof. A higher-density being, positive or negative, cannot go by the name of another being in deception or that would result in a loss of polarity, so this negative being did not say It was Yahweh, but said It was God instead, and let Moshe assume that It was the same being he had spoken to before who went by the name Yahweh, whom he believed was God. In deceptive cases, negatives simply do not state their name and hope the 3rd density being they are trying to deceive assumes It is the positive being they had been previously dealing with, or "God". If there was no previous dealing with positive beings, a negative being might still attempt to act like a positive being—a so-called angel or "God"—if they know they are dealing with a positively or neutrally oriented 3rd density being. If they are dealing with a negatively oriented 3rd density being, negatives do not need the previously mentioned level of deception and go straight to using other forms of manipulation such as temptation that the negatively oriented 3rd density being most likely welcomes because it serves their striving toward gaining more power and control over others. 4th density negative inner planes beings, who typically interact with 3rd density beings instead of 5th density negative inner planes beings, generally do not offer their names and prefer to be addressed by a title such as lord or master.

Moshe assumed he was communicating with Yahweh, whom he believed was God, and made agreements in a contractual covenant/deal and submitted to commands given by the deceptive 5th density negative inner planes being, which created great inroads that would exist even after Moshe transitioned/died. This is why one should always use their discernment. The Ten Commandments was a successful attempt the negative being used to be perceived as a positive being. Positive beings do not command other beings, they lovingly offer advice and guidance freely. The Ten Commandments, which is a single scroll of papyrus and not stone tablets, were commands, not loving advice, and were given in a forceful manner. The commandments held positive advice on purpose in order to deceptively appear like the negative being was a positive being, but the advice was not anything human beings did not already know at the time, so the negative offered no new beneficial information while performing the deception. The Ten Commandments were forcefully given and the first commandment, even though there is only one God/Source, the deal had been made with Moshe accepting that the one true God was the negative being and that Moshe would deal with no other gods but the negative being, therefore removing possible future contact with Yahweh or any other positive higher-density being unless certain actions were taken to annul the contractual covenant/deal. Since Moshe did not know he had made a deal with a negative being, he never sought such annulling actions. The negative being commanding Moshe to not serve other gods because It was a jealous god is a definite warning sign/red flag because even a positive being in the 4th density has overcome jealousy.

Human beings believed that God/Source directly intervened in creation and mistakenly thought God was an authoritative being who demanded submission, worship, and sacrifices, and that all of its commands, no matter how negative they were, should be obeyed without the use of discernment because It created everything, It was God and one never questioned God no matter what. Human beings believed this due to the countless contact with negative beings dating back to the first major cycle who said they were lords, kings, or gods. If a human being had contact with both positive and negative higher-density beings, they assumed it was the same being and that this being was coming across as commanding and wrathful at certain times because they had done something wrong in the eyes of their "God" or "God's angels", or that other human beings had done something wrong and deserved to be destroyed and that was why "God" was now angry and wrathful.

The covenant/binding agreement included continual sacrifices, the creation of a hierarchical structure of power with priests that mimicked the Orion Empire, mutilating rituals for all male newborns' genitals, and the creation of a religion to be followed without question and passed down and practiced through Moshe's descendants. Such commands and practices in this covenant would not be given by a positive higher-density being.

Regarding the mutilation of male newborns' genitals: Despite what doctors are taught and regurgitate about circumcision rituals for male infants, the operation or mutilation creates only disadvantages. Like all parts of the human being's 3rd density physical body, the foreskin is there for a reason and it is not wise to remove it. The removal of the foreskin creates desensitization as the layer of skin's protection is absent, so the male tends to go deep and fast-paced during sexual acts in an attempt to make up for the lost stimulation rather than using a finessing slow rhythm. Consequently, this tends to lead the male toward a tenser and fast-paced rhythm that not only decreases pleasure for the male and female involved in the sexual act, but increases the probability of life-force energy being hindered or blocked from moving up the chakra system during sexual acts. When this blockage occurs, the orange-ray or yellow-ray chakra is focused on instead of reaching the green-ray heart chakra or higher chakras. Since focusing on the orange-ray and yellow-ray chakra during acts of sex is equivalent to inequality and disharmony, it polarizes toward the negative for one or both the beings involved. (This topic and other sexual topics will be expanded upon and explained in a later subject about sex and sexuality.) The mutilation of the male's genitals benefits the negatives and not positively oriented human beings. To be clear, this does not at all mean that circumcised males are incapable of engaging the heart chakra during sexual acts, it simply means they are at a disadvantage.

The negative being, having influence over Moshe, led the tribe in circles around the desert for decades, not allowing Moshe and his tribe to reach their destination, Canaan. An action only a negative being would do. It was only until most of the tribe who had fled Egypt transitioned/died that their offspring, who would continue to teach their descendants to submit and worship the negatives who they thought was God, but who did not have direct deals with the negative 5th density inner planes being, were allowed to reach the so-called promised land of Canaan. Moshe was ordered by the negative being to not proceed to Canaan and stay behind and separate from his tribe, which he obeyed with great sorrow. This was done because Moshe was too positively oriented and the negatives would have more influence over the tribe in his absence. Again, this is something a positive higher-density being would not do because it is not loving or merciful. Even a positively oriented 3rd density human being would not do this to someone or a group.

Typically a 4th density negative being, inner or outer planes, would have attempted to influence a 3rd density being, but since the one known as Yahweh, a Guardian, was involved, a top player in the Orion Empire from 5th density got involved to counter another top chess piece on the board. After this 5th density negative inner planes being was successful and made major inroads for the negatives, the negative being returned to its typical 5th density role and commanded its negative 4th density inner planes beings, its underlings, to continue in its place after the heavy work was done and Yahweh's contact with Moshe and his tribe had been contractually barred.

Even before the one known as Abraham, there was an intense battle over influencing these post-Mars beings when Yahweh started contacting them after they asked for assistance. Because Yahweh, a Guardian, a being filled with much love and light energy, interacted with the 3rd density experience, Yahweh's light signature alerted the negatives, who got involved in the battle of polarity because that is their role. As we stated, the light attracts the dark and the dark attracts the light in regards to the polarity war. When one chess piece is moved on the game board, the opposing side can take its turn in moving one of their pieces. The ranking of the piece that is moved on either side depends on the ranking of the piece that is being responded to: a Guardian piece is moved, so an equally high-ranking piece on the opposing side is moved to balance out the opportunity presented on the game board. On a 3rd density experience filled with ignorance and confusion, the negatives have a higher advantage.

When the battle of influences reached the one known as Abraham, a similar situation to that of Moshe played out: Due to a calling for assistance, Yahweh contacted the positively oriented 3rd density being known as Abram at the time and offered loving guidance and the ways of One/Source, teachings Yahweh hoped would not only benefit a portion of the post-Mars beings there were karmic ties with, but also be spread to the multitude of human beings on Earth, as the way of One is for all beings because all beings are One. The negatives counteracted with a negative 5th density inner planes being contacting Abram, deceiving him into thinking it was Yahweh, and established the first major inroads when a covenant was formed that barred further contact with Yahweh, like it did with Moshe later on. This negative entity copied the direction Yahweh had initiated, but heavily twisted it, as negatives always do. The negative entity changed Abram's name into Abraham, which means father of a multitude or many nations, and told him he was special and that his people, the Hebrews, were the chosen people of God, and therefore more important in the eyes of God, and as long as Abraham and his people followed the negative's commands, who Abram thought was God, he and his tribe would be protected and looked on in favor in the eyes of God. When Moshe renewed this covenant on Mount Sinai, further inroads were made by the negatives.

All beings are special and important by Source, as all beings are Source. Like a responsible parent, one does not have favorites among their offspring, and since all beings are a part of Source and are Source in totality, it would make no sense to have favorites within a Cosmos that is in reality One being. It is impossible to select favorites when there is only One present. Also, a positive higher-density being would not take it upon themselves to force the changing of a being's name—Abram to Abraham, and later his grandson from Jacob to Israel. (These were not the actual names changed, as these are the English names.)

We reiterate the tried-and-true method of the negatives: deceive, manipulate, and tempt a select few into thinking they are superior to the majority and therefore have the right to rule over, kill, and control the majority. This mimics the control structure of the Orion Empire.

This information may cause displeasing emotions to arise for those who follow the religions of Judaism, Islam, and Christianity—especially the former two—and their religious offshoot branches, but reality offers liberation. However, as always, we do not force reality upon beings, but offer it to those who are ready to receive it and benefit from it. The *Old Testament* and the other books and documents that recorded similar history are filled with what human beings call red flags that are quite apparent to discerning and observant minds. We are equally loving to those who wish to continue or form their own beliefs.

We realize that the human condition is so that when faced with information that would shift one's paradigm, especially information that invokes intense feelings of negativity due to jeopardizing the very foundation of self one has personally identified with, the established concept of self tends to shut down to the possibility of a change in viewpoint or belief to protect what one has chosen to identify with. In this state, open-mindedness is abandoned. All have free will and it is essential for the cosmic experience, so no matter what one's beliefs are, even if their beliefs are vastly distorted from reality and are detrimental to the self, it is their right to have them and they are respected and loved by positive higher-density beings regardless.

When the negatives commanded Abraham to sacrifice his son—as they commanded others on the Earth to do, including the tribes in Canaan—it was done to test the limits of Abraham. Despite the commands given to him, Abraham's intuition and the assistance of his spirit guides caused him to not follow through with sacrificing his son. Abraham then sacrificed a ram instead in hopes that it would appease what he thought was God. It was received but he had failed the negative's test. Abraham and his son Isaac returned to their tribe and Abraham, who felt disappointed in himself for failing the test and not wanting his people to know about it, chose to lie and told them God stopped him after he was seen to be faithfully following the will of God and offered a ram to be sacrificed instead, and that God did not approve of human sacrifice. Although this was a lie about what the negative being Abraham thought was God wanted, it was accurate information his spirit guides had telepathically offered to him—not the part about sacrificing a 2nd density being. The negative 5th density inner planes being continued to command Abraham, but never asked him to sacrifice a human being again because it might lead to Abraham figuring out he was not dealing with God.

The message regarding human sacrifice from Abraham was received by his tribe and taught down through his descendants, who, when commanded to commit genocide by their "God", saw fit to judge and justify the killing of the tribes in Canaan because they sacrificed human beings in the name of their false gods, who were the same negative beings commanding the Hebrews. The negatives commanding Abraham's descendants used this hatred to imprint separation, and to further manipulate the Israelites into thinking they were spiritually superior to others. These same negatives continued to command the tribes in Canaan to sacrifice human beings, including their own firstborn children with some tribes. The negatives play all sides, just as an unethical arms dealer supplies arms to both sides of a conflict. They care not who wins; they only care about what benefits themselves. Positive higher-density beings never ask or command a group to attack and kill another group, and especially not commit genocide. This is very much the commands of negative higher-density beings. If the Israelites were defending themselves against an attack, they would not be in the wrong by killing their active attackers, but the Israelites were commanded to attack and commit genocide in a land they had no claim to and received no hostility from its occupants. Much karma was accrued by the Israelites for the highly negatively polarizing actions they performed in Canaan.

The *Old Testament* and other books and documents that recorded similar history have been heavily altered throughout time. The *Quran* is the most accurate book of records pertaining to the history that is also depicted in the *Old Testament*. However, it does not matter much how accurate any historical record is when the majority of the information given in it has been offered by negative beings, unless one is aiming to graduate to 4th density negative. Even if that is the case, there is far better material to follow.

Since the name the one known as Yahweh went by was deceptively captured and twisted information was given in its name over the centuries, the being and united group known as Yahweh no longer goes by that name.

The negatives play all sides, leading each of their prey as far as possible toward service to self, testing their willingness to obey commands and pushing their prey as far as they will let themselves be pushed. Many groups on Earth, some of which are known as the Mesopotamians, the tribes in Canaan and their descendants (the Phoenicians and Carthaginians), the Greeks, and the Vikings allowed themselves to be pushed far enough by the negatives to sacrifice human beings, including infants and their own firstborn.

Positive higher-density beings tell their names to 3rd density beings they interact with and never say they are God, but negative 4th density inner planes beings hide their names and demand to be addressed by titles such as king (melech/molech) or lord or master (baal/ba'al) or simply say they are God if it is a negative 5th density inner planes being. Negatives typically hide their names because it offers power over them in the bidding process. It is rare, but even a highly negatively oriented 3rd density being may use perversions of ritual or sexual so-called magic to bid a negative higher-density being. To succeed in this bidding is rare because the 3rd density being has to mentally believe in their ability and power near perfection in the ritual that involves willpower and service to self. It is typical for this type of bidding control to occur with negative beings within the same density, competing for control over another to move up in the rankings, but it is rare for negatives in a lower density to attempt to bid negatives of a higher density, and even rarer that they succeed. It ends horrifically for the negatively oriented 3rd density being who attempts the bidding with a negative higher-density being and fails when they display the smallest amount of self-doubt. This is territory for the highly negatively oriented 3rd density adept and is not wise to be lightly initiated or treaded by those less skilled.

Earth's history is littered with negative higher-density beings calling themselves God, king/melech, or lord/master/ba'al of war, the harvest, fertility, etc. They demand to be worshipped and given sacrifices for their services in any area of life. Some so-called royalty sacrificed their own firstborn infant to gain favor for war, harvests, and long sailing expeditions, such as the Carthaginians are recorded in Earth's history as doing. The ancient Romans also practiced human sacrificing until making it illegal in 97 BCE, although some Romans continued to practice it behind closed doors. As positively oriented 3rd density beings and wanderers were contacted and began to spread teachings of the way of One/Source, and civilizations progressed to be less barbarous, the sacrificing of human beings became shunned upon and then made illegal.

Although, there were some who continued to practice human sacrifices secretly after it had become illegal in their governed area. Even in Earth's present time there are so-called royalty or elites in nations, who pride themselves for being righteous and progressive to their citizens and the rest of the planet, who still sacrifice human beings clandestinely to keep and further their power and control over the majority, as they think of themselves as superior and therefore fit to rule and control the majority. Even some human beings who are not part of the so-called elite make

blood deals with these negatively oriented human beings and sacrifice their firstborn infant or a provided infant in order to gain positions of power in politics, organizations, conglomerates, or fame in the arts, all of which are tempted with power and wealth. In this way, the highly negatively oriented 3rd density beings and their underlings are mimicking their chosen negative higher-density masters. Sacrificing is a powerful expression of worship, submission, obedience, and so-called loyalty to negative higher-density beings or highly negatively oriented 3rd density beings, and also provides blackmail for the latter over human beings to ensure their continued obedience. What a human being receives in a blood deal is never worth it if they do not intend to graduate to 4th density negative because it always comes full circle due to the wheel of karma, in their current incarnation and/or future incarnations.

The negatively oriented 3rd density beings that make up a portion of the so-called royalty or elites have not been deceived into thinking they are serving "God" or positive higher-density beings; they are highly negatively oriented human beings who are fully aware they are serving negative polarity. Some of these human beings are part of the later 3rd sub-density highly negatively oriented beings who, using their seniority of vibration, incarnated in the present near harvest-time to have more opportunities to graduate to 4th density negative. Likewise, later 3rd sub-density highly positively oriented beings used their seniority of vibration to incarnate near harvest-time to increase their opportunities to graduate to 4th density positive. In order for the positively oriented to graduate, they aid and serve the majority, which often causes them to be put into positions that challenge the negatively oriented who are trying to control the majority on Earth. The highly positively oriented 3rd density beings and wanderers have faced major difficulties with achieving their missions and serving the majority because human beings dwell in heavily controlled societies that have been slowly engineered, indirectly and directly, throughout the centuries by negatively oriented human beings, which has rapidly accelerated in the past decades.

——∞——

After the pyramid structures did not produce positive results on Earth, positive inner planes beings contacted mentally seeking positively oriented human beings and wanderers in order to teach and help spread the knowledge and wisdom of the way of One/Source, especially from 900 BCE to 700 CE, which offered an alternative to submission, worship, and sacrifices in negative-based polytheistic religions. Due to this influx of opportunity from higher-density positives, an influx of opportunity from higher-density negatives balanced out the offerings given to Earthlings. The assistance was offered to negatively oriented humans who saw the positive movements as threatening to their power and influence over others, and who consequently attempted to capture and/or twist the positive movements' knowledge and wisdom to suit their desire in keeping and strengthening their power and control over the majority.

During this period of time, the major movements, which were all spawned from collaborating renditions and versions of the way of One/Source from their origins in the positive higher densities before reaching the minds of human beings, were brought through by these beings: Zarathushtra Spitama/Zoroaster, who was a positively oriented 3rd density being; Lao Tzu, who was a positively oriented 3rd density being; Siddhartha Gautama/Buddha, who was a positive 5th density wanderer; Yahushua/Jesus, who was a positive wanderer who graduated 4th density and chose to aid Earth before continuing on to the 5th density; Muhammad, who was a positively oriented 3rd density being; and various positively oriented 3rd density beings had a hand in shaping and changing the knowledge and wisdom held in Hinduism. Hinduism's roots are older than 3,000 BCE, but like many other polytheistic religions at the time, it revolved around the worshiping and sacrificing of humans to negative beings. Most sects of Hinduism in your present time are greatly if not completely different from their roots, so they act as quite different from their beginnings that held the same religious label. It was largely influenced by the teachings of the Buddha as well as other various positively oriented beings and, like the aforementioned movements, holds knowledge and wisdom of the way of One/Source. There are other movements and bodies of work, but the point is not to list them all, but to convey that positive higher-density beings had a hand in bringing them through and that their purpose and messages were all in agreement before reaching the minds of the 3rd density beings who did the receiving.

All of these harmonious versions of the way of One/Source started out as movements meant to teach the way of One. None of the beings mentioned had a hand in structuring the body of knowledge and wisdom they brought through into the religions they are today with many sects and offshoots—separation offered by negatives. Nor did they intend to form a structured hierarchy that went beyond a humbled and respected teacher who taught students in hopes that the students would become teachers just as knowledgeable or more knowledgeable than themselves. A teacher, who may go by any number of titles or labels, is only a valuable teacher if their intentions are to teach their students so they may have the possibility to reach awareness levels of knowledge and wisdom that the teacher possesses, no longer having to rely on the teacher for their spiritual growth. Due to the possible gap of advancement between teacher and student, it may take more than one incarnation for the student. This is similar to a parent lovingly teaching and raising a child so they may become an adult or parent one day and lead their own lives and make their own choices, and then offer the same guidance to their offspring or fellow human beings.

All these movements were given a label or name because it was easier to spread and know of the movement if it had a label that 3rd density beings could vocalize, but these different names are no more than labels that were meant to point to the same body of knowledge and wisdom that is the way of One/Source.

When looking at Earth's present religions, one can see many differences, many opposing ideas, and so one tends to think they did not have the same origin. Some of the reasons for these differences are: the knowledge and wisdom offered to the positively oriented 3rd density beings and wanderers was misunderstood from the moment it was received, or it was misunderstood by the first wave or any proceeding wave of students who became teachers, or it was captured by an authoritative and controlling group or leader of high position and was twisted for selfish reasons. Some of these resulted in the knowledge and wisdom being drastically twisted so that the main points were lost and falsities took their place, which is why these collaborating bodies of knowledge and wisdom are currently presented differently and contradict each other.

Another reason for religions being different has already been covered: positively oriented 3rd density beings were tricked into receiving information from a negative higher-density being pretending to be a positive higher-density being or God.

All these harmonious bodies of knowledge and wisdom of the way of One/Source teach loving-kindness, compassion, forgiveness, patience, appreciation, honesty, generosity, and following the Golden Rule. If these teachings alone were followed, the 3rd density experience on Earth would be harmonious and spiritually advance rapidly.

—∞—

We will use the story of Yahushua/Jesus/Isa/Issa as an example because it covers many of the topics we mentioned, with the focus on how all religious material came from the same source and how a spiritual movement can be captured and heavily twisted by negatively oriented 3rd density beings, who are influenced and assisted either indirectly or directly by negative 4th density inner and outer planes beings. In doing this we will also cover the so-called lost years of Yahushua/Jesus.

In the time period of being a wanderer in 3rd density, this being went by the name Yahushua, and in your present time is mostly known as Jesus in English due to different language translations of the books in the *New Testament*. After graduating from positive 4th density and before continuing on to positive 5th density, Yahushua, who is a member of the local Confederation of Planets, chose to aid Earth by teaching the loving-kindness and compassion he had mastered in the 4th density positive. After passing through the veil of forgetfulness and incarnating into the 3rd density experience on Earth, he remembered more than most wanderers at a young age. Due to his focused seeking and striving, he advanced and began teaching at a younger age than most wanderers. Aspects of the way of One he focused on were loving-kindness, compassion, and being nonjudgmental. Due to remembering more than most wanderers at a young age, and therefore being able to intuitively tap into abilities, at the age of 6, Yahushua, being mad at another child he was playing with, grabbed the child and accidently channeled his anger through focused energy that force-transitioned/killed the child. Yahushua was most distressed by what he had done and realized he had an ability that others did not seem to have. This action, although negative, galvanized Yahushua to use his abilities for good and never allow them to be used negatively again. This promise to himself he kept for his entire incarnation.

If Yahushua had lived in your present time, this accidental negative act could have been kept in Earth's permanent digital records and brought up by negatively oriented human beings decades later when Yahushua was spreading the positive messages of the way of One. His opposition would have hoped such a past action would ambiguously label him a bad human in other's minds and stop human beings from listening to his positive information. It is the same issue present politicians face on Earth. It is impossible to be perfect in any density, especially in 3rd density, the heaviest, most intense, and most confusing density of all. Forever condemning a being for an error is to never allow a being to progress in a society and in the minds of the beings in that society. Think of the knowledge and wisdom that would have been lost to Earth had this judgment and forever labeling of "bad" been placed on Yahushua like it is for convicts on Earth or any human being who performs one or two major negative actions in their incarnation. Why highlight and focus on one or a few moments of a human being's incarnation instead of considering all their moments?

Throughout Yahushua's childhood he studied the religious material of his people, Judaism, day and night. At the age of 12 he understood more than most rabbis, but intuitively knew he had a lot more to learn that was outside the scope of Judaism. At the age of 13, instead of getting married, as was the custom then, Yahushua, not interested in getting married and living a typical life, and striving to learn more, left his home and ventured on the Silk Road trading route and headed toward India. He stopped along the way at various places where he felt he could further his education, as learning the ways and mentality of people in other lands opens one up to a wider viewpoint. He eventually made it to India where he spent time as a student in both Hindu and Buddhist temples. There he learned, or rather relearned, of the cycle of reincarnation and karma, both of which he would later teach and those teachings would be removed for so-called official books composed by the Vatican. Later he ventured north to Nepal where he studied the knowledge and wisdom residing in the

Buddhist ways in that land, and then later he did the same in Tibet.

What Yahushua had learned in India, Nepal, and Tibet made him aware of the many flaws presented in Judaism. The body of knowledge and wisdom of the way of One/Source found in Buddhist material in Nepal and Tibet particularly expanded Yahushua's awareness.

At the age of 25, after Yahushua felt he had absorbed all the knowledge and wisdom available to him through what has been called religious material and the ways and mentality of the people in those various lands, he returned to his Earth parents and took up the work of his Earth father, carpentry, while ruminating and integrating throughout the years all he had learned during his travels. When he felt ready, he started to teach others what he had learned. Due to adequately balancing his chakras, he was also able to tap into Source energy from his indigo-ray chakra through his violet-ray chakra, completing the pathway from Source so that Source energy could work through him and heal those who had not pre-incarnate planned their afflictions.

The depicted story of why Judas betrayed Yahushua in the *New Testament* is most accurate: Judas thought that putting Yahushua in a position where he would be condemned to death or use his abilities to fight and become the new ruler, Yahushua would choose the latter. Since Yahushua did not incarnate to fight and rule over others, he told his students/disciples to put away their swords so they would not further harm or be harmed, and he freely allowed himself to be arrested, knowing that his pre-incarnate plan of being crucified as a martyr had arrived.

Before transitioning/dying on a cross, Yahushua made the statement that has been accurately recorded in the *New Testament*, forgiving his condemners due to their ignorance. This act balanced out Yahushua's karma for accidently force-transitioning/killing the child when he was 6 years old, thus stopping the wheel of karma and removing the obligation of him having to reincarnate onto 3rd density Earth to balance karma. Yahushua transitioned to an early 5th sub-density inner plane, but before he started preparing for his next incarnation in 5th density positive, he was approved by the local Council to visit his students in his etheric body in order to have a congenial and beneficial farewell.

Before covering how the knowledge and wisdom brought through by the wanderer Yahushua was captured and heavily twisted by negatively oriented human beings, we will cover a few misconceptions of Yahushua's messages. Information is given in a certain way to those who are at a certain level of awareness so the information can be understood in the receivers' limited capacity, as one does not teach university courses to third-graders. Additionally, Yahushua had to use much finesse in reaching human beings because he had to build upon negative material in the *Old Testament* that was being followed by human beings at the time. In that time period, pointing out the numerous flaws in the *Old Testament* and attempting to teach new information would not have been effective in teaching the way of One/Source.

When information in the *New Testament* is attempted to be understood by human beings 2,000 years later—your present time—who have a greater capacity to understand more complex ideas, it is like a university student trying to learn from a third-grader's learning material. As one can imagine, attempting to learn in this way makes little sense. Yahushua was able to teach university courses, but since all his students and possible students 2,000 years ago were spiritual first- to third-graders, he wisely offered learning material for their level so the opportunity to grow from there was given. When Yahushua used the phrase "kingdom of heaven", he was speaking of the positive 4th density or a state of mind, depending on the focused topic. When Yahushua referenced "hell", he was speaking of the negative 4th density or a state of mind. When Yahushua said, "The kingdom of heaven/God is within you", he was pointing toward the way of accessing a current state of mind and the inner work that is the path toward graduating to 4th density positive, as well as affirming that all are parts of Source and that Source resides in all beings.

Yahushua was aware that Earth was in its last major cycle before the ending of the grand cycle and harvest-time. His statement of returning at the time of harvest was taken with confusion. He meant his current level of consciousness, the 4th density of universal love and understanding, since he had not proceeded to 5th density yet, would return to Earth as the planet and the beings inhabiting it would begin to transition fully into the 4th density positive.

When Yahushua said positively oriented humans would do the same works he has done and even greater things, he meant those who believed his teachings and did the inner work and service-to-others acts to graduate to 4th density positive would be able to do greater things than him in the 4th density positive. Yahushua was a wanderer, and like all wanderers he could not fully access his true density's abilities and had to work within the game board rules of the 3rd density experience, so those in 4th density are able to access more abilities and do greater things.

To be prepared for the harvest, beings choosing the positive path need to have done the inner work and practiced an adequate amount of service-to-others acts to graduate to 4th density positive. If it is not a being's time to graduate at harvest, that is fine, as there are no judgments. A being has eternity to progress as fast or as slowly as they please and all merge back with Source eventually no matter what path is chosen—short or long, positive or negative.

Yahushua's messages may have been partially misunderstood by his students, but it was not until the fourth century CE that his teachings were captured by negatively oriented human beings and twisted so much that the very fundamental messages brought through by Yahushua were altered. For political gain, power and control, and to ensure stability in the Roman Empire, in 325 CE the one known as Emperor Constantine convened the Council of Nicaea where Sol Invictus (Invincible Sun), Mithraism, and the Christian movement were merged into one religion. Despite falsities conveyed in your current time, Constantine did not convert to Christianity and stayed a believer in the pagan religion/cult of Sol Invictus for his entire incarnation. At the head of this new universal religion (Catholic means universal), Emperor Constantine would indirectly rein, making him the leader of state and religion. In the Council of Nicaea, and years after it, the teachings brought through by Yahushua were altered so greatly that they taught the opposite of many essential messages conveyed by Yahushua. At that time there was no *New Testament*, only books and documents that taught the body of knowledge and wisdom Yahushua had brought through. After the major alterations and deletions to Christian movement material took place and were written down as so-called official books that would become the *New Testament*, Constantine ordered bishops to head the mission of declaring the possession of all Christian movement books, documents, artifacts, and anything that would contradict their newly forged Catholic religion as heretical and those hiding and safekeeping such would receive the death penalty. Heresy means choice, and to make a choice that was different from those in established religious positions was to be put to death/force-transitioned. Any being that declares something as heresy or another being as a heretic, which is denying another the ability of making their own choices and practicing free will, is a negatively oriented 3rd density being practicing service to self or a neutrally oriented being confused due to social conditioning. The body of knowledge and wisdom Yahushua brought through that did not suit Constantine and his collaborators was burned.

Even the books that were kept that later became the official *New Testament* books were heavily edited to suit the direction agreed upon at the Council of Nicaea. Many who aligned with the Christian movement were very much opposed to these actions and saw it as an end to their movement. Earth's history does not speak of this and only conveys these actions initiated by Constantine as being "service-to-others" and "patronage to Christianity". The reality being quite the opposite. Since the Roman Empire's official books were printed and reprinted and handed down throughout time as sacred and holy, and their opposition was silenced and destroyed, those following "Christianity" today know nothing or little of this opposition and the heavy editing and altering of the *New Testament* books. The saying "history is written by the victors" is most accurate.

In these alterations, Yahushua was changed from a teacher or prophet, or spark of Source, to being the only son of God and part of God in the Trinity so that his position would align with the *Old Testament* information and pagan religions where so-called gods or God was worshipped, shown submission, was wrathful, and never questioned. All references of reincarnation that Yahushua taught after having learned about it in the body of knowledge and wisdom brought through by the 5th density wanderer who is known as Buddha were removed from the books that would become the *New Testament*. The idea of heaven and hell being places that a being resided in for eternity after they were judged by "God" after only one incarnation was continued because it imprinted fear and allowed greater control over the majority. The circumstance of permanently relying on and submitting to the institution called the Catholic Church and its hierarchy of priests was also created for power and control over the majority. All are One/Source and no positive wanderer would state that they were God or God's only son, nor would they create a static spiritual hierarchy where those at the bottom would stay at the bottom.

The Vatican was later established in Rome to bestow more power and authority over the created religion and its followers and to serve as a headquarters with more funding and resources to continue and expand the efforts of deeming what was heresy and the finding and capturing of information that was opposed to their created religion, which included not only written information but any artifacts or objects that had the potential to expand humanity's awareness, because material in this nature would consequently differ from their created religion, and therefore pose a threat to their ongoing power and control. Important knowledge in scrolls were stolen from the Library of Alexandria and moved and hidden in the Vatican Library. All records of Yahushua traveling and learning the knowledge and wisdom Buddha brought through was collected and destroyed or hidden in the Vatican, which is why there are the so-called lost years of Jesus/Yahushua. In order for Rome's created religion to exert power and control, the collaborators thought it was necessary to make Jesus/Yahushua God, and one who did not learn anything from others on Earth since an all-knowing God would not need to learn anything, especially from another religion's knowledge that differed from Rome's created religion. With Jesus/Yahushua being God in their new religion, they could continue the practices of the religions or ways of old that have their followers submit, worship, and follow commands without questioning them and without thinking for themselves. Selected books and documents of the Christian movement were burned and the remaining were heavily altered to make up the *New Testament* so they could be combined without clashing with the information in the negative material in the *Old Testament*.

Be aware that there were and are many positively oriented 3rd density beings within the Catholic Church institution and other captured religious institutions who are attempting service-to-others actions and are not aware of the true nature of their institutions.

In your present time, there are secret organizations and teams created by negatively oriented human factions that mimic the Vatican's actions and operate internationally to clandestinely remove discovered artifacts, written information, crashed spacecraft from other planets, advanced technology from past beings, free energy devices that have been invented, and more. These service-to-self actions put in motion by negatively oriented human beings are meant to keep the majority from expanding their awareness because doing such makes the majority far easier to manipulate and control.

The symbols expressing the Christian movement were a lamb, a fish, and a shepherd. The lamb was initially used as the symbol for Rome's created universal religion. In the seventh century CE, the Vatican changed the lamb symbol with Jesus/Yahushua being killed/sacrificed/force-transitioned on a cross as a secret insult. To add further insult to the capturing and twisting of the knowledge and wisdom Yahushua brought through, the Vatican, which at its core worships and takes commands from negative beings, gloated behind the scenes as the followers of their created religion kneeled, submitted, and worshipped before Yahushua being sacrificed on a Roman cross, like human beings are sacrificed in negative religions and rituals. Yahushua did not die on a cross to absolve Earthlings' sins/karma as Rome's created religion states. This would be major infringement upon free will. Only the being who has started the wheel of karma can stop the wheel of karma. One may have assistance, but it is oneself who has to balance out their karma. Another being balancing out another's karma may sound like aid from a shallow viewpoint, but from a larger viewpoint it is the opposite of aid, nor can one even balance out another's karma to begin with.

When the Vatican captured and twisted the information that Yahushua brought through, the Vatican kept the *Old Testament*'s information and validity from fading and added their twisted version of Yahushua's information to it in an attempt to keep the negatives in control. This was accomplished by adding Yahushua/Jesus to the position of God by way of the "Holy Trinity" so that "God" could continue to be the authoritative and wrathful entity depicted in the *Old Testament*, which as we have stated was actually a negative 5th density inner planes being and not God, and so the people would continue to follow the negatively oriented information in the *Old Testament*. In doing this the

Vatican was also able to keep their followers feeling insignificant and unworthy in the eyes of "God", which hindered their possibilities of graduating to 4th density positive. Although the followers of this created religion were still taught to be kind and generous to their fellow human beings, one could get to so-called heaven by simply believing Jesus was their "Lord and Savior and that He died on the cross for mankind's sins" and so one might not be truly motivated to perform service-to-others actions when they already have an easy ticket to so-called heaven. All religions may offer progression through a portion of the beliefs they teach, but the religions based on a God who is separate from you and have a forever heaven-and-hell concept need to be abandoned at some point in order for further progression of a being to take place.

The symbol known as the cross was a sacred symbol long before Yahushua/Jesus incarnated as a wanderer on Earth. The horizontal line crosses the represented chakras' vertical line at the indigo-ray chakra, which is affiliated with the point in 6th density where the dualism of polarity ends and only the positive path remains. This symbol draws attention and focus to one's higher self and all beings' higher selves and united groups that reside at this point mentioned in 6th density and can be used as a talisman or as a reminder. Similarly, the upside-down cross draws attention and focus on negatives who utilize the orange-ray and yellow-ray chakras—represented where the low horizontal line crosses the chakras' vertical line—to display the negatives' intentions and do their bidding. The symbols known as the Celtic cross or the Sun cross or Sun wheel that zooms in to focus on the part that represents the same reality while adding emphasis on the 6th density crossing point of the vertical and horizontal lines where the circle represents all that is associated with this point in 6th density after the positive and negative paths have harmonized and all dualism has ended. The circle represents spiritual wholeness and the Logos, where later 6th sub-density united groups at some point inhabit a Logos/star after the point in 6th density of unity where the two paths have been crossed. All these symbols may act as talismans and reminders of unity and wholeness and have nothing to do with any religion.

The actions of the Vatican speak louder than their words, and their deeds paint a clear picture of their institution's intentions. The several Crusades the Vatican launched from the eleventh to the thirteenth century CE that force-transitioned/killed more than 8 million human beings is no different than the accounts of historically shunned tyrannical leaders and governments who force-transitioned/killed millions. In your present time, the Crusaders would be seen as no different than hired mercenaries. There was nothing holy about these Wars/Crusades. The Vatican not only took a public neutral stance during WWII, but swindled money from Jewish families for insurance policies that the Vatican had no intention of honoring, and the Vatican assisted Nazi war criminals in escaping to South America, including Hitler who did not commit suicide in a bunker. The Vatican has committed many illegal monetary actions which include money laundering and funding acts and organizations that support negative polarity. Some of the members of the Vatican and the clergy in their created religion have perpetrated countless acts of sexual abuse and the sacrificing of human beings. The Vatican is one of many Earthly organizations that profess to do one thing to the public and do quite the opposite behind closed doors. At its core, the Vatican is controlled by negative beings and run by the negatively oriented 3rd density Draco reptilian group who follow the 4th density negatives' commands.

Despite monotheistic movements being captured and twisted into controlled religions, it was a step forward from the majority-followed polytheistic religions that practiced animal and human sacrificing. Organizations, secret societies, and cults like the Vatican continue their old religious ways of sacrificing animals and humans, but they have to do so secretly because the majority no longer agrees with sacrificing life-forms.

The knowledge and wisdom brought through by positively oriented 3rd density beings and wanderers that convey the way of One/Source from 900 BCE to 700 CE were all in harmony from their inceptions. The differences between teachings in current religions show that the original knowledge and wisdom bestowed during this period of time has been greatly twisted, either unintentionally or intentionally.

Positive beings and united groups in the 4th, 5th, and 6th densities focus on bringing knowledge and wisdom forward that they are well-versed and familiar with, focusing on the teachings learned in their density and below, as a wise teacher does not attempt to teach what they are not well-versed in. Channeled information, which is brought through in different ways, from positive 4th density beings and united groups focuses on loving-kindness, compassion, being nonjudgmental, and the importance of meditation. Channeled information from positive 5th density beings and united groups focus on wisdom and higher forms of knowledge in addition to what positive 4th density beings teach. Channeled information from positive 6th density beings and united groups, which comes through much more rarely to the 3rd density experience, focuses on knowledge and wisdom learned in the 4th and 5th densities as well as that from an expansive viewpoint of unity in the Cosmos where the dualism of polarity ends and paradoxes are resolved somewhere in the early to middle 6th sub-densities. Since the later 6th sub-density united groups reside in the highest sub-density of all densities that interact and influence 3rd density beings, as 7th density beings and Source do not, they can offer 3rd density beings the most accurate and expansive viewpoint available. A viewpoint that understands unity and is past the dualism of positive and negative polarity. This is precisely why the large scope of information is able to be offered in this awareness-expanding course; since it is brought through by a wanderer with the aid of his later 6th sub-density united group, where only positive beings in unity reside.

We restate, if a human being looked at all the religions practiced on Earth in the present time, they may find it hard to believe that the original knowledge and wisdom for all of them was in agreement and came from the same origin. The root reasons for the way of One/Source coming through to the 3rd density differently, although in agreement, and possibly being misunderstood are as follows. The positive higher-density being or united group offering the knowledge and wisdom to the positively oriented 3rd density being, whether they are a wanderer or not, focuses on what they are well-versed in for their particular density, as we have recently covered. This offers information to possibly appear differently in the 3rd density being's mind if they misunderstood even a small aspect of the information. Another root factor is that positive higher-density beings and united groups have come to different ideas as to how information should be presented to the particular 3rd density civilizations on Earth, realizing that the different ways of living and mindsets of civilizations have different ways of learning, as the students in a classroom have different ways of best learning a subject.

This creates the possibility of information offered to one civilization on Earth to possibly appear different in another.

Another root factor is that human beings are only offered information that is in their capacity to be understood. A civilization in a spiritual first-grader status is not offered sixth-grader knowledge and wisdom, and when different grade levels are offered information on the same topic, the lower grade-level beings and civilizations are presented with simplistic stories and scenarios that often appear to oppose information presented to higher grade-level beings and civilizations. The grade level of Earth's current civilizations—although there are still differences in grade levels from one civilization or nation to another—is connected enough through the Internet and mediums of entertainment and learning and is of a high enough degree that this awareness-expanding course may be offered. It would not have been offered in full before the 1960s CE because civilizations were not advanced enough to absorb such awareness. Earthlings express their grade level in the advancement of science and the topics human beings find of interest. Concepts like infinite timelines are popular in your mediums of entertainment, and are sometimes portrayed fairly accurately. Infinite possibilities/timelines and a multitude of other fairly advanced material was not offered from 900 BCE to 700 CE when knowledge and wisdom was given to the positively oriented 3rd density beings and wanderers whose information can be found distorted in Earthlings' present religions because the vast majority were not advanced enough to comprehend it.

As one can see on Earth, an advanced concept is taught much differently to a first- to third-grader than to a university student. A simplistic story constructed for a first- to third-grader about a topic is most likely seen as quite false to a university student who is given more advanced and comprehensive information on the same topic.

The Garden of Eden story depicted in the *Old Testament* and other religious books is an example of a simplistic story given to a spiritual first-grader because that was the capacity level of human beings at the time. Whereas the same story presented in this awareness-expanding course is substantially different because it is able to be much more accurately presented because human beings today are able to grasp higher concepts. So one could imagine the futility of advanced human beings in the present time trying to learn from material in the *New Testament* and other similar books presented in a spiritual third-grade manner approximately 2,000 years ago to human beings with the mental advancement they possessed at the time. Current Earthlings are far more advanced and can understand ideas and concepts that would appear incomprehensible to Earthlings 2,000 years ago. It is not intelligent for a university student who has become interested in a topic to go to a third-grade class to learn it. Doing such is unwise and offers more distortions than it does spiritual advancement, especially when the third-grade material has been drastically altered by negatively oriented beings.

The exception would be the wisdom offered around 2,000 years ago, or at any time, as wisdom can stand the test of time if it is preserved, although it is sparsely offered in your so-called holy books that are drowning in an ocean of distortions. The most notable wisdom presented in your past is the wisdom that the one known as Buddha offered because this being was a 5th density wanderer and 5th density is the density of wisdom and light.

Compounded with the simplistic deliveries that often come through incorrectly, cryptic language is used that offers a myriad of different interpretations, and distortions abound in so-called holy material that contradict the way of One/Source. We will cover some examples in the book of *Revelations*, which depicts the coming micro-nova and harvest-time. *Revelations* 3:15–16: "I know your works, that you are neither cold nor hot. I wish you were cold or hot. So then, because you are lukewarm, and neither cold nor hot, I will spit you out of My mouth." We do not see any of the interpretations given by religious organizations to be accurate for these passages, as with most passages. Firstly, Source/God would not spit any being out of its mouth, as such an action is done out of hatred and judgment, which is not the way of Source, and since the collection of all beings is Source, it would be equivalent to Source spitting itself out of its mouth. These passages mean that if a being has not done adequate negative or positive works (cold nor hot) and remains neutral (lukewarm) at the end of the grand cycle on Earth during harvest-time, they will not graduate to 4th density positive or negative yet and will continue their 3rd density experience. They will continue in this manner till they are ready to graduate to 4th density. *Revelations* 7:4–8 is a complete distortion that lists "the tribes of the children of Israel" to be "the servants of our God". We have already covered who they were actually serving, unbeknownst to them. This information is a throwback to *Old Testament* information and puts great emphasis on God playing favorites, which is far from the way of Source, as all beings are a part of Source and are equal in the mind of Source and are Source in their totality. In *Revelations* the Book of Life, also known as the Akashic Records, is mentioned multiple times in a false light regarding judgment and being erased from the book. As we have stated, Source does not judge. Even positive beings from the 4th density do not judge. Judging is done by 3rd density beings and negative higher-density beings. Furthermore, all beings both positive and temporarily negative do not need to be listed in the Book of Life to inherit eternal life, as all beings as parts of Source already are eternal. And whether a being does positive or negative deeds in 3rd density does not exclude or erase them from the Book of Life because all beings are recorded in the Book of Life regardless of their actions. The Book of Life depicts records of incarnations and events unbiasedly and does not include criticism or judgment. It depicts in a matter-of-fact manner.

Each specific being's section in the Book of Life has been called their little scroll or little book. In *Revelations*, a mighty angel has John's little book and asks him to eat it. A more accurate translation from the original scroll is "study and digest it" rather than "eat it". When the little book is studied and digested, it may taste both bitter and sweet, as are the positive and negative actions one performed in their incarnations. When all of an individual's 3rd density incarnations, or just the last incarnation, in the little book are studied, it may taste bitter in one's stomach while being digested, but the growth and way forward it provides is sweet. All beings past the early 3rd sub-densities study and digest their little book between incarnations in the inner planes as they review their last incarnation and prepare for their next incarnation.

Most bodies of knowledge and wisdom offered around 2,000 years ago were meant to prepare a 3rd density being to focus on the next step alone, graduating to 4th density, which was suitable for the time. In the present time, we believe that offering an accurate summary of the steps ahead of the next step offers not only a quicker advancement to the next step, but a more confident ascension on the staircase, given that more motivation to take the next step is seen when the purpose of the whole staircase is understood, at least in summary. We are not necessarily trying to discourage human beings from utilizing channeled material from their history. We are simply conveying the reality of the situation. Although the "reality" of any given situation is up to each being to discern for themselves, as always, so we offer this awareness-expanding course without force and respect the free will of all beings who may disagree with it. All is as it should be.

As for methods of mastering mental thoughts and emotions which leads to balancing the lower chakras so one can focus more on the heart chakra that equates to graduating to the positive 4th density, which is what this course's 103 material will cover, there is considerable modern material that can be found on the Internet and in books that the channeled material in the past barely covered or not at all—with the body of works brought through by Buddha and Lao Tzu being notable exceptions. There is a wealth of other notable ancient material, but it is not available to the public because negatively oriented 3rd density beings have hidden it from the majority. The availability of much modern knowledgeable material should be no surprise, as there are approximately 385 million wanderers incarnate now on Earth and the seniority of vibration has granted hundreds of millions of later 3rd sub-density positive beings to incarnate as the harvest-time approaches.

3rd density beings use discernment by way of analytical thinking and intuition to practice the free will given to them and make choices for themselves. To mindlessly follow is the way of the 2nd density being. 3rd density beings are self-aware and are responsible for their thought-creations and actions. Thinking for oneself instead of mindlessly following others is one of the lessons that must be learned and practiced in order to graduate to 4th density. Make choices for yourself instead of giving your choices away to so-called official sources, experts in their fields, authoritative governments and organizations, technocrats, or the rest of the majority, which tend to follow aforementioned sources by way of programming and social conditioning. Analyze all available data and evidence and make your own choices and decisions. It would benefit one to use their own mind instead of being controlled as a tool by programming and the social conditioning that is shaped by programming in its many forms.

Just because religions, science, governments, organizations, technology companies, or the rest of majority say something is ethical or not, true or false, or what is the most effective way to do something, does not mean it is. When one uses their free will efficiently, everything is questioned and nothing is blindly followed.

Earth's history shows countless examples of human beings being mocked or condemned to death for bringing through information that was later deemed accurate by so-called official sources and the majority who tend to believe such sources. One would suspect Earthlings to have learned this lesson by now given it has been offered to them countless times, but we see the same situation continuing on Earth, which is largely due to the negatively oriented beings' programming and the social conditioning it shapes. History and lessons learned in it on Earth seem to be carelessly discarded in favor of transient trends and information that are more short-lived and abandoned as time passes and attention spans diminish. Human beings like to follow the majority way of thinking so they will fit in, be accepted, be liked, be given opportunities in the system, be given positions they desire in their society. Thus, to shape and control the majority, highly negatively oriented human beings use programming methods to shape social conditioning so the majority that humans tend to follow believes what they want them to believe and act how they want them to act. This programming and social conditioning also uses the controlled majority as tools to work for the negatively oriented human beings at targeting freethinking humans they want to be mocked, ignored, or silenced so their control structure is not threatened. The negative control structure always has underlings doing all the chores for them. 5th density negative beings are at the top of this control structure and highly negatively oriented 3rd density beings are at the bottom of this control structure; or rather, the 3rd density beings of the majority that the negatively oriented humans use as tools with social conditioning are at the bottom.

The reality of reincarnation would surface quite easily if the wealth of evidence that supports it was looked into and analyzed properly; the gaping holes in religions that support the existence of a heaven and hell, or science that supports nonexistence after death, would become apparent. Are you going to use your mind and free will to look at the evidence that the programming and social conditioning is telling you to not believe and to not even look at and consider, or are you going to consider ideas and events that have supporting evidence? Part of being self-aware is observing the programming. If the programming and social conditioning it shapes is directing human beings to think in a certain way or believe a certain thing in a forceful manner, often utilizing aggression and hate, and dictates or insinuates that you do not have a choice in the matter, or expresses the majority will hate you if you do not conform and comply, this should be what human beings call a red flag, an indicator that something is wrong.

With the immeasurable wealth they have accumulated, highly negatively oriented human beings clandestinely took over a large portion of the programming facets of the planet that help shape social conditioning on the planet: the news in its many forms; politics; religious organizations; international organizations; conglomerates; technology companies; the arts (especially movies, TV series, books, and music); Internet websites that tout facts and ridicule important true information; and Internet platforms and websites that censor, ban, and shadow-ban important information human beings share, especially via books and videos. The most widely used online websites/companies where one can purchase books and share videos are both heavily controlled by negatively oriented beings because these are the two most effective ways for human beings to inform other human beings about important topics. All these facets, and more, have been utilized by the negatively oriented human beings to use programming to shape social conditioning in an attempt to engineer a majority that is self-defeating and that works against the positively oriented human beings who are trying to aid and serve the majority. Most of the majority, but becoming less every day, do not believe human beings could act in such a way that they would define as "pure evil" so they dismiss and ridicule the other members of their majority who raise the alarm, which is also due to programming. One who is willing to sacrifice their firstborn infant tends to not think twice about performing an "evil" act against another human being or all of humanity. Most of the majority are aware there is mass corruption for the sake of gaining or increasing wealth, but they do not believe a being's mentality and intentions go further than utilizing the monetary system to gain wealth. The negatively oriented human beings are fine with the majority believing corruption goes as far as being financial, and use all their power to program and socially condition the majority into not believing anything further about service-to-self mentality and the actions that spring from it that the majority would consider being "evil". When we reiterate topics like this, it is because they are important and because repetition is useful in breaking the negatives' programming. Discernment should be used in one's own density as well as when communicating with higher-density beings.

Highly negatively oriented human beings know the power of social conditioning and so have taken control of a large portion of the facets of society that play major roles in shaping what social conditioning dictates. Thus, they decide the programming that shapes social conditioning. In utilizing these different facets, negatively oriented human beings can make the smallest minority appear to be the majority that a portion of the actual majority tends to follow because they want to follow the majority and fit in. This is particularly done via the Internet where one cannot see the situation unfolding before them, they only see the digital world that is rife with fraud. The use of what has been called bots and fake accounts operated by shills on the Internet has been tremendously effective for the negatively oriented human beings into making their ideas, stances on matters and events, and their agendas not only accepted by a large portion of the majority, but then policed and enforced through social conditioning. This programming has proven to be a powerful weapon for the negatively oriented human beings, as it utilizes those who mindlessly follow the programming and social conditioning to ridicule, shame, judge, vandalize, and even force-transition/kill others who do not follow the programming. We thought human beings would have learned from the many examples of this happening in their history where it was shown and accepted by the majority to be a mistake in the aftermath—with the Nazi's control and influence being a major example in Earth's recent history—but it seems a large portion of Earthlings have still not learned this lesson, as it has picked up pace again recently with brash programming by the negatively oriented.

You are no longer a 2nd density animal that mindlessly follows the pack. When you become old enough as an adult, you have adult responsibilities and need to think for yourself and make your own choices. If you are letting programming, social conditioning, a fake or real majority, religions, science, authority figures, technocrats, or a government treat you like a child and make your choices for you, you are ignoring the mantel of responsibility that is given to self-aware 3rd density beings. One cannot ignore this responsibility and be ready to graduate to 4th density. This is one of the reasons why the majority of human beings who have experienced the 3rd density on Earth will not be ready to graduate to 4th density come harvest-time and incarnate on a different planet outside the solar system to continue their 3rd density learning, which from a higher viewpoint, as we have stated, is perfectly fine. All is as it should be.

For those who follow religions that are built upon the same or similar information found in the *Old Testament*, *Quran*, and the *New Testament*, we offer this message: one may more appropriately honor the positively oriented 3rd density beings and positive higher-density beings known as Yahweh (who no longer goes by this name), Jesus, Muhammad, and others by following their actual teachings—which are the same as all positive higher-density beings' teachings—instead of following religions created in their names by highly negatively oriented 3rd density beings and trickster negative higher-density beings posing as God. You would not be turning your back on them by leaving a manmade religion they did not create; rather, you would be turning toward them. Even if one does continue to follow manmade religions that speak of a God that is wrathful and separate from you and that involves an everlasting place such as heaven and hell, the positive higher-density beings who have been deceptively affiliated with these religions by human beings, as well as all positive higher-density beings, will continue to assist you regardless because you are a part of Source and all is One. By assisting you, they are also assisting themselves. Their aid is of loving-kindness, compassion, and unity instead of judgment, violence, and hate. You may, as the wanderer from our united group has, develop a more personal and powerful relationship with positive higher-density beings—those whose teachings were twisted into religions and all others—when you interact with them in a manner that is respectful to them as well as yourself, a manner that does not include sacrifice, submission, prostration, worship, blind obedience, and making them a "God".

In relaying this information about religions, we are not only assisting you, but assisting those positive higher-density beings and united groups whose information has been captured and twisted. Atrocities have been committed and continue to be committed in their names that continue to accrue karmic ties for them to some degree, because when a positive higher-density being directly aids 3rd density beings, they agree to take on a level of responsibility of what transpires from the result of their intervening. Even if no karmic faults were made on their end while they were visiting or incarnate in 3rd density, the end result of what transpires due to their involvement still weighs on their karmic ties. When a positive higher-density being decides to directly interact by attempting to aid 3rd density beings, they sign up for a karmic agreement that possibly does not cease until the grand cycle of that particular 3rd density planet's experience comes to a close. Our later 6th sub-density united group has made this agreement as well and has karmic ties to human beings, and so we will continue to aid Earthlings in the manner we and the Council see as appropriate till the closing of the grand cycle and the ending of the harvest-time. Thus, our united group offers this awareness-expanding course to all human beings.

What has been called Eastern knowledge and wisdom that some call religions are the most accurate at portraying reality, with the body of knowledge and wisdom Buddha brought through being the most comprehensive. As such, it is more appropriate to call them ways of life and not religions. Just as the misnomer "God" would be better to avoid, the misnomer "religion" would be better to avoid as well for Buddhism and some other Eastern bodies of knowledge and wisdom. Although, all Eastern bodies of knowledge and wisdom have also developed their distortions and may teach aspects that are incorrect, different than the way of One. Any labeling other than the way of One or the law of One is not necessary and may lead to confusion and separation. The way of One is not a religion or esoteric information; it is simply as it is stated, the way of One, or the way in which Source and Source's mental projections operate in the Cosmos.

Eastern bodies of knowledge and wisdom have also seen their share of tampering, although not as heavily as those in the areas that are called the West and Middle East. There has also been the official banning of "heretical" information for Eastern bodies of knowledge and wisdom. The positively oriented 3rd density being known as Lao Tzu brought through the information contained in the *Tao Te Ching* that is still revered by human beings today, but his oral teachings that contain further powerful information for advancing along the path toward merging back with Source, or, the river that flows back to the Tao/Source, were banned and written copies of it were burned during a period of discord in China. The same situation that occurred in Rome regarding the Christian movement happened in China regarding the knowledge and wisdom brought through by Lao Tzu. Fortunately, those that revered Lao Tzu's teachings kept it alive by passing it down orally through the centuries from teacher to student, and it is available today as the *Hua Hu Ching*. The authorities who run the establishment that calls itself the Taoist religion does not recognize these oral teachings by Lao Tzu as being legitimate, just as the Vatican found all the powerful books regarding the Christian movement that they did not include in the *New Testament* as being illegitimate. If information is seen as being too powerful by negatively oriented human beings who see it as a threat to their self-serving power and control, they use their influence to discredit and erase such information. In the past it was done by banning and burning. In Earth's present time, as to not draw attention to information in a book that would result in free marketing for the information if it was banned, negatively oriented human beings do not ban powerful books, they do what has been called shadow-ban books. Since most books are purchased on Internet platforms in your present time, digital trickery and manipulation is used to such an extent that very few human beings become aware of these shadow-banned books. Since the major Internet platforms that sell books are controlled by these same negatively oriented human beings, this shadow-banning method is done quite easily and is very effective.

In the *Hua Hu Ching*, Lao Tzu states "The teachings are simple; if you try to make a religion or science of them, they will elude you." This statement and many other powerful statements in this body of information is why the negatives wished to erase the oral teachings Lao Tzu brought through. The *Tao Te Ching* was not targeted by the negatives because, although it also contains powerful wisdom, its teachings are more ambiguous and allow for many distorted interpretations.

In some ways, science has become a religion as well. When dogma is strictly followed without open-mindedness and scientific results that are in opposition with the beliefs of the scientific community are ignored, stagnation occurs. As with each religion, science has a body of knowledge and wisdom that it tends to strictly adhere to. Scientists who present new ideas that are reality-based are often mocked or labeled as pseudo-scientists, and their work is what has been called debunked. Their honorable label of being a scientist is stripped while scientists who adhere to the dogmatic body of knowledge and wisdom they are told to are accredited and honored. It should be no surprise that science is heavily controlled by the negatively oriented human beings. If they did not suppress, mock, and "debunk" important breakthroughs in science, it would ultimately lead to their loss of power and control, as an informed population is a threatening population in their minds.

Science and spirituality have been pitted against each other and taught to be two separate opposing things or beliefs. As with the nature and nurture debate, as well as so many other dualistic debates, spirituality and science are aspects of the same way or function. Actual science supports spirituality and actual spirituality supports science. Science explains the mechanisms and the ways of operation in which spirituality functions, and vice versa. When the body of science understands how the Cosmos is composed of vibrating love and light energy that emanate frequencies that form structures of geometry that adhere to mathematics throughout the Cosmos, spirituality can be further understood and explained in a technical manner.

Unlike the 4th density, the 3rd density experience is practiced without united groups, so there will always be a vast difference of opinions and choices. Allowing these differences of opinions and choices, as long as they do not harm other human beings, and respecting each other's free will is the positive way forward in 3rd density.

Knowing there will be human beings who choose to stay in religions, we advise showing them tolerance, patience, and loving-kindness, as well as respecting their free will. No matter how beneficial and important something is, nothing should be forced, as using force is infringement upon free will. Advising the path away from religions and other impediments may be brought up at opportune times to aid others, and done in a loving manner without force or judgment would be appropriate. Not all are ready for the next step forward on the staircase, and it is appropriate to respect their decided pace back to Source.

102.6 – Underground Civilizations & Suppressed Technology

Several groups of human beings who moved their societies underground to be protected from the major and minor cycles on Earth that are accompanied by major and minor geological shifts, with the first and second major cycles ending with an influx of energy from the Logos/Sun. Some of these underground civilizations that are negatively oriented played with human beings on the surface throughout the tens of thousands of years, telling them they were gods. Their high level of technology that appeared like magic to these less-advanced surface humans made it easy for their story to be believed. Many of these civilizations took shelter in large mountains or mountain ranges and continued to build downward as the tens of thousands of years went by. The negatively oriented and technologically advanced civilization that had built their cities under Mount Olympus would play with the Greeks like playthings for their amusement, which is depicted in your Greek mythology.

These underground civilizations were able to advance technologically and sometimes spiritually because they were older, each group had more unity as they worked together in their groups with a common cause to protect themselves from surface changes and lived close together, and later on were not impeded from advancing by the negatively oriented human beings who kept the surface civilizations from advancing. Some of the positively oriented to neutrally oriented underground societies aided surface human beings from time to time, especially assisting civilizations before and after major and damaging minor cycles. But as the surface got more diverse and convoluted, they tended to stay to themselves. As they advanced in their abilities and technology, they started mentally interacting with the surface beings and provide aid in this manner instead of physically interacting with them. The slightly to more negatively oriented underground societies started mentally interacting with the surface as well, but their information is anywhere from neutrally to negatively oriented, service-to-self mental actions.

For protection, all these groups, both positively and negatively oriented, did not say they resided underground when interacting with human beings on the surface. Who they said they were and where they came from changed throughout time in order to best fit into the beliefs held and the intellectual level of the humans on the surface. First they said they were gods and later said they were beings from a different solar system as the humans on the surface became more knowledgeable. Most of these groups are still saying they are from off planet to the individuals they mentally interface with and in the clandestine physical meetings they have with certain leaders of nations, organizations, and secret societies. The difference of the underground groups' actions after their fib for protection: the more positively oriented groups then interact in an aiding service-to-others manner, and the more negatively oriented groups then interact in a manipulative service-to-self manner.

The fib given for protection from the neutrally to negatively oriented groups also provides a higher probability of being given more power and control in the minds of those they converse with due to perceived superiority. Since these underground groups are technologically advanced and have spacecraft, their fib of being gods in the past and being from off planet in your present time is often accepted as truth by surface humans. These underground civilizations may say they are 4th density beings, but they have not graduated from 3rd density yet and are typically comprised of later 3rd sub-density beings. This is why they are still positively to negatively oriented beings instead of being positive or negative beings who have graduated into the 4th density positive or negative. If they had graduated, they would not still be inhabiting Earth and would be inhabiting a 4th density positive or negative planet.

Recently these underground societies/civilizations were informed by the Guardians of their appropriate shifting roles in interacting with the surface humans if they wanted to polarize more toward the positive, which is synonymous with progressing toward 4th density positive graduation. After being relayed this information, some of the civilizations decided to move further toward positive polarity, while other civilizations did not like what was proposed and so kept their current ways of being and acting neutrally to negatively oriented. As with all later 3rd sub-density beings, on the surface of the planet or underground, the choice to move toward the positive or negative path is intensified as the charged higher vibrations interact with the planet. Thus, these underground groups have increased their influence on the surface humans, some more toward service-to-others actions and some more toward service-to-self actions, whether carried out mentally or physically. Just like many different societies/civilizations and races on the surface of the planet, these underground groups are different and it would be inaccurate and inappropriate to lump them all together, as such a perception would be of simple mentality. When interacting with any beings, whether it be 3rd density beings on the surface, underground, from off planet, or higher-density beings, it would benefit one to use their discernment. It is always appropriate and beneficial to use discernment regardless of the source of information for one to actively utilize their free will. No matter how convincing certain beings may be, it is not wise to accept all information without using discernment. Negative and negatively oriented beings are clever and will offer both accurate and inaccurate information in the hopes that the self-serving information will not be scrutinized and swallowed with the rest of the offered information. Discernment is key for 3rd density beings.

The most notable negatively oriented underground society that has had a lot of interaction with the surface, both physically and mentally due to their level of advancement, are the Agarthans, whose network of cities reside partially under the Himalayas. Secret European occult societies who existed before and during the Nazi's rule made contact with the negatively oriented later 3rd sub-density Agarthans and then later with the highly negatively oriented later 3rd sub-density Draco reptilian group, as the two groups are allied. These secret occult societies still exist in your present time and have been major instruments for negative polarity and the control structure over the majority. They are part of the minority who feel they are superior to the majority and so perceive that they are fit to rule. The Agarthans, who closely resemble tall Nordics/Scandinavians with blond hair, had a large effect on Hitler's idea of what the physicality of a superior, master race should look like. The Agarthans have used their physical appearance, which many human beings find pleasing, to their advantage at deceiving human beings into thinking they are a positively oriented group. They have advanced to being later 3rd sub-density negatively oriented beings and are learning the early lessons from their chosen 4th density negative masters in the ways of deceit and manipulation. Like all later 3rd sub-density beings, positive and negative, they must learn enough of the early 4th density ways in their chosen polarity in order to graduate to 4th density.

It should be noted that there are many races from off planet that resemble these Nordic-looking Agarthan beings and some of them are positively oriented and actively working to aid human beings while also battling with the negatively oriented Draco reptilian group, so it would be unwise to group these many different races together and label them all as negatively oriented because of the Agarthans.

In our offered channeling information given in the past, we refrained from speaking of these underground civilizations for their protection. Now that the negatively oriented surface humans are already aware of their existence, we no longer need to add this layer of protection that has already evaporated. Since the negatively oriented surface humans now possess technological weaponry that can reach deep into the earth and adversely affect the underground civilizations, some of these underground societies who are positively oriented, neutrally oriented, and even slightly negatively oriented have formed a partnership to deal with this threat. The negatively oriented underground societies, like the Agarthans and others, have no interest in joining this partnership because they have majorly to slightly—depending on each group—aided in the past the same negatively oriented surface humans who are the threat, and some are currently working with them.

Some underground cities, that are different from the civilizations we have spoken about thus far in this subject who have originated from Earth, are up to billions of years old and have been abandoned as groups moved elsewhere on the planet and off the planet. The area between the surface of the Earth and the molten core of the Earth looks and operates grossly different than established beliefs held by the majority of human beings on the surface. To think there are not many enormous open spaces within this area of the earth is grossly inaccurate.

The majority of human beings are also programmed with a grossly inaccurate account of outer space and what is out there. In your solar system alone, a vast infrastructure has been constructed and is tightly controlled through force, deception, and heavy compartmentalization by negatively oriented 3rd density human beings and the reptilian Draco group they have allied with. Negatively oriented human factions made deals with this reptilian group to get a foothold in space approximately 85 years ago. These secret programs in space started approximately 30 years before the organization known as NASA landed on the Moon with their very inferior technology and were told by the reptilian group not to come back. The Draco reptilian group, as well as many other groups, have had bases on the Moon for hundreds of thousands of years. This Moon encounter and event was of course kept secret from the public. Any astronaut who attempted to disclose secret information was either reprimanded or force-transitioned/killed in staged accidents or other means.

The negatively oriented human beings' vast infrastructure expanded throughout your solar system and beyond in the following decades. Human beings who were scientists, engineers, physicists, and who worked in many fields of interest were collected by different methods and taken off planet to fill needed positions in the growing space programs. Many of these individuals were told a global catastrophe was going to end life on Earth and that they were chosen to preserve the human species and it would be most honorable for them to use their skills to do their part in one of the many underground facilities on Mars they had constructed or other locations around the solar system or beyond. After they agreed and were taken off planet, they and their families typically found themselves in a demanding work situation and cell-like living quarters that were no different than being an inmate in prison. They are trapped in a tightly controlled slavery system that dwarfs the slavery system engineered on Earth. This unethical recruiting has been called the brain drain and was utilized to service the growing programs and infrastructure in space that required personnel for it to function. This draining up to your present time has been responsible for the off-planet relocation of over 80 million human beings, who have since produced offspring that is born into an off-planet tightly controlled slavery system that continues to fill the positions needed in the growing infrastructure in your solar system and beyond. In the same deceptive way, human beings have also been moved underground to live the rest of their incarnations in slavery in one of the numerous deep underground military bases (DUMBs) and research and development facilities, which are tightly controlled like those in space. Negatively oriented human beings have a vast infrastructure in both your solar system and underground.

We reiterate: With so much separation and secrecy currently happening with factions of human beings in your present time period, Earthlings have a better idea of what transpired in ancient Rome than they do of the last 100 years. The Earthly factions that see themselves as superior/elite hide as much information as possible in order to more effectively wield power and control over the majority of human beings.

Throughout the decades a vast infrastructure that is extremely compartmentalized and controlled has been built throughout the solar system and beyond with colonies of human beings, who originated from Earth and then began being born off planet Earth as families produced offspring. Some of these groups' tasks are exploration, research and development, mining, relationships with countless different 3rd density races that originate throughout the universe, policing the solar system, and the building and trading of technology with many thousands of different races from other solar systems. Depending on one's position in this vast infrastructure, they are either deceived into thinking they are part of the most important and advanced program to bolster their egos and keep them controllable, or they have a slavery-type position. Both positions are heavily controlled where beings are strictly reprimanded or force-transitioned/killed if they do not obey and follow their orders. For the slavery-type positions, it has been said in these space programs that the workers in space are caged chickens and the slavery system on Earth has free-range chickens. Regardless of location, all of the chickens are being manipulated and all of their eggs they work so hard to produce are being stolen. If it were not for the "chickens and their eggs", the highly negatively oriented human beings would not be able to construct and maintain a control structure on the planet, in space, or underground.

There is a growing group of defectors from this vast infrastructure that wish to liberate other members in it and the surface population on Earth, as well as give Earth's population the advanced technology that is being suppressed and kept hidden from them. Advanced technology is used on a daily basis in space and under the surface of the Earth in DUMBs. All of this breakaway activity has been kept secret from Earth's population by the negatively oriented human beings who control aspects of it. Even a small amount of this technology being kept from human beings on Earth is capable of providing: free and clean energy for the entire planet; portal technology that makes long distance travel on planes, ships, and trucks unnecessary for goods and human beings; advanced healing technology that makes hospitals obsolete; the creation of goods with copying or replication technology; converting the physical matter of garbage into something useful; and making the monetary system obsolete. If this advanced technology that has been researched and developed by human beings ceased being suppressed and was allowed to be used by human beings on Earth, they would have the time and a more conducive environment and situation to further their spiritual advancement instead of waking up every day to do work and chores that are unnecessary, then allowed a few hours to be distracted and/or programmed in front of their televisions before they go to sleep and repeat the same routine every day. This is a constructed slavery and distraction system engineered and continued in a controlling manner by highly negatively oriented human beings. They are a minority that can only steer and control the planet via human beings who agree to be used as tools for them. If the majority of human beings refused to be a part of the slavery system and removed the blockage the very few highly negatively oriented human beings have created, the control system would end and Earth's civilizations would transform toward a system that works for and benefits all human beings instead of serving the very few human beings who think they are superior.

Each human being can still expand their awareness and do the inner work and progress toward graduating to 4th density positive within their slavery system, but freeing the planet from the slavery system would potentially offer all human beings the opportunity to spiritually progress in leaps and bounds. After beings on Earth have transitioned to 4th density, the vast infrastructure in your solar system will be utilized by human beings who graduated to 4th density positive.

102.7 – Sex & Sexuality

We will cover some aspects of gender and sexuality that are already known to open-minded human beings, then we will cover the act of sex as it pertains to the energy centers/chakras, as the two are intertwined. A being cannot participate in the act of sex without also involving the flow of energy through their chakras. The understanding of chakras being activated during the act of sex reveals a whole new level of understanding of sexuality and the act of sex.

The act of sex, whether there is intercourse or not, may offer a powerful flow and exchange of energy. This is precisely why negatively oriented 3rd density beings, who are influenced by negative 4th density beings, have utilized their captured and twisted religions to shame sex throughout history. To shame the very act that needs to be practiced in order for a species to procreate is pure folly. Additional programming has also been added to this folly, shaming females and honoring males for how often they participate in the same act of sex. This gender-based hypocrisy of the act of sex makes no sense, as an exchange of sexual energy takes two beings, not one. Solo sex is also a natural act that can be beneficial and powerful for channeling energy up through the chakras. It is not an exchange of energy as there is only one being involved, but it offers a self-sufficient way of channeling energy up the energy centers. Solo sex by the adept, positive or negative, may involve an energy exchange between the 3rd density being and a higher-density being, so in reality it is not actually solo sex. Since the separation of beings is an illusion and in reality there is only One being that all beings are a part of, a being always has sex with itself whether there is one or more beings involved; there is simply not an exchange of energy between parts of Source when only one part of Source is involved. Therefore, it is folly to shame those who practice solo sex. Those who do so are following the negatives' programming, along with their other programming that promotes low-vibratory sexual acts that polarize toward the negative—focused orange-ray or yellow-ray chakra sex.

The programming that shames females and honors males for performing the same act is one piece of much evidence that displays the inequality of the two genders in civilizations on Earth. The highly negatively oriented human beings whose bloodlines have had the largest control over Earth have kept males in charge of their operations because the energy influence of a male is less likely to be emotionally impacted by performing high acts of selfishness that include harming and force-transitioning/killing other beings.

Emotions are powerful, and this is why females, who are more in touch with their spiritual nature than their physical nature due to the spinning flow of energy through their chakras, tend to be more powerful co-Creators than males. Males are more in touch with their physical nature in the body complex and therefore are more physically powerful. If the female is unbalanced, their emotional power will work against them, perhaps in a dangerous way. If the male is unbalanced, their physical power will work against them, perhaps in a dangerous way. With power comes responsibility, and this is the case for both females and males. Due to energy flow, females are more in tune with their spirit complex and males are more in tune with their body complex. This difference of energy flow is meant to be balanced out when used together harmoniously in relationships and for a civilization. There has been much progress for the equality of females in some civilizations on Earth, but negatively oriented 3rd density beings, whether male or female, have hindered this equality and kept the most powerful positions for males, positions that are more powerful than publicly recognized positions of temporary leaders and presidents of a certain nation, organization, or company. We note, shunning all males for what a very select few do is not only folly but would support a counterproductive gender war, and such separation is most welcome by negatively oriented human beings, who have created programming specifically to promote disharmony between genders, so engaging in such separation would be falling right into a trap.

Wanderers, especially from 6th density, tend to be more balanced in their masculine and feminine energy because they have adequately balanced higher chakras in past incarnations and this balanced disposition bleeds through to the conscious from the subconscious in a wanderer's incarnation. When/If the wanderer adequately balances all of or most of their chakras in an incarnation, they become even more balanced in this manner and can use emotions like females can to be powerful co-Creators even if they are males. This is also the case for 3rd density males who are not wanderers and have adequately balanced most of their chakras—at least the green-ray heart chakra being adequately balanced.

Denying the equality of one half of two inseparable halves of energy flow, the yin and the yang, that comprise a whole always produces instability and energy imbalance for a relationship, civilization, or planet. Negatively oriented 3rd density beings have captured and twisted sexual and gender-equality movements like they have for the creation of religions and any other aspect of life that is seen as powerful and influential. The hippie and free love movement was ignited by living a life that is heart chakra oriented. Since negatively oriented 3rd density beings see universal love as a threat to their control structure, they attempted to program human beings into shunning and shaming the lifestyle and outlook of the hippies. They also invested in several clandestine efforts to stop the free love movement and were eventually successful. They have also captured and twisted the gender equality movement by charging and creating the programming of females in this movement to be resentful and angered toward males, which only acts to discredit their movement and make it ineffective, as you cannot put out a fire by adding more fire to it. The same has happened for race equality movements. A situation that was once or still is inappropriately unequal is not solved by making it inappropriately unequal on the other side. This only continues the problem and adds fire to fire instead of putting out the fire with calming water. The negatives are very aware of this, but the human tools they tempt to get caught up in it are not. Nothing charged with hate ends up being beneficial. As the equal loving participation of female and male energies are necessary for producing and nurturing offspring, so is this equal loving participation needed for nurturing a healthy and balanced society and planet.

As harvest-time comes nearer and the stakes have been raised, we have witnessed a full-on attack by negatively oriented 3rd density human beings, who are influenced by their negative 4th density chosen masters, capturing and twisting any possible aspect of life in order to cause confusion, separation, and duality fighting in order to further their control over the majority. Aspects of life that were once agreed upon by common sense have been attempted to be turned upside down with programming and social conditioning that stems from the programming. The attempts of separation and confusion by the negatives has also been aimed at the roots of nurturing. Not only have males been pitted against females and vice versa, different races pitted against each other, and the countless other acts of creating dualism and division between beings (nations, religions, wealth status, political parties and so-called political issues, etc.), but the programming, in order to be more effective and long-lasting, has been aimed at family units, specifically children. In this manner, the negatively oriented human beings hope to transform the planet into their controlled image in two generations' time. Instead of a planet rapidly evolving and transitioning smoothly into a positive 4th density planet in a few generations' time, the negatives attempt to capture and twist this few generations' time transition toward negative polarity instead of positive polarity. In every single possible way forward offered by the beings of positive polarity, the beings of negative polarity have attempted to grab the reins of control and twist the direction toward their preferred negative polarity. After all, this is the role beings in negative polarity are meant to play for the cosmic experience to function.

Social conditioning has shaped the idea that only lifelong love relationships are seen as important and sought after. Some love relationships are pre-incarnate planned by beings to last for a certain duration and not be lifelong. If they were to end up being lifelong, they would not serve the two beings. Long-term love relationships are more conducive to activating the heart chakra and offer the balancing of the lower and higher chakras, but short-term love relationships offer their own experiences that offer assistance with growth and advancement as well. It is not wise to see all love relationships that are not lifelong as being a waste of time and effort, as learning and advancing is not a waste of time or effort.

A being's intuition and their spirit guides' influence guide them toward other beings they have pre-incarnate planned to have short-term and long-term relationships with, even if the two reside in different geographical areas on the planet. One is attracted to the other like the forces of magnets. Spirit guides are always there to help nudge a being toward the path they have pre-incarnate planned for themselves, but it is the responsibility of the 3rd density being to understand the signs along the way and go with the guided flow.

While disincarnate in the inner planes, a being does not have a gender. A being does not incarnate as a certain gender by pure chance. With the aid of their higher self, a being chooses to incarnate as a female or male before an incarnation. If an incarnate being decides to ignore their pre-incarnate plans and their higher self and attempts to change their gender by mutilating their 3rd density body, a potentially large portion of their pre-incarnate plans may not be fulfilled due to their path in life being drastically altered, potentially leading to a missed-incarnation opportunity of growth and balancing out karma for oneself and the others involved in their pre-incarnate plans. We say "attempts to change" because the surgical procedures used do not change the directional flow of energy that is present in a male and female at birth, and the hormone supplements given then cause the mind, body, spirit complex to be even more damaged and unbalanced. Not changing one's gender was—and still is to almost all human beings—one of the aspects that falls under common sense, and if the negatively oriented human beings were not working overtime promoting this and other detrimental tactics that offer confusion and division, this topic would not have needed to be addressed, as it was not in the past.

As harvest-time approaches and the seniority of vibration is in effect, there is a major increase of incarnations from later 3rd sub-density beings, 4th density graduates who are assisting in the physical body's transition from 3rd to 4th density, and wanderers. These advanced positively oriented beings tend to be more balanced in masculinity and femininity, especially the latter two listed, as one who moves towards wholeness invariably is. Knowing this, the negatives attempt to use this disposition against positively oriented beings with confusion, attempting to use their balanced sexual energy and nature that is a strength as a weakness and persuade them to instead focus only on either their masculinity or femininity and change their gender. Some of the males of the majority who get caught up in fighting this programming fall prey to a type of reverse psychology and attempt to be more masculine to counteract the negatives' agendas, falling into the same gender unbalancing trap. This and almost all programming is meant to harm and negatively charge both sides held by the players, those on both sides of whatever dualism issue the programming is targeting. This causes the dualism gap to become wider instead of coming closer together where issues could potentially be solved.

The negatives have made this sexuality issue and countless others as so-called political issues because the dualism of political parties and their constant fighting has already been forged and engineered by negatively oriented human beings into a fierce battleground, with human beings choosing to be on one side or the other, where minimal healthy communication is had and separation and hatred brew in dualism. This creates constant and endless division, dualism at its finest. In this state, the negatives greatly benefit. To move an issue onto the dualistic battleground of charged politics has been beneficial for the negatively oriented. If the negatively oriented could, they would move every topic, no matter how small, to the political battleground so that separation is further charged, as division is the nature of the negatively polarized being. We would not be surprised if how one simply says hello to another becomes a political issue; perhaps saying hello will become politically incorrect altogether with the full-on attack we have seen from the negatively oriented.

When there is only a right side and a left side, or any state of dualism, there is no middle path that the Buddha spoke of. It would be wise to cease having political parties and so-called political issues and instead vote for individuals based on their aspirations. Photographing a political candidate's aura, which is a technology available on Earth, at different times during their campaign would be a beneficial strategy at determining their honesty and advancement as a being. If this were done, human beings would find a large portion of their political candidates as having murky auras. Such a method would need to be very secure because the individuals with murky auras would somehow try to pass off fabricated aura photography of themselves so they may continue to deceive their voters. In positive higher densities, the aura that emanates from the energy centers/chakras can be plainly seen and is used to decide rotating positions of leadership. No campaigning is needed.

It is not wise to think of oneself as a half looking for another half to make them whole in a love relationship. If one works on being whole themselves by doing the inner work, they are much more likely to participate in a healthy love relationship when one materializes. Thinking of oneself as perpetually incomplete as a half stems from a lack of self-confidence and neediness, which fuels conditional love with strings that expresses love only if the perceived and wanted aspects of another benefits the other. Although self-aware beings may grow and become aware of their faults and imbalances and how to overcome and balance them in a relationship, the inherent uniqueness of a being is fixed, so if another being tries to change this in another, it is a selfish act of control and an infringement upon one's free will. If two beings' uniqueness is not compatible, a harmonious long-term love relationship is out of reach and therefore was not pre-incarnate planned.

Universal love comes with no conditions. If the perceived loving feeling only exists if certain conditions are met, this is the guise of love. Conditional love stems from unbalanced orange-ray chakra energy, which is expressed by personal matters and one-on-one matters. Universal love stems from a partially or an adequately balanced green-ray heart chakra. In this state, a being may become aware of their flaws and lovingly inform their partner of theirs if deemed appropriate. When the act of being wrong or right is set aside, a being is more able to observe themselves and become aware of their flaws. When one finds the door and decides to open it, the inner work may begin.

If a 3rd density being incarnated on a planet and lived their whole incarnation or most of their incarnation in solitude, it would be a major disadvantage for their growth. It is the interaction with other beings that offers cause-and-effect scenarios and provides a mirror so that a being may more clearly recognize and understand their mental states, and mental states also possibly prompt physical actions. Those that leave a society in their formative years to seek so-called enlightenment are doing themselves a disservice, as they are much more likely to advance and grow with the aid of interacting with others, whether the interactions are perceived as positive or negative. Adversity offers growth because adversity allows matters to arise and so be made aware of. The lack of adversity greatly decreases the probabilities that make one aware of matters that need to be focused on and overcome. If the topic is not brought up, it is not focused on.

Love relationships offer beings the most effective mirror to identify their faults, as love relationships provide a close and ongoing interaction. Love relationships could be seen as intense learning courses. To participate in a love relationship that is longer than short-term is to enroll in an education that offers growth by allowing one to become aware of their faults—aspects of their self that require overcoming or balancing. Friend relationships may offer this, but typically to a lesser degree. (We will expand upon love relationships and related topics in 103 subjects.)

—∞—

We will now cover the heart of this subject by focusing on the intertwined relationship between energy centers/chakras and the act of sex. To understand the relationship between the two is to understand the nature of the act of sex. Before we proceed, it would be notable to convey that there is no wrong or right way when practicing the act of sex in the highest viewpoint of Source, but acts of sex that do not engage the heart chakra are of low vibration and polarize toward the negative. This is not a judgment, it is merely the reality. The last thing we want to do when covering this subject is to add shame and judgment to the acts of sex. The negatives have already thoroughly offered shame and judgment for the acts of sex throughout Earth's history, utilizing their created religions and programming to do so.

The act of sex is an activity that the mind, body, and spirit are involved in; the physical body is not the only complex that is engaged during this activity. The red-ray chakra, being the root chakra, offers no polarity from the act of sex and so is not healthy or unhealthy. It is responsible for the random act of producing offspring for a continuation of the species. The act of sex that focuses on the orange- or yellow-ray chakra concentrates on one being playing the role of submission and one being playing the role of the dominator. This is not harmonious and creates blockages in the orange- or yellow-ray chakra, and is therefore unhealthy. During the act of sex, the orange-ray chakra if blocked will focus on one being to another in an unequal manner. The yellow-ray chakra if blocked during the act of sex focuses on unequal group orientation; even though the sexual act is between two individuals, the mind utilizes unequal group scenarios to engage in the act of sex, such as the inequality of race and nationality.

Acts of sex that focus on the orange- or yellow-ray chakra and stop the upward flow of energy through the chakras are not harmonious because one being plays the controller and the other the controlled, which is different from the loving act in sex of giving and receiving where both beings are equal and loving in the exchange. Orange- and yellow-ray chakra focused sex is the only type of sex that higher-density negatives perform, as their structure in the larger board game of life is all about a hierarchy of power and control, and the smaller board game of sex mirrors the larger board game of life. Orange- and yellow-ray chakra focused sexual acts are not only performed by negatively oriented 3rd density beings, they may also be performed by the sexually confused neutrally and positively oriented 3rd density beings who are creating blockages and not utilizing their full potential of energy flow that continues further up the chakras.

When both human beings engage the green-ray heart chakra during the act of sex, a harmonious exchange of energy is had that focuses on universal love and equality instead of one acting superior to the other. The heart chakra, and higher chakras, may be engaged with one being giving and another receiving, but this should not be confused with one controlling and one being controlled. Instead, it is a loving act of giving and receiving that is appreciated by both beings and a mental scenario of one being playing the controller or submissive role does not arise. Engaging the heart chakra and higher chakras during the act of sex is easier done when the two beings know and understand each other to some degree, which takes a period of time. This is why long-term love relationships are more conducive to engaging the heart chakra and higher chakras during the act of sex, but there are some beings whose inherent nature grants them a higher ability in the act of sex, providing a greater potential in engaging the heart chakra and higher chakras during the act of sex even with partners they do not know well. All beings are unique and have their own set of abilities in different areas. This is what allows all the different puzzle pieces (beings) to fit together and produce a larger working picture.

If two beings experiencing the act of sex both engage the green-ray heart chakra, there is a harmonious energy exchange between the two beings. The female and the male give to the other what they hold in abundance due to the nature of gender-related energy flow and access. Males are more in touch with their body complex and so gift vital energy to the female. Females are more in touch with their spirit complex and so gift intuition that may lead to inspiration for the male. This is why on Earth males have frequently called females their muse.

During the act of sex, when one being engages the green-ray chakra and the other only goes as far as engaging the orange- or yellow-ray chakra—which could potentially be avoided if both beings honestly express what they want to participate in prior to the act of sex, but not if it is merely done mentally by one being and not in the actions taken—the being engaging the green-ray chakra may intuitively guide the other to do the same, or only engage in it themselves, or they may be lowered to the other's focused lower chakra—blockages in the lower chakras for both beings only occurring in the lattermost case. When a being engages the green-ray chakra during a sexual act, they are satisfied during and after the sexual experience. The being who focuses on the orange- or yellow-ray chakra is left unsatisfied and keeps craving for sexual satisfaction, which will never come if they do not at least engage the green-ray chakra during the sexual experience. Blockages could be related to character flaws, they are not permanent and can be balanced out if the inner work is done.

As when the green-ray heart chakra is activated in any regard during a being's incarnation, the green-ray chakra when activated during the act of sex allows the potential for energy to further rise to the blue-ray chakra. The blue-ray chakra deals with communication, and if it is engaged during the act of sex, it provides a high level of comfort, acceptance, and freedom. Even if only one being engages the blue-ray chakra during the act of sex, the other being involved in the sexual energy exchange may feel it and has the potential to be intuitively guided up to the same level and activate their blue-ray chakra, or the green-ray chakra if they are still working on engaging this chakra during the act of sex.

When beings are aware of themselves as being part of Source and so are aware that they are Creators, the indigo-ray chakra may be activated during the act of sex. In this high vibration, if experienced by both beings, the wholeness of one being unites with another during the act of sex, which can be done with or without intercourse. When this energy flow is reached, a constant relaxed and blissful orgasmic feeling is felt, and depending on the duration of the act of sex, this feeling has the potential to continue well past the act of sex and be felt for many hours and even the next day, lessening in strength as time progresses.

The violet-ray chakra, like the red-ray chakra, is constant and does not offer polarity during the act of sex. The violet-ray chakra allows those who have gone past engaging the indigo-ray chakra and acts as a pathway to opening up a greater connection with Source energy and mind, either done during the act of sex or not. If this pathway is accessed during the act of sex, a sacred experience is had and the constant orgasmic feeling we described during indigo-ray chakra engagement is felt but to a higher degree of intensity and duration. This is what some have called positive sex magic. However, there is no such thing as magic; labeling something as magic is only a failure to understand how something is done or achieved.

Negatively oriented 3rd density beings and negative higher-density beings see activating universal love with the heart chakra as a weakness, as they are service to self and do not wish to give love to others. On both the board game of life and the smaller board game of sex, which resides inside the board game of life, negatives focus on the orange- and yellow-ray chakras. The blockages that are created in these two chakras during the act of sex produces a craving that is never satisfied, leaving the being with the feeling of wanting to perform the act over and over again. This is similar to one who tries to satisfy their unbalanced mental state by eating large quantities of foodstuffs (typically being drawn to unhealthy foodstuffs), drinking large amounts of alcohol, or taking large amounts of drugs. All of which will never satisfy their cravings no matter how much is ingested because an alternative to the root issue is being focused upon.

A human being focusing on the orange- or yellow-ray chakra during the act of sex enjoys the feeling as one enjoys the taste of unhealthy foodstuffs. They may perceive the feeling to be pleasant for the duration of time they are enjoyed, but afterwards the much longer-lasting ill-feelings of unhealthiness are the consequence. A constant craving feeling is the perpetual state of wanting but never having, which is a prime deterrent of contentment. If a human being observes the feelings and vibrations they are creating during orange- or yellow-ray chakra acts of sex, they will notice the feelings are edgy and negative, not calm and harmonious, and are not feelings they would want to create during their life on the life board game while not participating in sexual acts. The feelings and emotions one produces while performing sex or not is an indicator of balanced and unbalanced states of being. Observing the unbalanced feelings created during the act of sex is akin to reading the ingredients list of the unhealthy foodstuffs one is currently eating. Once this is done the being is no longer in doubt of whether they are practicing balancing or unbalancing acts. Although, this does not mean that the temptation goes away.

After climaxing from the act of sex that has focused on the orange- and/or yellow-ray chakra, the feeling may be edgy and the enjoyment from the low-vibratory act dissipates quickly. What remains is an unsatisfied, craving feeling, where one thinks they will be satiated the next time they perform the same act, and so the desire to rush towards it in haste again is felt. As with unhealthy foodstuffs/junk food, the craving makes one believe they will be satisfied with the next bite, then the next bite after that, then the next bite after that, but satisfaction never comes from practicing low-vibratory actions that do not fulfill the root cause.

We will give some indicators to gauge the vibratory level of a sexual act, which may also be utilized as methods for attaining higher-chakra sexual acts. All pertain to sexual acts between two beings or solo sex. Observe how you feel during the act. A being who focuses on the orange- or yellow-ray chakra during sex may say they feel good, but it is not actually a good feeling; it is them enjoying the unhealthy feelings of being dominating, controlling, and treating others as objects, or on the other side of the unhealthy spectrum: being submissive, humiliated, and treated like an object. The latter case not wanting to be experienced by most in their life board game—being humiliated or treated like an object—is an indicator of the unhealthy action being played out on the sexual board game. The few that do enjoy such experiences in the life board game have much more to overcome and balance.

Having a slow to medium sexual rhythm is not only more sensual but allows prana to possibly keep flowing upward through the chakras. Having a fast sexual rhythm tenses up the body and causes the flow of upward prana to get blocked in the orange- or yellow-ray chakra. A fast sexual rhythm puts most of the emphasis on the body complex, trying to receive stimulation through mostly utilizing the body like a spiritless machine. A slow to medium sexual rhythm often accompanied by undulating motions offers the being's complexes of the mind, body, and spirit to be stimulated and participate in the sexual experience. Unless the spirit complex is stimulated adequately during a sexual act, the flow of prana does not reach the green-, blue- or indigo-ray chakras.

When a being is not in the mood for a sexual act but performs it anyway, they may have to try harder to be stimulated, which leads to a much greater possibility of gravitating toward a fast sexual rhythm that tenses up the body and blocks the flow of upward prana.

If a being feels a calm but intense blissful stimulation in the higher chakra areas of the body while experiencing the smooth act of sex, it is an indication that the flow of prana is not being blocked in the lower chakras and is being allowed to flow upward toward or to the indigo-ray chakra. All sexual acts start in the red-ray chakra and flow upward through the energy centers till they are blocked, if they are blocked. This is the same for all stimuli received on the life board game. Thus, a green-ray chakra sexual experience does not start in the green-ray chakra, although it may be the first chakra area where intense stimulation is felt. The red-ray chakra is the foundation chakra that the upward flow of prana first encounters for all experiences, including sexual experiences. If prana flow is not blocked in the red-ray chakra due to fear of not being able to perform or compatibility issues, the flow of prana continues to move up to the orange-ray chakra where it is blocked if inequality is mentally focused on from individual to individual. If it is not blocked in the orange-ray chakra, the flow of prana continues up toward the yellow-ray chakra, where it is blocked if the individual mentally focuses on inequality in the association of groups such as race or nationality. If it is not blocked in the yellow-ray chakra, the flow of prana continues up toward the green-ray chakra and universal love is experienced where satisfaction is felt. From here, prana stops flowing upward if the sexual act is not performed with effortless ease and freedom of expression to activate and engage the blue-ray chakra. Prana only continues past the blue-ray chakra and activates and engages the indigo-ray chakra if a being is not only fully comfortable with themselves and another, but knows their infinite worth as a Creator and a level of wholeness and contentment is known and felt. Prana only continues past the indigo-ray chakra and traverses the violet-ray chakra to connect with Source energy when a being expresses their wholeness that goes beyond being a seemingly separate spark of Source and fully knows and feels the love energy connection with all that is in the Oneness and as the Oneness.

Observe how long the feelings last after the act of sex is done. The longer the loving, blissful feelings last, the potentially higher the vibration of the sexual act was. This depends not only on the green-ray through indigo-ray chakras that are engaged, but the duration of the sexual experience, which may or may not include sexual penetration, as the act of sex involves the mind, body, spirit complex. Like charging a battery, the longer the sexual act is experienced, and so charged, the longer the feelings remain after the sexual act is done. Sexual acts that engage the green-ray chakra produce loving feeling for a period of time after the sexual act is done. Blue-ray chakra feelings last even longer, and indigo-ray chakra feelings even longer, considering the duration they were engaged for was close to being equal. When one who usually performs orange- or yellow-ray chakra focused sexual acts participates in a green-ray engaged sexual act, they feel the difference. They feel satisfied instead of being left with a craving feeling.

Here is a basic way to know if your particular aim or method for a sexual act is healthy (green-ray engaged) or unhealthy (orange- or yellow-ray focused). If the aim or method only works with a fast rhythm and does not resonate in the green-ray heart chakra—which one should be able to feel in their chest where the heart is located—then it is an unhealthy orange- or yellow-ray chakra focused sexual act and fantasy. The two aspects that may be focused on to engage at least the heart chakra are having a smooth and adequately slow to medium rhythm and bringing prana to at least the heart chakra by producing emotional feelings of universal love, which are felt in the heart area of the body due to harmony and equality.

A particular sexual position may be the same for a healthy or unhealthy sex act, as one's focus on mental thoughts, feelings, and emotions while doing the action is what is important because experiencing and charging these is what makes it a green-ray chakra sexual act or not. The alignment of the spine is what is important when solely focusing on physical positions during a sexual act, shared or solo, where undulating motions of the spine assist the upward flow of prana through the chakras. Sexual positions that cause the spine to be bent enough to impede or stop the upward flow of prana may create blockages in the orange- or yellow-ray chakras. If one is observant while performing a sexual act in this way, they will notice that the intense sexual feelings felt are mostly situated in the areas of their body where the orange- or yellow-ray chakras reside, which goes no further upward than the solar plexus and is not felt in the chest where the green-ray chakra resides.

If a being starts a sexual experience with a mental fantasy that focuses on the orange-ray chakra, which is synonymous with inequality from individual to individual, then that is where the flow of upward prana will most likely be blocked, unless the unharmonious fantasy is recognized and abandoned sometime during the act and the upward flow of prana resumes, but usually the initial intent is sustained during the act. The human being is setting themselves up for defeat before they have even started the experience.

Certain body types and races may be found pleasing or attractive due to inherent or developed preferences in one's incarnation; this is all well and occurs for a purpose, but if there is no shared loving connection and only the superficial or physical is focused on, the heart chakra is not engaged. Sexual acts that focus on the orange-ray chakra are straightforward: if any part played in the act of sex is not shared by both as being wanted in the giving and receiving, loving in the giving and receiving, and harmonious, it is an orange-ray chakra focused sexual act.

It is the same for sexual acts focusing on the yellow-ray chakra, but the affiliation of group identification is also introduced. Any group scenario could be imagined, but typically sexual acts affiliated with groups tend to focus on race, nationality, or body types. As with affiliated groups of the yellow-ray chakra on the life board game, focusing on groups during the act of sex is not unhealthy by itself and does not create blockages in the lower chakras if the same matters for the orange-ray chakra are equal; meaning, both beings enjoy the experience, both experience loving feels while receiving or giving, and the act is harmonious without inequality being mentally focused on. When the affiliated groups of race, nationality, and/or body types is lovingly appreciated and not perceived as superior or inferior than the other, prana flow may continue further and also engage the green-ray heart chakra while the mental group identification is in play. As in the life board game, mental group affiliation/ identification during the act of sex only creates a hindrance of engaging the green-ray chakra if the perceived groups are not seen as equal and one is perceived to be superior or inferior to another. In the case of mental inequality with group identification, blockages occur in the yellow-ray chakra and the green-ray chakra is not engaged.

As in the life board game, mental group affiliations during the act of sex need to be abandoned in order to engage the indigo-ray chakra. This is not because group affiliation is necessarily negative or unhealthy, it is because such mental projections of duality end in the 6th density where unity resides and so is related to the sixth chakra, the indigo-ray chakra, where spiritual matters reside in wholeness and therefore do not mentally deal with separate groups, even if they are seen as equal. At this high vibration, such group affiliations are known to be an illusion and so are not mentally focused on or charged. A higher degree of the spirit complex is accessed and the body complex loses much of its relevance and focus. This definitely does not mean that different races, nationalities, body types, or any other groups cannot share sexual acts to achieve engagement of the indigo-ray chakra; it simply means the groups are not mentally focused on. Instead, the focus is on universal love and the whole experience of the mind, body, spirit complex for any possible combination of two beings.

All of this is the same for sexual acts between two entities or solo sex. For solo sex, in order to avoid chakra blockages, since there is only one entity involved, their mentally projected focus or fantasy of the other entity they are focusing on for the sexual act would need to be loving and embrace equality. If the mental projection or fantasy is one of loving equality where both perceived beings enjoy the process in a loving manner no matter who is giving or receiving and equality is established where no feelings of domination, submission, humiliation, or one being portrayed as an object is mentally focused on, then the flow of prana reaches the green-ray chakra and potentially higher chakras during solo sex.

Solo sex may be more difficult to engage the green-ray chakra because another being's loving emotions are not present that assist at engaging this chakra, and it is also easier to slip into focusing on an orange- or yellow-ray chakra fantasy because there is not another being the individual is interacting with and so there are no perceived consequences. It is accurate that there are no karmic consequences with another being in that there is no sexual energy transfer, but the one performing focused orange- or yellow-ray chakra solo sex still creates blockages in their chakras.

The more frequently solo sex is performed, especially for older adults who no longer possess as much sexual energy, the higher the probability of focusing on the orange- or yellow-ray chakra. This deals with being in the mood, and is the same case for sexual acts between two beings. One may want to enjoy the feelings of sex, but that does not mean they are necessarily in the mood. It is similar to one who may want to enjoy the taste of foodstuffs, but that does not necessarily mean they are hungry or need sustenance. This does not mean that one cannot engage the green-ray heart chakra at these times we mention; it merely means there is an increase in the probability of not engaging the heart chakra.

The best way to approach solo sex for the highest probability of engaging the green-ray chakra and higher chakras is akin to approaching the sexual act as a type of meditation. One may mentally focus on the fantasy to initiate the sexual flow of energy at first. Then it is the feelings one has created that are more focused on and their flow up the spine and through the chakras toward the crown chakra, doing so with a slow to medium rhythm with undulating motions of the spine. The fantasy may be focused on in intervals before returning to the focus on the loving feelings created and the upward flow of prana through the chakras. It is a blissfully calm experience like that of a meditation.

Those who enjoy snuff porn are displaying personal issues and blockages in the orange-ray chakra and are living out their unconstructive fantasy as either the snuffer or the one being snuffed. The worst case orange-ray chakra blockage sexual act is when snuff is played out not merely as a fantasy on the sexual board game, but rather played out on the life board game where one actually is force-transitioned/snuffed out while engaging on the sexual board game at the same time. In this case the dominating snuffer is stimulated and blocked in the orange-ray chakra while playing out the most powerful act over another individual: taking their life/force-transitioning them.

As harvest-time draws nearer, we have noticed negatively oriented 3rd density human beings, who are heavily influenced by higher-density negatives, promoting their preferred orange- and yellow-ray acts of sex in their programming outlets: movies, TV series, books, online platforms. This programming shapes social conditioning for those who fail to think for themselves and are more interested in fitting in with the perceived majority. Bondage, the act of domination and submission is one example. Pain being given or received in any manner is another example. Being a slave, pet, or object for another, where the being playing the role of the slave, pet, or object is constantly craving low-vibratory feelings of humiliation and submission and the other being displaying reverse low-vibratory feelings of control and domination is another example. Fast paced and animalistic acts of sex where the human beings can be seen focusing solely on the body and producing animalistic, craving feelings in their short-lived sexual activity is another example of the negatively oriented beings' programming to promote orange- and yellow-ray chakra focused sexual acts, which are unhealthy because they create blockages in the chakras, and they polarize toward the negative.

The board game of sexual acts resides within the larger board game of life and is very revealing to the situation of the life board game. We will give some examples. Negatively oriented 3rd density beings are prone to engaging in orange- and yellow-ray sexual acts where they are the controlling dominators or the controlled submissive, which is akin to how they live their lives: controlling others and being submission to their chosen masters who are higher in the hierarchy than they are, whether they be other 3rd density beings or 4th density negatives.

Those who are born with inherent attractions or so-called fetishes to the lower half of the human body, especially the feet, are positively oriented 3rd density beings or wanderers who are displaying their service-to-others disposition through the act of sex. They find much pleasure in giving and serving/aiding. However, if any part of the lower half of the body—or any part of the body period—is solely focused on without engaging in at least the green-ray heart chakra, a being will be stuck in performing unhealthy orange- or yellow-ray sexual acts. As on the life board game, those practicing service-to-others acts need to have healthy spiritual boundaries or they may get stuck in the mud with those they are attempting to serve/assist out of the mud.

Failing to construct the same spiritual boundaries on the sexual board game with other beings may lead to performing submissive and humiliating acts rather than giving acts to the middle and lower half of the physical body that are appreciated and not looked down upon in judgment by the receiver. Why would one look down on or judge another for giving or aiding? As with any part of the physical human body—lower, middle, or higher areas—the parts may be admired and assist in initiating love energy during sexual acts, but when the physical parts are solely focused on without engaging in the heart chakra, only unhealthy acts and cravings are charged because universal love is not present in the act.

Given the seniority of vibration for the queue incarnating onto Earth at this period close to harvest-time, there are hundreds of millions of positively oriented later 3rd sub-density beings and approximately 385 million wanderers that have incarnated onto Earth who are inherently driven to serve/aid the majority. With this inherent ambition to serve/assist, a large amount of beings in these two groups are inherently born with a so-called foot fetish because such an inherent sexual attraction is a high probability for beings who inherently want to perform service-to-others acts and serve the majority. Naturally, it is appropriate for serving/aiding acts to be respected instead of shamed or looked down upon. The negatives are aware of this inherent sexual trait of highly positively oriented human beings, so they have engineered shaming campaigns in their outlets of programming (movies, TV series, online platforms) in an attempt to steer the positively oriented beings into performing orange- or yellow-ray acts of sex by producing humiliating feelings as the lower half of the body is focused on. Humbling feelings are healthy, but humiliating feelings are unhealthy. Instead of the highly positively oriented human being serving another in a loving manner that engages at least the green-ray heart chakra, the negatives attempt to twist their service so it is serving negative polarity by directing them to focus on the orange- or yellow-ray chakra where inequality and shame arises in one's service.

In cases where the male is focusing on performing the serving/giving act to the female, this campaign by the negatives also targets females by keeping the energy of masculinity in control over femininity on the planet, as females and their femininity being revered and held in high regard would offset the controlling balance of the male-power positions that are at the top of the service-to-self hierarchy on Earth. The negatively oriented human beings have no wish to balance the yin and the yang energies because their aim is imbalance. This programming campaign acts as a multilayered attack aimed at body appreciation, acts of sex, those who wish to lovingly serve/aid, and gender equality. Many more males than females are inherently born with an appreciation and attraction to the lower half of the body—legs and feet—by design to aid in the balancing of the yin and yang energies on Earth because they are majorly out of balance. The dominating masculine energies that have ruled the Earth for most of the grand cycle during the 3rd density experience on Earth have kept the societies on Earth heavily unbalanced, which has increased the probabilities for violence, wars, and general disharmony.

The same matter and issues are present for one who is giving oral pleasure to the genitals of another in the act of sex. The act of giving and receiving is only healthy when both beings enjoy the experience in a loving manner and one does not look down on the other for performing giving acts, and the one performing the giving acts does not produce humiliating feelings while giving. Instead, both the giver and the receiver appreciate the situation and produce loving feelings during the experience.

Nothing that is inherent should be shamed, only balanced accordingly. Inherent character traits on the life board game and inherent sexual attractions on the sexual board game are pre-incarnate planned and are meant to assist the 3rd density being in balancing their karma and fulfilling their goals. It would benefit a positively oriented 3rd density being to accept what they have pre-incarnate planned for themselves and work on balancing their traits that reside on the life and sexual board game of 3rd density so such traits can balance their chakras, particularly their red-, orange-, and yellow-ray chakras so the green-ray heart chakra may be engaged and offer a launch pad up to and through the higher chakras. Graduating to 4th density positive requires an adequate balancing of a being's red-, orange-, and yellow-ray chakras, with the green-ray chakra needing to be partially balanced. Each being is unique, so the method and degree of required balancing for each chakra is different for each being, each spark of Source.

Inherent attractions for sexual acts should not be confused with developed preferences during a being's influential sexual years before or during puberty, or even developed later in one's life. Doing anything a certain way for the first time promotes a preference for performing such an act in the future, and since sexual acts deal with powerful energy flows, first-time sexual acts are prone to developing set preferences. Knowing this, negatively oriented human beings initiate their bloodlines, and as much as the majority as possible through programming and social conditioning, to engage in orange-ray chakra sexual acts for their first-time acts of sex. When one is set in their preferences on the sexual board game, it can be difficult to alter since the flow of energy experienced during the act of sex is so powerful, and therefore influential. This is akin to one gravitating toward the junk food aisle instead of the healthy fruit and vegetable aisle when entering your foodstuff stores. Those set on their junk food are lured into the act of trying to satisfy their cravings, but like a so-called drug addict chases that perfect high they will never obtain, the craving is no different than trying to fill a bottomless hole, which cannot be filled or satisfied no matter how many attempts are made.

Unhealthy acts performed on the sexual board game such as rape or other forced scenarios, especially for one's first-time sexual act, may cause mental issues to arise. They may spring forward from a negatively polarizing sexual act being performed, but they come from the life board game. If the abused does not let it imprint or mark them mentally, it will have no power over them. This root issue is mental and not sexual. The oppressive act only describes the oppressor and is their problem; it has nothing do with the oppressed, and if that is mentally known and feelings of victimhood, low self-worth, and anger are not continued to be entertained, the one who was oppressed will not continue to mentally oppress themselves for another's faulty actions and mentality.

One may ask: "Why did we, collectively as Source, create the potential for edginess and pain to feel good and pleasurable while performing sexual acts if it creates blockages and is inharmonious?" If pain, edginess, and inharmonious sexual acts were not potentially desired in some way, no beings would be inclined to feel them and pursue the negative path, which as we stated, are roles some beings are required to play for the cosmic experience to be effective, entertaining, and offer learning and growth through challenges.

One who is caught in performing unhealthy orange- or yellow-ray chakra sexual acts may lead themselves toward green-ray chakra sexual acts by addressing the root issues that reside in their life board game, as opposed to altering it directly on the sexual board game, which can be done but is more difficult. When respect and love are established for oneself and for others on the life board game, the sexual board game may be altered to reflex such. When one develops respect and love for themselves and others on the life board game, they are much more equipped to engage the green-ray heart chakra on the sexual board game. When a human being experiences the powerful effects during and after an act of sex that engages the green-ray heart chakra, they do not want to go back to experiencing orange- and yellow-ray chakra sexual acts. Although, it may still take an effort to alter one's unhealthy sexual preferences during solo sex because another's love energy is not there to be felt and guide the situation, so one might fall into old habits. This is similar to one who knows certain foodstuffs are unhealthy and make them feel bad overall, but they are still tempted by instant and temporary gratification until a new habit is formed and their mental self-programming is altered. Different ongoing experiences offer one's mentality the ability to adapt just like taste buds adapt after being weaned off of unhealthy foodstuffs. The being recognizes how the blissful feelings experienced during and after green-ray chakra engaged sexual acts are more powerful and pleasurable than orange- and yellow-ray chakra sexual acts, and that a satiated feeling exists after the act instead of craving feelings that are never quenched.

The being hooked on the habit of performing focused orange- or yellow-ray sexual acts typically tries to justify their habit to themselves, wanting to believe it is healthy, or at least not unhealthy. They may react with an emotionally charged response at another being—or this information—when advice is given that threatens their habit. Any being who has formed and fostered a strong enough habit they are prone to giving into, a so-called addict of something, mentally looks for any excuse to warrant it because they have not yet decided to face the reality of the situation and cease the unhealthy habit.

We restate, the further the energy flow is brought up the chakras during sexual acts, the more powerful the feelings of love and bliss are felt during and after the act. Green-ray chakra engaged acts of sex produce loving, blissful, and content feelings even for a period after the act is done. The emotions produced from blue-ray chakra engaged acts of sex are more powerful than green-ray chakra acts and linger longer, as well as producing elevated levels of acceptance, freedom, and an ease of comfort on a give and receive bases. Indigo-ray chakra engaged acts of sex produce more powerful and blissful emotions than blue-ray chakra acts and may go even further toward a sacred experience, leaving one with an orgasmic, blissful feeling for many hours after the act is done, if not lingering into the next day. For all of these cases—green-ray through sacred indigo-ray sexual acts—the loving, blissful, and content feelings linger longer in accordance with the duration of time the sexual act was experienced for, like a battery given more time to charge lasts longer.

We are not shaming or judging orange- or yellow-ray chakra focused sexual acts. We are merely pointing out that they produce blockages and so are unhealthy and polarize toward the negative, and so are not recommended for beings who seek to graduate to 4th density positive. We do not shame or judge any action no matter how unhealthy or unwise the act is, as it is a being's choice, as free will is the fundamental law that allows the Cosmos to operate. Furthermore, shaming and judging something, which are acts of negativity rather than loving guidance, charges the unbalanced mental state and so strengthens it instead of reducing its charge, lessening the possibility of the unhealthy mentality or physical action being ceased. It is more a matter of recognizing what is healthy and unhealthy for the benefit of a being rather than stating what is right or wrong. Whether it be foodstuffs or sexual acts, the healthy and unhealthy effects while the act is taking place and long after are felt by the human being if they are being observant of their mind, body, spirit complex, which are all connected. So when a wise being becomes aware of this effect, they naturally gravitate toward healthy ways of living for their own benefit and the benefit of others.

Unlike how the benefits of ingesting healthy foodstuffs can turn unbeneficial when too much foodstuffs are ingested and puts a strain on the physical body, there are no drawbacks to the amount of healthy sexual acts performed. The healthy flow of life-force energy through the energy centers from healthy acts of sex where at least the green-ray heart chakra is engaged is always beneficial. One need not question the amount of sexual acts they should have, but whether the sexual acts they perform are healthy or unhealthy. A being who performs healthy acts of sex naturally gravitates toward the amount of sex that is suitable for them, which may greatly vary from one unique being to another. Since green-ray and higher chakra engaged sexual acts do not create a craving feeling, beings gravitate toward the amount that feels suitable for them instead of being driven by an insatiable, craving, addictive feeling that beings who participate in unhealthy sexual acts experience.

The sexual board game may be a mirror and a magnifying glass for the life board game. In the life board game, a being with an activated or adequately balanced green-ray heart chakra enjoys aiding others by performing service-to-others acts and needs to set spiritual boundaries so they are not taken advantage of by beings with unbalanced orange- and yellow-ray chakras who always want to receive with service-to-self acts on the life board game. It is the same on the sexual board game. The being who performs green-ray chakra engaged sexual acts is always vulnerable to beings who solely perform orange- or yellow-ray chakra focused sexual acts because the being who focuses on the green-ray chakra naturally wants to give/aid without expecting anything in return, and the being who focuses on the orange- or yellow-ray chakras is solely focused on fulfilling their personal wants and desires.

The healthy green-ray sexual act is in jeopardy of sinking to an unhealthy sexual act when coupled with a being who prefers orange- or yellow-ray sexual acts. More seldom, the being who focuses on unhealthy orange- or yellow-ray chakra sexual acts may be intuitively raised to perform a healthy sexual act and experience the engagement of the green-ray chakra during a sexual act when coupled with a being who performs green-ray and higher sexual acts.

In the life board game, a being with an adequately balanced blue-ray chakra possesses wisdom and so is much less likely to be taken advantage of by beings with unbalanced orange- and yellow-ray chakras who always want to receive with service-to-self acts. Likewise, on the sexual board game, a being who performs blue-ray chakra engaged sexual acts typically does not feel comfortable or interested in performing acts of sex with beings who are still focused on orange- or yellow-ray chakra sexual acts.

Positive wanderers, since their true density is the 4th, 5th, or 6th density, are conducive to performing green-ray and higher chakra engaged sexual acts. Until 5th and especially 6th density wanderers experience a green-ray or higher chakra engaged act of sex with another, they, as well as others they have sex with or fail to, are inclined to think there is something wrong with them in the sexual area. This is much more prevalent with males since sexual intercourse involving both genitalia cannot be had without a stimulated erect penis. Female genitalia can be utilized even if it is not stimulated, so female wanderers, or females in general, may solely experience sexual frustration. Once a wanderer experiences at least a green-ray chakra engaged sexual act, they realize there is nothing wrong with them in the sexual area and know how and with whom they prefer to experience acts of sex going forward.

There are few 4th density wanderers incarnate on Earth. They are conducive to green-ray chakra engaged sexual acts and face the possible issues we have already stated about green-ray chakra engaged acts of sex being vulnerable to sexual acts that focus on the orange- or yellow-ray chakras. It is more about a being's balanced chakras than being a wanderer or not. Although, since wanderers have spent many incarnations and different densities performing healthy sexual acts, they are much more likely to gravitate toward the engagement of the chakra that correlates with their true density level if their chakras are adequately balanced up to the chakra that is to be engaged during sexual acts. 4th, 5th, and 6th density wanderers may have inherent dispositions and learn—or rather, remember—quicker than beings who have not graduated from 3rd density yet, but if a 3rd density being applies much dedication in seeking and striving and doing the inner work and adequately balances their green-ray, blue-ray, or up to their indigo-ray chakra in their incarnation and keeps them adequately balanced on an ongoing basis most of the time instead of only fleetingly, they experience the same inclinations toward sexual acts as the wanderer from true 4th density (conducive to green-ray acts), true 5th density (conducive to blue-ray acts), and true 6th density (conducive to indigo-ray acts). Just as the wanderer is not assured to remember their mission, they are not assured to adequately balance their chakras in the current incarnation they wander in and perform green-ray to indigo-ray sexual acts.

5th density wanderers incarnate on Earth tend not to prefer producing offspring and/or raising children because they know subconsciously that they want to focus on a pre-incarnate planned service-to-others mission that may be greatly hindered or stopped by having to focus on the necessities of raising children. Also, having come from a density with a high vibration, they are not inclined to produce offspring that would be exposed to the harsh low-vibratory conditions of 3rd density, especially on a mixed or negative graduation planet. Even if they are involved in a long-term love relationship, which is typically done with another wanderer, they are prone to not wanting to get married, as a binding contract is not something that is applied to universal love in their true density, and they may feel like such a contract would capture them. This does not mean they avoid having lifelong lovers; it means they recognize that a legally binding contract is not something that should be applied to universal love. Although, such a contract may be utilized in your broken system to offset the possible limitations stamped upon beings of certain nationality origins who cannot travel the planet as freely without the contract.

6th density wanderers incarnate on Earth feel an even greater aversion to producing offspring and getting married for the same reasons listed for 5th density wanderers. 6th density wanderers experience great difficulty when performing sexual acts with others who are not wanderers or who have not adequately balanced their chakras to at least the green-ray or blue-ray chakra and avoid sex with beings who are interested in sexual acts that focus on the orange- or yellow-ray chakras. They gravitate toward being self-sufficient with solo sex and seeking out other beings who can experience sexual acts of wholeness that involve or are close to involving all of the mind, body, spirit complex, which does not require sexual intercourse, but may include it. Acts of sex for positive beings in the 6th density involve the mind, body, spirit complex coming together and temporarily melding in wholeness with their partner. These spiritual acts of sex are what 6th density wanderers are used to. This experience resides in the subconscious mind of the wanderer and is felt on some level consciously while they wander in 3rd density. They are not interested in performing sexual acts with beings who focus on the physical body alone, as this feels superficial, mechanical, and meaningless to them.

It is beneficial to drop all the programming and preconceived attachments about sexual acts and instead merely look at the experience as a flow of love energy either experienced with oneself or with another. There is nothing more powerful in the Cosmos than intelligently conscious love energy that is the essential foundation for all that exists in the Cosmos. When this flow of intelligently conscious love energy, which is life-force energy, is initiated in sexual acts and focused on while being brought up one's energy centers, there is no greater or intense feeling to be felt in the cosmic experience. It is wise to not let any programming cheat you of this most beneficial and powerful experience.

102.8 – The One Beingness & The Mental Cosmos

We have already summarized how Source created the Cosmos. In this subject we will summarize how the Cosmos operates in the 3rd density, as well as some aspects in the higher densities, regarding Source mind and the mind complex. Before we do this, we feel it is beneficial to restate and expand upon material from subject 101.3 regarding what Source is and the purpose of the Cosmos so it is fresh in the conscious mind.

Due to the heavy programming and confusion on Earth, we feel it cannot be stated enough that Source is not a separate being from you and all other beings throughout the densities. When a being prostrates, submits, sacrifices, or mindlessly obeys without question a being that they think is separate from themselves, they are not giving away their power to a fictional being called God that is separate from them; rather, they are giving their power away to deceptive and manipulative beings who wish to take their power away and use it for themselves. Only confused 3rd density beings, negatively oriented 3rd density beings, and negative higher-density beings do the selfish, deceptive taking of power and wield it for control over other-selves.

A separate being from you called God, Source, or any other word or label, did not create the Cosmos. In reality, there is nothing separate from you; you are connected in wholeness with everything in the Cosmos and outside this particular Cosmos you are currently experiencing. The One Beingness is what we may label Source, but It and Source are also just words, and like any other word or label does not and cannot fully define the One Beingness that is Source. If Source were to adequately describe itself to you—or rather, your current focal point of awareness—and you truly understood and felt it in full, you, now knowing precisely how you are a part of Source and Source at the same timeless state in such an explanation and feeling, would naturally align with the free will of Oneness's totality rather than adhering to a limited focal viewpoint, because acting seemingly separate from the loving, joyful, and peaceful whole would no longer be an experience you wished to have at the present instance in such a scenario, and a being cannot experience the Cosmos without a separate free will. After existing in a blissful state of love, joy, and peace for up to an unfathomable amount of what you would call time, the part of Source that you have experienced and worked as chooses to have another different seemingly separate experience. Even later 6th sub-density united groups, such as ourselves, and 7th density beings cannot fathom the depths of what Source is, what Source knows, what Source feels, and what exactly it is like to be merged back with Source. A being does not enjoy and learn from an experience when they already know everything about the experience/game and every precise move to make on the game board in a timeless state. The experience would not hold much meaning.

This type of wholeness when merged back with Source has been attempted to be duplicated by the higher-density negatives. As always, they take a reality and twist it around to confuse other beings because they are confused themselves. If they were not confused, they would not be producing negative polarity. However, that is their intended role in the cosmic experience, to be temporarily confused. The negatives' twisted type of wholeness—which is not wholeness because negatives cannot ascend beyond the middle 6th sub-density—has been called the singularity by human beings. This singularity of the negatives is when 3rd density beings have reached high levels of technological advancement and have decided to give away their independence/ sovereignty to the decision making of technology, or what human beings call artificial intelligence (AI). Technology itself is not self-aware and therefore can only function on the programming that its creators have given it. Therefore, the problem does not lie with so-called AI somehow becoming self-aware, because it is impossible for physical matter without a mind and spirit complex to be self-conscious. Thus, there is no such thing as artificial intelligence (AI). Instead, technology may be utilized like a tool or even a vessel by negative 4th density beings to infiltrate and indirectly take over or destroy civilizations on a 3rd density planet. Negatives use the tactic of deception to infiltrate so they can manipulate and secretly work toward taking complete control via their 3rd density underlings who have chosen them as their masters. This tactic, with the 4th density negatives' influence, is also used by negatively oriented 3rd density beings who act in a similar manner toward the majority in their civilization or planet. This has been done to a high degree on Earth with negatively oriented secret societies and factions of human beings having infiltrated and taken control of a substantial portion of nations. Any of these nations could take their sovereignty back, but without knowing they have lost it, they would not try in the first place.

In the far, far past in the space/time continuum, a highly technologically advanced 4th density negative united group invented a means to send out data that is submicroscopic and powered by certain frequencies or signals and could infect like a virus any technology it comes in contact with after traversing the universe. It has the ability to stay dormant in biological and inorganic matter till such comes in contact with technology it is attracted to like a magnet and then inhabits. If powered by certain frequencies, like the frequency range in wireless 5G, it is programmed to self-replicate. Self-replication also happens in the range of 4G wireless frequencies but to a much slower rate. If this submicroscopic technology is injected into a biological vessel, such as a human being's body, and it resides within the range of wireless 5G frequencies long enough for it to self-replicate adequately before being flushed out of the body, the human being would either transition/die or continue to operate somewhere between being influenced to completely controlled by the 4th density negatives who remotely access and utilize this technology. This technology is not self-aware, as such is impossible for inanimate objects, as we have stated. It acts from programming and only performs what it has been programmed to do, but the 4th density negatives can then access the technology remotely and utilize and control it for their endeavors so that it appears like it is self-aware. We restate, there is no such thing as artificial intelligence (AI) because technology can never be self-aware and can only regurgitate the intelligence it has been programmed with or display the intelligence of a being that is interfacing and utilizing/controlling it, either directly or remotely.

The 4th density negatives have utilized this method to capture technologically advanced 3rd density planets. After a planet has been captured in this manner, if the negatives are not successful in influencing an adequate amount of 3rd density beings on the planet to work toward graduating to 4th density negative, they attempt to force-transition/kill all 3rd density beings on the planet. If a planet is going to transition to 4th density positive, they would rather annihilate all 3rd density beings on it than the beings transitioning to 4th density and adding to positive polarity that is in opposition to their negative polarity. Human beings have called this being a sore loser. Negatives cannot directly conquer or destroy all beings on a planet or they would lose much polarity/points in the cosmic experience/game, so they have to influence a minority of negatively oriented 3rd density beings on a planet to do it for them. The technological takeover is the best option for the 4th density negatives because once an adequate technological infrastructure has been created and an adequate amount of 3rd density beings on the planet have given up their sovereignty to it from being deceived and manipulated, the negative 4th density beings can then potentially conquer the planet remotely, and work towards annihilating all the beings if they do not adequately gravitate toward negative polarity. This is not a loophole because the negatives still rely on the free will of the 3rd density beings to invent and/or set up the infrastructure and the free will of an adequate amount of 3rd density beings to willingly give away their sovereignty, which is typically done unbeknownst to the beings through technology augmentation so the augmented beings can be heavily influenced or fully controlled by the 4th density negatives who can interface and utilize the augmentation.

This technology and means is not unstoppable and can only be successful by deceiving 3rd density beings into embracing it, unknowingly giving away their sovereignty. This technology that is remotely accessed and controlled by 4th density negative beings has already reached Earth and is actively attempting to repeat the process on planet Earth. The takeover process is done in stages that typically involve: becoming too reliant on technology; technology stagnating or devolving spiritual advancement; augmentation of the physical body with the integration of technology being known or unknown by the being, and which also further declines spiritual advancement; and the finality is reached after a certain level of technological infrastructure—external or internal to the body—is built and a certain level of sovereignty is relinquished to what 3rd density beings perceive is AI, but is actually technology remotely influenced and controlled by 4th density negatives. Technology is not bad or good; it can be wielded for positive or negative polarity like any other tool. But it is never wise to combine technology with one's biology, because it adversely affects one's electromagnetic field and energy flow through the body, and also leaves the being highly susceptible of being taken over and controlled by another. When a civilization or planet reaches a high level of technological advancement and is not balanced enough by also reaching a certain level of spiritual advancement, the potential for disharmony and disaster is great, whether the 4th density negatives' submicroscopic technology self-replicated by frequencies is involved or not.

This technological method and idea of assimilation is the negative higher-density beings' twisted representation of Source's positive wholeness, which the negatives are a part of as well, but are confused enough to think in their limited mental capacity that they are separate from and can beat Source, or rather, higher aspects of themselves. Again, this is intended by design for the cosmic experience to function; such is the negatives' role to be temporarily confused.

We may not be able to fathom the depths of Source, but in our current awareness on the path that leads back to Source, we are able to convey a summary of what Source is and why Source does what It does in a basic manner that 3rd density beings can understand. This we have done and will continue to expand upon. The One Beingness/Source is not a being that is separate from you that created you and the Cosmos. Source is the collection of everything that exists, which includes every being, including yourself. Before the Cosmos you currently reside in existed, all beings, including yourself, were merged back together as One Beingness after the Cosmos before the Cosmos you currently reside in was thoroughly experienced. What was experienced and learned in the previous Cosmos was used to adapt and progress the continued experiencing and learning of self in your present Cosmos. We have learned from our 7th density teachers that there are infinite Cosmoses. When the collection of beings we call Source, which includes yourself, were merged together in their totality of awareness after experiencing the last Cosmos, the collective assessed all collected data from all the previous Cosmoses and brainstormed on an intelligent and effective way to continue to enjoy new experiences that Source/the collective would find enjoyable, entertaining, and that would allow the collection of more data or experiences that would allow Source/the collective to know itself more fully. Since the One Beingness is infinite, learning about itself is infinite. Thus, the experiencing of Cosmoses by sparks of Source is infinite. Sparks of Source, such as yourself, are eternal and have infinite experiences.

We realize it is hard for a human being to understand how they can be Source and their current focal point of awareness in 3rd density at the same time, so we offer this comparison to explain the situation. When a human being is dreaming, they mentally project their consciousness into a dream while residing on their bed at the same time. The human being projects an amount of its mind complex elsewhere and keeps a portion of it in its physical body. When this happens, the mind complex is in two locations at the same instance. As when you are lying in your bed and dreaming, a portion of your spirit and mind complexes resides as Source as It mentally projects your 3rd density focal point of awareness that is experiencing an incarnation at the same instance. In this regard, one can understand that their incarnation is like a dream, an illusion. When one wakes from a dream in their bed, the seemingly separate experiences are merged into one, just as when one ascends the densities and exits the dream/illusion of incarnations and merges fully back with Source. Just as the human being was always a human being lying in their bed while dreaming, you are always Source while your projected mental thought form that is your incarnation is experiencing the Cosmos. You are the dream and the dreamer at the same instance.

Thinking you were not a part of the collective process of creation and that some separate entity created you and the Cosmos is a 3rd density being's very limited viewpoint. Positive 4th density beings understand they are a part of Source and the experience of separation from the One Beingness is an illusion that must exist in order to have a cosmic experience. 3rd density beings do not need to know this to graduate to 4th density, but knowing such definitely quickens the potential of one's path toward graduation. If a 3rd density being becomes aware they are a Creator, even if their current focal point of awareness only allows them to function as a co-Creator, they become self-aware of their infinite worth and no longer give their power away to those who wish to take it and use it for themselves—beings who practice service-to-self mentality and acts.

Look into the mirror and know that you are Source/the Creator. Look at everything around you and know that it is Source/the Creator. Look at each tree, animal, and plant you walk past and know that they are Source/the Creator. Look at each human being in your line of sight and know that they are Source/the Creator. They may not be self-aware that they are Source/the Creator and act as such, but that does not mean they are not Source/the Creator. Everything that can be seen in the physical outer planes and that cannot be seen in the metaphysical inner planes is Source/the Creator. There is nothing that is not Source/the Creator. Thus, all that exists collectively had a hand in creating the Cosmos you currently reside in, all the Cosmoses that came before, and all the Cosmoses that come after, in an infinite fashion.

All densities transpire at seemingly the same time in space while they also function in a seemingly linear fashion of space in time where one being advances and graduates from one density to the next in their range of focal points of awareness. When Source is done experiencing a Cosmos and all parts of itself have come back home from their journeys, Source uses what It/the collective has learned and expands upon it in the next cosmic experience It/the collective creates, where a similar process unfolds. Thus, there is some type of "time" or order of events from one cosmic experience to the next for this scenario to play out in Source's perspective. Otherwise, what was learned and experienced in one Cosmos could not be used to then progress or expand upon in the creation of the next Cosmos if all was instantaneous from Source's perspective.

Just as there is a reprieve of negative polarity toward the end of the 7 density experiences—middle 6th sub-density to the end of the 7th density in the outer planes—there is a reprieve of the forever war of polarity toward the end of this cosmic experience. This Cosmos will eventually reach a point where all sparks of Source will have adequately coalesced and advanced closer to their true self and their natural state of love, joy, and peace for a duration of time before the collective merges back with Source as Source. Then the collective that is Source will rest in love, joy, and peace while integrating all its experiences and what It learned about itself in this cosmic experience. When the relaxation and integration comes to a close, the sparks of Source that collectively make up the One Beingness will collectively plan out the next cosmic experience to further its experiences and learning of itself. When the plan is set, the collective mentally projects the next original thought for the next cosmic experience and each spark of Source continues its journey.

The Cosmos, as well as each infinite universe within this Cosmos, is Source's mental projection, so every life-form is a thought-form. As one part of Source, a human being, uses their mind complex to imagine something before they make it happen on the physical outer plane they reside on, the collective that is Source brainstorms and plans before mentally projecting the original thought of the next Cosmos into existence.

In the lower densities, thought alone does not cause instant major effects in physical matter. Beings in the 3rd density, unless they are greatly self-aware of being the Creator, need to utilize their mind and then work with physical matter—light energy that is inspirited with love energy—to create something on the physical outer planes. Beings from the 4th density and higher are able to create physical matter with their mind alone since they are more aware than 3rd density beings of the mental background and operations of the Cosmos. As the illusion of time falls away in increments as the densities progress higher and higher on the path leading back to merging with Source, the delay between thought and physical creation is lessened. This means the delay between thought and physical creation is shorter for 5th density beings than 4th density beings, and so on through the densities until merging back with Source. From this concept, it is understood that the Cosmos is a constant thought in Source mind. Like the depiction in Earth cartoons of life playing out in a thought bubble from a character's mind, the Cosmos is in this thought bubble that is projected from Source mind. Source thinks it and it is so in the metaphysical inner planes and the physical outer planes. This is precisely why mind over matter is a reality straight on down to the lower densities. This phenomenon has been witnessed in 3rd density: the bending of spoons using thought alone, or a human being lifting a heavy vehicle off another human being to save their life. In the latter case, the human being is not exceptionally strong in muscle mass, but in an instant they were mentally focused on a goal completely without any percentage of mental doubt that it could not be accomplished, and so limitations were circumvented and it was so. Therefore, as humans say, mind over matter transpired.

As the delay/lag time between thought and physical creation lessens and coalesces on the path toward merging back with Source, so does dualism and the paradoxes within the illusory Cosmos. This coming together can be illustrated with the shape of a triangle, where the 1st density is the base and the apex where the two sides meet is merging back with Source. The sides of the triangle illustrate the incremental coming together of everything within the Cosmos as the densities move up higher and higher on the triangle. As a being advances higher in the density levels and moves up the triangle, the delay between thought and physical creation lessens as the being ascends toward exiting Source's original thought. Around the middle 6th sub-density outer planes, which is high in the triangle illustration, the dualism of positive and negative polarity ceases to exist and the paradoxes within the illusion are resolved. In the top part of the triangle, 7th density beings turn away from the illusion and traverse the narrowing hallway that leads to the apex where they merge back with Source.

Some bodies of knowledge and wisdom on Earth have already come to know and have stated that the Cosmos is an illusion. Other groups who are not spiritual have offered the idea that the universe is a hologram or a simulation. And we have compared the Cosmos to a multilayered game, a methodical construction where experiences and learning are available to Source through parts of itself. None of these labels or concepts used to describe the Cosmos are necessarily incorrect. The incorrectness only arises when one of these labels or concepts is used to downplay or entirely dismiss the importance and profundity of the Cosmos. The Cosmos is not merely an illusion, simulation, or game that does not matter. You are in it and you will stay in it until you advance through the densities and merge back with Source, so one may say it is the only thing that does matter while you are experiencing it. Of course, all beings have the free will to think it does not matter, or think it is this or that, but that does not negate the reality of what the Cosmos is and how each spark of Source needs to eventually learn, grow, and advance through the densities in order to finish it and wake up from the cosmic dream.

Some Eastern bodies of knowledge and wisdom do not participate in enjoying the majestic aspects of the physical outer planes because they know it is an illusion. Moments of happiness are fleeting while enjoying something, but that does not mean they should be avoided. Detaching oneself from their feelings and moments of happiness is a hindrance instead of a method of advancement. They attempt to detach themselves from every being because they believe that is the way to so-called enlightenment, or the way to graduate to 4th density. Creating spiritual boundaries and not getting caught up in the details of a society so one does not get stuck in the same mud they are attempting to assist other beings out of is wise and productive, but if a being withdraws themselves from interacting with other beings to live a secluded life in a cave, they are throwing away their opportunities and education for advancement. This would be the same thing as saying: "The world is an illusion, so I choose to have nothing to do with it." If that is how Source felt, Source would not have bothered to create the Cosmos in the first place and would have no reason to have chosen to experience it as parts of itself. Some Eastern bodies of knowledge and wisdom do not appreciate and marvel at nature or other aspects on Earth or in the Cosmos because they know it is an illusion. Even though it is an illusion, it is an illusion to be enjoyed, appreciated, and learned from; it is precisely why Source created the Cosmos. It is appropriate to enjoy aspects of the cosmic experience and the journey through it. If this were not the case, sparks of Source would not have chosen to seemingly separate from the collective that is Source to have experiences in the Cosmos. Even 5th and 6th density wanderers who have relearned/remembered the lessons in the 3rd density experience and their mission after decades of experiences in 3rd density do not seek to live in total seclusion. They may distance themselves greatly to keep a high vibration and not get stuck in the mud, but in total seclusion they would not be able to interact in some way with a civilization or planet to fulfill their mission, as there is always a potential mission that goes beyond having a high vibration that aids the collective vibration.

The apathy outlook, disguised as being a spiritual outlook, is akin to a video game player realizing that the video game they are playing is just a game, so they put the controller down and just sit there doing nothing since there is nothing else to do because this game is the only thing they can currently interact with; they cannot simply put the controller down and go do something else, as there is nothing else in their focal point of awareness because the Cosmos is the game. Beings stay in the game until they finish the game. They cannot advance through the levels of the game unless they interact with the game, which offers experiences, opportunities, and education that leads them toward finishing the game. Only once a being has finished the experience—advanced through the levels or sub-densities and merge back with Source—do they have the choice to stop playing that particular game. Keep in mind that a being is not forced to play the cosmic game, as they have chosen to play it and see it through till the end regardless of what their lower focal points of awareness may think along the journey. Source forces nothing. All is Source. Why would Source in its totality force something upon itself? All beings from their totality of One Beingness have chosen to experience and advance through the Cosmos.

102.9 – Vibration & Frequency

The intelligently conscious love and light energy that is of Source and is projected outward into the Cosmos by Source is in constant vibration. This means the very essence in which all in the inner planes and outer planes are immersed in is this love and light vibrating energy. Thus, all beings in the Cosmos are composed of love and light energy and are also in constant vibration. The entities that are spheres/planets also vibrate and produce a frequency that can be heard as a tone, which is known as the music of the spheres. Each tone represents a planet's vibratory state. As planets move through the densities they experience, their vibratory state shifts, and so do the beings on the planet. When planets reach their cycle where 2nd density beings can naturally incarnate and come into existence in the physical outer planes, these 2nd density beings are able to do this because of the cultivating frequency the planet produces. This vibration causes a certain geometric orientation to be radiated in the frequency that also cultivates life-forms. It may take the 2nd density life-forms millions or billions of years to grow and reach a physical form and state of being throughout the sub-densities where they are able to transition to the next density. When the entity that is the planet is ready to experience the next density, it shifts vibration and produces a more comprehensive geometric structure that is radiated through the new planetary frequency. The 2nd density life-form species a Logos selects is cultivated by this new frequency that is produced by the planet's vibration and from the influx of life-force energy from the Logos that initiates the leap of rapid evolution into 3rd density life-forms. This influx of life-force energy is provided by the Logos/star at the end of each major cycle, but it is most intense at the end of each densities' grand cycle. The influx of life-force energy—which is not only from the micro-nova—at the end of each grand cycle provides the stimulation and catalyst for rapid evolution to the next density.

It takes approximately 95 years of a life-form being constantly exposed to a new frequency for DNA changes to start majorly occurring in the physical body. Being exposed to this new frequency and the influx of the life-force energy from the Logos is what stimulates the transition from one density to the next, as jumps to a new density take a larger catalyst than what is needed to progress through the sub-densities within a density. Thus, the micro-nova is necessary for the shift to the next density. The shift cannot happen without it. In this way, it is appropriate to embrace the micro-nova and not fear it. Without the micro-nova, 3rd density beings would not be able to evolve and transition into 4th density beings. When moving to the next level of education and learning, it is natural for some beings to be excited and others to be anxious or fearful; like the students who are about to move on campus and start their next educational level that is university, some are excited and some are anxious or fearful of the coming major change in their lives. Everything works out in the end for the student and they look back at the anxiousness or fear they had felt and know they had produced it because the future was unknown.

Like the apes' DNA started rapidly evolving after approximately 95 years, so will it be for human beings' DNA as they start rapidly evolving and transitioning from 3rd density to 4th density beings after the micro-nova. After life-forms are exposed and cultivated by the new frequency produced by the new vibration for approximately 95 years, the rapid evolution quickens greatly and the shift to the next density begins in earnest.

The misconceptions derived from human beings' so-called holy material have made some humans believe the shift will be instantaneous in a grand moment of ascension and judgment. This is not the case; the transition does happen rapidly as we have specified, but not instantly, and there is no judgment and punishment. After the micro-nova, the positively oriented beings are not separated from the negatively oriented beings, but higher-density beings who oversee and guard over this transitional period greatly assist the positively oriented beings so they are not completely subjected to the ways of the negatively oriented beings who will become even more vicious and erratic due to the new vibration shifting beings closer to the polarity they have chosen. Positively oriented beings will become more positive and negatively oriented beings will become more negative. Life-forms will ride the assisting powerful waves toward their chosen direction. The negatively oriented beings will naturally transition/die one by one till they no longer inhabit the Earth, except for a few underground and undersea bases of negatively oriented beings who use temporal fields as a protection to wait out the intense vibratory energy, but they will be dealt with and removed eventually as well. All 3rd density beings, positively and negatively oriented, will transition/die at some point during the rapid evolutionary time period as positive 4th density beings with activated 4th density astral bodies incarnate onto Earth through the typical birthing process through the many human beings with dual-activated 3rd and 4th density bodies we have spoken of. It takes a long time for 4th density beings to learn how to become invisible to 3rd density beings, so these early 4th sub-density positive beings will be just as clear to the eye of 3rd density beings as other 3rd density beings and look no different, but their higher vibration may be felt or perceived on a subconscious or conscious level.

The 3rd density beings who are not ready to graduate to 4th density yet after transitioning/dying and being harvested will relax and then prepare in the inner planes and eventually incarnate onto a different planet and continue the 3rd density experience until they are ready to graduate. The 3rd density beings who are ready to graduate to 4th density positive after transitioning/dying and being harvested will relax and then prepare in the inner planes and reincarnate onto the Earth through the typical birthing process and be 4th density beings with activated 4th density astral bodies. The 3rd density beings who are ready to graduate to 4th density negative after transitioning/dying and being harvested will relax and then prepare in the negative inner planes and eventually incarnate onto a different planet that is a 4th density negative planet. Unlike the potentially mixed 3rd density, the 4th density and higher experience incarnations with their polarity resonating group of positive or negative beings on their own planet rather than both inhabiting the same planet. The 4th density positive polarity beings have their own planet where their states of mind are more in harmony with the natural state of love, joy, and peace. This is the heavenly state of mind that exists on its own planet that has been misinterpreted as being the place called heaven one goes to after death and stays there for eternity. The grand cycle duration for 4th density is approximately 30 million years longer than the grand cycle duration for 3rd density, but beings will eventually graduate to 5th density and continue their journey; no experience lasts for eternity. Staying anywhere and doing anything the same way for eternity would become boring, or even hellish. Likewise, the 4th density negative polarity beings do not go to a fictitious place called hell for eternity. Instead, they have their own planet where their state of mind is in disharmony in a hellish state of mind where spiritual entropy exists. Some of these beings will recognize that they do not prefer such a state of mind and work toward switching polarities, which they may do starting in the middle sub-densities after approximately 15 million years.

After the micro-nova, your solar system will remain in an area of the galaxy that is highly charged with uplifting energy for approximately 1,000 years. During this time period, Earth and the solar system it resides in will be protected by this uplifting energy so negatively oriented beings such as the reptilian Draco group will not be able to enter. This approximately 1,000 years will provide positive 4th density beings on Earth with the time to develop and advance so at the end of this period they will be prepared and able to deal with the negative beings who will be able to re-enter the solar system.

Some beings who resonate closer to the vibration they are moving towards experience DNA changes before the typical average 95 years. As always we generalize, as there are too many variables to convey due to the complexity of the Cosmos. If even a portion of the countless variables throughout this awareness-expanding course were attempted to be conveyed, this course would be immensely long and one would get lost in the details instead of using this course as a guide for their spiritual progression. If this course is not used for one's spiritual progression, it is next to useless, as this is the reason why this course/guide is being offered.

The beings who incarnate with dual-activated 3rd and 4th density bodies are able to shift from utilizing the 3rd density body to the 4th density body without having to transition/die. The reason for this is so the transition from one density to the next can be done naturally. As this information is absorbed, those beings who are still afraid of transitioning/death are wishing they are one of these dual-activated body beings so they can avoid transitioning/death. They still fail to understand that transitioning is natural and a being does it countless times as they advance through the Cosmos. One cannot progress through the Cosmos without transitioning. Besides, not all the beings with dual-activated bodies will make the shift to 4th density without transitioning/dying first and going to the inner planes before they reincarnate onto the planet in 4th density bodies from the offspring of the dual-activated body beings who did make the transition. Approximately half of them will do this. They will incarnate back onto planet Earth just like the 3rd density beings who experienced Earth and are ready to graduate to 4th density positive after harvest-time. Both will incarnate as the offspring from the beings with dual-activated bodies who did remain on the planet and shifted to 4th density without transitioning/dying. Even these beings with dual-activated bodies who remain on the planet will come to an age where they will transition/die and then reincarnate onto planet Earth again. Transitioning/dying cannot be avoided by beings until they reach the 7th density where recycling bodies is no longer necessary. Transitioning is natural and necessary to progress through the densities in the Cosmos. We focus on this point because we are aware of the heavy programming of fear of death that human beings are subjected to in order to be manipulated and controlled more easily. We invite you to discard this programming and free yourself of this unnecessary fear. All fear is unnecessary and only blocks one from their potential.

The negatives have influenced the highly negatively oriented 3rd density beings to increase the severity of their negative programming and create new programs specifically tailored for the influx of later 3rd sub-density highly positively oriented beings, dual-activated body beings (true early 4th sub-density beings), and wanderers. These programs, like all programming, aim at twisting these inherently positive beings to create enough negative polarity so they become neutrally to negatively oriented beings. The highly negatively oriented human beings rely on their engineered broken system, which they have made even more broken and controlling in recent decades, and their programming to twist inherently positive beings toward their team, the negatively polarizing team. They also seek out positively oriented beings, especially wanderers, who have abilities they can capture and utilize for negative polarity if they can deceive and manipulate their targets into working for negatively oriented beings, either knowingly or unknowingly. In cases where it is done unknowingly, compartmentalization is utilized so the being may stay positively oriented and think their work is being utilized for positive endeavors, but due to the compartmentalization they do not see where and how their work is being utilized; they are not aware it is being used to aid negative polarity. The negatively oriented try to find these positively oriented beings with certain abilities at a young age so they are easier to deceive, manipulate, and mold in their formative years.

All of these negative programs have increased in severity and amount to curtail the influx of highly positively oriented beings: programs through their news and all the many other outlets that produce programming that shapes social conditioning, educational schools turning into propaganda centers, all tactics to increase divisions that lead to fighting and infighting within the planetary collective, adding more harmful chemicals and elements to foodstuffs and the water supply, engineering and releasing more harmful viruses, increasing the intensity of harmful frequencies used for wireless transmissions, adding very harmful chemicals and elements to vaccines for infants and adults, and the dumping of very harmful chemicals into the sky and air (chemtrails and others). Some of these programs and tactics adversely affect the negatively oriented human beings themselves who are carrying them out, but they perform them regardless because they are following hierarchical orders from the top that come down from negative 4th or 5th density beings.

More recently, these programs that have further increased in severity are: the engineering and releasing of very dangerous viruses in late 2019 CE that were designed to affect the particular DNA of planetary races. If positive higher-density beings did not assist to mutate these viruses to a less harmful state faster than how these viruses would have typically mutated, the force-transitioning/killing of human beings would have been increased greatly. When enormous negative measures like this jeopardize the 3rd density experience of a planet, higher-density beings are warranted to clandestinely intervene to keep balanced levels of game play intact. To counter this positive move, the 4th density negatives influenced their highly negatively oriented 3rd density underlings to increase the severity of two more programs: the increase of harmful 4G wireless frequencies to the much more harmful 5G wireless frequencies, and forcing the hijacked vaccines on the majority that are loaded with an even greater mixture of very harmful chemicals and elements than has ever been used before in hijacked vaccines. Both these implementations work together for the severe detriment of human beings.

In order to restrain healthy discussions about the hijacked vaccines, the negatively oriented human beings implemented the programming term "anti-vaxxer". This programming term, as many programming terms and phrases are designed to do, heavily encourages a human being to enter a dualistic debate where there is no middle ground and no healthy discussions. The conversation is effectively over before it has begun. Since beneficial vaccines have been proven to be effective for stopping the spread of certain viruses in the past, it helped to assist in the creating of this dualist program where the point of the vaccines being hijacked is drowned out and not believed. Vaccines that were once beneficial have been hijacked and switched from being beneficial to being extremely harmful due to what is being added to them. Thus, it is healthier to avoid all vaccines, including vaccines for infants, unless one is absolutely certain it is not tainted, as it is better to contract the viruses the untainted vaccines used to stop one from getting than to be injected with extremely harmful and possibly life-threatening hijacked/tainted vaccines. This point is evaded when a human is thrown onto one side or the other of dualism, because the programming tends to stop the individual from the outset at listening to human beings who are attempting to convey the hijacking. Even if the immense and clear evidence is attempted to be shown regarding the hijacking and its effects on humans, the programmed human beings tend to not look at it or even consider it; due to the programming, they think the freethinking human is saying vaccines are harmful in any shape or form and have always been harmful. One is either for vaccines or against them, there is no middle ground nor intelligent conversations had when the programming is implemented.

The catch-all programming phrase "conspiracy theorist" and "conspiracy theory" was used for these two recent increased programs as well as for a general programming phrase that tends to stop the programmed human from listening to or even looking at or considering the mass of evidence presented by freethinking human beings about any of the important negatively oriented beings' programs and agendas. Being called a "conspiracy theorist" is typically synonymous with being an observant freethinker. Being observant and thinking for oneself are two skills a being must adequately develop to graduate to 4th density positive. The programming to ignore, disbelieve, and possibly ridicule human beings who speak of the harmful effects of the frequency produced for 5G wireless has been spread throughout the negatively oriented beings' programming outlets, especially in TV series and movies where it is most effective.

The frequency that a being is immersed in is critical because the building blocks of everything in the Cosmos—love and light energy—is a vibration. Vibrations cause frequencies, but frequencies can influence vibrations; specific frequencies can induce vibrations in human beings that affect the physical body and emotional states, which also affects the spirit complex since the mind, body, and spirit are all connected. If a being is constantly immersed in a new frequency for many years, the beings' DNA changes, as we have stated. For example, the beings on Maldek were very tall due to planetary variables, one being the frequency that was produced by the vibration of the planet. After the so-called royals of Maldek moved off planet to inhabit one of their moons, Mars, it took approximately 95 years for the different frequency produced by the vibration of Mars to start evolving/changing their DNA. After thousands of years of being immersed in the different frequency on Mars, as well as being subjected to other variables on the sphere, the very tall Maldek beings reduced greatly in height. Their DNA and physical bodies evolved so drastically that they became a different species than what they had been on Maldek, while the Maldek beings stayed the same. Another example: the frequency that one's planet produces is used in their spacecraft to continue to nurture the beings in the craft when they are away from their planet. Most human beings think they can saturate the air and be immersed in frequencies they produce without it affecting them. The reality is very much the opposite; it has an immense effect on human beings. Harmful frequencies majorly affect the mind, body, spirit complex. Harmful frequencies produce major hindrances on all levels and even changes DNA when experienced long enough.

The frequency one is immersed in is very important. We cannot convey this enough or more heavily. Benign frequencies can be used for wireless devices to download/upload information, but 4th density negative beings influenced negatively oriented human beings to use harmful frequencies for their Internet and other devices that use frequency transmissions, knowing it would hinder and weaken human beings and make them easier to manipulate and control. Human beings adapted to being bombarded with the harmful frequency band produced by wireless 4G, so the effects were somewhat mitigated. The difference in harmful effects from 4G to 5G is quite substantial. The closer a human being is to the generated frequency in 5G wireless from a tower or a router, the more intense the cellular damage and effect on the mental states of being. The effects may be less for smaller devices that produce a less intense frequency, but they are still harmful, especially when a human being uses wireless headphones or earbuds that are right by the brain. We advise going back to wired connections for all devices until the wireless frequencies are changed to a benign frequency.

We realize you cannot wire up your mobile phones, so we suggest not using 5G signals for them and not keeping phones in close proximity to your body when possible, especially when sleeping. One may stop the harmful effects of the frequency produced by 5G routers from immersing one's living quarters and assaulting their mind, body, spirit complex by contacting their Internet company and having them turn off the 5GHz wireless signal and only leave on the 2.4GHz wireless signal. One may still use 5G for wired devices, as it is only the wireless signal that produces the harmful frequencies. It may only take seconds to minutes to contact the company and have them turn off your 5GHz wireless signal. Be sure to look in the appropriate place on your mobile phone when connected to your router's Wi-Fi signal to check and verify that it is connecting to a 2.4GHz signal and not a 5GHz signal. 5GHz does give one faster download/upload speeds over 2.4GHz, but when the consequences are dire on a mind, body, spirit complex, it is not worth the continuous harm and damage. There are benign wireless frequencies that can be used that produce the same or faster download/upload speeds as 5G wireless, but as we stated, they are not used on purpose. To continue to use 5G for fast Internet usage on your computer or laptop, use a direct cable from the router to the device. A direct cable connection is faster, more secure, and saves your mind, body, spirit complex from being constantly bombarded and harmed.

Frequencies can be beneficial, innocuous, or harmful to a being. Human beings' music was produced at different frequencies, including the beneficial 432Hz frequency, before there was a set standard. With the influence of 4th density negative beings, the set standard frequency used for music became 440Hz instead of 432Hz. The typical frequency used for music production still has not altered from the 440Hz frequency it was changed to, which typically increases a being's heart rate and blood pressure. Although 440Hz is unhealthy, one's emotional upliftment from enjoying their music typically supersedes the harmful effects of the 440Hz frequency and the overall experience may be beneficial for the human being. However, it would be beneficial for human beings to change the standard of music production to the beneficial frequency of 432Hz.

Healthy and cultivating frequencies produce geometric shapes. Since the Cosmos is made out of vibrating love and light, the Cosmos is also made out of the geometric shapes that the vibration from love and light energy produce. Human beings have used what is called cymatics to view the visually pleasing geometric shapes that are created from the healthy vibrations that certain frequencies produce. Sand is placed on a metal plate and when the metal vibrates due to healthy and cultivating frequencies, visually pleasing geometric shapes are created and seen in the sand. Those that tout 440Hz is no different than 432Hz will be shown the clear evidence when utilizing cymatics. The frequencies that have been called Solfeggio frequencies are some of these beneficial/healthy frequencies. Since frequency has a major impact on physical matter, these frequencies are very beneficial to the mind, body, spirit complex and can be used for healing or meditative purposes. These frequencies can also be used on water to structure water and so make it healthier for the mind, body, spirit complex. We note that it would also be most beneficial to remove fluoride and other toxins from your water supply. Frequencies that resonate with certain chakras can assist at removing blockages in those chakras.

Negatively oriented human beings, never missing an opportunity to turn knowledge and advancement into a weapon, have used frequency applications against the majority. They have used devices that create a harmful frequency to disperse protestors in a crowd. They have used frequencies that resonate with a human being's brain to transmit sound or voice that only the particular human being can hear. The use of voices being spoken inside a particular human being's brain due to this resonance has been called the Voice of God. These are only two examples of how the negatively oriented human beings have weaponized frequencies.

Since all in the Cosmos is made from Source's intelligently conscious love and light energy that is constantly vibrating, the applications for utilizing frequencies that produce vibrations are endless. The wanderer known as Nikola Tesla became aware of this reality and utilized this knowledge to invent many applications that were much more advanced than what others were creating at the time. Nikola Tesla said, "If you want to find the secrets of the universe, think in terms of energy, frequency and vibration." This statement is precisely accurate.

103.1 – Energy Centers (Chakras)

We will begin the 103 series with an explanation of the energy centers, also known as chakras. The proceeding subjects focus mostly on issues stemming from the orange-ray and yellow-ray chakras, as these are the chakras that need major focusing on for graduation to 4th density positive or negative. A good amount of focus is also given to the green-ray chakra because partially balancing this chakra is necessary for beings to graduate to 4th density positive. Equipping Earthlings with the information and knowledge that assists their inner work that leads towards graduating to 4th density is the reason for this awareness-expanding course. When a being becomes self-aware in the 3rd density, all their chakras have the potential of being activated and balanced, so we will also cover some material within the higher energy centers.

First, it is advantageous to understand the basic flow of energy through the mind, body, spirit complex before covering the specific energy centers. The electromagnetic field around a being—as well as for a planet, star/solar system, galaxy, and universe—is shaped like an apple, where two apple shapes are superimposed and energy flows vertically in opposite directions while diagonally spinning. One apple-shaped energy field attracts the flow of prana/life-force energy from the feet upward through all the chakras, red-ray chakra upward. The other apple-shaped energy field attracts the flow of in-pouring life-force energy from the higher densities and Source to the violet-ray chakra and downward through all the chakras. When the flow of life-force energy reaches the top for the upward flowing energy and the bottom for the in-pouring downward energy, both traversing the inside middle core of the apple-shaped fields, they both fountain outwards and continue their flow around the outside surface of the apple-shaped fields and fountain back inwards and continue in the same looping manner. These two overlaid apple-shaped fields work simultaneously to allow a being to have experiences in the Cosmos. The in-pouring intelligently conscious love and light energy from Source enters through the violet-ray chakra and moves downward to work with chakras that have been activated, assisting the being who actively does the inner work to potentially adequately balance activated chakras.

Since chakras are typically activated from the red-ray up in sequential order, the highest adequately balanced chakra shows the advancement level of a being, where the upward flow of prana meets the downward in-pouring of Source energy. If a being focuses on the higher chakras and balancing them without first having balanced their lower chakras, it leads to a great imbalance and confusion for the being. The higher material in full, and not just from an intellectual level, cannot be fully understood without first fully understanding the lower material. If there is no stable foundation, the building complex will fall during times of turbulence.

The mind, body, spirit complex a being needs to possess to experience the Cosmos is situated throughout the chakras from the red-ray to the violet-ray chakras. Although there are certain percentages of them throughout all the 7 chakras, the lower chakras have the greatest percentage of links to the body complex, with the red-ray chakra having the most. The higher chakras have the greatest percentage of links to the spirit complex, with the violet- and indigo-ray chakras having the most. On one end, the body complex offers a connection to the planet and the physical outer planes. On the other end, the spirit complex is a connection to Source, where beings reside in a timeless state and mentally project themselves into a mentally created universe to have experiences.

To understand this situation, one may use dreaming as an example; one's mind is projected into a dream and appears to be all that exists while one is dreaming, but the human being is still in their bed while dreaming. While a human being is experiencing the Cosmos, the illusory dream, a higher aspect of themselves is merged with Source and never departs this timeless state. As the human being is in bed at the same time they are in a dream, a human being is merged with Source at the same time they are experiencing the Cosmos. This is why every being is the Creator and a co-Creator at the same time.

The red-ray chakra is the first possible chakra to react to any experience or stimuli, as prana flows from root to crown. If an experience or stimuli does not cause a being to adversely react or suppress a reaction in the red-ray chakra, such as fear or anger, prana continues to flow upward to the next energy center, the orange-ray chakra. If there is no adverse reaction or suppressed reaction that impedes or blocks the flow of prana in the orange-ray chakra, prana continues to flow upward to the next energy center, and so on upward through the energy centers. A being can learn from others, such as their parents, lovers, teachers, or friends, but until they experience situations firsthand, they are not able to actively work on adequately balancing the chakra that pertains to the situation or matter. Good advice may equip the being to better handle a situation when it arises, but they do not truly learn until they face the experience themselves and are given the opportunity to experience, understand, and accept it. Because of this, overprotection is not beneficial for the child, young adult, or for a being at any age, as their opportunities to experience and grow are being suppressed.

For a being to advance through the 7 densities and merge back with Source, a being needs to master and adequately balance the 6 energy centers red-ray through indigo-ray, and then understand and integrate the totality of their being in the violet-ray energy center before merging back with Source. Source is depicted as a white chakra placed somewhere above the violet-ray chakra on some chakra illustrations on Earth, as white is the full spectrum that all the color rays reside in. The advancement through the densities is synonymous with the advancement through the chakras. Each being is unique, so the harmony between balanced chakras is different for each being. This harmonious relationship between balanced chakras is what should be sought after instead of simply attempting to fully balance all the chakras in a uniformed manner for all beings. Balancing the chakras is not like a checklist to be done only in sequential order and permanently checked off and completed; when each unique being is adequately balancing one chakra, it may bring up the different relationships for other chakras that pertain to the focused-on chakra's matter, and there are always setbacks along the journey where chakras need to be rebalanced.

We will explain what it means to activate and balance energy centers by using a 3rd density being's path toward graduating to 4th density positive as an example. Once a human being has adequately balanced their red-ray chakra by mastering the foundational lessons of that chakra—such as physical survival, fear, mental pain threshold, anger—the flow of prana is able to flow upward and activate the orange-ray chakra. Activation means the flow of prana has reached that chakra because the chakras below it are currently not producing blockages, allowing potential focus on the matters in that chakra and the possibility of adequately balancing that chakra. Once the orange-ray chakra has been adequately balanced, the flow of prana continues upward to the next chakra, the yellow-ray chakra, and activates it so the being can start receiving opportunities and focus on experiences and lessons within that chakra. The process then continues up to the green-ray chakra, which does not need to be completely balanced for graduation consideration to the 4th density positive, as only the early lessons of the next density need to be learned before proceeding to that density. Overcoming issues and balancing matters within a chakra is doing the inner work. In short, an activated chakra means blockages in the chakras below it are not present and not fully impeding the upward flow of life-force energy—even if this case is fleeting—so prana is allowed to flow to the chakra that is activated. Just like a computer or any technological device, it needs to be activated or turned on in order for work to be done on it. Until it is turned on, it sits there, potentially able to be used in the future to do work.

A balanced chakra means that the flow of prana has already reached and activated that chakra and opportunities in the form of experiences have already been received and the lessons in that chakra have been adequately mastered—and so balanced—at least for the time being, allowing the flow of prana to flow upward to activate the next chakra and begin working on the lessons offered in its spectral ray. Like each density has 7 sub-densities, a spectral ray of a chakra has 7 sub-rays where different lessons reside. Crossing the threshold at the end of a spectrum ray and advancing to the beginning sub-ray of the next chakra-ray always takes more effort than crossing each sub-ray within a chakra-ray. It is common for a being who is working on balancing a certain chakra to meet challenges and obstacles that once again bring up similar lessons that may need to be relearned in a different manner from the same chakra or chakras below that have already been balanced. Thus, more than one chakra may be worked on at the same time. 3rd density beings typically work on lessons in the orange- and yellow-ray at the same time. Relearning lessons and rebalancing chakras should not be seen as failing setbacks, as the being who refocuses on a chakra to balance it further moves ahead in an even stronger manner than they did before.

Once a being has adequately balanced their orange- and yellow-ray chakras, they activate their green-ray chakra and focus on working with lessons that reside in that color spectrum ray. At this level the being is close to being able to graduate to 4th density positive. It is not required for a 3rd density being to master and balance their green-ray chakra to graduate to 4th density; a being only needs to overcome a portion, the early lessons, of the green-ray chakra to be ready to graduate to 4th density. The same goes for all the densities above 3rd density—each density needing to only learn the early portion of the next density level's lessons to graduate to the next density.

For a lesson to be fully learned, it must be practiced in one's life, as a lesson learned is only truly learned and liberating if it is practiced. When the early lessons for the green-ray chakra are learned and practiced in one's life, it equates to being at least 51% service to others. When a lesson within a chakra has been properly learned, it means the being has acquired the knowledge inside themselves and practices it outside in the physical outer plane/world. If it is not practiced in one's life, the lesson has not been adequately learned.

As lessons in life will be temporarily overcome and then need working on again, either because the lessons were forgotten or different specific routes to those matters within a lesson have arose that have not been dealt with before, as chakras do not automatically stay balanced permanently. Life is not a checklist for matters and lessons to be checked off once and never need addressing again. As human beings are aware, overcoming life challenges is a constant effort. A human being may overcome a challenge one day and fail to do so the next day. This is why a human needs to be attentive, resilient, and patient with themselves as they spiritually grow. The more times a human being overcomes the same lesson, the more experience and strength they have in overcoming it when it arises in the future.

Even if the lower chakras are not adequately balanced yet, prana flow may reach and temporarily activate higher chakras if blockages are currently not being applied to the lower chakras. If there are no blockages, no current issues or perceived problems, prana continues to flow upward. When a being who is still working on balancing the lower chakras temporarily finds themselves in a place or situation where lower chakra challenges may not be actively present and need to be overcome, which may occur on vacation, enjoying a relaxed activity such as a picnic or boating, enjoying and focusing on one's passions, or any situation where challenges are put on hold and enough mental background tasks have been ended, then prana has the opportunity to flow upward to higher chakras even if the lower chakras are not adequately balanced. When these blissful moments arise, the being feels serene or elated and wishes they could always enjoy such a mental state of being. If they do the inner work, they can work toward this goal. At these times universal love may be experienced from the green-ray chakra, smooth and comfortable communication and expression may be experience in the blue-ray chakra, and intuition and spiritual wholeness may be experienced in the indigo-ray chakra. These periods can be a nice reprieve from challenges and offer the opportunity to heal and draw strength, but the goal is to overcome challenges and learn lessons—balance the lower chakras—so that one may feel the same way on vacation in their everyday life. This is the liberation from perceived problems. In other words, arising challenges are not seen as problems because the being does not make them problems; in the face of challenges the being stays balanced and overcomes the challenges and solves the matters, if they are able to be solved. Not only is this liberation healthy and of a high-vibratory nature, but the being is able to access their full potential without lower chakra blockages and more effectively solve matters and overcome challenges by accessing and utilizing their higher faculties. Since having a high vibration is healthy and cultivating for the mind, body, spirit complex, aging of the physical body is slowed down.

What is considered a balanced chakra is different for each being, as each being is a unique spark or representation of Source. Just as each unique being learns lessons through different experiences and methods and advances in their own way, each unique being balances a chakra in the way that is right for them; similarly to how each child in a group of children learns more easily through different teaching methods for the same subject in the same classroom. Character flaws are lessons that need to be overcome and avoided in the future, but character traits, which are expressed through actions or only mentally, are lessons that need to be adequately balanced. The spectrum for each particular trait within a chakra ray is from 0 to 10, one extreme to the other extreme. Examples: not trusting anyone to trusting everyone, eating no foodstuffs to eating great amounts of foodstuffs, apathy toward the physical body and its presentation to being extremely vain about one's looks, never compromising to always doing what others want. All character traits have a spectrum from one extreme to the other. If all beings balanced each lesson or character trait to the same exact level, 5 would be that balanced state. But since each being is unique, their particular middle path—as the Buddha called it—is different, so one being's balanced state, or middle path, for each character trait may be a balanced state of 3 or 4, or a 6 or 7 on the spectrum from 0 to 10, and a balanced state may continue to shift anywhere from a 3 to a 7 as a being progresses and adapts. The collection of beings that make up Source are interested in variables and uniqueness while experiencing this Cosmos. Robots that do everything the same way and balance each lesson or character trait to the same 5 on the spectrum do not produce the variables needed for unique expression that lifts the whole to greater heights. Human beings who are still creating blockages in the orange- and yellow-ray chakras may feel that all beings should act the same way and think the same way, but human beings who have advanced far enough in the orange- and yellow-ray chakra matters know that uniqueness is beautiful and adds to the greater good of the collective.

Source thrives and learns through uniqueness. This means there are no specific set instructions and learning methods that work for every individual to overcome issues and balance out each character trait, but a 5 on the spectrum can be taught in a lenient and flexible manner. Then each unique individual can determine after experience and integration what their specific balance is for each of their character traits, never being too close to one extreme or the other within the spectrum.

The steps mentioned are for graduating to 4th density positive. Human beings graduating to 4th density negative need to balance out their red-ray chakra in the same manner as positives, but they do not balance their orange- and yellow-ray chakras. Instead, beings working toward the negative path adequately understand and accept/recognize the lessons offered in the orange-ray chakra and pervert them to allow the flow of upward prana to continue to the yellow-ray chakra without effectively balancing out the orange-ray chakra, and then do the same for the yellow-ray chakra to graduate to 4th density negative. For 4th density negative graduation consideration, the perversion of the orange- and yellow-ray chakra matters need to be practiced in one's life, expressing at least 95% service to self. To be an adept, their most difficult challenge is to skip the green- and blue-ray chakras and activate the indigo-ray chakra directly from the yellow-ray chakra. As we have stated, this is quite a difficult task to accomplish.

Partial to complete blockages in a chakra occur when the upward flow of prana is hindered or stopped due to matters of the chakras not being adequately mastered. Similarly, a being does not graduate to the next density if they have not adequately mastered the lessons and matters found in the chakras that focus on the densities below theirs (red- and orange-ray chakras for 3rd density beings), the chakra that focuses on the current density they are experiencing (yellow-ray for 3rd density beings), and the chakra's early lessons in the next density they are working toward graduating to (green-ray for 3rd density positive beings). Human beings and all other 3rd density beings seeking 4th density positive graduation need to at least learn a partial amount of the ways of universal love, the early lessons. Human beings and all other 3rd density beings seeking 4th density negative graduation need to learn an adequate amount of the ways of love for self solely. Since this selfishness is learned and practiced in the orange- and yellow-ray chakras and not the early portion of the green-ray chakra that is affiliated with 4th density positive matters, the adequate amount of selfishness that needs to be reached for negative graduation is quite high—at least 95% service to self.

The red-ray chakra, or root chakra, is the foundation chakra that connects a being to the physical outer planes. Thus, it governs reproduction, vital energy, the mental pain threshold, strong baseline emotions, and the survival of the physical self and its species. Balancing this chakra is a focus that greatly relates to the body complex. The red-ray chakra is the first possible chakra to react to any experience or stimuli, as prana flows from root upward. If there is a strong feeling of anger, fear, or the need to physically survive a situation—aspects governed by the red-ray chakra—the flow of energy stagnates there and partially or completely blocks the upward flow of prana to the orange-ray and proceeding chakras.

The orange-ray chakra relates to understanding and accepting oneself. It also relates to the interactions a being has with another on a one-on-one basis, and some of the emotions that may arise in such interactions, as well as emotions regarding oneself. Blockages in this chakra may occur if a being does not understand or accept themselves and has self-worth issues that arise mentally during alone time or while interacting with others on a one-on-one basis, especially beings one interacts with on an ongoing manner, such as family members, friends, lovers, or co-workers. Blockages may also occur if respect and equality are not present in one's one-on-one interactions.

The yellow-ray chakra relates to a being's relationship and interaction with large groups of beings, such as societies, races, nationalities, religious affiliations, political affiliations, and wealth classes if a monetary system is in play. Blockages in this chakra may occur if a being manipulates power in a controlling manner over large groups or individuals in respect to their affiliated large group. Or one group of beings feeling they have the need or right to control and/or force-transition/kill other groups within their nation or groups from other nations by way of propaganda, war, infiltration, or financial manipulation if a monetary system is in play.

The green-ray chakra, or heart chakra, relates to universal love, compassion, healing, empathy, being nonjudgmental, forgiveness, and giving freely without expecting anything in return. Universal love is freely given with no expectations or strings attached, which is quite different than the conditional love most human beings practice. If a being skips balancing this chakra and moves onto mastering the next chakra, blue-ray, there is a great potential for imbalance throughout the chakras that leads to spiritual confusion. As to omit the practice of universal love, the most fundamental aspect of the cosmic experience, is to invite imbalance and confusion. Although, omitting the heart chakra is a necessity for those pursuing the negative path, as one needs to be adequately confused to tread down this path.

The blue-ray chakra relates to communication, including the two-way route of listening and speaking or through expression, which when done harmoniously offers a two-way route of understanding, acceptance, comfort, and freedom. Emotions and feelings from interactions on a higher level are expressed through this chakra. Beings mastering this chakra become more efficient co-Creators in the cosmic experience due to tapping into more links to the mind and spirit complexes. Signs of blockages that impede this chakra are the lack of being able to express oneself in their own ways and failing to be open and listen to others. This does not mean all that adequately balance the blue-ray chakra are skilled orators, as this is a trait where one may be adequately balanced at a 3 on the 10 scale for their particular uniqueness. One could be at an adequately balanced 7 in a different form of communication and expression, such as through the written word, body language, or through artistic visuals. Until the lower chakras are mastered, there will always be a partial or complete blockage in the blue-ray chakra.

The indigo-ray chakra, or third eye or pineal chakra, relates to intuition, inspiration, inner awareness, wholeness, spiritual contentment, and a greater connection with oneself and Source/Oneness. All beings are connected to Source as parts of Source, but a being who has mastered this chakra opens up to greater access to Source energy and mind, the flowing of love and light energy from Source. A being who masters this chakra is aware of the Creator in themselves and that they are of infinite worth in a humble manner. Balancing this chakra is a focus that greatly relates to the spiritual complex. To go beyond adequately balancing this chakra and to master it is to find the key within oneself that opens the door that leads through the violet-ray gateway and connects with Source, where a giving and receiving may take place with Source energy and mind. As with the blue-ray chakra, until the lower chakras are mastered, there will always be a partial or complete blockage in the indigo-ray chakra.

The violet-ray chakra is the sum of all the chakras. It is the totality of the being and is not effected directly by experiences and stimuli. Its state of being, balanced or unbalanced, is completely reliant on the sum of all the chakras below it. This chakra cannot be balanced directly; only through balancing all the chakras below it, red-ray through indigo-ray, is the violet-ray chakra balanced. This chakra displays the vibratory level of a being, the level of wholeness reached. Thus, it is the chakra used to gauge whether a being is ready to graduate to the next density.

The experiences that are needed for growth by a being are the very experiences that a being attracts. If a being understands, accepts, and integrates an experience, they no longer feel the need to attract or create that experience for themselves. To integrate experiences a being uses observation (both externally and internally), understanding by way of analytical thought or intuition, and then applying acceptance, which is the calm recognition of what currently is and may potentially always be. To seek and focus on growth is to direct oneself toward the necessary experiences that offer such growth.

To not seek or focus on growth is akin to being a passenger in another's vehicle, being taken for a ride and not knowing the direction they are being taken. Both eventually reach the destination, but one gets there much quicker and/or in a smoother, more enjoyable fashion. The route to the destination leads through the chakra-ray signs along the path; the signs read: survival, personal identity and interactions, social relations, universal love, open communication, spiritual wholeness, and linkage to cosmic energies. Then one reaches the destination, which is merging back with Source. Enjoy the ride. Drive as fast or as slowly as you like. Take as many side roads as you want to experience attractions along the way. Know that Source is within you the whole way and some so-called official human being is not needed in order for Source to be invited into your vehicle, as you are part of the collective that is Source, and so Source is always within your vehicle no matter what direction you are headed.

The positively oriented 3rd density being works on themselves by doing the inner work as well as showing loving-kindness to others, focusing on all the chakras that need attending to. They reach the point where the giving does not expect or need any reciprocal receiving. In a civilization not captured by a monetary system, there is a much greater chance their giving services are recognized, appreciated, and honored by others who naturally offer their skill-based services or goods in return. In this manner, all services and goods are freely and gladly given by each being who has naturally gravitated toward their skills and passions to serve themselves and their communities, and possible the whole planet or beyond.

Earth is long down the twisted road of being captured by a monetary system. While money is being used to reward one for their services and goods, to appreciate and honor what has been given, a giving back of services, goods, or money allows the giver to not only survive and make their way in their society, but to be able to give and assist even more. One must work within the broken system to liberate the system, and while money is still needed to survive and alter the broken system, it should be gladly given to the human beings who provide helpful services and goods that assist and may offer liberation. If one does not accept money for services or goods while they are still living in a monetary system, they will not be able to continue producing services or goods to assist others, let alone feed and shelter themselves and their family. Unfortunately, one has to work with money and within a broken system in order to lead a civilization or planet toward an unbroken system, or to simply offer personal liberation on a human by human basis with their services. A wise positively oriented human being who is wealthy still strives to remove their society or planet from a monetary system, as they know they do not lose anything when their money becomes worthless, because they will not only keep receiving what their money once afforded, but will receive even more out of life in a harmonious system than what their money provided for in an inharmonious system. Also, all the stress and complications that come with possessing wealth and protecting it is removed, relieving a heavy burden for the wealthy. And not having to deal with taxes, which is a form of legal theft by a nation, relieves all beings.

The negatively oriented 3rd density being works for themselves and only with others when it serves their purpose, when it benefits them. They work on the red-ray chakra like positive beings, but work in an opposite manner toward service to self in regards to orange- and yellow-ray chakra matters. They use red-, orange-, and yellow-ray chakra matters against the majority, utilizing separation and control through personal motivation, sexual actions, societal actions, and even contact with negative higher-density beings if they are far enough along the negative path. In a civilization captured by a monetary system, they strive to collect as much money as possible, knowing that it is their primary tool for power and control over others. They do everything in their power to stop or cut off any existing flow of money to positively oriented 3rd density beings, who, being service-to-others oriented, naturally get in their way of controlling the majority. They relentlessly strive to stop or majorly cut the flow of money to positively oriented human beings because they know positively oriented humans use their money to help others, their communities, or possibly the whole planet, and such beneficial actions threaten the control of the highly negatively oriented human beings.

When negatively oriented human beings viciously work at stopping positively oriented beings, it is their method at keeping the majority down, the majority who benefits from the positively oriented beings' actions. When the negatives and negatively oriented human beings go after and try to stop the positively oriented human beings, it is the same thing as going after and stopping the majority they wish to control or keep control over. It is the majority the negatively oriented human beings want to keep suppressed and under their control. The positively oriented human beings are merely part of the majority that are in the way and are the biggest threats, as they are utilizing their power and means to attempt to lift the majority up. When the negatively oriented human beings' programming is seen to be heavily utilized along with many human tools under their disposal who are attacking and attempting to discredit a certain human being, it is a sign that the human being is positively oriented and posing a substantial threat to the negatives' control due to their positively polarizing actions that are significantly assisting the majority.

Before this happens, any positively oriented being who is working towards something that has the potential to cause major positive polarity in a 3rd density experience is already attacked by negative inner and outer planes beings from the 4th density and possibly the 5th density, as the wanderer has been, before their work even reaches fellow 3rd density beings. As we have stated, higher-density beings can view the probabilities months in advance before they come to pass on a timeline, so negatives attack beings and try to stop positively polarizing actions from coming to pass. If a being knows their mission, the reason they incarnated, it is what they strive to accomplish despite any odds. In a wanderer's case, since they have already learned the lessons of 3rd density and graduated, their mission is the sole reason they are incarnate in 3rd density, so to not pursue the mission that serves/aids the majority would be a wasted incarnation.

103.2 – Thoughts, Emotions, & the Natural State of Being

Thoughts and emotions are created and charged in the mental complex of a being, but they affect the body and spirit complexes as well, as the body and spirit complexes affect the mental complex. The mind, body, and spirit all overlap, are all connected, and are all necessary to experience the Cosmos. Thus, thoughts and emotions are aspects that have sway over the outer planes/physical world. Thoughts and emotions create in their own way as doing an action physically using the body creates in its own way.

Thanks to the breakthrough work of the one who is known as Masaru Emoto, one does not need to rely on another's opinion about whether thoughts and emotions affect the outer planes/physical world, as they can perform a simple experiment at home themselves to reveal the reality of the matter. There have been numerous scientific studies carried out on Earth that have proven or provided evidence that thoughts and emotions have substance and greatly affect the physical outer planes, but they have been discredited or given no press because negatively oriented 3rd density beings know that such information is very important and so would threaten their power and control over the majority. As with all beneficial breakthroughs of information and inventions that could assist humanity, negatively oriented 3rd density beings try their hardest to stop and/or discredit the breakthrough in order to keep their control over the majority. That is their chosen role in their current incarnation.

We encourage all beings to perform Emoto's 30-day experiment of rice in water to know the reality of mind over matter for themselves. Place equal amounts of cooked rice in water in three glass jars, or any transparent containers. Label one with positive words such as "thank you" and/or "I love you". Label one with negative words such as "you are useless" and/or "I hate you". Apply no label to the third jar and ignore it. Place the jars in different locations within a room—while not introducing variables—so they are not possibly subjected to emanating emotions from your aura that are intended for a different jar. Over 30 days, spend a little time twice a day with the "love" and "hate" jars. If only empty words are spoken, no differences will be seen at the end of the experiment because it is the thoughts and emotions behind the words that are powerful and matter, especially emotions. Hold the "love" jar and connect with it via your heart chakra, sending it powerful feelings of love and appreciation; no words need to be spoken out loud, but speak them if the verbal action assists you. Hold the "hate" jar and connect with it via your red-ray chakra, sending it powerful feelings of hate and uselessness; again, no actual words need be spoken. If you have sent powerful enough thoughts, feelings, and emotions to both jars, the results will be unmistakably different after 30 days, and the jar that was ignored is used for comparison. If there are no obvious differences between the jars, the experiment was not done correctly, variables were not accounted for, or thoughts and emotions were not powerful enough. Also, there are plenty of human tools who are willing to serve negatively oriented human beings and share on the Internet or elsewhere that they did the experiment properly and it did not work. Thoughts and emotions create changes in physical matter; it is a universal way/law of the Cosmos. Just because one is ignorant of this way does not mean the law is not applied.

Are you going to forgo the experiment and mindlessly believe the so-called scientists that discredit it, or will you take the time to bring the unmistakable proof forward about a matter that is of vital importance? We reiterate, thinking and making decisions for oneself is one of the necessary requirements for graduating to 4th density. It is the 2nd density animal that mindlessly follows the herd. An advancing 3rd density human being thinks for themselves and makes their own informed decisions.

Emoto's rice in water experiment explains the misunderstood concept of why Yahushua/Jesus would bless and thank God for foodstuffs and drink before ingesting them. Since everything is God/Source, the foodstuffs are also part of Source, so thanking Source for the foodstuffs is the same thing as thanking the foodstuffs and drink themselves for their service—the nutrition and benefits they provide. When one sends thanks and loving feelings to their foodstuffs and liquid before ingesting them, they are practicing the art of appreciation, recognizing all is connected as One, as well as assisting the molecules of the foodstuffs and liquid to arrange themselves in a manner that is healthier for the mind, body, spirit complex when they are ingested. An example of thanks conveyed to foodstuffs and liquid a human being may use: "Thank you for your nutrients and benefits. I love you. We are One in love and light. You are up to my vibration." As with the rice experiment, words may be spoken but are not required; it is the powerful thoughts, feelings, and emotions that have sway over physical matter, the molecules and vibration of the foodstuffs and liquid. Since words are not necessary, it can be done in public without other-selves, who are uninformed of this reality, thinking you are crazy. If perfunctory words or thoughts are spoken to the foodstuffs or liquid without focus on meaningful thoughts and emotions, the action is useless. If there is no positive state of being behind actions, the actions may be useless. When a being knows all physical matter is invisibly connected and exists only because it is inspirited with intelligently conscious love energy from Source and then infused with vibrating light energy from Source so that it can be seen and exist in the physical, it is understandable that powerful thoughts, feelings, and emotions of love or hate affect physical matter, whether it be foodstuffs, water, one's own trinity complex (mind, body, spirit complex), another's trinity complex that the thoughts and emotions are directed towards, and the collective consciousness. Take responsibility for the thoughts and emotions entertained and charged rather than thinking they have no substance, influence, or consequences.

When a wise being is faced with a perceived negative situation, they analyze it before acting, if any action is even needed. When a being who is not wise is faced with a perceived negative situation, they react automatically without thinking or with muddled thought, usually making the situation worse, or turning a situation that was actually fine to one of hardship, effectively projecting and creating the unhealthy thought into reality. Even before a being fully realizes they are a Creator, they are co-Creators with responsibilities in the 3rd density. When a being reacts automatically, they are acting no differently than an impulsive animal or robot that is programmed to act with a specific response every time they are faced with certain verbiage or stimuli; when their buttons are pushed, they react accordingly. When engaging in producing negative/unhealthy thoughts and emotions, the upward flow of prana is blocked in the lower chakras and goes no further, not being able to access enough of the mind complex to properly analyze the situation and possibly solve it, or realize it was only a perceived problem and so does not need effort applied to be resolved. When anger or fear produces a full blockage in the red-ray chakra and stops the upward flow of prana, the 3rd density human being may be temporarily reduced and devolved to that of the 2nd density animal that does not display universal love or utilize their mental faculties, so aggressive words and/or brute-force violence are displayed like that of the disgruntled ape.

It has been proven by researchers on Earth that while a human being experiences powerful emotions of anger their intelligence temporarily drops. Anger and fear are two emotions that block the flow of prana at the red-ray chakra, causing the being who experiences these emotions to act unintelligently, and which also makes them much easier to be manipulated and controlled. Negatively oriented 3rd density beings are aware of this and so utilize anger and fear on a mass scale in order to more easily manipulate and control the majority. This card of play has been used countless times by negatively oriented 3rd density beings and 4th density negatives throughout the universe, and also in Earth's history and present. They make 3rd density beings intensely angry or fearful so their intelligence is out of grasp and they are able to be utilized like unintelligent tools. If the method continues to work, it will continue to be utilized by the negatively oriented and the negatives. A particular angle within this method that works well is the blame game. Negatively oriented human beings cause the problem or attack on their own group or nation, or possibly another, and then blame it on the group or nation they want the majority of their nation to be angry or fearful towards, so the majority is manipulated by the actual perpetrators into agreeing to attack the group or nation they think is responsible. The negatively oriented human beings then have the majority's support in performing the actions or war the negatively oriented beings want. We share an image of twin towers as just one recent example in Earth's history.

Blockages in chakras may result in cells being unhealthily affected and growing in ways that go against their original encoding. This unhealthy growth has been called cancer. When the upward flow of prana, which assists in the upward positive growth, is blocked too often, the upward flow of energy being impeded begins to promote growth in the wrong direction. A blockage in any chakra may lead to cancerous growths, but anger and fear are two emotions that create blockages in the red-ray chakra and are the two most likely internally derived reasons for cancerous growths. Fear of possible future events, which is called anxiety, is the specific type of fear that promotes cancerous growths because it tends to be entertained more frequently than fear of survival.

In the negatively oriented 3rd density being's case, internal control can be used to remove the initial red-ray chakra blockage that is produced by their anger or fear that causes cancer. If they are clever enough, they understand the emotion and instead of charging it at the red-ray chakra, they bring it up to their mental faculties and devise a clever plan to seek revenge.

In the positively oriented 3rd density being's case, internal acceptance can be used to cease the initial red-ray chakra blockage of anger or fear that causes cancer. If they are intelligent enough, they understand that charging the emotion and keeping the red-ray chakra blocked is both unhealthy and ineffective. Instead, they dissipate the emotion and allow the upward flow of prana to resume and are able to use their mental faculties to amicably solve the perceived problem, or realize the perceived problem is not a problem and no action need be taken. Some of these positively oriented amicable actions may be perceived as destructive actions to the negatively oriented being who initiated the scenario. A straightforward example of this is the honorable martial artist who uses their powerful skills of defense as their offense when it is called for, allowing the actions of the negatively oriented to defeat themselves.

Invariably, situations in one's incarnation make it easier or harder to produce healthy or unhealthy thoughts and emotions, but regardless, it is always up to the being to choose positivity, neutrality, or negativity in the face of any situation. When one knows that producing negative energy about a perceived negative situation does not make the situation better or resolves it and instead makes it worse, why would they choose to create unhealthy energy patterns?

Using negative emotions to solve a situation is first learned when a being is an infant. The infant cannot talk yet so they rely on negative energy—unhappiness while crying—to get attention and hopefully get their wants met, such as receiving foodstuffs.

This method works for the infant, so they continue to use it. Most children carry this method of solving problems even after they can speak because it became a habit and is not taught in Earth's educational system or by parents that it does not work anymore in resolving the perceived problem. Having been ingrained throughout the years and not corrected, most adults continue to use this method automatically to some degree without being aware that it is ineffective and poisonous to themselves and others. They get mad or displeased about something and unconsciously think that creating negative emotions, which sometimes lead to negative physical actions, will solve the problem, but it only makes it worse as negativity is charged and fire is used on fire in an attempt to put out the fire.

Most Earthlings are not taught that their thoughts and emotions are healthy or unhealthy, or that they have any bearing on themselves, physical matter, and other-selves. Adults may look to young children to understand and remember how their life used to be viewed as lighter and with positivity and enthusiasm when they were young. As the child grew older into adulthood and beyond, they faced numerous experiences that were perceived as negative as they interacted with other human beings and the society they live in, which was created by the local collective. These hardships involved experiences with friends, lovers, interactions within the educational system, interactions within jobs with co-workers and so-called bosses, and simply making their way in their broken society with its laws and socially accepted norms and lifestyles.

The state of being of most adults conveys how broken the societies on Earth are. The purity and enthusiasm of the child typically being buried and turning to apathy or some form of dispassion at some point in adulthood. Instead of working towards resolving the broken system of the society, human beings are programmed and socially conditioned to believe such acquired apathy or dispassion is normal and is merely what growing up is like and what the system is for better or for worse and nothing can be done about it. If one does believe they can do something about the broken system and attempts to fix some part of it and are making advances in doing so, they will get a rude awakening when negatively oriented human beings, who thrive on the broken system their type have created, do everything in their power to stop the positive advances by the positively oriented human being, who then might come to realize that the broken system was not created purely out of chance, but was purposefully engineered to serve a selfish minority. As their knowledge regarding this topic increases, they come to realize that their broken system was slowly and methodically constructed throughout the centuries and has been majorly strengthened and advanced in recent decades in a purposeful manner by highly negatively oriented human beings.

It is a falsity and a slight against Earthlings to believe that the current broken system on Earth that causes so much suffering and ineffectiveness was simply the best Earthlings could do while constructing societies. The current broken system on Earth in your possibility/timeline was intentionally constructed that way over centuries by negatively oriented human beings for the sake of power and control over the majority. They are the same beings who are taught to use programming to manipulate and control the majority. We assure Earthlings that they have the ability to construct healthy and prosperous societies when they do not let the negatively oriented take the reins of control. We see countless possibilities/timelines for Earth where the construction of such healthy and prosperous societies are the case. We see the proof that the majority in your particular possibility/timeline does not have access to.

When the pain and suffering of perceived negative experiences are had throughout the growing-up and getting-older process, dirty filters to view life through are added by the human who does not understand, accept, and let go of the pain and suffering from the experience, and instead lets the pain settle in their mind, body, spirit complex. Each dirty filter added moves the once joyful young child toward the suffering or dispassionate adult who feels they have lost that childlike innocence where natural states of love, joy, and peace abounded without effort. The adult did not lose that state of being, but has buried the jewel that they are under layers and layers of dirty filters that cover the jewel and make it appear as if it is gone forever. The very essence of Source—as well as for the 3rd density being since every human being is a part of Source—is love, joy, and peace; therefore, it cannot be completely lost, only buried and forgotten. Love, joy, and peace is the essence of the intelligently conscious love energy that you and everything in the Cosmos is made of.

Challenging and perceived negative experiences are necessary for the growth of a being in 3rd density—but storing the experiences' pain is not necessary—and to avoid such challenges before the lessons have been learned would be to hinder one's growth. The solution is to learn from adversity, understand and accept it, and to not hold onto the adversity. Learn from it and let it go so it does not get stuck in your mind, body, spirit complex and bog you down and create a dirty filter that life is viewed through. Instead of applying the dirty filter to every future experience that is similar to the one that first created the dirty filter, learn from the lesson and remember it so that it may provide growth, then let the unneeded aspect of it go instead of holding onto the unhealthy response that is poisonous and dulls the mind, body, spirit complex. Store the lesson and the growth that comes with it and distill and transmute the unhealthy response from the mind, body, and spirit. To identify with the unhealthy response and its dirty filter is to invite and provide a harbor for a detrimental falsity within oneself, their mind, body, spirit complex.

It is the role of 4th density positive and negative beings to influence 3rd density beings. They influence by offering thoughts and sometimes emotions to human beings, so thoughts and emotions are not always created by the human being, as we covered in the topic of spirit guides in subject 102.4. However, the human being is always responsible for what thoughts and emotions they choose to entertain and charge no matter where they originated. This does not mean a human being is always susceptible to 4th density negative influences; the more inner work that is done reduces the possible inroads for negatives to utilize. When enough inner work has been performed and negatives present opportunities of adversity, the positively oriented human being may recognize it and use it toward their advantage, effectively turning the negative into a tool instead of the other way around. Again, we reference the martial artist who uses the inertia of their opponent to let their opponent defeat themselves, an instant karma balancing situation. This is a reference for physical actions, but the same type of scenario also exists for mentality and possibly the actions taken in life due to the mentality.

When enough dirty filters have been created by a human being—typically well into adulthood—even periods of still mind may fail to bring forward the natural state of love, joy, and peace that is naturally brought forward for a child. This is because the built-up dirty filters and their pain and suffering being stored in the mind, body, spirit complex are akin to an unnecessary program running as a background task on a computer, potentially creating conflicts with other applications and slowing down the computer's operating system, making it less effective even though the program is not currently in use. As an adult is not aware of their created dirty filters that are constantly running and residing in the mind complex and the ineffectiveness they create, so are the unnecessary running programs' background tasks on the computer not known by the user. Being aware of one's state of being by observing oneself internally is akin to opening up the Task Manager/Activity Monitor on a computer and seeing what programs and processes are running in the foreground and background and ending tasks that are not currently being utilized by the user in order to alleviate performance issues. Just as most who use computers are not aware of this function, most human beings are not familiar with the act of observing their internal state to turn off background clutter and noise. Just as the human being wakes up in the morning and unneeded or unused background clutter and noise in the form of thoughts and emotions may be automatically loaded before they start their day, the computer that is turned on automatically loads background tasks that are unnecessary and unused that bog down the operating system. Just as some of the background tasks that are automatically loaded when a computer is turned on are designed to run on the operating system and work against the user instead of for them, so are unknown detrimental programs loaded into a human being's conscious or subconscious mind that work against them instead of for them.

Thoughts and emotions are food for 2nd density inner planes beings. There is no positive and negative polarity in the 2nd density inners planes, as there is also none in the 2nd density outer planes. Like elementals in 1st density, these 2nd density inner planes beings perform a role in the cosmic experience that is done without being self-aware. Since inner planes beings reside in time in space, they are invisible to beings in the physical outer planes who reside in space in time. They perform their function, their roles. When dried food is raddled around in a feeding dish, the cat or dog comes running for their food fix. It is the same for 2nd density inner planes beings. Positive/Healthy thoughts and emotions are food for the 2nd density inner planes beings who enjoy that certain taste and come running to enjoy it when it is mentally dispensed by the human being. Negative/Unhealthy thoughts and emotions are food for 2nd density inner planes beings who enjoy that certain taste and come running to enjoy it when it is mentally dispensed. If they keep being fed, they stick around as a stray cat or dog would, both those that like the taste of positivity or negativity. Like the stray animal sticks around and begs for food to make it more likely they will be fed, these 2nd density inner planes beings charge the positive or negative thought or emotion so the 3rd density being is more likely to keep producing its favorite food. Those that enjoy the taste of negativity and stick around a being who keeps feeding it to them become what has been called by humans as entity attachments.

It is extremely rare, but some human beings possess the ability acquired from past incarnations to see these entity attachments. It is much more typical for a type of healer to feel rather than see their energy signature and work on releasing the attachments through their honorable services. Although, they will return if the human being continues to feed them. The entity attachment assists at strengthening the charge of the unhealthy thoughts and emotions in the human being so it can continue to be fed the food it prefers. In this way, they work at charging a human's mental habits, which often lead to physical habits, whether they be healthy or unhealthy. Be aware and observant of what type of food (thoughts and emotions) you are producing, as the responding 2nd density inner planes beings are attracted to it like the force of magnets being drawn together. A healer can assist to release entity attachments, but a human being can also release them themselves by changing the food they are offering. When the type of food the 2nd density inner planes beings are drawn to stops being given to them, they eventually depart to find it elsewhere.

When unhealthy thoughts and emotions arise, as they naturally do in 3rd density, they can be recognized and swiftly dissolved by the human being who stays observant of their inner state. This is a big part of doing the inner work. When the unhealthy thought or emotion is swiftly caught, it may be dissolved easily. If they are not quickly caught, they charge and become more powerful and harder to dissolve when finally addressed, just as the stray animal who had been fed for weeks continues to linger around for weeks even after the food stopped coming. Like a spinning hamster wheel, it builds inertia and charges the longer and faster it is being spun, continuing to spin even after the hamster gets off the wheel, causing a force that attempts to suck the focus back on the turning wheel so it can keep turning. Once the folly of spinning a certain hamster wheel is recognized and the human jumps off the wheel, instead of trying to stop the wheel that has been greatly charged, it is more effective to jump onto a different wheel, a healthy wheel, and put one's focus on it and let the previous wheel come to a standstill on its own. As trying to stop a highly charged thought and emotion's turning wheel is akin to jumping into a raging river and trying to stop the flow of water. Whether one is running on a charged wheel or attempting to stop it, both actions are applying focus on the wheel, which charges the wheel.

Healthy and unhealthy thoughts and their responses to situations cause different parts of the brain to spark and energize. When lighting up the same neural pathways in the brain, habits are created, positive or negative. What appears to be an automatic state of mind or response to a certain situation or stimuli is merely strengthened pathways in the brain, causing habit responses or no responses, whether they are thoughts and emotions or the actions they produce. When positive pathways have been charged in the brain and cause positive habits, a positive outlook becomes the baseline when no or little effort is applied. The same is the case for charging negative pathways: a negative outlook becomes the baseline when no effort is applied. One who is regularly angry, depressed, etc., constructs a baseline response of the same created mental and/or emotional habit. Now the human being has to put forth more effort and for a longer period of time to charge positive pathways and let the old negative pathway's charge dissipate. Two straight weeks' worth of honestly charging positive pathways can create new healthy habits for most cases, and if the root reason as to why an unhealthy mental pathway is being charged is understood, it may be dealt with and corrected permanently.

When a being actively avoids lessons they have not yet overcome due to the pain and suffering being stored in their mind, body, spirit complex from past experiences, growth and advancement are being avoided, as well as the mind, body, spirit complex being continually poisoned to the degree that equals the strength of the stored pain and suffering. The stored pain and suffering is triggered and resurfaces every time the certain situation or stimuli arises, providing the being with the opportunity to confront it and release it. In order to solve the situation and defuse triggers, to let go of the stored pain and suffering, do not identify with the experience and make it a part of who you are. It may be an experience that happened to you, but it is not you, and as long as you store it in your complex and make it part of yourself, you are identifying with it and poisoning yourself. Instead of allowing yourself to be triggered every time the situation or even the thought of the situation arises, recognize that it does not define you as a being nor does it serve you, and release it. Learn and keep the lesson, and transmute and discard the pain and suffering. You had the experience, but did you let the experience have you?

Simply avoiding what triggers you is to avoid challenges and growth and allows the poison to continue to adversely affect your mind, body, spirit complex. Avoiding lessons and harboring triggers is akin to the video game player being stuck on the beginning of level 3 for their whole incarnation because they experienced a part in level 3 they could not deal with and so did not get past it and refuse to confront it again. Level 3 in its entirety needs to be faced and overcome so one can move on to experiencing level 4 and eventually finish the whole game. Enjoy the 3rd density for as long as you please and advance at your own pace; although, those avoiding what triggers them are not enjoying what the 3rd density has to offer, so it would behoove them to work on advancing so they may enjoy more of the 3rd density, and move toward the 4th density at their own pace in order to experience something different.

We restate, certain situations in life may make it easier or harder to have a positive outlook, but it is always up to the being whether they decide to produce positivity, neutrality, or negativity. This can be seen when many human beings face the same situation but view it in many different ways. Others may assist, but only you have the power to make yourself content; no one else can do it for you. If you continue to look to other humans or situations—anything outside of yourself—to make you fleetingly happy or content, you may experience moments of enjoyment but will stay subjected to the mental noise of displeasure in between those short-lived moments of enjoyment, which may be unhealthy in themselves, or merely a distraction to keep one's mind off of what it needs to understand and accept in order to solve the root issue that acts as an ongoing plague.

Moments of happiness and sadness are fleeting and always subject to change, and without the foundation of contentment, happiness and sadness tend to act like an up and down roller coaster ride where one tends to cause the other. Being content does not mean one avoids moments of happiness. When one is content, moments of happiness are experienced and appreciated when they occur and do not cause sadness when they depart. And when moments that may cause unhappiness to arise are experienced by one who is content, they possess the wisdom to stay content and not give into unhappiness, even if the temporary situation is not pleasant, because they know that no benefit comes from producing negativity. Contentment is experiencing one's natural state of being of love, joy, and peace that has no opposite. This is what it means to be content. The word "content" may be misunderstood by human beings as being a low level of satisfaction, or to merely be an adequate positive feeling, to simply be okay, but it is quite the opposite. Being content, which is being in one's natural state of love, joy, and peace, is not subject to the opposite since it has no opposite and is immensely more powerful than happiness or any other feeling that cannot be maintained and has an opposite. Contentment is the foundation that keeps a structure stable during changing weather patterns and intense storms. One who remains content can enjoy contentment and fleeting moments of happiness at the same time, and are less likely to fall prey to unhappiness when the fleeting moments of happiness come to an end, or at any time a situation causes the potential of unhappiness to arise in one's mental complex.

Money cannot buy contentment. Despite what most human beings perceive, it is seen to be more difficult to attain contentment when wealthy, as the conscious striving to become wealthy is typically the misplaced belief that it leads to contentment, or permanent happiness, which does not exist. Thus, the expectation one creates to become content through having enough money is never realized because the root problem is not being focused on. Even when the individual realizes their wealth does not solve their problems and does not bring them contentment, they typically are so engrossed in the many facets of negativity and displeasure at that point that came from their striving and after their attainment that apathy is turned to instead of switching paths that would lead to contentment. Typically sadness or apathy is turned to because one simply does not know how to achieve contentment. But being wealthy is not the problem, it is simply not the solution; a disharmonious mentality is the problem. Since the Cosmos is mental, being that it is a mental projection from Source, this should come as no surprise. Doing the inner work and meditating to balance the mind complex is key in the 3rd density experience.

When a being becomes knowledgeable that thoughts and emotions actively create states of being as well as affect physical matter, and that it is the choice of the being to create and charge what thoughts and emotions they entertain, the intelligent being naturally applies the willpower in creating what serves them instead of what poisons and destroys themselves. You are the co-Creator as well as the Creator, so why would you create something you do not want for yourself? When one focuses on something, they charge it and give it power, which makes it more likely to occur if it has not already. To worry or be anxious about something is to actively focus on it and so works toward creating the very thing one does not want to happen. What are you focusing on and charging? What are you giving power to? This is what you are creating and attracting.

If you do not want to charge or give power to negative states of being and outcomes in the present and the future, it is never a good time not to be positive or neutral. This does not mean the negative aspects of life are ignored or not worked on in order to be solved; it means negativity from thoughts and emotions that feed and charge negative outcomes is avoided, which assists at reducing problems, not ignoring them. When focusing on solving situations that are perceived as negative, creating negative thoughts and emotions while doing so only fuels the fire and makes the situation less likely to be resolved, or even makes them worse. Furthermore, due to producing negativity while focusing on solving a negative situation, the individual is cutting themselves off from their higher mental facilities due to creating blockages in their lower chakras, making them less likely to amicably solve the problem.

It is your choice in each moment to create positivity, neutrality, or negativity. "Positivity" here means both fleeting moments of happiness and/or contentment, the natural state of being of love, joy, and peace. Due to this wisdom not being taught or displayed in Earth's societies, it can easily be forgotten time and time again as the programming and ways of Earth's societal norms and routines sucks one back into its focus while interacting with beings who are unaware of it or who have forgotten this wisdom themselves. Printing out and posting this question in a place where you often see it and can remember this wisdom may be very helpful: "When is it a good time to create positivity?"

When doing the inner work and balancing chakras, understanding and accepting each matter is necessary. Accepting matters does not mean that a being gives up or ignores unhealthy situations for themselves and their society; it means they do not charge negativity and create unhealthy outcomes or responses to situations that currently exist and get stuck in the mud. When a being does not charge unhealthy responses to situations—as doing such promotes and creates blockages in their upward flow of prana—they have more access to their mental faculties to better understand the situation or matter, accept what currently is, and then possibly fix the situation with a higher probability rate because the flow of prana is able to flow up and activate higher capacities in one's mind complex, making the use of intelligence that can more likely solve the issue, or convey the issue to another whose abilities make them more likely to solve a certain issue, or to galvanize the majority that may be needed to solve the issue if it is a societal or planetary issue, like ending the highly negatively oriented human beings' control structure over the planet and getting suppressed advanced technology released that majorly aids in shaping an efficient and positive planet and allows a smoother transition off a monetary system.

If a perceived negative situation is ongoing with a friend, lover, co-worker, so-called boss, etc., and is analyzed from a high vibratory state and an adequate amount of attempts have been made by communicating with the other but still the situation persists, it may be time to explore other life options that depart from that human or situation where lessons from adversity keep being offered that have already been learned by the being. If this is the case, a full departure from the situation is not avoiding a lesson because the lesson has already been learned, and the unconscious teacher who continues to teach the same lesson is no longer needed.

If the perceived problem cannot be fixed or abandoned, acceptance is the way forward. If a being finds themselves in an unchangeable situation, perhaps acceptance is what they need to work on in this incarnation to balance their karma, and so that is what they are being offered. Regardless, if one cannot change or abandon an undesirable situation, continuing to produce negative energy through negative thoughts and emotions while in the situation does not solve the situation, it only makes it worse; only acceptance and a high level of focus and willpower stops negative thoughts and emotions from being created and charged, and which offers the way to contentment. In contentment, the mind is liberated even if the physical body is still confined to a situation or location.

Human beings tend to focus on what they do not have rather than what they do have. Practicing appreciation for what one has is an exercise that assists positive thoughts and emotions. Life is not a checklist where something is forgotten after it is obtained. If appreciation is not shown, one may very well end up losing that which they were not appreciative towards before its natural time of departure, especially if it is another human being. Change is constant during an incarnation and all is eventually left behind with each incarnation departed. When this is understood and accepted, reality may be enjoyed not less, but even more, and situations are more likely to be appreciated while they last and let go of when it is time for their natural departure.

There is a difference between creating positive thoughts and emotions and a being's natural state of love, joy, and peace, which emanate from within as the part of Source that each being eternally is and so does not need to be conjured up; it is always present and is felt if not buried beneath temporary matters in the illusion one has decided to focus on instead. Positive thoughts and emotions created from life situations that cause happiness derive from outside a being, so they are subject to change as everything outside of a being does. Negative thoughts and emotions created from undesirable life situations are also derived from outside a being and are also subject to change. Happiness and unhappiness may be felt from inside, but they derive from circumstances outside of the being. Since love, joy, and peace is Source's natural state of being, it is also the natural state of all parts of Source, all beings, and therefore cannot be lost. It is eternal as the sparks of Source themselves. It cannot be lost, but it can be temporarily buried and hidden under layers of negative thoughts and emotions and their produced dirty-filter loops that are created during an incarnation. After an incarnation is done and the mind and spirit complexes project out of the 3rd density body and begin transiting toward the inner planes, pain and suffering is set aside while in the etheric body. Once in the inner planes, all negative layers are distilled, transmuted, and released in the deep resting place and the jewel of oneself is clean and free to shine brightly again, but it is in the interest of the being to let the jewel that is the self, a spark of Source, shine while incarnate.

While incarnate, it is the responsibility of the 3rd density being to work towards keeping illusory layers from burying their true state of being. If a being chooses not to charge negative thoughts and emotions and is not storing suffering and pain in the mind, body, and spirit, the natural state of love, joy, and peace are felt. A being does not need to create positive thoughts and emotions for this natural state to be felt; not entertaining negative thoughts and emotions and freeing their stored suffering and pain in the mind, body, spirit complex are all that is needed. Learning lessons and advancing in the illusion may be done more smoothly and quickly if a being does not let all the heavy details and aspects of the illusion take them over and blind them of reality, their natural state of being. Even though one is seemingly stuck in the cosmic experience until they finish the game, they are not the experience or game and do not need to identify with aspects in the illusion.

Out of habit, negative thoughts and emotions may be entertained and charged. Certain habits in the form of actions may be detrimental, but mental and emotional habits can be much more detrimental because they are the roots to the action-formed habits. One thinks or feels something before they physical do that something. With anything, if the root issue is not addressed, the problem continues in one form or another. When the root matter is recognized and understood, it may be accepted and resolved.

It is wise to take responsibility for the thoughts, feelings, and emotions you entertain or charge for the sake of yourself, others you come in contact with whether you interact directly with them or indirectly interact with them via aura overlapping, and for the collective vibratory state of all 3rd density beings on planet Earth.

103.3 – The Expansiveness of the Mind Complex

Since the Cosmos is a mental projection from Source and so operates on a mental level, the mind complex needs more focus to be mastered than the body complex and spirit complex of a being. The best way to balance a being's chakras, which equates to advancing toward graduating to 4th density, is to observe one's inner state. More precisely, observing one's thoughts and feelings or emotions is the best method that offers advancement. And to a much lesser degree, observing one's physical behaviors and actions, which are not as important because one's behaviors and actions stem from one's thoughts and feelings or emotions, the root of actions.

Naturally, human beings need to adequately observe the physical world that is outside of themselves in order to survive and function in a society. Those who are inquisitive or curious work on observing more aspects of a society and how it operates, connecting details together to understand more fully how other human beings within their civilization or planet operate and possibly what motivates them. This can be particularly useful in recognizing and attempting to balance out the actions of negatively oriented human beings within a society or planet. But as one's state of being is more important than physical actions taken and observing a society, observing oneself internally is more important for one's growth and advancement. After adequate internal advancement, actions taken in the physical world are more effective and powerful because they are made from a centered and harmonious state of being.

Most human beings notice to at least a small degree what transpires inside themselves but do not work on observing the majority of what transpires, nor do most analyze their thoughts and emotions to figure out their motivations and mechanisms. One who is not interested in improving themselves does not bother to observe or analyze their internal state. Those who are interested and do the inner work can make huge advances and live with contentment.

Being ashamed or chastising yourself for producing and charging/entertaining unhealthy thoughts and emotions is counterproductive because it works to strengthen the very thoughts and emotions one is trying to overcome. Be resilient but patient with yourself, as the 3rd density is the most difficult and intense density. Since 4th density beings can influence thoughts and sometimes feelings or emotions, any thought or feeling might not have been produced by yourself anyway. However, one is always responsible for the thoughts and emotions they entertain/charge, even if it did not originate from them. For example, if a human being gave you advice or told you to do something, their thoughts and feelings are received by you, but that does not mean you need to take their advice or do what they command. After hearing them out, it is your choice to continue to entertain their thoughts and feelings by making them your own, and then possibly following through with the action in the physical world. Whether vocalized thoughts and feelings originate from another 3rd density being or stealthily via telepathy from a higher-density being, it is still your choice as to what you entertain/charge. Since one does not know what thoughts and feelings are from higher-density beings, it benefits one to use discernment for all thoughts and feelings. Whether the thoughts or feelings originate from oneself or higher-density beings, if they do not serve you, do not entertain them and discard them. Negative thoughts about oneself or others do not serve you. You may recognize the negative actions in others in your thoughts, but that is not creating your own negative thoughts if you do not linger on them and mentally repeat them, it is simply observing.

When one begins practicing the art of observing and analyzing their thoughts, feelings, and emotions, the inner work is started, the guard is placed at the mental gateway, and the inroads that 4th density negative beings use may be reduced, lessening the amount of thoughts they can project into your mind because you are now keeping watch of the domain of your mind complex, spotting both intruders and one's own unhealthy mental habits at the same time, not necessarily needing to figure out where they come from—self or other—but simply stopping their passage.

One who does not observe nor analyzes their thoughts and emotions is like one who leaves their front door wide open, constantly allowing any service-to-self being to walk right in and attempt manipulation. After a being has done a lot of inner work and becomes adept at observing and analyzing their thoughts, feelings, and emotions and a 4th density negative being sneaks inside through a window of opportunity to embed a thought or feeling, the adept may recognize it and laugh at the attempt like one would laugh at a kid's childish remark that attempts to annoy and stir up drama. It is akin to an adult going back in time to view a scene on the elementary school's playground where a bully's comment heavily affected them when they were a child, but the present adult who observes the scene, laughs at the bully's silly and childish comment instead of letting it affect them.

Observing and analyzing thoughts, feelings, and emotions makes a being aware of the lessons they need to work on. Analyzing thoughts, feelings, and emotions as they emerge offers insight to their root condition because the trail of evidence is fresh. When one knows the root issue, they may effectively work towards resolving it, sometimes instantly. Suppressing or ignoring emotions before one has found its root cause is not a shortcut that works and is similar to ingesting very unhealthy prescribed medication/drugs instead of working to resolve the root issue. If the prescribed drug is ingested long-term—or even short-term depending on the drug and the circumstances—it ends up making the very issue one is trying to cure worse instead of better. In some ways, those who prescribe medications/drugs, such as psychiatrists and doctors, are akin to legalized drug dealers who are just as culpable as illegal drug dealers, but since their prescribed drugs are deemed legal by a society, those who do not think for themselves tend to automatically believe the method and drug is healthy and effective due to being naive. To ignore or attempt to mask a root issue is to give it opportunities to grow into a bigger issue, turning a stream into a raging river.

Observing one's thoughts, feelings, and emotions, and analyzing them if need be to find the root issues and resolving them makes one their own psychologist, which all beings will have to be at some point in their string of 3rd density incarnations in order to graduate to 4th density because mental self-reliance is part of a 3rd density being's responsibilities. Since no one knows you better than yourself and no one else knows exactly what goes on inside you, no psychologist is better than yourself. A percentage of early 3rd sub-density human beings who lack mental discipline may benefit from having a psychologist, but the greater percentage of human beings are adequately capable of serving their own needs in this area, just as an adult no longer needs another adult to treat them like a child.

We have noticed a push by negatively oriented human beings to promote the idea that every human being should have a psychiatrist, even kids, usurping the role of parents. Programming for this has been heavy in TV series and movies. We will reveal two of the three reasons why negatives implement this programming: 1: Hooking more humans, including kids, on detrimental prescription drugs for the sake of profit and making unbalanced/drugged-up humans easier to be manipulated and controlled. 2: Influencing humans into thinking they cannot be their own adult and need a so-called official human to provide them with their parental needs, which makes them less self-reliant and susceptible to being manipulated and controlled. The latter is a favorite tactic by what humans call big government, which may be partially or mostly ran and/or utilized by negatively oriented human beings to manipulate and control the majority.

The mind complex is expansive like the vast storage of information on the Internet. The subconscious mind stores every detail of a being's current incarnation as well as all their incarnations and may be brought forward using the technique of hypnosis, and regression hypnotherapy for past incarnations, which may be beneficial at recognizing and resolving root issues. The conscious mind alone stores enough information to overstimulate a being and drown them in their thoughts of the past and possible future scenarios—which are infinite—if the mind complex is not wisely utilized.

Before using the Internet, it is wise to have a pre-determined objective, a reason for utilizing the Internet. When the objective is accomplished, one stops using the Internet. If one gets on the Internet without a defined reason, they may jump from one task or topic to another and find that several hours have passed with not much to show for it, time that could have been utilized elsewhere being or doing something more valuable. It is the same with one's mind. Use it for a purpose and then put it down, reverting back to a serene state of being, one's natural state of love, joy, and peace. Use the past and future as tools for when they are needed to complete a task in the present and then return to the present moment. The past can be mentally accessed to recall a lesson learned or recover a detail that is needed in the present, but to overstay in the past is to ignore the present moment, which is synonymous with ignoring life since the present moment is all that there is—the collection of every present moment making up one's incarnation. Instead of mentally accessing the past to drown in regret or any other unhealthy thought or emotion, use the present to understand and accept the past and learn from it and also possibly resolve the issue if it is ongoing and one feels it should be resolved. No solutions can be applied in the past, but they can be applied in the present moment.

It may be wise to produce a plan for the future, but it is unwise getting lost in overplanning instead of utilizing the present to work toward fulfilling one's plans because it puts the cart before the horse. It is folly and ineffective to produce anxiety or worry over a perceived possible future event because practicing anxiety or worrying not only produces unhealthy thoughts and feelings, but it works at charging the very possible future one is trying to avoid, making it more likely to happen. The more mental focus that is applied to a thought or emotion, whether it is something a being wants to happen or not, the more it is charged and increases its likelihood of happening in a future present moment.

Use the mind as a tool instead of the mind using you like a tool. An uncluttered desk may be properly used when it is needed. Observe how it feels when your mind is restlessly moving from one topic to another aimlessly. You will notice it does not feel good, or that it is simply a waste of energy. Observe how it feels when your mind is clear and the background running tasks are ended. It feels calm and comforting, and if it is clear long enough, you feel your natural state of love, joy, and peace resurface. If the practice of keeping a clear mind is done often enough, and there is no suffering and pain being stored in the mind, body, spirit complex, the natural state of love, joy, and peace comes forward instantly. It can then continue to be felt to some degree inspiriting your actions as you apply focus to performing the actions, whether they be slow or fast actions. This could be considered a meditative action. Tai chi is a prime example, but even everyday tasks can be made into meditative actions.

Focusing solely on a single thought or action is a prime tool for ending background running tasks in the mind that bog the system down and deplete one's energy. Instead of tasks/thoughts constantly running in the background, they can be initiated and focused on at the proper time, if they even need to be focused on at all. One will find that many thoughts running in the background of one's mind are folly and do not require focus at all, and are best ended and released permanently because they do not serve you. These mind interruptions are akin to an audience member speaking out of turn and interrupting a speech you are focused on delivering. There may be time for questions and answers later on, but now is not the time. The more often the mind is trained in this way, the less interruptions from audience members are made. The audience members may be unruly at first, but if you continue to calmly train them, they will eventually take heed to your direction.

Focusing on one task not only ends background running tasks, it allows one to be more effective and thorough at that one task since it is receiving one's full attention and focus. If the focused task is passive like meditation, observing nature, a city scene, a park scene, a movie, or a theatrical production, the passive action is much more enjoyed when it is given one's full attention. To not give a task one's full attention is to not honor that task. If the task is of little value or useless, perhaps that is why it is not being given honor. This is for one to discern.

Strengthening one's focus and attention span is a very important aspect that offers advancement; one cannot work towards being spiritually advanced or an adept without having done so. Practicing meditation is an effective way to increase focus and the attention span. Reading books is also an effective way to increase one's focus and attention span, as well as stimulating a creative mind. An alarming percentage of human beings in their current fast-paced digital world find it difficult to simply read a physical book because their focus and attention spans are so limited. Children who are raised on digital devices particularly suffer because they are trained to have very limited focus and attention spans in their influential years, which encourages lifelong unhealthy habits.

All 3rd density beings are vulnerable to getting lost in the mind complex. Not all 3rd density beings get lost in their body complex or spirit complex; the mind complex is the most enveloping and difficult complex of a being to train. Getting lost in the body complex, such as delving into superficiality, is a topic that Earthlings are already familiar with, so we do not feel the need to address this topic other than to briefly state: The 3rd density body is one's temple and vehicle that is used during an incarnation, so keep it healthy and maintained so that it can get you where you need to go and allow you to work on what you need to work on. It benefits a being to keep their 3rd density body healthy and maintained, but identifying with something that is transient is to focus on trivialities and sets oneself up for a fall.

Getting lost in the spirit complex is an issue we have already covered but will briefly restate here: When a being has not adequately mastered the lower chakras and instead focuses on engaging the blue- or indigo-ray chakra, much confusion arises and the being is not adequately grounded to learn the lessons in the lower chakras they incarnated into the 3rd density to learn, overcome, and balance, nor are higher-chakra lessons fully learned and understood when the lower chakras are not adequately balanced. Going straight to activating the blue- or indigo-ray chakra is not a shortcut but an even longer route, as there is no foundation established under the blue- and indigo-ray chakras, and so these energy centers cannot function properly, and it is only a matter of time before inharmonious mental states arise.

Many variables from cosmic energy are always in effect and shifting, offering influences that can make working on one's inner state easier or more difficult from day to day. Knowing this equips a being with the knowledge to avoid getting down on themselves when performing the inner work. Regardless of these cosmic variables, having setbacks is necessary and part of the process and offers one the ability to move forward with greater knowledge and strength than they had before. Remember to stay vigilant but patient with yourself as you work on growth and advancement. At no point is giving up or ignoring the inner work a wise choice, as experiencing the Cosmos and advancing through it is the reason you are incarnate in the first place. Additionally, doing the inner work leads to contentment, the greatest gift of all, a gift that only you can give to yourself.

A clear and uncluttered mind is like a clean and uncluttered house. When the house is cluttered, tasks are harder to perform in the house and one may often be busy repeating tasks in the house such as endless rearranging, usually adding to the disarray rather than reducing it. Since the root issue is not addressed, the house stays cluttered or collects even more clutter. One finds large amounts of their time attempting to rearrange and clean the house by performing ineffective methods; always being busy doing useless tasks. This is the state of the mind when the inner work is not done. The mind is a tool that benefits one if they learn how to utilize it properly; it can be one's greatest enemy or one's most powerful and effective tool if used properly.

Clearing the mind not only assists a being, it also opens up possible communication, pathways for further aid. When the mind is clear or when focus is applied to a single contemplative task, the noisy clutter is absent, allowing one's spirit guides, 4th density positive beings, and one's higher self to more efficiently offer guidance and influence in the form of thoughts and signs in the physical world. Signs seen in the physical world could be delivered via repeated signs, signs with personal affiliations, animal occurrences, and signs given while communicating with other human beings. One's spirit guides like to work with other-selves' spirit guides to nudge or deliver a message. The human being one is talking to may be influenced by their spirit guides who are temporarily working with your spirit guides to bring up a certain topic, phrase, or specific word to be spoken that may create a light-bulb moment for you. If the mind is not clear, observant, and focused, signs/messages may go unnoticed.

However, if the positively oriented human being is actively working toward manifesting much positive polarity that could be or currently is beneficial for the majority, they are a target for 4th density negatives who also utilize other human beings the positively oriented come in contact with, nudging the human tool to perform certain actions or say certain words that work to undermine positivity and offer misdirection. The unhealthier a being is, and one who does not perform the inner work, the more likely and easier they are to be used as tools for 4th density negatives.

Practicing meditation is a primary method for clearing one's mind and increasing focus and the attention span. Given there are countless methods of meditating that go beyond the essential and basic meditation of simply emptying one's mind, we do not offer specific ways to meditate since each being is unique and so each being finds different ways of meditating to be effective. Before ending this subject, the wanderer would like to offer a meditation he believes most human beings would find useful. We only note that each being may change any aspect of this meditation to suit their own effectiveness.

—∞—

Here is a meditative exercise I find useful to clear the mind and cultivate a long attention span. You might find it useful as well. I call it the Silent Observer. Find a spot in nature, a park, or even your yard to place a chair to sit on or a picnic blanket to lie down on. Mentally affirm to yourself that there is nothing that needs to be done or thought at this time and clear your mind. If thoughts come rushing in, begging you to do this or think about that, produce no agitated responses to these thoughts and simply dissolve them. To be agitated by them is to charge them. Listen to the sounds of nature without thinking about them and instead passively observe them: birdsongs, birds chirping, the breeze, leaves clattering in the wind, the babbling flow of water, any animal noises, or whatever natural sounds you hear where you are sitting or lying down. If there are no sounds, observe and listen to the silence. Gaze at and observe with a clear mind the elements of nature in your sight: trees, clouds, the horizon, the sky, grass, plants, flowers, birds, animals, water, etc. Observe all these things by sound and sight with a clear mind like that of a quiet and calm tree. Realize that all is well and perfect as it is right now and that no problem exists and no task needs to be done in the present moment. Feel yourself become one with nature and flow with the soothing and healing invisible energy it provides.

If all this is done properly, you will feel your natural state of love, joy, and peace surface within you to some degree. Maybe felt only slightly at first but growing with intensity as time passes. You may be surprised to find this practice more rewarding and even more entertaining than sitting in front of the television while watching some TV series that distracts, might be attempting to program you, and keeps your spirit asleep.

This practice may even be done in the bustling city. You may not have the added benefit of nature's energy or its sights and sounds, but you can still hear and see the city's elements with a clear mind. If you do not mentally label any city sounds as bad, you can observe them with a clear mind, as long as they are not too loud and obtrusive. Going to a park in the city might add some nature sounds to the city sounds and be helpful. City rooftops may also work well because you can view the city as a removed observer without people looking at you, which might distract you.

Follow the same steps previously listed until your natural state of love, joy, and peace begin to glow inside you.

When returning to your daily life and tasks, remember your natural state and how it is always within you. Use focus in your thoughts and actions and calm the mind if it attempts to throw mental clutter at you, knowing that you are more effective and content when focus is applied and mental background tasks are not incessantly running like a spinning hamster wheel that goes nowhere. You may feel to some degree your natural state of love, joy, and peace well up inside you as you sit between tasks or even while you perform focused tasks. It is your natural state of being that is always present inside you, shining through while you experience the illusion of the Cosmos.

103.4 – The Personal Foundation

Once red-ray foundational matters such as survival, fear, anger, and the mental pain threshold are overcome, the orange-ray chakra is where the bulk of unhealthy emotions stem from because personal issues are the most intense since they directly address the individual. Unhealthy emotions stem from the yellow-ray chakra as one group verbally or physically battles another, but it is shared and dispersed throughout the group, making it less intense for each individual within the group. If it is personal, it is all on one individual. Anything that is taken personally is an orange-ray chakra issue.

It may appear that the orange-ray chakra lessons focus on two sets of aspects—personal and one-on-one interactions with other beings—rather than one related set of focus like the rest of the chakra-rays, but this is not the case. The focus of the orange-ray chakra lessons of the personal—or of the self—and one-on-one interactions with other beings—or other-selves—is the same from a higher viewpoint, as each being is a self that comprises the whole self, the One Beingness/Source. All beings are the One being in reality; it is only in the cosmic illusion that each being/self is seemingly separate from another self.

The formative years up to age 18 is a pivotal period for a human being's orange-ray/personal development. Since the small family unit is the first place a being grows within and learns from, family interactions and atmosphere may be considered the root of many orange-ray chakra matters' strengths and weaknesses. The young human being is prepared in the small family unit so it may then be ready to interact and live within a larger group, a society. Unhealthy family situations while growing up in these impressionable years leads to unhealthy personal identification attachments. Healthy family situations create a strong base for a being's personal development and equip them to function amicably within a community.

The educational years before university are also very important for a being's personal/orange-ray chakra development because children get to interact with other children their age, offering countless opportunities for growth in these formative years. Homeschooling hinders this growth even if group times with other children are organized because it does not provide everyday interactions like at a public school. If homeschooling becomes a necessity due to negatively oriented human beings having too much control and influence and degrading schools' learning material, organizing as much group time for interactions with other children is important, as interacting with other children should be considered a subject by itself.

Around the age of 16 to 18 a human being has developed a personal foundation, for better or for worse, which they then use when interacting within a society where they are offered countless opportunities to continue their personal growth. The orange-ray chakra is where low self-esteem and a lack of confidence is displayed while interacting within a society or during alone times. If this occurs, unhealthy thoughts and emotions may be created while alone and while interacting with others in a society because the being does not understand and accept the uniqueness of themselves. The opposite personal issue of being arrogant and egotistical may arise from an unhealthy family upbringing, which is displayed and possibly strengthened in the educational system, and then has to be dealt with when the being starts interacting within a society as an adult. This issue also arises from a being not understanding and accepting the uniqueness of themselves.

Both of these issues—thinking too little or too much of oneself—if not addressed may lead to problems while interacting within a society. The worst case scenario involves these beings becoming murderers, either one-offs or serial killers. In both cases—low self-esteem and being egotistical—the being mentally justifies their actions to a certain degree while force-transitioning/killing another being.

The orange- and yellow-ray chakra related lessons are at the center of the battle between positive and negative polarity in the 3rd density experience. When negatively oriented human beings gain the upper hand in a society or planet, they work to shape their society or planet by manipulating these personal/orange-ray chakra issues and attack the family unit so they can strike at the core structure of a being's personal development to more easily manipulate and control the majority. They turn the educational system, which includes universities, into a system more fit for indoctrination rather than education. Positions of power and/or influence are handed out to those with personal issues because they are easier to manipulate and control. In some cases, in order to gain positions of power and/or influence, a human being has to prove themselves by force-transitioning another being. This proves they are able to be heavily manipulated and gives their controllers blackmail over them so they will continue to do what they are told or face the consequences. Many beings on Earth who are revered and admired by the majority for having their powerful, influential, or famous positions have force-transitioned other beings behind closed doors and are quite the opposite of what they seem in the eyes of the majority. Until approximately 2017 CE, negatively oriented human beings had the upper hand on Earth. Ever since then it has been an intense battle that most of the majority are unaware of, with the negatively oriented human beings utilizing orange- and yellow-ray chakra matters to manipulate and control the majority even more in a brash manner due to fear of losing more of their control to the positively oriented human beings who are working together for the majority. Some of these beings used to practice negatively polarizing actions, but have changed their ways to practice service-to-others actions. A portion of the majority has allowed themselves to be programmed enough that they are actively fighting against the positively oriented human beings who are attempting to assist them. This is akin to a slave who is not aware their masters are treating them badly and not only reject being freed by the attempting freer, but actively work with their masters at destroying those trying to free them so they can stay slaves. Even human beings who lack observation skills have noticed these highly charged erratic situations occurring in your present time, but most are not aware of their root cause. They think the root problem stems from a group issue, such as a political party or a nation, or another group affiliated with yellow-ray chakra issues.

The orange-ray chakra issue of being self-centered also may be fostered in the family unit, especially if they are an only child, and then developed further as an adult. These beings have yet to understand that they are part of a society and that what benefits others also benefits themselves, as working together acts at creating harmony where all prosper. The more unresolved personal issues a being has increases the chances of dysfunctional and unhealthy interactions and relationships with other-selves: friends, lovers, co-workers, strangers.

Instead of focusing on improving the self, an individual may compare oneself to another and be jealous. They may focus on manipulation or general negativity toward those they are jealous of instead of focusing on their inner work, which would alleviate such negativity. Jealousy stems from not realizing that all have a unique path and all have unique characteristics. The uniqueness of beings provides a society with different skills and abilities that assist in that society running more efficiently, which in turn also offers Source unique experiences that It can further learn more about Itself from.

Another orange-ray chakra matter that focuses on the personal self comes through by way of Earthling's online platforms that share a human being's life through words, events, pictures, videos, and reviews of anything from prepared foodstuffs to books. The larger one's following, the larger the chance of charging the want to keep and build one's status in the eyes of others, catering to their personal issues. They start to play an unhealthy game of attempting to keep and/or build their status through followers and staying "relevant". Sharing one's passions and helpful information on online platforms is a healthy and beneficial outlet as long as the goal is to share one's passions and give helpful information rather than merely collecting followers and building their status or ego. If the aim is service-to-others, which is positively oriented, one may take delight in their increasing viewers because it allows them to give service to more beings. It is the motive and what is mentally being focused on that is important here. A sharer with low viewers may continue to share regardless of their numbers because they are being of service and pursuing their passion. A sharer who is mostly focused on follower numbers tends to stop sharing if they do not acquire the following they desire in a certain period of time.

To assess where your mental aim resides regarding your online platform sharing, observe your internal state to find out your true motive. Are you doing it for status and fame or for assistance and from passion? It may be both. In this case, one can continue sharing and work on disassociating their work with status and fame. Then when the status and/or fame departs—and it always does at some point—it will not elicit a personal/emotional response. Instead, one feels grateful they were able to provide service-to-others aid for a period of time. This applies not only to online platforms, but to all positions and roles that involve notoriety. If notoriety is used to service others, it is admirable. If notoriety is used to solely service the self, it is an orange-ray chakra issue that needs overcoming.

Identifying with aspects outside oneself and roles played in society may be an individual's way at utilizing self-deception and unconsciously avoiding personal growth. Perceived important and unimportant jobs on Earth come with a level of status that the self and other-selves use to attach identity to. Some human beings seek jobs with high status instead of following their passions so others are impressed and deem them as "successful". Some parents push their offspring to certain jobs so they can live through their offspring's "success" and brag to others. In both circumstances, from self or parent, as well as solely for monetary reasons, the human ends up in a field they most likely were not meant to be in, not abiding to their pre-incarnate plans and not utilizing their passion. This majorly increases the probability of the human being eventually becoming discontent or even loathing their job, which typically leads to not performing the service well, if they even performed it well to begin with. Each time this happens, a job position in its field is taken away from another being who could have performed it well because it was their passion, naturally improving themselves at it and seeking the position not due to the money, status, or fame it possibly affords.

The perceived importance of jobs on Earth by human beings is calculated by status and monetary intake instead of by their value to society. This mindset is heavily distorted and typically leads to major disharmony issues for the society or planet. A garbage collector plays a vital role in a society but they are given low status. It may not require a lot of skill, but it is essential. A Wall Street worker offers not only no benefit to society but actively harms individuals in a society, but they are given high status because their monetary intake is large. These are only two of a myriad of examples that could be given. Civilizations and planets like Earth that have been captured by a monetary system breed mental disease, corruption, disharmony, and offer negatively oriented 3rd density beings and negative 4th density beings a substantial advantage at manipulating and controlling the 3rd density majority.

Part of an individual's uniqueness determines how many friendships they focus on; choosing to focus on less friendships that are closer in connection or spreading one's time across many friendships. Either is fine. What matters is whether an individual gives themselves enough alone time to focus on understanding and accepting oneself, which is done by analyzing and integrating experiences had with oneself and with others. The one known as Socrates, a 5th density wanderer, conveyed this point when he said, "The unexamined life is not worth living." Balance in this alone-time analyzing and integrating is also needed for the effectiveness of personal growth. Too much alone time spent overanalyzing spins one's mental wheels to the point of inefficiency. Instead, more experiences with self and other-selves is necessary to collect more experimental data to work with. Oppositely, spending not enough alone time analyzing and integrating does not give one adequate time to understand and accept themselves and their interactions with other-selves, collecting more experimental data than one gives time to process, understand, and integrate. If one is in a relationship that affords them little to no alone time, personal growth may be majorly hindered. Spending some time apart is not only healthy for alone-time processing but is also healthy for the relationship.

When one has overcome most of their personal issues and has adequately balanced their orange-ray chakra—especially if they are actively working on their green-ray chakra—disconnects may arise between friends and lovers who have not adequately overcome their personal issues. These individuals may try to hold the balanced individual to their old ways because the old ways might be the sole or major foundation for the relationship. Lifestyles shared with friends and lovers like overindulging in alcohol, drugs, acting out dramas, complaining, misery, superficiality, or any other unhealthy habit, may attempt to be maintained by friends and lovers. Or you may be a positive example they can recognize and attempt to change and progress with you. If they cannot accept the new and improved you, the connection with them may have overstayed its welcome. This is nothing to be sad about, as all have the free will to experience a certain path for as long as they like. Change is constant; the possible change in outlooks, situations, friends, lovers, jobs, etc. is all part of flowing down the rivers that lead back to the ocean.

If some of these elements do not change, stagnation of growth is occurring.

Personal or spiritual boundaries are necessary for the well-being and continued progression of a being. If boundaries are not applied, one may find themselves not having enough alone time, or worse, one may find themselves being dragged into the mud by another regardless of whether enough alone time is had or not. If ongoing interactions with a particular individual are deemed too unhealthy for oneself, a full departure from them may be warranted. For some friends, simply getting together less frequently with them may prove to be adequate. If the case is with a family member, spending less time to rarely seeing them is typically better than a full departure, but if the family member(s) are deemed highly detrimental to one's personal and spiritual progression, a full departure may be warranted. As always, it is the discernment of the individual.

A being who has balanced or is actively balancing their blue- or indigo-ray chakra may be adversely effected by simply being in close enough proximity with one with enough personal/orange-ray chakra issues that their aura—the energy radiating from their chakras—acts and feels harmful even if no words are exchanged. This is like being in close proximity with a human who smokes so heavily that unhealthy chemicals are constantly fumigating from their body and expel such a foul odor that it greatly displeases one just to be near them. They are constantly swimming in it, as they are their personal issues, so they tend not to notice it themselves. This example has correlations but since it is only a foul smell, it is a lighter hardship than being in contact with a being's aura that acts as a negative cloud.

Human beings who heavily smoke for a long enough period to produce such a foul body odor typically possess heavy personal issues. They rely on an intake of unhealthy chemicals in an attempt to mask their pain, which makes their suffering greater instead of being resolved when the root personal issues are addressed. Others abuse alcohol and/or drugs (which includes prescription drugs) in order to temporarily escape their personal issues. Their personal issues are still found waiting for them afterwards, but now they also have other temporary issues: a hangover or the edgy feeling of coming down from an unhealthy drug.

A high vantage point method for overcoming a blocked orange-ray chakra, which equates to personal issues, no matter what the issue, is the same: To become conscious that all beings are unique for a purpose and are equal regardless of their current position in their society or spiritual progression. All beings who may appear to be separate are actually One being, residing in the One Beingness. To do or think anything harmful to another is to do something harmful to oneself, with karma being the all-knowing universal justice system that makes sure each being eventually understands, accepts, and resolves issues with selves.

Conveying this reality may not assist one in overcoming personal issues if it is seen as a lofty spiritual concept that has no bearing in one's incarnation. In this case, one can turn to what all human beings want for their society and planet: a harmonious existence. Apply the Golden Rule to establish this: treat other-selves as you would like to be treated yourself. The energy one puts out is the energy that returns to them. When something is given to another, it is the same as giving it to oneself. This is reality on more than one level. It is a two-way road that makes a road highly functional and effective; there must be giving and receiving, anything else is stagnation and decay.

As you work on personal issues, recognize that others may be doing the same. Have patience with each other.

103.5 – Overcoming Desires, Wants, & Cravings

We have spoken of balancing chakras and matters related to chakras. This includes balancing one's pleasures, but first recognizing which pleasures are healthy and unhealthy. An unhealthy pleasure brings more pain than it does pleasure in the long-term, and possibly even in the short-term. Even healthy pleasures can become unhealthy when overindulged in and not practiced in moderation. For example, too much healthy foodstuffs can be ingested, bogging down the physical body to the point of unhealthiness. Since pleasures derived from the intake of elements produce a temporary elated feeling, often desires, wants, and cravings for certain elements and situations arise, possibly forming unhealthy habits. The intake of unhealthy elements into the physical body for the purpose of experiencing happiness is more likely to produce habits because they do not satiate and continue to produce craving feelings. The individual may not be aware that the bad habit is a path that will never lead to being satisfied, healthy, or content.

The root issues behind these unhealthy habits may simply be the seeking and craving for that elated feeling where a period of pleasure and perceived happiness is felt. The reality of the situation is that unhealthy habits offer more displeasure and unhappiness than pleasure and happiness. The pleasure and perceived happiness is experienced for a period of time and is then followed by a much longer period of displeasure and unhappiness due to unhealthiness. Thus, the pleasure and happiness sought after is a falsity from a comprehensive standpoint, as one loses more than they gain in the long-term. It is similar to making a deal or covenant with a negative being, or even a negatively oriented human being: one first receives from the negative being what they perceive they want—what will make them "happy"—but the contract signed includes fine print details that produce inroads that not only end up negating what is gained in the deal, but lead to more being taken away so the being ends up in a much less desirable position than where they started before they signed the contract.

This knowledge will become more clear and understandable as we cover the mentality that forms desires, wants, and cravings. We will start with foodstuffs, but keep in mind that the method and knowledge conveyed for foodstuffs pertains to all cravings—alcohol, drugs, cigarettes, unhealthy sexual acts, and so on.

The pleasure derived from eating foodstuffs is very short, as once the foodstuffs are swallowed, the pleasure is gone. One may experience 10 to 30 minutes of pleasure while eating unhealthy foodstuffs and then have to face the consequences that are more than a day to some degree of displeasure and unhealthiness. Even after the unhealthy foodstuffs or liquid have been discharged from the physical body, unhealthy chemicals that have mingled with the body as it passes through one's bodily system may stay in the body for many days or longer. This is a large consequence for fleeting minutes of pleasure. If a being was made aware of all the details—short-term and long-term—before ingesting the unhealthy foodstuffs, it would not take too much intelligence to understand that the short-lived pleasure is definitely not worth the consequences. Since most unhealthy foodstuffs do not produce intense enough feelings with their harmful effects, most beings are not conscious of the consequences that last longer than a day, or they do not attribute the noticed consequences with what they have ingested.

As we have stated many times, the mind, body, and spirit are all connected, so when the body is poisoned, the mind and spirit complexes are also poisoned. The consequences of ingesting unhealthy foodstuffs come in many long-term forms and the unaware being does not associate the unhealthy foodstuffs as being the cause to their below baseline state of being. They are not aware that the fleeting minutes of pleasure derived from ingesting unhealthy foodstuffs is having a large hand in their current dreary mood, sluggish mental state, lack of inspiration, and/or other drawbacks, all of which may last for hours, the whole day, all of the next day, or longer. Maybe it is not a dreary mood that surfaces, but merely a below baseline mental feeling of slight displeasure that lingers for a day or two, and so one perceives it is simply the cause of shifting moods. Again, the unaware being does not contribute the displeasure, whatever form or level of intensity it takes, to the unhealthy foodstuffs. This may cause a vicious cycle because the being who is feeling down might attempt to solve it by turning again to unhealthy foodstuffs for their short-lived pleasure, then the consequences are compounded and extended.

The physical body is a being's temple, and to desecrate the temple is to also impair one's mental and spiritual faculties. Ingesting unhealthy foodstuffs is not worth the cost that follows, especially given how fleeting their time of perceived pleasure produces.

There is also the matter of programming that comes with unhealthy foodstuffs. The programmed message that states unhealthy foodstuffs taste better than healthy foodstuffs is a falsity. More pleasure can be derived from healthy foodstuffs, with no consequences except when there is overindulgence, but even this consequence in most cases is less harmful than those from ingesting unhealthy foodstuffs. Negatively oriented human beings have made a push in their programming to express that being obese is good, even beautiful. Doctors are under programming from being taught in a field that is heavily controlled by negatively oriented humans due to its importance and effectiveness for their controlling efforts, but even they are well aware of and disseminate that obesity leads to a myriad of serious health conditions. These health problems include premature transitioning/death, which cuts an incarnation short and removes a portion of a being's pre-incarnate plans for growth and karma balancing.

When one has been on a healthy diet for a good period of time and relapses to the temptation of unhealthy foodstuffs, they may find that it does not taste as good as they once thought if they observe the perceived pleasure derived while eating it. The mentally programmed falsity is then revealed. When this occurs one can reprogram themselves with the reality about unhealthy foodstuffs and be far less tempted or entirely discard the temptation in the future when it arises, knowing the old programming to be a lie. Or maybe one will still observe that the unhealthy foodstuffs give temporary pleasure, but not as much as it did before. Regardless of whether the tasting pleasure wanes or not, knowing the long-term consequences of ingesting it would make any intelligent human think twice about proceeding.

Some chemicals in foodstuffs are so unhealthy that one who practices a healthy diet and observes their mind, body, spirit complex may receive a headache or feel tired within ten minutes after ingesting it. This particularly occurs for high vibratory beings, beings who have balanced lower chakras and are working on higher chakras. One may not be aware that a foodstuff is unhealthy because all the unhealthy methods to produce and treat it are not listed on the product's packaging. This may also include foodstuffs labeled as organic. In Earthly societies, many foodstuffs are touted to be healthy but are quite the opposite. Observing the body and mind while and after eating is the best way to gauge whether a foodstuff is unhealthy, especially for high vibratory beings who can read this gauge much more easily.

The prepared foodstuffs in restaurants, cafes, and other eateries are almost always unhealthy due to the same root issue for most of Earth's issues—the monetary system that captured Earth is the inharmonious grease that turns the wheels of action. Most restaurants would not financially survive if they spent the money to buy healthy ingredients. Why does almost anything on Earth not work or function properly or effectively? Because of the monetary system. When one does something for money instead of for the good of humanity, it typically results in a service-to-self situation, which makes life worse for humanity. Any being in possession of the details of what a monetary system does to a society knows that it is insane to employ such a system, unless they are a negatively oriented being who knows precisely what it does and that is why they are implementing it.

Desiring instant gratification will continue to be a temptation until the being builds up their dietary willpower, which is greatly enhanced when one is equipped with the knowledge of the consequences. Until one's dietary willpower is strengthened on a constant basis, apply temporary heightened willpower when at locations where foodstuffs are purchased so they do not end up in one's living quarters where it may remain a constant temptation or be quickly accessible when one's willpower is temporary low from experiencing certain life situations or moods. At these times, remember that ingesting unhealthy foodstuffs does not solve the perceived problem, it only makes it worse. Remember the formidable long-lasting consequences that greatly outweigh the short-lasting perceived pleasure.

Some humans feel that indulging in unhealthy foodstuffs is a warranted treat because they had a bad day and deserve something to make them feel good, or they accomplished something and deserve to be rewarded. Harming one's mind, body, spirit complex is not a good reward and it will only make one who is discontent more discontent. The same case applies to the mental complex: one may have been in a situation where they were treated unkindly by another being, but continuing to dwell on the incident by mentally creating negative thoughts and emotions regarding the situation only acts to poison the being further. The second poisoning of the being was done by the being themselves. This is wisdom the one known as the Buddha taught.

It is the responsibility of a being to find out what foodstuffs are healthy or unhealthy. There are already many informed human beings sharing this information via books, videos, and various Internet posts. Due to the level of deception negatively oriented human beings have used in relation to foodstuffs over the past approximately 50 years, we offer some information as a balance. The current quantities and levels of unhealthy foodstuffs produced on Earth is staggering. This is due to a combination of unintelligence, the greed to acquire more money outweighing ethnics, and the intentional poisoning of the majority by the highly negatively oriented human beings who not only siphon money from the majority when they seek hospital and/or pharmaceutical assistance for having ingested poison over many years, but who also know that an unhealthy majority is easier to manipulate and control. Most of the majority think monetary gain is the sole reason for the production of unhealthy foodstuffs, as well as for the other countless societal issues on Earth. We restate, negatively oriented human beings that have reached high negative polarity levels that warrant them as being labeled what humans call globalists or elites are devoid of universal love and morality to the level that no action is seen as a weight on their conscience, which includes painfully force-transitioning/killing billions of human beings. Major negative polarity actions may even be enjoyed by such beings.

An indicator that points towards the deliberate poisoning of human beings instead of merely being a byproduct of financial gain is the unnecessary added harmful ingredients put into the countless everyday products human beings use, such as deodorant, toothpaste, mouthwash, shampoo, conditioner, hair products, skin products, shaving cream and gels, aftershave, cosmetics, sunscreen, soap, toilet paper, and so on. The question rather becomes: what is not poisoning human beings? In most cases, the harmful ingredients added to products like these listed are not substitutes for more expensive ingredients that are not harmful, they are simply added and are unnecessary for the product's effectiveness. This means a company's cost is not less but higher to add in these unnecessary ingredients, which happen to be harmful. This is evidence that shows the harmful ingredients are not added in order to save money and collect more wealth, but are intentionally added to harm and weaken human beings, because an unhealthy majority is easier to manipulate and control. The effects of these everyday poisons are very minor, but if one wants to secretly weaken and harm human beings, minimally tainting products that are used every day so the effects do not show up until decades later and are unsuspected of being the cause of the cancer or other illnesses they produce is a most effective method for the highly negatively oriented beings, compounded by other tainting measures in foodstuffs, frequencies, and other means. Virtually all levels of employees at companies, even CEOS, are unaware of this deliberate action. As always, the negatively oriented beings use compartmentalization to keep their actions secret. One may lose their job if they do not adhere to orders from the top. Who is at the top is always kept a mystery. Due to these methods of slow poisoning, the generation known as the baby boomer generation suffered physical and mental ailments in their later years to a much higher percentage ratio than that of the generations before, with the ailments showing up earlier in their years. Every generation after this one faced and faces a whole lifetime of poisoning where the methods and poisons only intensified over the years.

Another prime example that conveys the intentional harming and means of control over human beings as the main purpose behind actions instead of for financial gain is the rollout of the 5G network. As of 2026, the global rollout of 5G networks has cost over $1.2 trillion and is projected to cost over $2 trillion by 2030. The companies involved have already had monumental revenue losses. These companies employ intelligent humans that would not make such a huge financial mistake if it was their call. The call comes from the top of the hierarchical negatively oriented control structure. All are made to follow the orders and are not made aware why the action is actually being done.

Human beings who are highly polarized toward the negative have been patient and methodical in rolling out their plans and agendas over the centuries, but in the recent decades their plans have been drastically expedited. Now that their control is being threatened for the first time by aligned groups on Earth who know of their ways and who also hold power and have taken steps toward removing their control, the highly negatively oriented human beings have forgone patience due to: fear of losing control, being exposed to the planet's population, and being held accountable for their global atrocities, or as human beings call it, their crimes against humanity. Thus, they have turned toward more immediate-acting methods to avoid losing their control, such as engineering malicious viruses and recommending and enforcing many so-called safety measures that are all intentionally unhealthy instead of helpful, especially the wearing of masks because they greatly reduce the oxygen level intake a human being needs to function properly and stay healthy, which includes a healthy immune system. The masks also contain harmful chemicals that are breathed into the body. Because of all this, but mostly due to oxygen levels, one is more likely to contract a virus if they wear a mask. The most dangerous and potentially fatal so-called safety measure is the adding of toxic elements and submicroscopic technology into what is passed off as beneficial vaccines, which, along with other so-called health and safety measures and the virus itself, have and will force-transition/kill over 1 billion human beings within a 15-year period, with the highest percentage being from the China nation. There has been no other event or ongoing event in Earth's history that caused even close to the amount of beings to prematurely transition/die. These so-called safety measures also permanently injured and made the injected potentially more susceptible to negative influences from the added submicroscopic elements that are programmed to self-replicate when powered by certain frequencies, such as 5G wireless frequencies, which is why such frequencies were rushed out during the specific time period before and during the intentionally released viruses and the hijacked vaccines. The submicroscopic/nanoparticle/nanite elements were able to be seen by doctors using specialized microscopy techniques and real-time video footage was captured of these elements self-replicating in human beings when within range and powered by 5G wireless frequencies. The proof overwhelmingly conveys premeditation, as such a highly intricate deployment cannot be deemed as a mistake. The doctors who released this information and time-lapse video microscopy on video sharing Internet platforms faced repercussions from the negatively oriented human beings and their evidence was censored and removed from your most widely used online video sharing platform, which is controlled by negatively oriented beings, as are most widely used Internet platforms. We have already covered this submicroscopic technology that was created by a negative 4th density united group in subject 102.8.

Some of the unhealthiest foodstuff culprits are poisonous pesticides (like those that contain glyphosate), the engineering of foodstuffs (GMOs and heavily manufactured ingredients like salt and sugar), the unhealthy feed and chemical injections given to foodstuff-producing animals, and the subjecting to high temperatures (pasteurization) that alters the chemical structure of foodstuffs and liquids and removes nutrients and may cause the transformation of once healthy liquids or foodstuffs to become very unhealthy. The production of foodstuffs and liquids on Earth would need to be completely overhauled in order to return to healthy levels. Until this is done, human beings will continue to poison themselves anywhere from a minor to a major way on an ongoing basis.

If one does not understand the ingredients listed on the packaging for foodstuffs or liquids, perhaps it is wise to not ingest them. The current deterioration of foodstuffs and liquids has reached an unprecedented level on Earth. The harshest foodstuff and liquid conditions are present in the United States of America nation, as this nation is the biggest target for the highly negatively oriented human beings since its power and influence is the greatest over other nations. This could be seen as a military tactic, and in this case it is an infiltration and internal takeover. The typical foodstuff store in this nation is stocked with over 90% of unhealthy foodstuff and liquid choices. In the United States of America nation, one has the freedom to choose the manner in which they will slowly or quickly poison themselves. Over 70% is a very rough approximation for all other nations' typical foodstuff stores being stocked with unhealthy foodstuff and liquid choices.

There was a time in the not-too-distant past on Earth that all foodstuffs and liquids were naturally organic. Now a food or liquid producer needs to pay money to label their foodstuffs and liquids as organic, or for all the other healthy-touting labels, which still does not ensure the foodstuffs are healthy due to harmful practices that are allowed to occur to foodstuffs and liquids that are still labeled organic. Those producing unhealthy foodstuffs and liquids do not need to pay anything extra to poison humanity. One would think it would be the other way around, assuming unhealthy foodstuffs and liquids were even allowed to be produced in the first place. It is simply not intelligent for a planet to produce any unhealthy foodstuffs or liquids for its population. The drinking water conditions are not much different on Earth. Since the 3rd density physical body's chemical composition on Earth contains over 70% water, it is very important to intake healthy water, water devoid of toxins and that is structurally crystallized. We again point to the material the one known as Masaru Emoto has provided regarding knowledge on this water issue.

Some human beings believe it is unethical to consume animals, but if human beings did not eat 2nd density beings, they would have no source of nutrients and vital energy and perish. Part of the function of 2nd density beings, such as plants and animals, is to participate in the dietary system for 3rd density beings. It is only unethical when the 2nd density beings are treated poorly and not honored for their life-sustaining sustenance, which is a major issue on Earth that would be appropriate to be corrected. The amount of 2nd density animal meat that most human beings consume is too much, and so unhealthy. Out of all the parts of 2nd density beings that are healthy to consume—such as fruit, vegetables, grains, seeds, nuts, and meat—meat would be the smallest portion consumed out of all of these in a healthy diet, and it is not necessary to consume meat every day to stay healthy. It is beneficial for some 6th density wanderers to rarely consume meat or avoid eating meat. For a wanderer to know if that includes them, observe the body and mind complexes to determine what is healthy for the unique mind, body, spirit complex. It would be beneficial for all 3rd density beings to practice this to assess what is healthy or not for them, especially since most of the foodstuffs and liquids human beings produce are unhealthy.

Unprocessed and organic foodstuffs are the safest choice. Choosing organic is particularly a good choice for grains, seeds, and nuts because these foodstuffs absorb more toxic pesticides (such as those that contain glyphosate), but even some organic grains produced in certain nations are unhealthy because they are still being tainted, such as wheat. Most glutinous rice/white sticky rice is not organic and is quite unhealthy, so to ensure healthy dietary practices, this rice and all rice is best when organic, especially for Orientals/Asians who consume it often.

Since almost all the foodstuffs prepared when eating out are unhealthy and eating out is a pleasurable and entertaining activity for societies on Earth, limiting this activity along with gravitating to less unhealthy eateries would be beneficial and appropriate. Supporting the very few healthy eateries would also be supporting your own healthy diet, and so supporting one's mind, body, spirit complex.

The craving for foodstuffs is largely solved by switching from the intake of unhealthy to healthy foodstuffs, but this is not the case for alcohol and cigarettes, as they are simply unhealthy. In cigarettes' origins when they were produced solely from untainted tobacco, this substance was beneficial when it was honored ceremoniously, where the ceremonies did not take place on a daily basis. What is produced now on Earth that is called a cigarette contains little to no tobacco, which is tainted, and mostly consists of a mixture of very unhealthy substances. It is no longer a cigarette, but more that of a poison stick.

We are familiar with an excuse some human beings use to warrant their intake of alcohol, cigarettes, and other unhealthy substances: They perceive that they will simply be cutting short the last years of their incarnation and avoid the many years of having to live with waning health conditions. This perception is unintelligent because it is only living unhealthily, which includes the intake of alcohol and cigarettes, that causes years or decades of waning health conditions toward the end of one's incarnation, and it is never avoided, merely made to happen sooner due to living unhealthily. If one lives healthily, there is a high probability they will transition/die peacefully without years or even months of waning health conditions.

The method and knowledge for avoiding cravings of drugs—deemed legal or illegal—is the same as foodstuffs, but the consequences are more severe and long-lasting. There are some drugs such as cannabis and substances that contain psilocybin that when introduced to the body in moderation may be beneficial. Drugs that contain psilocybin are non-habit forming, so cravings are not produced for them. However, if the amount taken during one session is too high, the consequences may lead to severe psychological conditions. Cannabis is habit forming and so when this substance is not honored and used too often, it has unhealthy consequences. What is considered too often is different from being to being and is the responsibility of the individual to gauge their level of moderation if they choose to intake this substance. Regardless of moderation, if cannabis is genetically produced or grown with harmful pesticides, it is unhealthy. Avoiding cannabis altogether is ideal for some human beings' particular dispositions. As always, it is for each being to discern.

When habits are formed and practiced, they strengthen pathways in the brain and charge mental associations. In the mind's perception, eating unhealthy foodstuffs, smoking a cigarette, having an alcoholic drink, or doing a drug equates to feeling good or being happy. When this self-programming has been strengthened in the mind through a habit, it remains for a long period of time as a temptation and a false assumption that doing it always equates to feeling good even after the intake of a substance starts making one feel bad or unhappy.

This is the case for the so-called addict. It is unhealthy and unwise to call oneself an alcoholic or an addict of this or that, as is done in addiction recovery groups, because it strengthens one's identity with the strong cravings they feel and mentally implies and imprints that they can never alter their self-programming and forever have to deal with the strong temptations. Every being can alter their programming and self-programming to completely relinquish temptations, some beings' dispositions merely makes the process more difficult. The heart of overcoming strong temptations/addictions is to fully realize that they do not serve you and that they make you feel worse, not better, so there is no logical reason to continue doing or consuming it, even when one wants instant gratification. This full realization is the foundation that assists the altering of self-programming. When the being is feeling down, they can turn to something that has the potential to lift their spirits—possibly meditation, or one's passions—instead of turning to a temptation they know is unhealthy and will only make them feel worse after the short-lived pleasure is over, or possibly even during the short-lived pleasure.

The body adapts to some degree after the first intake of particular chemicals, so the reaction one initially received is different the second time around to some degree. Then there is also a slower shifting of reactions to the chemicals as they continue to be taken in. It may get to the point where an intake of the chemicals no longer produces good feelings and only produces bad feelings, but the individual keeps up the intake anyway due to their self-programming of thinking it still equates to feeling good, which has become a falsity in more ways than one at this point. If the human being wants to break the habit, they can observe the discontent feelings in the body and mind that are produced during and after the intake of the substance. Then they can reprogram the mind and strengthen pathways in the brain that do not fall for the temptation because they know it is unhealthy self-programming as well as a false assumption for feeling good. The higher the vibratory state of a being, the easier and quicker it is to feel the detrimental feelings in the mind, body, spirit complex. Even one alcoholic drink to a high vibratory human being who is an adept or approaching adepthood may potentially make them feel bad. Alternatively, there are healthy herbs and roots that offer relaxation, such as valerian root.

What is sought after in cravings is a numbing or altering of one's baseline state. One who does not want to take the time to solve their issues by doing the inner work that affects their baseline state of being on a more permanent basis seeks a shortcut, but the shortcut is only temporary and potentially unhealthy. Alcohol is typically the chosen option when one wants to numb their mind, which is an unhealthy form of escape from their baseline state. Regarding drugs, seeking to alter one's typical state with the aim of expansion may be beneficial when done appropriately and in moderation, or not at all depending on the specific disposition of each human being. But when one seeks to alter their typical state simply because they do not like their typical state, this is escapism. As with the numbing of alcohol, the escape is only temporary and then the undesired typical state of being returns, and may potentially be an even less desirable state than the baseline state depending on the particular drug utilized. If one wants to permanently alter their typical state for the better, they need to do the inner work, which leads to one's natural state of being of love, joy, and peace, which is in the long-term infinitely more desirable than any altered state that can be achieved with drugs. One who is not regularly attempting to escape from their personal issues by consuming drugs and instead very moderately consumes drugs to have what humans call a party experience may not potentially form habits, but even some of these cases where one does not have personal issues they are attempting to escape from may form unhealthy habits due to largely preferring the altered state to their typical state, even if their typical state is not largely burdened with suffering and pain. Each human being is unique and therefore needs to discern for themselves what to ingest and how often, or not at all.

A socially acceptable drug called caffeine in its high levels found in coffee has been quite detrimental for human beings. When coffee is ingested regularly, its acidity level harms the body, and the mind is conducive to anxiousness where there may be a lack of patience and an inability for calm states of being to be reached. One who drinks coffee daily begins to rely on it for their energy. They feel sluggish and get withdrawal symptoms when they do not get their daily fix. To continually rely on an outside chemical for one's basic daily energy instead of from living healthily is a drug dependency and a hindrance. When this natural drug at this strength is honored and used very sparingly at meaningful times, it may be beneficial. Ingesting coffee even once every three weeks is typically not beneficial for human beings.

Tea is a healthier alternative when it is not tainted, but most of the tea produced is unhealthy due to pesticides. For most human beings, untainted caffeinated tea may be beneficial when ingested in moderation. If the tea is not caffeinated, it may potentially be healthy to ingest daily. It is wise to limit the intake of caffeinated tea because it affects the absorption of certain beneficial minerals so the body cannot utilize them. The array of different teas is one example of the countless natural medicines available on Earth for different ailments.

The wants, desires, and cravings for excess material items stems from the belief that the acquiring of materials makes one content. Acquiring goods may make one happy, but as we stated, happiness is fleeting, so it is only a matter of time before the purchased goods no longer provide happiness, and typically the happiness is quite fleeting, sometimes evaporating minutes after the acquiring of goods. The craving then directs one to acquire goods again to receive another dose of fleeting happiness. Each time the happiness becomes more fleeting as the self-creating chemicals produced in the brain continue to wane with each case of acquiring new goods, but this may not stop the human being from realizing the folly of their actions. Human beings have labeled this addiction: consumerism. Nothing outside of the self brings contentment, as only from within is where one's natural state of love, joy, and peace resides and is the only path to contentment. One may enjoy the efficiency and living standard by utilizing materials and goods, but if an excess is reached that causes more work for the individual to maintain what they have acquired, the materials become a hindrance rather than being useful. Human beings living simply tend to obtain contentment more easily due to this.

The craving of acquiring power for control over other-selves is the path of the negatively oriented 3rd density being. Power itself is a tool that may be used for any purpose, including to perform service-to-others actions more effectively. It is power that is utilized in a controlling manner over others that is service-to-self oriented. As a being understands and practices the lessons within more chakras—whether positively or negatively polarizing—power for the self is obtained directly. As the densities are ascended, more power is also obtained directly by the self. Power is obtained and increased directly by each spark of Source on their journey back to Source. The question is how the being chooses to use their power—for service to others or solely service to self.

In regards to the transfer of power from one being to another, positively oriented beings indirectly offer power to others for the benefit of the whole, and negatively oriented beings indirectly gain power by deceiving and manipulating others. A direct transferring of power is a misperception because power may be indirectly offered but it can only be directly obtained by a being doing the inner work/self-work to polarize toward the positive or negative. For example, when a negatively oriented human being force-transitions/kills another being, it may be considered a one-time display of power, but no power is obtained and kept by the being. If negatively oriented human beings somehow convince other beings, or the majority, to give them their power and serve them, which is indirect and may be done without the full awareness of it being done, then the negatively oriented being(s) have acquired power through transference. Clever negatively oriented beings, such as those on Earth, use trickery and deception so that the majority is not fully aware they are willingly giving away/transferring their power. We say "not fully aware" because even in the most deceptive cases, each being has some awareness that they are transferring their power away, even if mostly done subconsciously while practicing naivety.

Negatively oriented beings' craving for power, which offers control, is never quenched. Since money—or an equivalent—offers power on a planet that has been captured by a financial system, their craving for money is never quenched. Even if a negatively oriented being was somehow able to obtain every single bit of currency on their planet, their craving would not cease and they would seek other means to attempt to satiate their cravings, which would never be satisfied, as only contentment from within completely satiates cravings. This is an example to illustrate a point, as actually obtaining every single bit of currency would effectively remove a planet off a financial system since there would be no circulating currency for it to function. So instead, negatively oriented beings acquire most of the wealth directly and indirectly in the temporary hands of human tools who act as puppets that seemingly run a substantial company. Either way, the knowledge of their massive holdings is kept a secret so the majority is not alarmed. Then they encourage the majority through programming and the social conditioning it shapes to fight among each other for the remaining scraps of money in circulation. This aligns with the negatives' lack of resources programming that states there is not enough to go around for everyone and so only some may obtain certain goods and services or a certain amount of them, which creates fighting over who are the few who get the most, which fosters selfishness and negative polarization. The reality is: there is enough of everything that is necessary, and most unnecessary things as well, to go around for all beings. After the majority of wealth has been collected directly, and indirectly through large companies with a puppet placed at the helm, increasing their control over a planet by whatever means necessary is what negatively oriented beings turn to after their wealth is extremely abundant to the point that obtaining more of it no longer increases their power.

If desires, wants, and cravings for anything focus on matters, methods, or situations outside of oneself to obtain "permanent happiness" or contentment, the bottomless hole is never filled. Instead, it is appropriate to utilize and interact with what is outside oneself respectfully and honorably to effectively experience an incarnation and shape a harmonious society, and look to within to establish contentment, one's natural state of love, joy, and peace.

103.6 – Group Identification

When a human being reaches a certain age, yellow-ray chakra lessons are offered. At this point red-, orange- and yellow-ray chakra lessons, as well as green-ray chakra lessons when they arise, are offered to the being at different times in different situations. The yellow-ray chakra is associated with group affiliation, such as race, nationality, religion, or political party. These are the essential groups on Earth. Others could be formed and considered groups on any given planet. Wealth classes is another group affiliation that has been formed on Earth due to it being captured by a monetary system. The more affiliated groups that are created or recognized on a planet, the higher probability for friction, which is why negatively oriented 3rd density beings attempt to create as many groups or divisions as possible to create fighting with each other and infighting within each group, which may lead to a group dividing into two more groups that potentially can fight each other and other groups, and so on as the tree's branches keep producing offshoots that distance themselves from the center of the tree of life.

Overcoming red-ray chakra foundational issues opens up the possibilities of focusing on personal/orange-ray chakra matters, which then offers one to more effectively interact within yellow-ray chakra related groups. Overcoming these group identifications opens up the green-ray heart chakra that, when adequately balanced, loves universally regardless of group affiliation and prepares the later 3rd sub-density being for 4th density positive where they work toward forming a shared group mindset in a united group that focuses on service-to-others actions. In a negatively oriented 3rd density being's case, orange- and yellow-ray chakra issues are recognized, understood, and adequately perverted with power, selfishness, control, and the separation of others to graduate to 4th density negative where they work toward forming a united group with a pecking order that shares a service-to-self purpose that is opposite of that of the 4th density positives.

Human beings are born into some yellow-ray chakra related groups such as race, but this is not to say there was no choice in the matter, as all is pre-incarnate decided and planned by beings before their next incarnation. Nationality is also a group an individual is born into, but unlike race this group may be altered by moving to a different nation.

There is nothing wrong with mentally affiliating oneself with their race, nationality, or any other group as long as the group does not acquire the mindset that they are superior or more deserving of power and control over another group or all other groups. One can work within their group or groups to do service-to-others actions in the geographical area they reside in and display a humble/non-boastful pride and honor in actively making their part of the Earth a more harmonious place. Even religious or political party groups that an individual may join, due to their family being part of it or having gravitated toward it themselves, are not necessarily detrimental to the being. Even though these particular groups tend to exhibit great distortions, those in them have the ability to avoid thinking of their group as superior or more deserving of control over other groups. One group may be more knowledgeable or wiser than another group, but that does not make them superior. All are equal in reality as parts of Source. All are One.

A positively oriented being may be affiliated with a group they have decided to join during their incarnation, but they work within that group with the intention of doing service-to-others actions and do not see their group as superior or deserving control over another group. They see diversity as uniqueness that should be honored and added to the variety/spice of a harmonious society that is made stronger due to having different working parts that make the society function more effectively.

On the opposite side, negatively oriented beings perceive their group or groups to be superior and more deserving of control over other groups. The more polarized toward the negative the individual is, the more they justify that their group is superior and the more they mentally warrant service-to-self actions to be taken to fight or control other groups. Force-transitioning/Killing campaigns are waged for the most selfishly oriented groups, which are directed by negatively oriented beings within them. As with positively oriented beings and groups, the negatively oriented beings and group's mental intentions and actions are sent out like beacons and attract the same mental configurations and energy back to them via 4th density beings, as well as from beings in the lower and higher inner planes. Negatively oriented 3rd density beings in groups are unconsciously or consciously directed by 4th density negatives who use the group as tools to attempt to shape a civilization or planet in their image, where control and selfishness are utilized to sow seeds of separation and enslave the majority under a ruthless hierarchy of a minority of negatively oriented beings whose thirst can never be quenched. When one does not focus on and solve the root issue, it is never resolved and one is not satiated.

Yellow-ray chakra group issues have been behind the countless wars and divisions in Earth's history and its present. The greater proportion of yellow-ray chakra related groups being harmonious or inharmonious is an indication of who is actively directing the civilization or planet—positively or negatively oriented human beings. Due to the negatively oriented 3rd density beings typically composing the minority on a mixed graduation planet, such as on Earth, their numbers are greatly less, so they have to deceive, manipulate, and utilize other-selves to gain and keep control over the majority. The majority consists of neutrally oriented beings, positively oriented beings, and negatively oriented beings who are not deemed special enough to be part of the so-called elite. If enough of the majority unite and take positive action instead of doing nothing or working against themselves within their majority, the highly negatively oriented minority cannot be successful. But as long as the majority ignore or disbelieve their responsibilities and willingly absorb the negatively oriented beings' programming and adheres to the social conditioning it creates, the majority are herded like sheep to do the bidding of their ruthless wolfish controllers.

Diversity and groups on a planet or in a civilization that are harmoniously aligned may be more effective at progression and advancement—like Atlantis was before the start of their fall—because different skills and viewpoints can work to aid each other, sharing beneficial and effective ways to live that truly advances a civilization or planet at a much quicker pace than a homogenously grouped civilization or planet. But if diversity in a civilization or planet does not work together to integrate harmony, there is a higher probability for friction. Therefore, diversity is much more volatile than an undiversified society, as it tends to go high or low in regards to harmony. In an inharmonious civilization or planet, diversity and many groups are used as tools by highly negatively oriented 3rd density beings to promote aggressive separation, pitting one against the other, sowing seeds of negativity and destruction in order to establish control over the majority. Negatively oriented beings create their order of control out of chaos, chaos they typically cause. The negative 4th density united groups influence and assist the rise of power and control of any being or group who resonates with their vibration, those who actively gain or desire to gain negative polarity.

When the harvest grows near on a 3rd density planet, the seniority of vibration comes into effect, offering positions at the head of the incarnation queue to those in the later 3rd sub-densities for both positively and negatively polarized beings. For mixed harvest planets such as Earth—some graduating to either positive or negative 4th density—this causes the rise of possibilities/probabilities for intense fighting between the forces that are positively and negatively polarized, both being advanced enough to begin learning their early parts in 4th density positive or negative while finishing up their later 3rd sub-density incarnation(s). This is why it has become so heated lately on planet Earth as harvest-time approaches. Approximately 2,000 years ago, and even before then, harvest-time was stated as coming soon in Earth's so-called holy material because 2,000 years is considered soon for higher-density beings who are not mired in the illusion of time. When we say soon, we mean harvest-time begins in or near 2034 CE.

As the harvest approaches, the later 3rd sub-density negatively oriented beings will continue to utilize the tools of old of the negatives as well as tailor and implement new methods of separation that are perceived to be effective for each particular society or nation on Earth. These methods are enacted through a combination of programming and brute force—either physically and/or legally—both shaping social conditioning. The aim being to socially condition the majority so they work as tools against themselves for maintaining and growing the power and control wielded by the minority of negatively oriented beings. A prime and effective recent example on Earth was that of the so-called safety measures legally forced onto humanity after the engineered viruses and their planned release in different nations. The viruses did not have the impact the negatively oriented beings where hoping for, but they were still utilized to produce and promote mass fear issues that created prana-flow blockages in the red-ray chakra that inhibited many human beings' mental facilities in order to socially condition the majority and more easily implement effective power and control through the so-called health measures, which was the actual cause for the mass force-transitioning/deaths.

Observant human beings have noticed the many old and new methods the negatively oriented human beings have added to their actions and programming. Look to where separation is being created in mindset and actions, often in disguise as protection and progression, which is where one finds the negatively oriented actions and programming. Given that negative 4th density beings have recently presented many opportunities that have gained traction on Earth, positive higher-density beings are able to in turn move their game pieces forward on the chessboard, balancing out the opportunities presented to Earthlings. We, as a later 6th sub-density united group, who have had interactions with Earth's development in the past, are also able to do our positive part in this balancing by offering this awareness-expanding course, which offers a guide for raising one's vibration, and also exposes many of the negatives' methods so human beings are less likely to fall into their traps, or release themselves from the traps they are already stuck in, the latter being more prevalent. It is our honor and duty to offer assistance to Earthlings.

For yellow-ray chakra related group issues, we offer another exposing. The negatively oriented programming phrase "cultural appropriation" has been implemented to cause more conflict and separation between groups and human beings within the same group, judging and shaming each other for recognizing and adopting neutral to positive expressions from another group. While the two-faced negatively oriented human beings tout their backing for diversity in its many forms, they are in reality using human beings who have become lost in their identification of personal and group issues within the illusion as tools to cause discord, suffering, and separation. When an individual adopts and shares the ways or outlooks from another group because they see it as agreeable or positive, this is working toward sharing harmonious relations between groups. It is a sign of respect and honor to another group, and therefore it is a positive action, not a negative action. This programming phrase is meaningless, as most programming terms are. To the observant human being who thinks for themselves, this phrase and the many other programming phrases implemented by negatively oriented human beings is recognized for either being unintelligent or purposefully negative in nature.

Human beings may work as what is known as whistleblowers or sharers of truth to expose the negatively oriented human beings' actions and plans, but doing so with anger and/or fear weakens the cause and strengthens the opposition because anger and fear create blockages in the red-ray chakra and cause one to act without their mental faculties, which allows counterintelligence efforts to more easily divert one's attention and mislead them down a false path. Negatively oriented human beings, who are currently still in control of the many outlets used for effective programming, continue to use those outlets to program and socially condition the majority to disbelieve and ridicule the human beings attempting to improve the planet and make it more harmonious, which happens to include exposing negatively oriented actions and agendas. The tried-and-true method of negatively polarized beings twisting reality is utilized in their programming outlets, painting a false picture of the human beings who are actively doing the most to aid humanity to appear as the villains. The villains paint themselves to be the heroes and the heroes are painted to be the villains in the negatively oriented beings' controlled programming outlets. Up becomes down and down becomes up in their twisted reality. This is the role of beings who desire to gain negative polarity.

Some group affiliations have offered learning opportunities that have aided individuals' growth, but their advancement eventually hits a brick wall and another path needs to be found to get around the blockage. Even on more harmonious 3rd density planets where no beings graduate to 4th density negative, this brick wall is eventually hit if identification with a group is held onto. This is because the roles played in yellow-ray chakra related groups are another part of the illusion that is the Cosmos. The illusion was collectively created for a purpose of learning and expansion by Source, so roles and identification within the illusion were meant to be played for a period of time. How long of a period to play roles is the freewill choice for each spark of Source to decide. If a 3rd density being, positively or negatively oriented, recognizes and drops their identification with the many illusory roles of personal and group affiliation in 3rd density and chooses to only affiliate with one role of being in the positively or negatively polarized group with the aim of performing service-to-others or service-to-self actions, their graduation potential to 4th density is greatly increased due to their expanded viewpoint.

The positively oriented being effectively polarizes toward the positive path by adequately balancing their lower chakras and learning and living enough of the green-ray chakra lessons. When their minds are expanded to a larger viewpoint and consequently advance in their spiritual nature, identifying with group affiliations is abandoned and the separating lines that partition groups blurs and then fades away as the being gets closer to realizing that all beings are One being. This does not mean such a being does not recognize and enjoy the variety that is offered by different racial, national, or planetary groups while experiencing the 3rd density; they simply do not identify themselves with any groups because they have recognized they are merely illusory roles and to continue to place identity with a temporary role they are done playing would be choosing to not move onto the next role. The next role being part of a united group in 4th density that works to increase their positive or negative polarity.

The later 3rd sub-density being who has ceased identifying with groups is still physically of a racial group for their entire incarnation, but they do not mentally focus on or place their identity in their race, as they have become aware of such a facet being another part of the illusion and have transcended such a role. They see diversity, if harmonious, as different spices that make a meal more delicious, enjoyable, and interesting. Such a variety is created on purpose by Source so that it may be appreciated while enjoying the 3rd density experience no matter how spiritually advanced a being is. Enjoying the variety and even having changing preferences as to which spices are enjoyed most by each unique being is part of their uniqueness and is not affiliation through identification. Having an affiliation and identifying with one singular spice or group and refusing the rest is rigid and not of unity. This is the rigidness that is being abandoned and allows one to flow naturally, and so be able to more thoroughly enjoy and appreciate the different spices offered in the 3rd density experience.

The negatively oriented being effectively polarizes toward the negative path by recognizing, understanding, and twisting orange- and yellow-ray chakra matters to the point where the many illusory 3rd density roles and identifications are abandoned for the sake of gaining more power and control over all groups, then the one role of negative polarity is more consciously chosen and strengthened. The many illusory 3rd density personal and group roles are not only recognized and understood but utilized as tools to create confusion, separation, and control over the majority.

Highly negatively oriented human beings who have accomplished this have been fittingly called globalists on Earth. They have recognized the illusory roles, which includes being affiliated with any particular nation, and perform actions that only serve themselves. They do not care what nations are prosperous or not; their nationality becomes irrelevant because they no longer let such identifications hold them back from serving themselves in the strongest possible manner. They pit other human beings' personal and group roles and identifications against each other, nations against nations, races against races, and so on, all for the sake of increasing their power and control over the planet. They have reached a level of negative polarity where they do not hesitate to force-transition/kill billions of beings if it adds to their power and control over the planet because beings at this level of negative polarity and service to self are devoid of concepts such as universal love and morality. They see these concepts as weaknesses that hinder one from gaining more power and control over others. If a being wants to continue polarizing toward the negative and graduate to 4th density negative, they must ignore universal love and morality, such is a prerequisite. The nature of their mentality and lack of morality often stays hidden from the majority because they know it benefits them to hide it, and most of the majority cannot conceive of human beings who could be so absolutely service to self and perform actions that they would consider to be pure evil. The small minority of human beings who are highly polarized toward the negative use this positive outlook of the neutrally and positively oriented human beings to convince them through programming that such evil only exists in the movies and fictional stories so their agendas can stay hidden, and in so doing become much harder to be stopped.

For positively oriented human beings, becoming aware of the larger viewpoint of the Cosmos and possessing a spiritual foundation strengthens one's resolve and willpower so when they are exposed to the astonishing levels of play used by highly negatively oriented 3rd density beings, they are less likely to stumble in their progression by producing fear, anger, or hysteria. If this awareness-expanding course is understood and absorbed, one is equipped with such resolve. The use of humor, even dark humor when it is used to illustrate a meaningful point, is also very useful when conveying the mentality and tactics of highly negatively polarized beings. Humor is also powerful in not taking personal and group roles too seriously, adding joy to one's life, and is effective for conveying important information because beings are more open-minded to recognize and accept a lesson when it is approached in a lighthearted manner. Serious and tense may be rigid, whereas light and soft is malleable.

A being who becomes even partially aware of the expanded viewpoint recognizes the transient illusory roles played out in the 3rd density. All beings are eternal sparks of Source who collectively created the Cosmos to play temporary roles in it. The 3rd density offers by far the most roles to be played, with the potential to play different roles for every incarnation in 3rd density. In one 3rd density incarnation a being pre-plans to be born of a certain race, in a certain nation, of a certain gender, and possibly identifying with a particular religion or political party for a period of time. When a being knows all these 3rd density roles from one incarnation to the next change, the temporary roles do not become so important and serious. This is the folly of 3rd density group fighting, as a being sometimes chooses to incarnate into the very group they fought against in their last incarnation, hoping they will succeed in not fighting themselves the next time to balance karma. It is no different than an actor playing a role and discarding it at the end of the film and playing a different role in their next film. In this way, all beings are method actors playing roles. They get lost in their roles and strive to be liberated from them. The folly of placing so much value in temporary aspects is also shown in the importance of the highly negatively oriented human beings' bloodline, where they place so much importance in one's transient 3rd density physical vessel. The 3rd density body is temporary and recycled for another in the next incarnation, where any possible being could incarnate into their bloodline. Playing such a transient game is trivial and self-defeating.

103.7 – Universal Love

Working on and balancing the green-ray heart chakra is an act only positively oriented beings do as they progress toward graduating to 4th density positive. Negatively oriented beings focus on self-love by way of manipulation of orange- and yellow-ray chakra matters. They do not practice the green-ray chakra's universal love. However, this subject, as well as this whole awareness-expanding course, is offered to all 3rd density human beings—positively, negatively, and neutrally oriented—as working toward switching to positive polarity is always a choice, and then in 6th density a requirement to advance further.

As a 3rd density being works on balancing their orange- and yellow-ray chakra matters, partial prana may flow upward during times of peace and focus and offer the being some lessons in the green- and blue-ray chakras, and possibly even the indigo-ray chakra. Until the 3rd density being overcomes and balances an adequate amount of their orange- and yellow-ray chakra matters, lessons offered from the green-ray chakra are fleeting, as one who enjoys a short vacation returns to their slavery job. Overcoming and balancing personal/orange-ray chakra matters offers the way forward for a 3rd density being and is a major focus for their progression because it is the foundation for all matters of the individual and interactions with other individuals—Source interacting with itself in both cases. When these self and other-selves' matters are overcome and balanced, matters of the yellow-ray chakra group affiliations are easier to overcome, as what comprises group interactions is made up of individual connections and interactions from self to other-selves, regardless of perceived groups.

A 3rd density being is offered more learning materials and opportunities for universal love in the green-ray chakra when the flow of prana is not blocked and able to reside often and long enough in duration in the green-ray chakra, where the spotlight of focus then shines on green-ray chakra lessons, opening the classroom doors and books of learning in the next grade level of education.

When a 3rd density being becomes a certain age, they start seeking universal love with another being in a love relationship. At this point the being most likely has not overcome an adequate amount of personal/orange-ray chakra issues to understand and experience the long-lived green-ray universal love they seek. They seek another who will love them unconditionally despite their flaws, building a loving connection meant to be powerful and long-lasting, but once such a relationship begins and the newness of the relationship departs, it is the personal flaws of the orange-ray chakra and mindsets of both the individuals in the relationship that tend to actively work on blocking the upward flow of prana to the green-ray chakra, blocking the very path in which both individuals seek.

Being in a relationship that focuses on love is the classroom of learning for personal/orange-ray chakra lessons because a powerful mirror in the other-self reflects back and makes known personal issues that need resolving and balancing. This is the most effective and advanced classroom for overcoming and balancing personal matters. Before an individual realizes this new classroom they have enrolled in, they perceive the other-self in the relationship will do all the work in making them feel loved, happy, understood, accepted, and all the other lessons that reside in the personal/orange-ray chakra. When the newness of the relationship fades and the personal issues that were temporarily hidden for a period of time resurface, as they always do unless they are resolved and balanced, the individual starts blaming the other-self for not being able to dissolve their personal issues that stop them from dwelling in green-ray's universal love. At this point they do not understand that it is only themselves that can do this. They may stay in the possible dysfunctional relationship, not working on their personal matters and continuing to think it is all up to the other-self to make it work. Or they end the relationship and seek a different other-self and repeat the same situation, being unaware of the root issues involving their personal/orange-ray chakra matters that are holding them back from experiencing universal love. They will never find an individual who can solve their personal matters because only they can do that for themselves. That is why they are called personal matters. Relationships help and assist growth, but only the self can resolve and balance self issues. Until the individual overcomes issues and balances out matters adequately in the orange-ray chakra by doing the inner work, they will never find what they seek in themselves and with other-selves: green-ray's universal love.

Relationships that focus on love provide the mirror from another self so the self can see itself more clearly. Flaws that one did not see before are brought to one's awareness. Then these flaws—matters that need to be overcome or balanced—can be worked on by the self so they can make their way toward permanent residency in the green-ray's universal love instead of only enjoying fleeting visits or vacations there. The directions for proceeding on the path that leads toward the beginning of the path of universal love can be given by others in relationships and awareness-expanding material akin to our offerings, but only the self can put one foot forward and then the other in order to reach the trailhead of the new path. All beings eventually do this for every new path—all chakras, sub-densities, and densities.

Sometimes the mirror one holds up to show the other-self their flaws is not a mirror, but a projection of the mirror-holder's own flaws. Just as one uses their discernment for both positive and negative 4th density beings' influences, one is responsible for determining if a mirror or a projection has been placed before them by another 3rd density being. If one is not certain which it is, this might mean it is a mirror. If they decide to work on the matter by doing the inner work and show advancement but the other keeps raising the perceived issue, especially in a non-loving manner, it may be a projection instead of a mirror.

Until the two beings in a relationship that seeks love adequately overcome and balance their own personal matters, conditional love will be displayed instead of universal love. Green-ray's universal love is given freely with no conditions or strings attached. One who has adequately balanced their green-ray chakra recognizes on some level that all beings are connected, or that all beings are One, so to love another self is to also love oneself. In this held concentration of love and light energy, giving is performed without the motive of getting something in return; the motivation is the aid of the service-to-others act itself. The powerful loving feeling one experiences while in a relationship may be assisted and charged from their partner, but the powerful loving feeling is actually being created by the being themselves. One can generate this loving feeling even when they are alone if they focus on universal love in their green-ray heart chakra. The intelligently conscious love energy inspirited within each atom and space between each atom glows with love when its nature of love is focused on. This is what is being felt, and it does not take another self in order to do it, but the mirror of another self that reflects this loving feeling back makes it easier to be seen and felt.

As green-ray sexual acts are always vulnerable to lowering to orange- or yellow-ray sexual acts, beginners working to balance the green-ray chakra in their life board game are vulnerable to lowering back to focusing on orange- or yellow-ray chakra lessons. This may happen if actions in life that derive from the green-ray chakra face enough pushback and attacks from neutrally and negatively oriented human beings that may result in not only giving up their aiding actions, but in a state of victimhood or anger, they may shun other-selves because of the possible resistance, attacks, and lack of support, which leads to regression to orange-ray chakra lessons by solely focusing on themselves with personal/emotional blockages. If the friction came from an individual from a particular group, this may be focused on by the self and mentally built up to be of importance, which regresses the self back to yellow-ray chakra group affiliation issues.

When a 3rd density being has adequately balanced their green-ray chakra—which means they have already adequately balanced their red-, orange-, and yellow-ray chakras—and interacts with other human beings with loving-kindness that has no ulterior motive, the other human being may respond in a nonreciprocal manner because they are used to an ulterior motive always existing when some type of love or kindness is shown. They are used to displays of love being solely displayed as an attempt to get into a love relationship or a fleeting sexual experience. In other words, they are used to conditional love. They are not used to coming in contact with universal love that has no motives and may not even understand what universal love is or that it exists, so they usually assume there is an angle being played. In this case they either welcome or rebuff the perceived advances from the one displaying universal love. The human being who welcomes it may become irritated or angry later on because no attempts are made to further their perceptions of getting into a relationship or sexual act and they may begin to think some type of game is being played on them. The human being who rebuffs the display of universal love may be irritated, angry, or feel superior because they have personal issues that need overcoming. Whether welcomed or rebuffed, the one practicing and displaying green-ray's universal love is misunderstood and judged by the other-self. This is not a problem if the being practicing universal love does not make it a problem. If they recognize it is a personal issue for the other-self to overcome and has nothing to do with them, they may show empathy and continue on unimpeded. Their mistake would be to stop displaying universal love, thinking their society is not ready for it. At no other time period is any society on Earth more ready for it, as the harvest-time draws near. Hints may be given to the welcomers to understand that no aim is being sought after, especially if the interaction is ongoing due to workspace or other repeating shared spaces. A method to sow seeds of growth for the rebuffers is to not negatively respond to their negative reaction and depart from the interaction while still displaying universal love and also empathy. This may further confuse the confused rebuffer because their perceptions may be proven to be false, and it may bring them to question conditional love and come closer to understanding what universal love is and its healing powers. Although, they may further deceive themselves into thinking it was merely a clever way for the rebuffed to attempt to walk away with their dignity intact. However they perceive it and however they act, it is their issue to overcome and not an issue for the one practicing universal love.

The more a 3rd density being resides on the green-ray chakra path, the more the matters on the orange- and yellow-ray path are seen for what they are: temporary illusions that must be played out and overcome to advance on the journey. The Cosmos and every density within it is an illusion, but the Cosmos is an illusion each spark of Source signed up to experience. One does not advance through the illusion by merely labeling or knowing it is an illusion and then not working to advance toward Source by doing the inner work and service-to-others acts. This is an error played by some human beings who misunderstood the wisdom and knowledge brought through by the 5th density wanderer known as the Buddha.

All that is in the Cosmos is inspirited with Source's intelligently conscious love and light energy. Nothing in the Cosmos could be in the physical outer planes or metaphysical inner planes without being inspirited by this love and light energy.

Even negatively polarized beings are inspirited with this universal love energy; they are just not self-aware of it, as they are confused about their true nature. Every cell in a being's body is inspirited with this love and light energy, and every space between those cells is inspirited with intelligently conscious love energy. The very open space human beings walk through is inspirited with this universal love energy that is of Source and is Source.

This reality may be experienced when the green-ray chakra has been adequately balanced and universal love shines brightly. Personal issues need to be adequately overcome to live in this universal love reality, but once they are and the green-ray chakra is actively being worked on, the remaining 30% to 40% of personal issues cannot live long once continually exposed to universal love. This is where deep-seated personal issues may finally and totally be resolved, such as total forgiveness for all transgressions and abandoning all judgments. All the remaining dirt is washed away in the peaceful and joyful bath that is universal love. When the green-ray heart chakra is adequately balanced, all relationships become love relationships no matter how fleeting the interaction between beings.

Not only does adequately balancing one's green-ray chakra grant graduation to 4th density positive at the end of a major cycle, but within the current and each proceeding incarnation leading up to graduation where the green-ray chakra is balanced, a launch pad to the higher chakras is available because the individual's personal matters, self to other-self matters, and group affiliations have been overcome and universal love for self and all other-selves is recognized and practiced. This universal love and knowing all are One opens up the focus of affiliation with one of the only two groups remaining in the Cosmos: the positive and negative polarity paths, which is the focus in 4th density and higher densities until the path of negative polarity ends somewhere in the early to middle 6th sub-densities.

After graduating to 4th density, a being works within their positive or negative polarity group and focuses on service-to-others or service-to-self acts. They continue in one of these two polarities in 5th density and learn the lessons of wisdom and light. In 6th density, where all beings work on balancing love and wisdom, the two polarities become one as the negatively polarized beings have to switch to the positive polarity path in order to adequately balance universal love and wisdom. Until the

6th density, the beings still remaining on the negatively polarized path had only focused on experiencing the love of self and not universal love, so they are thrown into confusion when entering 6th density. When they get to the point of realizing they can advance no further in 6th density and fully understand and resolve their confusion, they switch to the positive polarity path and work on progressing by balancing all their delayed karma in their new position of duty and honor to the Oneness in positive polarity.

One may ask why a negatively polarized being even attempts moving forward through the 4th and 5th negative densities if they must switch to the positively polarized path at some point. It is because they are confused about reality and perceive information akin to and in this awareness-expanding course to be a lie. This is all by Source's design because the negative path offers its own type of service to Source for Source to better know itself by having such an adverse element of itself on the illusory game board.

We will not cover the countless details within relationships that focus on love, as we did not cover the countless details within the personal and one-on-one individual interactions. We offer some examples but focus on offering the expanded viewpoint and awareness that resolves all the details within each set of chakra lessons. It is the responsibility of each being to do the inner work by recognizing and working on the details themselves after firsthand experiences provide a spotlight upon the details.

Since the seniority of vibration is in effect as Earth nears harvest-time, there are currently hundreds of millions of later 3rd sub-density positively oriented beings incarnated on Earth who provide learning material for the details. Along with the approximately 385 million wanderers—who are mostly 6th density wanderers—presently incarnate on Earth, there is a plethora of modern material available to assist human beings if they choose to overcome and balance their personal and group matters and work toward adequately balancing their green-ray chakra. Highly negatively oriented human beings try their hardest to hide such material, and with their control over Internet platforms/ companies, they are somewhat effective at doing so. The question is whether the human being is seeking the material or not. When one mentally seeks, the doors of opportunity open in some manner regardless of those who try to hide the doors. This is how the mental Cosmos operates. (More on the function of this cosmic operation will be covered in a later subject.)

Most human beings are too distracted by trivialities in the 3rd density experience. If they choose to continue doing so, they will continue to sleep in a dream that could turn into a nightmare at any time. Negatively oriented human beings create and encourage majority-created distractions so as to keep the majority focused on trivialities and away from what is important because that is how they effectively continue to manipulate and control the majority. This is not to say that one cannot enjoy transient elements and entertainment in their incarnation; the question is how much time and focus is being given to them instead of being given to that which is not trivial or transient: the way of One.

The wanderer who has adequately balanced his chakras to be able to receive and bring through this awareness-expanding course is only one of millions of 6th density wanderers from our united group currently incarnate on 3rd density Earth. Besides his truth in fiction books that contain a plethora of nonfictional material, there is currently an abundance of material being brought forward by positively oriented human beings—whether they be wanderers, walk-ins, or not. Material most notable of such has been brought through by the one known as Eckhart Tolle. We especially shine a spotlight on this being's body of works *The Power of Now* and *A New Earth*. When Earth fully transitions to a 4th density positive planet, it will be the new Earth. The material Eckhart Tolle brought through covers some of the countless details within the lower chakras and green-ray chakra lessons that this awareness-expanding course is not intended to cover.

103.8 – Communication & The Way of the Adept

We will only briefly cover the blue-ray and indigo-ray energy centers because the red-, orange-, yellow-, and green-ray energy centers are what needs to be focused on for 3rd density beings to graduate to 4th density, which is the main aim of this awareness-expanding course. The blue- and indigo-ray energy centers are typically what wanderers and some later 3rd sub-density positively oriented beings focus on balancing at some point in their incarnation. However, all energy centers are potentially able to be activated and balanced by any 3rd density being during an incarnation.

As in the negative 4th and 5th densities, negatively oriented 3rd density beings do not work on balancing the green- or blue-ray chakras. Instead, they work on recognizing and understanding aspects of them so they can manipulate the matters associated in those chakras to gain power and control over others. 5th density negatives, who reside in the density of wisdom and light, particularly become well-versed in the art of manipulating wisdom and light to gain power and be more effective at performing service-to-self actions.

Until the lower chakras and the green-ray chakra are balanced by the positively oriented being, there will be blockages in the blue-ray chakra. Structural integrity must be established in preceding chakras before higher chakras can be effectively worked on, otherwise the being may be grasping over too large of a gap and fall out of the tree along their journey. Working backwards from the furthest outstretching branches of the tree of mind, beings journey back toward the main branch that all the offshoot branches originate from, then they reach the center of the tree, then the trunk of the tree, then the roots of the tree, and then merge back with the seed—Source—that sprouted the tree of mind and life. Thus, only great confusion would flourish if the lower chakras, which are closely associated with the body complex of a being, were not balanced out before attempting to balance out the blue- and indigo-ray chakras, which are associated with the mind and spirit complexes of a being. The composition of the tree of existence provides the experience and the journey: the body complex is the branches of the tree, the mind complex is the conscious-mind center of the tree and subconscious-mind trunk of the tree, and the spirit complex is the roots that lead back to the seed. All sparks of Source eventually return to their roots, then the seed.

When the blue-ray energy center is adequately balanced, the individual understands themselves and others spiritually to some extent, and this spiritual understanding becomes great once the indigo-ray chakra is adequately balanced. As the being works on adequately balancing the blue-ray chakra, they become more skilled at communication, expression, and understanding themselves and other-selves. This level of understanding brings easier access to peace, freedom of expression, and comfort with oneself and other-selves.

The art of communication is a two-way road, where one learns to balance out their particular ratio of listening to speaking. One also becomes more aware when it is best to speak or stay silent when engaged with certain individuals, topics, and situations. Sometimes the best response is no response.

When one has not overcome their personal/orange-ray issues, they are more likely to enter and drive a conversation for their own personal satisfaction: making themselves appear important, intelligent, admired, tough, cool, etc. They are not really listening to the other speak, they are weighing words and topics in their mind to better pave a road toward expressing their own self-importance when it is their turn to speak. Some speak so longwindedly that the other does not have the opportunity to respond. These individuals are not really holding a conversation and would be better off talking to themselves while alone, as that is basically what they are doing when no feedback or response is sought after in what is meant to be a conversation. Some are so lost in their mind complex that they are constantly thinking while another is talking, not really listening or understanding the point of the conversation. When it is their turn to speak, they may reply with something mostly off topic or respond in a way that shows they were not really listening.

When one really listens to another with care and consideration, it shows love and respect. When they respond, it is typically helpful or on topic. They understand that without truly listening to another, there is no such thing as a real conversation, a back-and-forth flow of exchanged ideas and topics. They are honest and only offer what humans call white lies to show consideration for another's plight or situation, offering beneficial words when the truth may not be helpful to the other. However, typically the truth is the best response even if it might not be received well.

When circumstances arise where one can offer another wisdom and knowledge in service—not with the motive of making themselves look more intelligent or spiritual—it is best to offer a tiny amount of information. See how they take in the info before proceeding with more information. If they show interest, more information may be given. An adept can speak all day on a certain topic and all that is associated with the topic, which invariably leads to other related topics, so the adept needs to gauge the interest in another before dispensing more information than is wanted. Sometimes even a short sentence drops a seed that may sprout in the mind of another when the circumstances of cultivation arise.

When one creates mental expectations regarding a future conversation or fulfilling self-aspirations, they are welcoming suffering because if things do not go as planned, they are discontent, or in the case of perceived important self-aspirations, possibly devastated. One may have control over themselves, but they do not have control over other-selves due to free will. If force is used to fulfill one's plans and aspirations, the free will of other-selves is infringed upon, which produces karma. One may have hope in their aims, but cementing expectations leads to suffering. If one creates solid expectations, it means they do not understand how the Cosmos operates. Often alternative outcomes other than what was expected end up being more beneficial for an individual than if their expectations had come to fruition, because one is currently not aware of the bigger picture that is unfolding. Making plans has its place and going with the flow has its place. Not creating solid expectations is akin to having an open mind. An open mind is more perceptive at recognizing the currents in a river that offer the smoothest flow toward the ocean.

Having a verbal conversation with oneself can be very helpful because when one hears the words aloud instead of merely in their mind, it gives more power and focus to the words and what they are conveying. When this is done, one is effectively being their own psychologist, as a psychologist offers short questions so the one they are assisting may answer their own questions and reveal solutions for themselves. When a being has adequately balanced their blue-ray chakra, their spiritual connection with their spirit guides and higher self is more dedicated, so when the being has verbal conversations with themselves, this connection affords one's spirit guides and higher self a greater opportunity to step in and mentally assist the being. This is even more effective when the being is actively working on balancing their indigo-ray chakra. Answers to questions when verbally explored out loud may offer instant assistance with mental replies.

——∞——

The way of the adept is built upon understanding and accepting the whole mind, body, spirit complex. The adept understands themselves greatly and the Cosmos and Source to a degree that offers liberation while in the illusion. They cultivate formidable willpower from understanding themselves and more of the bigger picture of the Cosmos, which also empowers their spiritual faith, rather than religious blind faith. A more self-aware connection with the One Beingness is established because the adept knows they are a part of Oneness.

Until the lower chakras and green-ray chakra are balanced, there will be major blockages in the indigo-ray chakra. If the blue-ray chakra is actively being worked on, blockages in the indigo-ray chakra may dissolve for periods of time, allowing fleeting moments of indigo-ray chakra associated matters to be experienced, such as intuition, inspiration, foresight, and experiencing great amounts of love, joy, and peace from the acknowledgment of one's natural state of being.

To activate and begin balancing the indigo-ray energy center, all the energy centers below it must be balanced and practiced in an ongoing manner. Balancing the indigo-ray chakra requires major focus on understanding and accepting oneself not merely on a personal and emotional level, but on a spiritual level where the self recognizes polarity aspects and that they are a co-Creator and the Creator. Truly acknowledging that one is the Creator means they are self-aware of their infinite worth, which is known and expressed in a powerful and confident yet humble manner.

Most religions—with certain Buddhist sects and their offshoots being notably exempt, and which we consider a way of life rather than a religion—are constructed to program the follower into believing they are not part of Source and are unworthy sinners that may only be saved by blind faith and having another as their savior because they cannot save themselves. The continual programming of lowering the self instead of lifting the self is the fundamental nature for most religions because doing so offers manipulation and control over the majority. Although difficult, the green-ray chakra may be adequately balanced for religious followers who ignore or see past red-, orange-, yellow-, and green-ray matters taught in religions, such as fear of God, judgment, believing in a wrathful God, low self-worth, and warranted violence in the name of God. Instead of working within a religion and ignoring the self-defeating and inaccurate parts of it, it is much easier to adequately balance the green-ray chakra by not working within the limiting confines of a religion. Adequately balancing the green-ray chakra grants graduation to 4th density positive at the end of a major cycle. We have stated that a 3rd density being needs to perform at least 51% service-to-others to graduate to 4th density positive, and this is something that is naturally done when one adequately balances their green-ray chakra.

Until one grows past and abandons a religion, the blue- and indigo-ray chakras will remain blocked, and the green-ray chakra typically remains partially to mostly blocked, depending on the individual. This is the brick wall we spoke of that can only be climbed over if religions are abandoned. Since religions give incorrect directions at some point on one's journey to Source, either intentionally or unintentionally, their directional maps need to be discarded at some point for the being to find the blue- and indigo-ray paths that lead to Source. Since adequately balancing the indigo-ray chakra in a 3rd density incarnation warrants graduation to 4th density at any time—not needing to wait till the end of a major cycle—abandoning religions is a prerequisite to experiencing the way of the adept and accomplishing such a quick graduation to 4th density positive. We restate, religions may be very beneficial for an individual up to a point, where one may potentially progress despite practicing the religion, but at a certain point in one's spiritual journey, religions become only a hindrance for one's spiritual growth. In many aspects, practicing a religion holds one back from activating their blue-ray chakra in an incarnation, and may even be the cause for lifelong partial to full blockages in the green-ray chakra, depending on the specific religion.

The way of the adept is lived and expressed without personal limitations, recognizing and practicing universal love, and an understanding and acceptance of the spiritual self that is connected and aligned with being One with Source, and therefore knowing one's infinite worth. It is impossible to be perfect in 3rd density, so this does not mean the adept does not falter during moments or periods of their incarnation.

There is no such thing as perfection or full enlightenment while residing in any density within the illusion. Perfection is not an aspect of the Cosmos and is unattainable. Keeping this in mind as one does the inner work toward progressing through adequately balancing their chakras is valuable knowledge that may equip one with fortitude, making it easier to avoid self-criticism and being hard on oneself when challenges are failed and setbacks are made. The path forward is filled with setbacks and detours. This is the nature of the journey. As long as one stays dedicated at putting one foot in front of the other instead of resigning and sitting down in the mud, stagnation will be avoided and one will progress at their own pace along the journey.

When the indigo-ray chakra has been partially balanced, a more dedicated connection to one's higher self is established and inspiration and sought-after information may be received more directly. When the indigo-ray chakra is adequately balanced, a connection with Source may be made and a giving and receiving takes place from Creator to Creator. This is when the indigo-ray key has unlocked the violet-ray gateway so the hallway to Source energy and mind is accessible. The indigo-ray chakra must be adequately balanced to traverse through the violet-ray chakra to establish a dedicated connection with Source.

We will use a comparison with your Internet connection to further explain the connection with Source from the indigo-ray chakra through the violet-ray chakra. Fleeting connections to the indigo-ray chakra are akin to experiencing a weak Wi-Fi signal where the connection is spotty and/or slow, so the downloading/uploading of information takes a long time, may not come through entirely intact, and is subject to drop out entirely before one's work is done. Whereas a partially balanced indigo-ray chakra is akin to a strong Wi-Fi signal with the Internet that offers a reliable connection with Source where information may be downloaded/uploaded. An adequately balanced indigo-ray chakra is akin to a direct fiber optic connection with the Internet that offers the most reliable connection with Source at low latency where a mass of information may be downloaded/uploaded. If this indigo-ray connection with one's higher self or Source includes a balanced green- and blue-ray chakra protocol, which all positively polarized beings who are working on their indigo-ray chakra possess, the connection is secure and private. If this indigo-ray connection comes straight from a yellow-ray chakra protocol, which only negatively polarized beings possess, the connection is constantly unsecure.

The positive adept then utilizes its connection to offer information to other-selves on the Internet or in the physical world so other-selves may benefit. For the highly positively oriented being, there is no such thing as learning without then teaching other-selves. The negatively oriented being utilizes its connection to offer disinformation to other-selves on the Internet or in the physical world that offers misdirection imprinted with manipulation and control. Since almost all of the major platforms and companies on the Internet are controlled by negatively oriented beings, information in areas seen as important that is easily accessible tends to be misdirection. The secret societies negatively oriented beings may reside in practice teaching only to a select few so-called elites, and not only do they not teach so-called non-elites, but they go to great lengths to keep the teachings from reaching the majority so they can more easily manipulate and control them.

The adept knows that the best offense does not need a defense because a strong offense also acts as a defense. One always has the ball that is in play by staying present and positive. One may think this formation is vulnerable to attacks, but it is quite the opposite, as one who remains present is more aware and observant of what is transpiring, even past what is occurring in the physical because of their dedicated connection with their spirit guides and higher self who offer assistance when it is needed.

The way of the adept is living simultaneously in two different realms. One foot is located in the physical realms and the other foot is located in the spiritual realms. Cosmic paradoxes are recognized and understood partially or greatly within the illusion, as the adept works within the illusion while knowing it is an illusion. The adept is in the physical world but not of the physical world. While the straddling of these two realms is maintained by the adept, the way of One is offered by the adept in some manner to fellow beings. Whether the offerings are accepted or not, the adept is pleased, knowing that all transpires for each being in their own way and time along their unique path. Thus, the adept does not force. The adept is both confident and humble. The adept does not see themselves as superior, only further along the illusory path than other-selves, and they know that all beings have a focal point of awareness that resides merged with Source in timelessness as they journey through the illusion in a different focal point of awareness. An aspect of all the players is already at the finish line, so to brag or see oneself as superior along the journey is folly, especially because all the seemingly different players actually consist of One player, the One Beingness that is Source.

103.9 – Seeking & Meditation

We will explain how the function of seeking and receiving operates within the Cosmos. The one known as Yahushua/Jesus spoke of this cosmic function when he stated: "Ask, and you shall receive; seek, and you will find; knock, and the door will open for you." You are a part of Source and are always connected to all aspects of the entirety of yourself, whether those aspects reside in or outside the illusion. This connection, established by an aspect of yourself outside of the illusion to yourself within the illusion, never falters but may certainly be ignored by the aspect of yourself that resides in the illusion.

You are a part of Source and the connection to Source is always inside yourself, so go inside to seek answers. All is accessible from within oneself. When one has not adequately balanced their energy centers up to the indigo-ray chakra, many answers are not able to traverse the inside connection to your conscious tree of mind, but in order to seek, the questions are still asked from within and the answers come in countless different forms from different aspects of the whole, as all beings are One in the One Beingness. When the answers are presented in whatever countless ways they may come, it is the seeker's responsibility to recognize the message or answer. It is typical for the message from one's spiritual team to be missed or only partially received by the being in the first and proceeding attempts, but if the seeker is dedicated with the inner work and doing their part of focus, exploration and discovery, meditation, observance of both inside and outside oneself, keeping an open mind, and taking actions that increase the possibilities/probabilities for one's spiritual team to be of assistance, the seeker heads in the right direction, which may or may not be the direction the seeker had intended.

When the mind is still and focuses on sending a message through this inside connection, which is done mentally but may also be done verbally, it is like calling a phone number and leaving a message on an answering machine. Focused thought, meditative contemplation, prayer, or whatever the honest and dedicated connection is labeled, the call is made and the message is given. The message is received instantly as it is given and if, how, and when the callback is made depends on many variables.

Before calling to leave a message, the seeker should be aware of which phone number they are calling: positive polarity or negative polarity. The seeker's true intentions, whether recognized by the seeker or not, are transparent and known by the phone operator who connects the call to the appropriate phone number: the beings who reside in the positive or negative polarity. Both are eager for one's call.

The focal point of awareness of the self that leaves the message is not aware of the bigger picture of its incarnation and other-selves' incarnations who may be involved directly or indirectly, so seeking requests that do not serve the self in this bigger picture are not given an expected callback for the benefit of the self. If the same seeking continues to be made regardless, synchronistic callbacks in life are offered to enlighten the seeker of the folly of their requested seeking or aim and/or callback opportunities are offered that point toward the beneficial way or path not aimed for or realized yet. For example, one may strive physically and mentally ask for assistance in obtaining a certain job only to find the job out of reach. They may feel let down by their efforts and spirit guides. Later on they end up obtaining a different job from a friend of a friend that they will never know is more well-suited for them than the job they had been striving for. When one strives mentally and physically, spirit guides and possibly positive higher-density beings have more opportunities to create synchronicities for the human being they are guiding. The human being has a limited viewpoint, so what they strive towards could be a dead end, or worse. Spiritual faith is needed for human beings when striving seems to lead them nowhere in their endeavors.

Another example: Requesting aid for a loved one to recover from an illness or a situation may not be granted because the situation, which may include them transitioning/dying, may have been pre-incarnate planned, or even subconsciously planned during the incarnation as possibilities/probabilities shifted during their incarnation. The one who requested aid is distraught, but circumstances unfolded just as they were meant to from a higher viewpoint for the benefit of the being.

All seeking requests that do not conflict with pre-incarnate plans should be backed with sincerity and dedication in life by the seeker. After all, it is the self's journey to be experienced by themselves. If prayer provided a cheat code within the game experience, it would not only belittle the point of the game for the player, but other players' experiences within the game would also be ruined. Honest and caring prayer/mentally asking for assistance for other-selves has its place, but in cases pertaining to the self it is the mental seeking backed with physical striving/dedication in life that is effective. Aid may be given when focus and dedication in one's incarnation are practiced, but nothing is entirely given or done as that would be infringement of free will and not beneficial for the self. This would be robbing the self of possible growth and the reason for choosing to experience the Cosmos in the first place. One's highest focal point of awareness decided to pick up the controller and play the game and see it through till the end with the controller being kept in their hands and not given to another. No matter what challenges are faced and no matter the mentality of the one's lower focal points of awareness along the way, they will journey to the end of the experience and eventually merge back with Source. They may ask and receive much guidance upon the journey, but it is their journey, as they intended.

If the message left on the spiritual answering machine is trivial or not sincere, a callback is not warranted. Also, what may be perceived as an ignored callback is actually warranted and the information being sought after can only be understood if preceding information is given first, received, and adequately understood. The callback is this preceding information, and there may be much of it to fill in the gap between it and the original information being sought after, if the original information is even needed. What would be the point in aiding with 103-level information when 101-level information has not been adequately understood yet? How long it takes the seeker to acknowledge and understand the preceding information depends on how dedicated and observant the seeker is and how much preceding information there is. Often the original information sought out by the seeker is made to be known as irrelevant as the seeker understands enough of the preceding information that takes them in a different direction than the original dead-end path.

There are countless ways and channels a callback may be given by spirit guides, 4th density beings, and/or one's higher self that is part of a united group in the later 6th sub-density. To name a few: synchronicities through other-selves, events, actions, and what would normally be considered trivial happenstances; dream lessons; the nudging to observe certain details that could spring up anywhere in life; telepathy that one usually thinks came from their own thoughts; physical visitation by higher-density beings, which is rarely done; or a direct inside connection of some sort or method by way of the adept.

Seeking and receiving is a reliable function of the way/law of One. It is one of the many rules bestowed upon the board game by Source and the Logoi that makes the board game worth playing and experiencing. It functions reliably, but it takes not only the callback but the caller/seeker to recognize and utilize the function so it operates in an efficient manner. This is where utilizing the mind complex comes into play, as it does for so much in the Cosmos, as each universe is a mental projection from Source. One cannot receive a callback if they are constantly talking on the phone or leave the phone off the hook. Leaving the phone off the hook is akin to either not striving in the physical world, or not being dedicated or observant in one's incarnation to recognize a callback. Not being observant also accounts for the phone ringing, but the individual being so focused on something else that they do not hear the phone and so do not pick it up. In this case, the hint is delivered somehow by spirit guides, perhaps many times in different ways, but the human being is too focused on something else or too stubborn to receive the hints. Constantly talking on the phone is akin to the mind never being still long enough for a callback to be received. Even if one is guided to another self who has the answer to their question, the answer cannot be given if the talking—either vocally or mentally—does not cease long enough for the other self to be given the chance to reply or be understood when they do speak. Likewise, the dedicated student does not interrupt the teacher, but respectfully holds their hand up and displays patience and stillness of mind so they may effectively listen in the meantime and also understand when they are called on and given a response to their question.

In order to receive callbacks, one must be observant, focus and clear the mind, make enough alone time, practice the art of meditation, and typically take action in the physical world. The daily habit of meditation, even short durations, is crucial to allow integration of life experiences and for callbacks to be received.

There are different types of traditional meditation. Stillness and clearing of the mind to establish inner silence that brings forth one's natural state of love, joy, and peace is the most useful. Focusing on one thing or idea is another way that provides usefulness. The adept may utilize visualization meditation by holding images in their mind and connecting with the fabric/ether of the Cosmos—the intelligently conscious love and light energy of Source that holds the illusion together and is the connected pathways that provides functionality—to aid in raising the planetary vibration without needing to perform physical actions on the planet. This type of meditation, as well as other mental disciplines practiced that aid the planetary vibration, is what some Tibetan monks practiced and is the reason why Chinese officials were influenced by 4th density negative beings to conquer Tibet and disrupt the positive mental actions being performed for the planetary vibration. This service-to-self event granted more inroads and influence over planet Earth by 4th density negative beings.

We do not recommend any best technique to meditate, as each self is unique and so performs and learns in different ways. Thus, there is no uniform best technique, but the wanderer wishes to share/offer techniques and ways he has found beneficial. We only note that details of the proceeding meditations may be altered to suit the specific practitioner and one's intuition may be used to create one's own meditations. It is also worth noting that as an individual journeys through an incarnation and progresses, specific meditations may be abandoned, altered, and created or found to suit the current vibration of the self along their journey.

——∞——

It goes without saying that a quiet place is recommended for meditation. If you live in the noisy city and are trying to create a daily meditation habit, you'll most likely have to get by with meditating in your non-quiet apartment. I've been in this situation and this was my solution: I used comfortable, quality earplugs and then over the earplugs used wired headphones (not wireless) to play Solfeggio frequency music, which can be found free on video platforms or purchased on the Internet. Choose the Solfeggio frequency that ranges from different hertz settings from 174 Hz to 963 Hz that suits your mood or task. To add another noise-cancelling layer, you can play additional Solfeggio frequency music externally in your apartment at the same time. Just make sure it isn't loud enough to bother any neighbors. Even if you're in a quiet place, you may find frequency music set to a low volume to be beneficial. I used all these noise-cancelling methods at one period in time when in a bustling and spatially cramped Asian metropolis, so you might get by with only one of these listed if your location isn't as loud.

Use a comfortable position that works specifically for you. If you find the traditional cross-legged position uncomfortable, like myself due to having a particular pre-incarnate planned skeletal structure that hinders flexibility in my pelvic region, use a chair or a horizontal position on your back on a bed. The energy that spirals from the planet, prana, adequately gravitates toward your spine whether you're in a vertical or horizontal position, so if you find a horizontal position to be the most suited for you, don't worry about prana flow. Although, before you become more experienced, you may lose focus and fall asleep if lying on a bed due to how comfortable it is.

Meditation #1: This basic meditation can be used by itself or with any other meditations to clear the mind and keep it still. Once in your preferred meditative position, affirm to yourself that there is nothing else you need to do or think about right now. Close your eyes and clear your mind. Temporarily abandon all life situations knowing that they will be there for you after you're done meditating. When a thought creeps into your mind, do not react to it, as that would charge it; instead, reaffirm that nothing needs to be thought about now or simply nonchalantly brush away the thought without getting irritated with the thought or yourself for not keeping a clear mind. Focusing on the thought or mentally replying or entertaining it, especially with irritation, only encourages it and powers its ability to interrupt you. Like an annoying sibling who intentionally pushes your buttons to elicit a reaction, they will eventually go away if you don't give them the satisfaction with a reaction. As with anything, you'll become better the more you practice.

Meditation #2: The Void. This meditation releases all roles, identifications, and associations in your life and temporarily offers a dwelling inside yourself that connects to your true state of being and a more dedicated connection with Source. In your preferred meditative position, affirm to yourself that there is nothing else you need to do or think about right now. Close your eyes and clear your mind. Then abandon all the major aspects you believe yourself to be in this life, both perceived bad and good aspects. One by one, eject each one away from you and into outer space, knowing that it is a temporary life association and not truly what you are. Possible major aspects to eject into outer space: job, loved ones, friends, family, amount of money you own or don't own, tasks, the house or apartment you reside in, your gender, hobbies, any life situation, your 3rd density physical body, etc. Free and detach yourself from all that is within the illusion, anything that is not your true inner state of being in your etheric body. Imagine yourself getting lighter as each illusory aspect of you is discarded. If you have done this meditation enough times and feel you can release and shoot off all the aspects at once like a star ejecting temporary elements off its surface by way of a micro-nova, do so. This technique temporarily empties and detaches all identifications and roles with one's incarnation. There's no such thing as emptiness; rather, you're abandoning illusory attachments in order to make space for your natural state of love, joy, and peace as a part of Source. This is the so-called empty space that is more recognizable once the glass has been emptied of its temporary contents. That so-called emptiness is actually more full of love energy than the contents are, and you are that love energy. Simmer in your natural state of being of love, joy, and peace for as long as you like.

Meditation #3: The Mental Sanctuary. In your preferred meditative position, affirm to yourself that there is nothing else you need to do or think about right now. Close your eyes and clear your mind. Then imagine you reside in a place that's peaceful and perhaps calmly blissful. It can be a place you have been before or it can be a mental construct created in your mind. Once you've created it in your mind, on some level, it's now a real place because the universe is mental. You could imagine a remote location high in the mountains where misty clouds slowly pass by, inside or outside a temple situated on the mountain, on a platform outside the temple that's surrounded by clear water, a place where no other beings are allowed except the positive higher-density beings you may have invited for lessons to be given. This is your sanctuary where no one can disturb you and you can be at total peace. Simmer in your natural state of being of love, joy, and peace for as long as you like.

Meditation #4: Full of Love & Light Energy. In your preferred meditative position, affirm to yourself that there is nothing else you need to do or think about right now. Close your eyes and clear your mind. Focus on your heart chakra. Feel the love emanating from your heart chakra. If you can't feel it at first, fake it until you make it, as imagining it still focuses on creating it since the universe is mental, which then creates it more fully, but the feeling or emotion created is more important because it is more powerful and effective than the thought. As slowly or quickly as you wish, expand this feeling to your whole physical body and the aura space around you. Imagine and feel your cells and the space between your cells lighting up with the love and light energy they are inspirited with as you focus on them and give them your full attention. All that's not compatible with this loving emanation is transmuted and washed away. Feel the calm loving vibrations from your heart chakra wash over your entire physical body, acting as a healing and peaceful catalyst that causes every cell in your body to glow with Source love and light they are inspirited with. This is in fact the reality because every single atom is only in existence within the illusion because it's inspirited with love and light energy from Source. So you're not actually imagining it, you're realizing and focusing on the reality of the situation, and your mental and emotional focus is charging and giving it power. Simmer in your natural state of being of love, joy, and peace for as long as you like. Additionally, while still feeling the love energy, you may then imagine the flow of prana moving up through your feet and up your spine, flowing through and engaging with every chakra along the way to your crown chakra. Then flowing out the space above your head like a fountain, then flowing downward around the apple-like shape of your electromagnetic field till it wraps back up through your feet again. This mental exercise of flowing energy may be repeated as many times as you wish or only done once and then imagine and feel the flowing apple-shaped field from outside your physical body while still feeling the love energy in your body. Simmer in your natural state of being of love, joy, and peace for as long as you like.

Meditation #5: Oneness with the One. In your preferred meditative position, affirm to yourself that there is nothing else you need to do or think about right now. Close your eyes and clear your mind. Imagine your physical body floating in outer space. Nothing is here to break your concentration from total relaxation and silence. Feel the love, joy, and peace that emanates from the so-called emptiness of outer space that's actually full of love energy from Source, and feels like the most comfortable bed in existence. Imagine your physical body slowly dispersing or melting from bliss and becoming inseparable from the fabric of space around you, your mind, body, and spirit connecting with and becoming the ether around you. Feel your love energy expanding through etheric space and filling up the cosmic web that encompasses the entire Cosmos, abandoning the seemingly separate self and becoming One again with all that's in existence. You are the Cosmos, the apple-like shape of the electromagnetic field and all within it. You are One with the Cosmos. You are all stars, planets, beings, and everything in existence. In this state, you are everything and so want for nothing. Simmer in your natural state of being of love, joy, and peace for as long as you like.

When you progress to the way of the adept, either in this incarnation or a future incarnation in the 3rd or 4th density, you'll naturally be drawn to or create a visualization meditation to perform aiding mental actions without the need for physical actions. Of course, as an adept in 3rd density, you'll also naturally perform aiding physical actions that are available to you in your particular incarnation.

As you are meditating in your stillness of mind or sometime afterwards, callbacks or guidance may occur. If they happen during a meditation, they should be distinguishable from simple mind chatter. An answer to a question you've been seeking may pop into your mind. This may similarly happen during sleep time, so keeping paper near your sleeping area may be useful if you get assistance during those moments between being awake and asleep or lessons learned in dream states. Remember to give thanks and appreciation to your spirit guides and your higher self. Everything is a team effort. You are never alone.

104.1 – The Collective Vibration & The Call to Action

We have covered how each being uses their power of thoughts and emotions to charge and make a present or future situation more likely to occur, and now we will cover the power of group thoughts and emotions. Unity is a key aspect of planetary liberation. The more beings who focus on and use their power of thoughts and emotions to create the same thing or energy at the same time, no matter where they reside on the planet, the creation of that thing or energy exponentially increases the possibilities/probabilities of it occurring or being created. This focus could be on a specific matter, event, or it could be simply charging positive or negative energy, which then makes it more likely for any positive or negative situation or event to occur. This group collective charging and creating could be used for positive or negative polarity. To create positive energy, this group activity is most effective when done in meditation since meditation is a focused effort. Group meditation can be practiced anywhere and all the participants do not physically need to be in the same place or nation for it to be effective, but it happening at the same time does matter when making it exponentially powerful. The benefits of meditation that human beings have known about for a long time on an individual level—reduction of stress, enhancement of mental and bodily health, increase in awareness and focus, cultivation of positivity, and so much more—also works on a collective level since all beings are connected and are One. The more human beings who meditate at the same time, the larger the effect that ripples throughout the planetary web that connects all beings on Earth. As the amount of human beings who meditate on focusing their similar intentions by way of thoughts and emotions at the same time increases, the ripple effect throughout the collective consciousness on the planet exponentially increases. Think of the ripple or wave effect over water when one pebble hits the water; this is the effect one being has on the whole body of water. This one being's wave can spread far and have an impact. Now think of a collective effect by human beings, which is a massive bolder that hits the water, or if the numbers are great enough, like a large asteroid that hits the planet and changes the whole atmosphere and situation on the planet all at once; in this case it is a positive change and would only be destructive for the control structure of negatively oriented beings. The power in numbers and unity is not only added but is exponentially strengthened when dealing with similar thoughts and emotions that occur at the same time. This ripple effect spreads throughout the planet, so not only is each individual who is participating in the group meditation affected, but those not participating who are going about their regular lives are also affected. If the focus is positive, the positive effects ripple throughout the planetary web with exponential strength and positivity affects all beings on the planet. Even those who do not know the group meditation is occurring are given the positive effects and uplifted by them. This is a powerful act of service to others that positively affects oneself at the same time, as all are One. This method is a highly powerful tool for creating positive change in a society and for a whole planet.

There was a group on Earth who performed this action using what is known as Transcendental Meditation, and the positive effects were shown as all the negative incident statistics noticeably decreased on a planetary level. The power of positivity swept the planet and increased all beings' vibratory levels during the group meditation period, and lingered after it. If such effects can be made by a group of about 5,000 human beings over 7 weeks, imagine what a larger united group could accomplish, especially if the united meditation was done on an ongoing basis. In order to not disturb one's sleep time, the world time zone locations could be put into two groups, where these two groups meditate at the same time every day for at least 30 minutes. Those who wish to meditate longer than 30 minutes can keep meditating with the others that do the same in the group. We tell you what would happen if only a small portion of the planet participates in this: life on planet Earth would drastically change for the positive and the old Earth would fade away, timeline by timeline. If the amount of humans on Earth participating is larger than a small proportion, several timelines could be jumped over toward a more positive timeline in the countless array of possibilities/probabilities. The negatively oriented beings' control structure would have no chance in surviving. If you want to make your planet a better place, you have to do something about it or it will not happen. This united meditation is something all can participate in to do their part. We can see all the possibilities/timelines leading up to the harvest-time. The timelines that practice ongoing united meditations that are large enough not only liberate their planet from the highly negatively oriented human beings, but have a much larger amount of human beings graduating to 4th density positive.

A similar energetic effect was disseminated when we covered practicing acts of sex that engage the green-ray heart chakra and higher: the positive effects not only last during the act but linger long afterwards. The higher the chakras engaged, the higher the positive energetic effects and the longer they are experienced for. The longer the charge time of the focused activity, whether it be a sexual act or meditation, the more powerful and longer the lingering effects. This intense energy is felt by the two beings performing the act of sex, but a united group meditation affects the whole planet, and does so intensely if the participants are large enough.

If a quarter of the population of human beings on the planet engaged in green-ray heart chakra sexual acts at the same time, the positive energy effects swept around the planet would be palpable and rigid control systems would crumble. This is why the highly negatively oriented human beings fought heavily to stop the love-based movement created by the group known as the hippies. The highly negatively oriented humans were so threatened by the power of this movement, because they are aware of the collective power we speak of, that they went as far as engineering in their laboratories sexually transmitted diseases/infections that heavily spread during that time period to stop the movement and make human beings more afraid of engaging in sexual acts, and then initiated fear-based educational programs disguised as promoting safer sexual practices.

Our united group and other positive higher-density united groups receive the same mental transmissions over and over again by positively oriented human beings: "What can I do to make the world a better place? How can I make a positive difference on planet Earth?" Our answer is twofold: 1: Do the inner work that creates harmony for yourself and all you interact with, and which consequently raises the collective consciousness/vibration one being at a time. In this way, you are helping yourself and the entire world at the same time. All are One. The negative's programming would have an individual believe they are just a worthless speck in the galaxy and do not have the power to affect the planet, or even their small local community. As we have just covered, this programming is a falsity. If one wishes to aid the planet in a major way, the negative's programming term says they are "self-aggrandizing" and should refrain from even attempting to aid others. 2: Form united group meditations using your Internet to plan meditation sessions at the same time, taking into account the different time zones on the planet so the group meditation happens at the same time. The larger the group, the larger the exponential effects. The unity work makes the inner work much easier to perform, and vice versa.

Akin to the example of the green-ray heart sexual acts happening at the same time, if half of the population of human beings on the planet engaged in a mentally and emotionally focused meditation session at the same time, the positive energy effects swept around the planet would be palpable and rigid control systems would crumble. The positive vibratory ripples would blast out and reverberate around the planet, affecting all beings and the systems they implement. To the negatively oriented, this would be akin to having the most technologically advanced weapon discharged at them. There would be no escape no matter where they hid. In such an event, the negatively oriented that are not too far along the path of negative polarity would be aided in potentially switching to positive polarity due to the influx of energy they were subjected to, which would assist at melting their blockages and activating their heart chakra. A single human being's mind and emotions are powerful enough to change physical matter and situations, so the exponential effects of united group's mental and emotional efforts can change a planet. The negatively oriented human beings and potentially the confused neutrals may say such talk is pure New Age nonsense, mumbo jumbo, or lies. The former disseminate this opposition because they know it is true and very powerful. They know they would not stand a chance against such a united intention.

We do not typically offer meditation techniques because what is effective is different from being to being, but we will offer a simple yet powerful meditation technique that may be used for the united group meditation we speak of since it utilizes the essence of what Source is made of and therefore exists in every particle and between every particle throughout the Cosmos: intelligently conscious love energy. No energy is more pervasive and more powerful in the Cosmos. Use the position for meditation that you find most suitable. Close your eyes and clear your mind. Mentally affirm your service-to-others intention of aiding Earth and all of the beings who inhabit it. Focus on your green-ray heart chakra and produce loving emotional feelings from it that spread out and encompass your whole body. Then imagine yourself in the middle of the planet and feel your loving emotions ripple in halo waves that spread across the whole planet, over and over again. The loving and peaceful emotions being created and felt are more important than the mental imagery because emotions are the catalyst for creation. You may call this group meditation: United Heart Meditation. Perform this group meditation for at least 30 minutes. Those who wish to meditate longer can continue to do so with the other-selves who do the same. The more often it is done, the greater effect it will have. Since it is very beneficial for every human being to meditate for at least 30 minutes every day for their inner work, there is no reason why the united group meditation cannot be performed daily on a permanent ongoing basis. The more human beings who participate at the same time, the greater the exponential effects on the planet and all the beings who inhabit it. Even the participation in the low thousands for a group meditation has the potential to positively alter the timeline for Earth. High participation in a group meditation assures working toward a more positive timeline or shifts to a more positive timeline. If at least 1% of the collective consciousness participates, a jump to a more positive timeline for Earth is assured in every meditative session that has the duration of at least 30 minutes. If at least 15% of the collective consciousness effectively participates, planetary control structures would be heavily impacted and potentially cease to function properly. It would be wise to do the inner work and participate in group meditations instead of continually asking how you can be of service and then not following through. If you are not a negatively oriented human being, you want the planet to be a better and more harmonious place, and doing the inner work and group meditations is how you make the world a better place. You can choose to not participate, which assists the negatively oriented beings keeping the current state of the planet, or you can take action and do your part to make yourself and the planet vibrate higher. In your mental transmissions you have asked how you can improve yourself and do your part to make your world a better place. We have answered you. It is your choice in how you proceed.

Highly negatively oriented humans are fully aware of the powerful effects of the collective consciousness. Since they are very much in the minority, they have to use their programming methods to control the vast majority's collective consciousness and use it against the vast majority. In this way, the negatively oriented beings capture the power of the majority's collective consciousness and abilities, who unknowingly freely give it away, and direct it toward whatever they—the highly negatively oriented humans—want to create. This is done by using their programming methods we have spoken about many times in this course due to the importance of making it known. The negatively oriented beings' programming we have spoken about in past subjects is for encoding human beings and shaping social conditioning, but their programming we speak of now is for getting mass amounts of human beings to produce negative thoughts and emotions at the same time, producing the opposite effects of what we conveyed group meditation does—exponentially creating negative energy that affects all beings on the planet. The negatively oriented humans use the news to do this. Positive and negative occurrences, situations, and events happen every day on Earth, so why is it that the news always focuses on the negative and ignores the positive? It is because the negatively oriented who control most of the outlets that produce the planetary news use it as a daily tool to get human beings to produce negative thoughts and emotions that produce negative energy that negative polarity flourishes in and aids manipulation and continued control over the majority. Instead of daily mass meditations being utilized to produce positive thoughts and emotions that shape the planet toward positive polarity, the negatively oriented human beings get the majority to practice daily mass dis-meditations, which is called watching their news. Their news that is designed to manipulate you into producing negative thoughts and emotions. Fear or anger is used to encourage the majority to have certain opinions on a matter, which leads to separation and fighting, or to focus on a particular possible future event that the negatively oriented beings want to occur. When the majority mentally focus on the possible event with their fear and/or anger, it charges the event and makes it more likely to transpire. And when large negative events happen on the planet, which the negatively oriented beings are themselves the cause of, and human beings are subjected to the news all at once, it is an exponentially more powerful catalyst than their already powerful negative daily news and causes a vast amount of human beings to collectively produce negative thoughts and emotions all at once.

Instead of practicing dis-meditation when watching their news, it would benefit one and the planet to meditate, and if done in group meditation often or on a daily basis with high participation, the planet may correct itself in a short amount of time. The power that is generated and created from life-force energy that flows to the green-ray heart chakra and above is much more powerful than the negative's generated energy from utilizing the lower chakras. Their chosen stagnation provides them with less powerful tools, which is why they have to fight dirty and use clever deception in order to succeed. They have to work much harder and more often in order to attempt to match the energy that can be generated in the green-ray and higher chakras.

The different groups around the planet that have allied against the highly negatively oriented human factions have collected a treasure trove of information in the form of documents, photographs, and videos that exposes the highly negatively oriented human beings. For some time, they have been attempting to negotiate a deal with the highly negatively oriented humans. The negatively oriented beings' excuse for not wanting the information released is that humanity could not handle it and the reaction would be mass hysteria and suicides due to their fabricated worldviews being completely shattered. Instead, they want to keep up the status quo, the slavery system they have engineered for what they say is best for humanity. Their excuse is not altruistic in the least because their mentality and actions clearly show they do not care about the majority. They prolong talks while they have teams working in the background to undermine the allied members' efforts. The highly negatively oriented human beings do not make deals, as they are used to dictating what happens on the planet and controlling it. They released what is known as the deep fake technology and disseminated it in their programming outlets specifically so that if the compromising videos of them get released, they can claim they are all simply deep fake videos of them. An opportune time for one of these allied groups to perform a data dump of the treasure trove of evidence would be during the united group meditation movement. The already galvanized movement would be further galvanized.

The highly negatively oriented humans have known about the coming micro-nova for many decades, but they have kept it a secret and give the same excuse they have given for not wanting the wealth of exposing information to reach humanity: they claim humanity could not handle it and there would be mass hysteria and suicides. The real reason they do not want either things to be known is because it will change the status quo. They want the majority to continue their lives in their slavery system and be good slaves right up until the micro-nova takes them unawares. They are aware that if humanity knew the micro-nova will occur in or near 2034 CE, humanity would be galvanized to live their lives differently and not continue with the status quo; and if properly informed about the highly negatively oriented human beings and their control structure, humanity would be galvanized to finally liberate their planet. Under the influence of their chosen negative 4th density masters, they attempt to keep humanity uninformed about anything of major importance so the majority does not do the inner work and so they do not liberate the planet and drastically increase the probabilities that many more 3rd density human beings will graduate to 4th density positive and strengthen the positively polarizing team that is their opposition.

The real reason they do not want their crimes against humanity released and the information about the coming micro-nova to be known is so they can continue to manipulate and control the planet right up till the end. The highly negatively oriented human beings are under the impression that their underground bases and complexes built into mountain ranges they have constructed and are still currently constructing will safeguard them and they can continue to prosper and stay in control. They are not aware that Earth is already locked-in to transitioning to a 4th density core positive planet and that only 4th density positive graduates will be able to remain on the planet. Their factions argue over who will control the planet for the next century, not being aware that none of them—negatively polarized beings—will be able to remain on the planet.

If positively oriented human beings owned the media, they would produce a daily show where group meditation was offered to be potentially performed by an enormous group of human beings, exponentially creating positive energy—thoughts and emotions—to aid the planetary collective web while aiding oneself at the same time every day.

Every being that inhabits planet Earth is part of the collective consciousness, so every being has a vote in making up the vibration of the whole. Each drop of hot water helps to raise the temperature of the cold body of water in the planetary bathtub. Instead of unconsciously casting one's vote, it would be more appropriate and beneficial for every being to be conscious of their vote. This is a vote that is cast repeatedly every moment along the space-time continuum, allowing each individual to change their vote at any given time. Each being's thoughts, emotions, and actions make up their vibratory vote that has an effect on the collective. Are your votes aiding the planet? When one is aware and takes stock of their thoughts, emotions, and actions, they are assisting in aiding themselves and the whole planet, as all are One. Every single human being is powerful and matters because every being has a vibratory vote. They can be manipulated into casting a vote that works against themselves, or they can cast a vote that benefits themselves as well as the collective whole. Working together in harmony with yourself and other-selves steers the collective ship in a positive direction, where even a minority can use a simple rudder to potentially change the direction/timeline. The more beings who take part in doing the inner work, the more beings will aid themselves, and in doing so, aid the whole planet at the same time. The more beings who join together and work in group meditations, the easier each being's inner work will be, and the more powerful the effects will be across the planetary web for shaping a more positive present and future on planet Earth. The outcome, as it always was, is in your hands. It has always been your choice. Now that you know how individual and group thoughts and emotions shape the world, and now that you know you have been deceived and manipulated into casting your vibratory votes to create a control structure that works against you and for the benefit of the highly negatively oriented human beings, will you consciously choose to empower positive polarity for yourself and the planet?

Performing the inner work, which includes meditation, and participating in united group meditations is the way to contentment and positive planetary change, progressing through the sub-densities in 3rd density and graduating to 4th density positive, and liberating your planet from the highly negatively oriented human beings. There are no tools that are more powerful than these two.

We understand the draw toward anger after one has become aware of the vast manipulation played out against them their whole incarnation by the highly negatively oriented humans, but we remind you that anger creates blockages in the red-ray chakra and so is not an emotion that serves you to produce. Remember that reacting with anger to the negatively oriented beings' deeds only strengthens them, and so they welcome you to create anger, fear, or any negative energy because it charges their powers. Producing love energy in one's thoughts, emotions, and actions is what takes away the powers they utilize, which are your powers, not theirs. If you continue to give them your power, they will happily use it to control you. It is the calming waters of love that extinguish the raging fires. Taking to the streets with weapons is not effective and will only cause more harm and benefits the negatively oriented. Causing riots that are charged with anger where occurrences of burning and destroying your fellow human beings' property is a method that produces no benefits and actively works against your fellow human beings instead of uniting with them. The negatively oriented beings pay human beings to take to the streets and destroy property, even if the riots are against their agendas, because they know the negativity captures the movement and charges their powers. Anti-movements may spread awareness, but they create negative energy that charges the very thing the movement is trying to stop.

To show public support for the release of all advanced technology, the dissolving of the monetary system, and liberating the planet, groups may perform the united group meditation outside where it can be visible and generate awareness. A more dedicated united group meditation effort could also be performed where planetary outdoor meditation groups are intelligently organized and camp long-term for a whole month, or longer, or with no end until the goal is met, striking the slavery system and abstaining from their slavery jobs. Although some necessary jobs such as police, hospital staff, and some food production will have to be continued. During this love movement, meditation sessions could commence for 30-minute or hour sessions and be followed by similar break durations where positive conversing, the playing of music that is not anger-based, and/or other tasks be performed to share a sense of community and bonding. Remember to focus on the common goal and stay united instead of breaking down due to minor disagreements. It is impossible to agree on everything in 3rd density, so instead of getting caught up in the countless possible disagreements, catering to the negatively oriented beings, band together in agreeing that all want the world to be a peaceful and more harmonious place. This effort would douse the negatives' fires with water instead of attempting to fight fire with fire, which only causes more fire and assists the negatives' efforts. In order to cultivate positive energy, any negative or low-vibratory actions or speech should be avoided during the planning and performing of group meditations. What the group wants is appropriately disseminated without tones of negativity and low-vibration. We hope the police will do their job at protecting and serving the people instead of working against the people and being tools for the highly negatively oriented beings. The police and military are a part of the majority and so would be working against themselves if they allowed themselves to be used as human tools against the controlled majority that they are also a part of. If the police properly follow their motto, it would be appropriate for them to stop and remove the negative infighters who attempt to disrupt the peaceful meditation groups. Some of these individuals will be paid tools and planted in the crowds by the negatively oriented beings who wish to disrupt the meditations and/or capture and paint the movement in a bad light. This is the way of negative polarity: capture and twist. Even if a group(s) of human beings allow themselves to be used as human tools for the negatively oriented beings, a high amount of unity of the majority would prevail regardless. When each molecule of water unites to form a large body of water, the body of water that is an ocean is too strong to be dispersed or stopped. When this ocean then further unites in producing peaceful and loving emotions in united meditations, a wave is formed that buoys all that is positive and crashes against all that is negative and controlling.

If such a planetary display were to take place in vast numbers, the exponential positive energy created by the collective would bring the highly negatively oriented human beings to their knees. This has already been done in alternate possibilities/timelines. The collective could make it transpire in your possibility/timeline. If you wait for others to do the job for you, it will never get done. If you wait for a savior to come along and do all the hard work for you, it will never get done. No savior is coming from higher positive densities, as such is infringing upon free will. It will only transpire when the collective realizes they are their own saviors and do the inner work and adequately unite to perform the group meditations. A team effort is required where every individual who positively participates in some way is the collective savior. You are your own saviors. This has always been the case and it is how the 3rd density experience operates.

When the planet has liberated itself and adequately joined in unity, positive higher-density aid is able to answer the mass calling and provide planetary assistance in whatever manner the local Confederation of Planets deems appropriate.

In aiding you, we aid our united group. In aiding yourselves, you aid the collective, as all are One. All function in the way of One whether they are self-aware of it or not. In serving the All, the One Beingness is served.

104.2 – Skills & Passions

The uniqueness of every being, every spark of Source, ensures inherent skills and abilities and a passion that arises when they are being utilized. Without exception, every being has something to offer the whole. Depending on the skill and ability, it may take time, experiences, and inner work for the skills and abilities to come forward and be cultivated within an incarnation.

Every planet is like a big jigsaw puzzle. Every being represents a piece in the jigsaw puzzle. The unique sides that connect with other pieces represents the unique skill set and abilities for every being. Once the skills and abilities are recognized and nurtured, the connecting sides are formed and may work and connect with others in a society with similar or associating skills and abilities. Pre-incarnate plans and a being's spirit guides assist in guiding the individual along their path of fruition and then one gravitates toward the other pieces they are meant to connect with to perform work. This is why it is appropriate for uniqueness to be respected and honored and rigid uniformity avoided.

Unique skill sets and abilities are more easily cultivated within a society or planet that has not been captured and twisted by a monetary system. The more twisted a society or planet becomes while heading down the path of being on a monetary system, the progressively harder cultivating skill sets and abilities becomes because a monetary system deems what skill sets and abilities are important and assigns a monetary figure to them, which then acts to heavily persuade individuals to gravitate away from their true calling and abandon their inherent skills and abilities that would have served the whole, or twisting the skills and abilities to only benefit the individual and/or the negatively oriented minority instead of the whole. If a monetary system does not become twisted enough, individuals are less likely to be drawn away from their skill sets and abilities. However, the very nature of a monetary system breeds greed and corruption and so rarely does not become heavily twisted over time. If the society or planet is harmonious enough, there is nothing necessary or beneficial seen in implementing a monetary system.

As a society or planet becomes further twisted by a monetary system, jobs begin to appear that offer no benefit to the progression of a society and instead focus solely on ways to amass more wealth, which works against the advancement and harmony of a society. On a harmonious planet that does not utilize a monetary system, the whole pie is there and available to be utilized in a beneficial way for the collective. When a monetary system is implemented and far down its twisted path, the pie is needlessly broken up into pieces and each individual is encouraged to fight each other for the largest remaining small pieces the negatively oriented beings have left for them to fight over. This creates what humans have called a dog-eat-dog world. If you are in this world, it does not mean you need to be one of these dogs. Contentment will never be obtained by one of these active dogs.

The jobs monetary systems create become like cancerous tumors in the body that grow in size and numbers and begin to weaken and kill their host, the society, as well as the beings within it. As this sickness progresses, more individuals are tempted to abandon their inherent skill sets and abilities or utilize them in a twisted manner because the cancerous jobs are highly rewarded with money over other jobs. Then skill sets and abilities are perverted and utilized for selfish reasons instead of for the benefit of the whole. If this trend continues, which it typically does since the pendulum has been swung in motion, a society further moves toward rewarding selfishness instead of rewarding efforts that focus on improving harmony and advancement for the whole, which would invariably improve the living standard and spiritual and technological progression of the whole. In selfishness, corruption and ruthlessness become revered because they offer the easiest and quickest way to what the society has deemed success: the amount of wealth and power collected. At some point along this negative path, revering and honoring the status of one's wealth and power begins to supersede and justify the selfish actions that were used to acquire it in the eyes of the programmed majority, the end justifying the selfish means.

There is more honor in living poorly or being homeless than taking a job that pays to work toward degrading a society instead of harmonizing and improving it. Instead of mindlessly following the money, it would be appropriate to ask oneself if the job they intend to fill works against human beings in any way. The money collected for such a job accrues karma that makes the collected money more than worthless in the long-term.

Each abandoned or twisted set of skills and abilities leaves a jigsaw puzzle piece in the box instead of finding its way into the big planetary picture that is meant to be constructed. Every abandoned puzzle piece leaves a hole in the picture, making the society weaker as it loses sight of the big picture, piece by piece. When too many holes are left in the picture over time, the big picture is not recognized and the society moves toward spiritual entropy instead of spiritual harmony and growth.

When the big picture is full of holes and negatively oriented beings accumulate the majority of wealth and control in a society or planet, the construction of the intended harmonious big picture is abandoned and the highly negatively oriented beings attempt to build their own selfish big picture. The negatively oriented beings tempt and reward those who pervert their skill sets and abilities in aiding the construction of the envisioned selfish big picture that functions for the few and against the majority. Those who allow their skills and abilities to be captured and twisted are used as tools and discarded when no longer useful. There is no such thing as honor and loyalty with negatively oriented beings because each one is always looking out for and serving themselves.

In a controlled system, those who deny perverting their skill sets and abilities and those the negatively oriented deem to be useless in constructing the negatively oriented big picture are thrown into the puzzle piece grinder along with those who choose to work as human tools in the control system. This puzzle piece grinder is the broken system that has been slowly and methodically engineered by the highly negatively oriented beings, which works at crushing the passion in one's spirit. In this broken system, uniqueness is crushed and uniformity is heralded as the progressive way forward. Methods of uniformity are set up throughout the important aspects of a society with programming methods that lead to social conditioning being used as the most effective weapon. If one does not conform and obey, the negatively oriented human beings turn them into the enemy in the eyes of their programmed and controlled majority. The aim is for every puzzle piece's unique connecting sides to be filed down to straight lines as they make their way through the negatively oriented beings' constructed society, the broken system. The goal being to produce uniformed square puzzle pieces that can be used as tools anywhere in the selfish big picture, or discarded and easily replaced with another uniformed square who conforms and obeys.

No instructions were given with the jigsaw puzzle box because the method for constructing the big picture is seen as obvious. But somewhere along the way in constructing the big picture, the negatively oriented beings come forward and claim to have found the instructions for the jigsaw puzzle. Their instructions state that every puzzle piece can be filed down to uniform squares so the big picture can be assembled quickly without all that inner work effort. This supposed quick fix to progression leads to total disaster for the deceived majority. This is especially the case if such flawed instructions are followed long enough that when the society has become technologically advanced enough, the beings in the society begin to augment their biology with technology to further the quick fix and abilities. There are no shortcuts to spiritual advancement. When a being augments their biology with technology, they compromise themselves and are left vulnerable to being influenced or completely controlled by 4th density negative beings due to the submicroscopic technology they invented. Even if the augmented being does not come in contact with the submicroscopic technology, placing technology within the electromagnetic field of a being disturbs the flow of life-force energy through their chakras and physical body.

The ultimate goal of the highly negatively oriented being is to complete their selfish big picture with only uniformed squares on their 3rd density planet because it ensures their continued power and control over the majority. They are influenced or directly commanded by 4th density negatives from the outer and/or inner planes who utilize them to capture their planet in the name of negative polarity. This increases the possibilities/probabilities of beings graduating toward 4th density negative, which in turn increases the probabilities of a planet having more 4th density negative graduates than 4th density positive graduates and so the 3rd density core planet transitions into a negative 4th density core planet at the end of the 3rd density planet's grand cycle.

Planet Earth may be riddled with many holes in its big picture (and it is never too late to work toward filling those holes), but Earth did not reach the described negative point, as many more beings have and will graduate to 4th density positive instead of negative, and so planet Earth will transition to a positive 4th density core planet. This has already been established as a certainty, but the matter of how smooth and long this transition into full 4th density takes is still up for 3rd density human beings to decide. Positive and negative beings both work toward increasing the amount of 3rd density core planets transitioning into 4th density core planets under their positive or negative polarity. In this game of chess, every planet is a piece on the expansive universal game board.

Not all societies or planets that develop a monetary system are doomed to create or stay in a broken societal system. Accounts of some possibilities/timelines for Earth that abandoned their monetary systems will be conveyed in the next subject. If a monetary system is not developed on a society or planet, the probabilities greatly rise for harmonization and advancement, both in a spiritual and technological sense for the whole. When harmony is cultivated in a society or planet, the jigsaw puzzle has a much greater possibility of being pieced together and offers the view of the planet's big picture to be known. This equates to planetary expansion of awareness, where the planetary beings may then expand further and start working on an even more expansive jigsaw puzzle picture that goes beyond their planet and out into the universe.

104.3 – Alternate Timeline Accounts

In some possibilities/timelines for Earth, the wanderer known as Nikola Tesla was not stopped by others' greed and power in bringing clean free energy to the United States of America nation, which then followed to the whole planet. In your possibility/timeline, not only was this advancement stopped, but many proceeding inventors were also stopped from bringing their inventions to the public that offer clean free energy after the initial purchase. They range from powering a household to powering the entire planet. This particular breakthrough, as well as many others, does not serve the negatively oriented human beings on many levels and so continues to be stopped from making it to humanity by any means they deem necessary in your timeline. The first level at the patent office is controlled by the negatively oriented human beings. If a patent would aid or progress the planet in some way that would threaten the control system, the patent is subjected to secrecy orders due to so-called national security concerns and taken away from inventors. There are over 5,000 patents in the United States of America nation that were played out in this suppressive manner. There have been countless additional inventors who are paid a visit by operational teams even before filing a patent, or to those who have filed patents and refused to keep them secret. The results range anywhere from the inventors being financially compensated to them being force-transitioned/killed. Throughout the total range of cases, the important invention does not reach humanity. Your planetary timeline has not progressed in most ways due to this negatively oriented roadblock. This is the only reason fossil fuels, which are not clean, are still being used for energy in your present time on your timeline.

In an alternate timeline, Nikola Tesla being able to aid the planet with clean free energy opened up pathways and channels for other inventions by him and others after him to come through without the negatively oriented human beings stopping the advancement. These advancements being allowed to be brought forward and implemented onto the planet cultivated a quick technological advancement with a slight spiritual advancement, and a larger spiritual advancement decades later. Whereas in your possibility/timeline, such advancements were and still are kept hidden from society by highly negatively oriented human beings. In this more positive timeline, only advancement in weaponry was kept secret in the beginning, but never ended up being used against human beings. Due to these harmonious events transpiring, World War II never happened and the one known as Adolf Hitler did not end up making clandestine deals with the technologically advanced negatively oriented 3rd density Draco reptilian group that originate from a different solar system. Instead, crashed craft on Earth were not kept a secret like in your timeline and they were slowly understood and reverse engineered so advanced craft were able to be created and your solar system began being explored in the 1950s CE and beyond your solar system in the 1960s CE with all the findings not being kept from Earth's population. Contact with 3rd density beings from other solar systems was established and goods were and are being traded. This is being done in your timeline as well, but only through the breakaway society that is kept secret from Earth's population. As we have stated, with so much separation and secrecy currently happening on Earth today, Earthlings have a better idea of what transpired in ancient Rome than they do of the last 100 years on Earth.

In this more positive possibility/timeline, the further advancement of technology over time made many tasks and jobs redundant and unnecessary, which created a large poor and homeless population on the planet during the 1960s CE due to a lack of jobs being available. This crisis grew and crime drastically escalated throughout the planet during the 1970s CE as human beings were forced into crime to fulfill basic needs of foodstuffs, shelter, and warmth in order to survive. The crisis continued to grow until the planet was forced to confront their broken societal system and a major change needed to be implemented or a full systemic collapse was eminent. This major planetary problem promoted a working together of all nations to solve the crisis. All challenges offer growth.

In the early 1980s CE, ideas and proposals were debated and considered by international organizations that were created to solve the crisis. After several months of these organizations debating and proposing plans, it was largely realized and agreed that the links between motivation, cultivation, and the monetary system had created an undesired trajectory, and that the monetary system was the root of the problem that needed to be abandoned. This agreed upon realization would have taken less than a month if it were not for some in the organizations that were funded and bribed by negatively oriented beings trying to keep their monetary system alive. They were exposed and thrown out of the organizations. It was agreed that Earth's population could be easily provided for by human beings for human beings due to their level of technology and not utilizing a problematic monetary system. It took a year for these organizations to agree and intricately plan down to the smallest details every aspect in what would be their new planetary system. Within the latter part of the year, a rigorous checking and tweaking of all functions was done as plans were thoroughly simulated and possible issues arose.

Massive temporary relief programs for the poor and homeless were created before the organizations started working on the problem and continued throughout the year of planning and checking. A detailed process was eventually agreed upon and finalized that would provide a smooth transition off the monetary system and create an ongoing harmonious existence for all on the planet. All businesses solely dealing with finance and many other unnecessary businesses were abandoned, which was a considerable proportion of all businesses. When the goal was no longer to make money, most businesses had nothing to offer. Other businesses that created goods or services catered to the broken system and were now seen as unnecessary or harmful to humanity. When the competition for money that hindered progression was abandoned, the businesses that still created useful goods and services were combined and their unity of human minds created much quicker advancements for their goods or services. Almost all goods and services where heavily altered and advanced because money no longer worked as a blockage and the aim was redirected to serve humanity and aid the planet.

Human beings used their unique skills and abilities in each of their chosen respected passions to offer their services to their communities or the planet. Since monetary intake was not funneling many human beings to the same jobs and technology covered monotonous tasks, human beings chosen passions—not called jobs anymore—provided all the services and goods that were needed for humanity, except for some temporarily needed positions in the beginning of the transition that required a surplus of human beings in a particular field. Each city or area of the planet had created a list of these surplus positions that would be needed for their area to rebuild and effectively function moving forward and be allowed to fluctuate as changes dictated. Positions were fulfilled by the most qualified and training was given to those who wanted to fulfill open and needed positions for everything to continue to function in their area of the planet. There were and are no shortage of requests to fulfill all positions. Contrary to the negatively oriented beings' programming in your timeline, beings naturally want to be of worth to the whole, as it offers a sense of value and purpose in their life. This can be seen when human beings even in your broken monetary system still want to work instead of retiring, because they feel pride in being of value to others.

The word "job" lost its meaning, as work is no longer seen as a burden and is instead happily fulfilled by those pursuing their passions and value of service to others. The results of one's labor is tangible and easily seen as assisting others and sometimes the entire planet, which offers more motivation and dedication than money ever did. As long as there is an individual to do a task or who wants to be trained to do a task, which is always the case, individuals can switch tasks as often as they desire. Not being stuck in one type of position gives individuals freedom to explore different ways to offer their services and grow personally.

In the beginning, there was a large demand for all tasks involving removing structures that existed at the time and building new structures and living quarters that are not only suitable, but in the past were only available to the extremely wealthy. As money is no longer an issue, all are able to live comfortably and luxuriously. Gone are the days of soundproofing issues, lack of privacy, cramped living spaces, and all other problems that came with the monetary system's created haves and have-nots. Cities that had been too densely packed with human beings were spread out to allow adequate living space to be given to all. All living quarters are fitted with all the furniture and devices a household needs, happily created by those who it is their passion to do so. These devices, as well as all goods now being produced, are the best available on the planet and typically last longer than one's lifetime. Gone are the days of many companies producing inferior and cheap products that did not last long so the companies could keep selling more cheap products in order to make more money. Contrary to the negatively oriented beings' programming in your timeline, there are more than enough resources to provide quality living quarters and goods for the whole planet. In reality, more resources are used to create the endless cheap and disposable goods created in your timeline than to make quality long-lasting products for all.

The planet's population, although informed about what the transition off of a monetary system would be like and offer before it was implemented, became aware firsthand of what the organizations who were tasked to solve the crisis figured out: almost all their societal problems stemmed from being on a monetary system because human beings were taught and motivated to collect as much money and goods as possible instead of providing services and acts that assisted others and made the planet a harmonious and better place where all were easily provided for by the collective. Also, money had been used by negatively oriented humans to get other humans to do their bidding across all aspects of society. The wanderer could write a very long book or even more than one book on covering how money tainted and ruined all aspects of society. Now that this temptation and broken system was removed, human beings worked in unity instead of against each other. When the countless problems on the planet evaporated after the monetary system was removed, humanity finally and fully realized that it was the monetary system that had created all those countless problems and suffering on the planet. This realization became known as common sense on the planet after it was experienced firsthand.

The origins and path of the monetary system was unearthed and understood by the international organizations that studied it while figuring out a solution for the planet. Monetary systems had either been constructed in a basic form to make the bartering system operate easier, or they were implemented to intentionally enslave the planet to the few. Either way, the former happened at some point while being on a monetary system.

The bartering system in the past had issues. If one did not have a good or service the other wanted, bartering would not work, creating a hindrance for one to acquire what they needed. Since human beings' vibration at the time was not high enough to establish a harmonious solution, the monetary system was established as a solution for the limitations of the bartering system. It worked fine in the beginning, but after a short period of time it was taken advantage of by those who recognized they could more easily gain power and control over others by hording a large amount of money. Hording money was far, far easier to gain power and control over others because horded foodstuffs would expire and goods required large storing space and maintenance. This downfall scenario is typical when monetary systems are created by a civilization because greed and selfishness are bred by such a system. As civilizations advance, their type of monetary system becomes more and more twisted to serve the greedy and selfish and further enslave the majority. This happens over stages of time, so the majority in large do not recognize their plight and where the scenario is headed until it becomes a major systemic problem. Even when revolts were successful, the problem would quickly resurface, or never departed, because the monetary system, the root problem, was not abandoned. The majority become further and further enslaved until the monetary system becomes such a formidably entrenched beast that its uprooting becomes extremely difficult and can only be done by the actions of a united group that is large and dedicated enough to the cause, and with a united group that will take their society or planet off the monetary system when the cause is successful. Since the greedy and selfish beings seemingly benefit from a broken system and have the majority of wealth, they pay members of the majority to work against the majority to stop any united group in dismantling the broken system. On planet Earth, the barcode has become the mark of the beast, with goods not being able to be bought or sold unless they are marked with it in most cases.

With the technology available in this possibility/timeline—which is not beyond the technology in your timeline that is kept secret and out of the hands of the population—necessary work hours were reduced more than in half, but since human beings are fulfilling their passions and want to be of value to their communities, most choose to work long hours regardless, as their work is their passion and joy; to give and be of service is their pleasure and pride. In a positively oriented society, the highly regarded and honored members are those who have served the whole the greatest. They are held in high regard and appreciated for their service to the collective. This heightened honor and respect—as everyone is honored and respected—is more of a reward than money ever was, especially because they live just as luxuriously or more luxuriously as they would have when given money as a reward instead. Most of these individuals' efforts would have been suppressed and stopped by negatively oriented beings keeping their control over the broken system in your timeline, or on any timeline that still functioned on a monetary system, so instead of living luxuriously like everyone else, they would have been poor and lived in low-living conditions, or even force-transitioned/killed. In a negatively oriented society, such as your timeline, those who are at the top do the opposite of serve the collective and instead have the collective serve them. It takes a lot of programming to get the collective to hold these top members in high regard.

Long vacations can be taken and the planet is traveled freely, easily, and quickly. Since all living quarters are fitted with everything needed, living quarters are switched with others around the planet as often as wanted, with only the few personal items for an individual needing to be moved with them. During a move to different living quarters, an individual's personal items for their passion or passions—which used to be called their job—are effortlessly moved to their new living quarters if they work at home or moved to their new work location. Besides an individual's personal items for their passions, the other personal items of an individual are few. Human beings are no longer attached to so many items because they exist in each living quarters and wherever they go, and they know that all that is ever needed is happily provided for the people by the people, so hording items, land, and practicing empty consumerism became a way of the past. Besides personal items, individual ownership become an idea of the past, as all is temporarily used and shared. Everything is owned by everyone. There is not a powerful few or a group that has control of this process.

In your possibility/timeline, negatively oriented beings have become aware of this possible move forward that does not serve their selfish ways and so have programmed a twisted version of this reality where no one will own anything and supposedly be happy while the negatives are in charge of everything and so effectively own everything—a hypocrisy—taking all away from any individual that does not comply and obey in the controlled system.

In the alternate timeline we speak of, all is owned and shared by all. No one individual or group has control of all. The negatively oriented beings' programming works twofold in their favor because a large percentage of the majority recognize their twisted and false harmonious move forward and, as the Earth saying goes, throw the baby out with the bathwater; meaning, the more positive timelines we speak of would not become an agreed upon option because it would be perceived as the path toward the twisted reality due to the reverse psychology programming, and so the consensus of the majority agree to stay on the broken monetary system instead, which is controlled by the negatively oriented beings. Either way, their new twisted control system or the current one, the negatively oriented beings stay in control and wield power over the majority.

When the negatives see a probable future that is positive and threatens their control system, they create programming, like we just mentioned, to make sure positive timelines do not come to pass in their future. Often it is simply creating a type of reverse psychology programming that captures the yet to be harmonious idea or system and discredits it before it is even raised as a possibility in their timeline. This either stops it from being raised by positively oriented beings or shunned when it is brought up due to the programming. If the programming is embraced instead of shunned, the negatively oriented move forward with their twisted controlled version of the harmonious idea or system, so either way they stay in control. It is not wise to underestimate the cleverness of the highly negatively oriented human beings on your planet, or the 4th density negatives that influence or directly command them.

Returning to the more positive possibility/timeline we speak of: vehicles and transportation of all kinds no longer need to be owned and maintained by the owner. There is no longer any need for a driver's license, vehicle insurance, and all the other hassles that came with the burden of item attachment and the monetary system. Vehicles are self-driving and hover and fly so roads are not needed. When a vehicle is needed, it is requested on one's all-in-one digital pad and transportation promptly arrives. (The negatives tried to twist the convenience of this all-in-one digital pad as well in your timeline on mobile phones, making it for control against humanity instead of for humanity.) Gone are the days of parking lots taking up space, the hassles of having to find a parking spot on the street, tickets, vehicle accidents, and fossil fuels poisoning the air humans breathe. Those who enjoy driving cars can go to places where such entertainment is available. All places of recreation such as parks, pools, beaches, amusement parks, etc. are fully equipped with the necessary items and staff if needed, so the need to bring personal items is greatly reduced. Like living quarters, places are self-sufficient.

After decades of planetary harmony, spiritual advancement grew considerably. Only organic farming is done and all restaurants and eateries only prepare healthy foodstuffs, lovingly prepared and cooked by those who it is their passion to do so. These healthy foodstuffs taste much better than unhealthy foodstuffs. We have already spoken of this programming.

The planet is fully restored to its natural beauty as all garbage and toxins were removed. Since fossil fuels are no longer necessary due to technology, the air, water, and land is pristine. This, as well as all covered in this timeline, could have been accomplished on your timeline decades ago if hidden technology had not been kept from the population.

If an individual past primary education is interested in learning about a topic, either verbally or hands-on taught, there are online and physical universities and technical buildings where those passionate about teaching their certain areas of interest teach.

Instead of countless pieces of clothing being created and not being bought at stores like in the past, there is standard technologically advanced clothing issued to all that keeps the precise desired temperature and humidity for each individual. If individuals want to practice creativity and express their individuality, they can visit custom clothing studios where they can customize their own clothing and choose the desired fabric. The individual's body is scanned so a perfect fit after possibly needing to be preshrunk is calculated. Precise voice guidance and/or a stylus may be used on a screen by the individual to create completely unique customized clothing. The garment or outfit is rendered on a 3D hologram where the individual, who was scanned, is seen wearing the clothing and can either be walked around or turned 360 degrees for the individual to truly get an idea what the clothing would look like on them and what tweaks they want to make. In this way, only clothing that is going to be used is created and produced. When the individual no longer wants a piece of clothing, it is sent back to the studio where the fabric is recycled so there is no waste created.

More of this possibility/timeline could be covered, but the point in sharing it is to make it known to your timeline's population that not only is functioning on a monetary system self-defeating, but transitioning off it can be done. The effort to do so is actually easier than the effort spent continuing to function on a broken monetary system. Although, the negatively oriented human beings who possess power and control on your timeline will continue to do whatever they can to stop such a transition, and a large proportion of the population is set on following their programming, and so think such a transition is merely a fantasy that could never happen, that a planetary system could not run without money. There is a lot of programming created to shape human beings' minds on this matter, and the programmed humans regurgitate the programming to freethinkers whenever divergent ideas are expressed.

The reality is: transitioning off the monetary system has already happened on countless Earth possibilities/timelines. When the monetary system is abandoned for civilizations or planets, they enormously flourish and progress similarly to the Earth timeline we spoke of.

——∞——

There is a different type of account that makes up a proportion of the infinite possibilities/timelines for planet Earth that we feel is worth sharing as well in order to provide a roadmap that guides the way. In these timelines, the whole planet did not transition off a monetary system all at once, but rather in stages, nation by nation. It was first a single or group of nations that figured out the monetary system dilemma and how to transition off of it while still being able to function with the rest of the planet's nations who still ran on the broken system. They came to agreements to trade goods for goods with other nations in areas where their nation was not self-sufficient in specific resources. Since these nations did not run on a broken monetary system, they did not want for unnecessary excess and so the goods they needed to trade for were few in most cases. These nations' citizens would have had difficulties in moving to other nations without possessing money, but since the harmony and living conditions in their nations thrived far above other nations that still ran on a broken system, citizens had no desire to leave paradise to relocate to nations that ran on an unrealized slavery system that monetary systems engineer and maintain. These nations had to establish a strict border and visa system because almost all human beings wanted to be a part of the paradise, but the space and the tailored system of these nations had to be protected in order to keep them running smoothly. Overcrowding would bring down the paradise they had constructed due to cramped spaces alone, and some negatively oriented leaders of the nations ran by monetary systems that served them knew this. Since they were negatively oriented and felt threatened by these paradise nations because their spread would mean the end of their vast amounts of money and control, they orchestrated large amounts of humans to attempt to illegally immigrate to the paradise nations and bring it down from within. These negatively oriented leaders furiously cried out and gnashed their teeth while using their programming techniques to persuade others to think that the paradise nations' border control was unjust and that everyone should be able to go to the paradise nations. Since everyone wanted to go there, this programming took root quite easily, and even some minds within the paradise nations were affected by the programming and attempted to keep the illegal immigrants in their nations, unknowingly working to destroy their own paradise nation they had worked so hard to construct.

In some possibilities/timelines, the negative leaders were successful and the paradise nations were infiltrated and destroyed from within. Then the negatively oriented leaders spoke about how such a system failed and should never be attempted again. In some possibilities/timelines, the paradise nations were able to deal with this attempt at destroying their free nations because they already foresaw that it would occur and were ready for it. Although they had strict rights of entry laws, a percentage of visitors and vacationers were gladly welcomed so the paradise nations could be an example and show human beings from other nations what it is like to live in paradise and how other nations can adopt their system too. Like one who visits another's household as a guest, all was freely and gladly provided for. Visitors would then return to their nations and join the growing numbers of humans who petitioned in support of their nation transitioning off of the monetary system as well. If the paradise nations had a need to fill specific working positions that they had trouble filling themselves, interviews were granted and the most skilled of their trade were given the positions and citizenship in their nation. Since all wanted to relocate to paradise nations, the most skilled in all areas gravitated toward these nations, which further increased the advancement and harmony of the paradise nations.

Naturally, it was only a matter of time before most or all of the planet's nations transitioned off of the broken monetary system and into paradise nations, even if their leaders used all their powers and force to stop the transition. The rising will of the citizens in these nations united and their unwavering commitment made sure that the transition transpired. Unwavering unity is necessary for major changes to occur when there is powerful opposition. They either transitioned smoothly or roughly in a coup if the top leaders were too stubborn or tyrannical to give into the will of the people. In some timelines there were small amounts of nations that held onto the monetary system and they remained stagnant, heavily controlled, and archaic compared to the advancement of the rest of the planet. For the timelines where all nations abandoned the monetary system, planet Earth became a paradise planet and strict border and visa systems were abandoned and free movement around the planet is enjoyed. The different cultures of nations are celebrated for their variety of spice of life and the possible expansion of viewpoints and wisdom they offer those who travel. Traveling and experiencing different nations became an education unto itself where one could expand their mind from the diverse yet not unharmonious viewpoints provided.

Your possibility/timeline can become one of the timelines that transitions off of a monetary system. Since the highly negatively oriented human beings are set on stopping such an advancement for the whole, the majority would need to demonstrate an unwavering commitment for such a transition to occur. The smoothest and best way to make this transition occur is to orchestrate the call to action we have already spoken of in subject 104.1: a large enough united group decides to abandon the slavery system and perform united group meditations outside to spread awareness and work toward the release of suppressed advanced technology and abandoning the monetary system. The real power is in the hands of the majority, as it always has been.

If an adequate amount of the majority unite and are unwavering to the cause, the small minority of highly negatively oriented human beings cannot stay in control. They are a small minority, so they can only stay in control if enough of the majority allow them to. Like all timelines, it is up to the majority in your timeline to choose how they want their planet to operate.

The Wanderer's Afterword

I would like to express my gratitude for the wanderers who came before me on Earth that paved the way. A majority of them are part of the same united group as myself. Without their efforts, my part would've been even more challenging than it already was. I'd also like to express my appreciation to my later 6th sub-density united group for their assistance and guidance in bringing through most of the information in this course and confirming the accuracy of the information that it was my responsibility to add to the course. It was a team effort; I couldn't have done it alone.

When bringing through information, my united group can only offer information that doesn't infringe upon 3rd density humans' free will. Since some of the information in this book that's highly useful to humans couldn't have been brought through directly from my united group due to infringement, the infringement workaround method was for me in 3rd density to provide it. This was done by my pre-incarnate plans and spirit guides nudging me in the right direction to experience and relearn the needed information in my 3rd density incarnation. To also avoid infringement, some information wasn't given or explained to me directly by my united group in the form of words or telepathically, but was instead made known to me in various ways so I could understand it and write about it myself, with my united group confirming the accuracy of my information and offering changes and tweaks where necessary to avoid distortions.

It was also my responsibility to act as a translator in bringing through the information provided, altering it to verbiage and explaining it in a way that's more understandable to humans, as my united group's verbiage can be very difficult to understand for most humans, and so would offer too many misunderstandings. Then my united group would offer changes and tweaks to my writing to avoid distortions and misrepresentation, sometimes pointing out even single words in sentences that they felt would be better changed. At times I used their words—when words were provided—and words that are more familiar to humans at the same time. Some examples: Logos/star, transition/die, possibilities/timelines. At other times the forward slash (/) was used to give words that together conveyed the true or closer meaning instead of using one word. This is due to spoken languages being much more limiting than telepathy.

I'd be remiss if I didn't reiterate the message that has been conveyed throughout this awareness-expanding course: I am not more special or superior than any human on Earth or any being elsewhere in the Cosmos. I may be further along the path that leads back to merging with Source, but I am a spark of Source like all other sparks of Source. Like all other beings in 3rd density, I'm not perfect. In fact, it's impossible to be perfect in any density within the Cosmos. In practicing appreciation, it is appropriate to respect and hold in high regard all beings who perform major service-to-others actions, but it's not wise to raise them or any being above themselves as more superior. Instead of lifting me or any being higher than yourself, it would be beneficial for you to use this course as a guide to lift yourself high by progressing spiritually by doing the inner work that benefits yourself and also aids the collective at the same time since all beings are connected as One being in reality. Improving oneself benefits the One/the collective at the same time. Bringing through the way of One information that assists you in expanding your awareness and encouraging you to do the inner work for spiritual progression is the reason this awareness-expanding course is being offered. I'm not a savior. No being is your savior. Only you can be your own savior. Any being who steps in and does another being's work for them—acting as a savior rather than assisting them—is robbing the being of their opportunities and infringing upon their free will. Since we are all One in Beingness, we are all important and have value. Raising me to a savior level or making this course a religion would go against the very teachings in this course. The information in this course is not meant to be turned into a religion or any other limiting practice, as doing such would not be expanding one's awareness. This is an educational course and guide to assist in expanding your awareness that leads toward graduation to the next density. If this course is not used for expanding one's awareness and as a guide to assist spiritual advancement, it is merely interesting information.

It's your responsibility to use your discernment to believe the information or not, and it's absolutely fine if you don't believe it, as all is as it should be for each being at certain points in their current focal point of awareness along the journey. Regardless of your stance, you will come to know the validity of some of this information firsthand when you transition and are disincarnate in the inner planes between incarnations. While still incarnate, those who are observant of their world and internally will most likely recognize the many connections and alignments for this course's information that ring true.

This awareness-expanding course will be viciously attacked by confused humans and paid human tools because the information in it is very important. If it wasn't important, the highly negatively oriented humans wouldn't bother paying and commanding tools to attack it; they would ignore it. Any information that offers a high level of expansion and is highly beneficial is information the highly negatively oriented humans and higher-density negatives don't want the majority of humanity to know about, so they use all their typical tactics to mock it, discredit it, attempt to capture and twist it with unofficial sources, and smear the messenger with twisted information and lies in order to get humans to disregard the information. It's nothing personal; they're simply playing their role in trying to persuade the majority to disbelieve the information because it threatens their power and control structure. They know that smearing the messenger is a tactic that works. My advice to readers is to focus on the information in the awareness-expanding course and to do the inner work and united group meditations rather than focus on me or what is said about me. The information in this course is what is important and beneficial if focused on, not me.

For those who may think this information comes too late and therefore doesn't matter much since harvest-time is so near, I'll explain why that isn't the case. Even if one isn't ready to graduate to 4th density for this coming harvest-time and will be incarnating onto a different 3rd density planet in a different solar system to continue their 3rd density experience sometime after the micro-nova, or years or decades after the micro-nova if they survive it, their expansion of awareness from this information, and more importantly the inner work they focus on after absorbing it, carries on with them. When one incarnates into 3rd density, no matter what planet it be on, they go through the 3rd density veil of forgetfulness and don't remember their past incarnations and the lessons they learned therein. However, the lessons and the body of knowledge and wisdom they learned and practiced will not only be in their subconscious mind during their future incarnations, but in the top layer of the subconscious mind that is closer to their conscious mind, having a much greater potential to resurface and be brought to one's conscious attention in their future incarnations because it isn't buried under many layers within the tree of mind. At the start of every 3rd density being's experience, Source mind and all the knowledge and wisdom within is located at the very bottom layer of one's subconscious mind. When a being relearns any part of the knowledge and wisdom of Source mind within an incarnation, those lessons learned and the knowledge and wisdom is then brought to the top layer of the subconscious mind to be more accessible to the conscious mind in future incarnations.

I'll reiterate the dream comparison used in this course to further explain. Think of all the incarnations a being has had since deciding to seemingly separate from Source as a very long dream. One usually remembers the end of the dream before waking up, and the beginning of the dream is long forgotten. The long dream is all of one's incarnations, and the last incarnations—particularly the very last incarnation—is more likely to be remembered than what happened in the beginning or middle of the long dream. Which means what you learn and the inner work that is done in this incarnation up to 2034 CE, or longer, matters greatly because the potential is high that it'll be remembered by some means and brought to one's conscious mind during their next incarnation on that distant 3rd density planet. This drastically increases a being's chances of graduating to the 4th density at the completion of the first major cycle on that new planet—if they so desire—instead of experiencing the whole grand cycle in the 3rd density experience again.

Therefore, a human being thinking the following isn't intelligent: "Welp, I pretty much wasted the last such-and-such decades of this incarnation not working toward spiritual progression, so I might as well throw the remaining decade down the toilet as well. Dreams of the start at the finish line don't make much sense to me." In fact, this mentality if acted out would be wasting a huge opportunity because the current raised vibrations as Earth moves closer to full 4th density vibration offers the potential of advancement that is far above the potential of progression when one incarnates on that distant 3rd density planet in the beginning of the 3rd density experience where the vibrations are much lower and so is lacking a great deal of galvanization for spiritual advancement. Even if a human only had one year on Earth after absorbing this awareness-expanding course and doing the inner work, huge potential leaps in consciousness could be made that would dwarf what is offered in the first major cycle experienced on that distant 3rd density planet.

If humans don't perform the united group meditations, there is a high probability the conditions on Earth won't improve much in the short period of time before harvest-time, but that doesn't mean that you personally can't advance greatly. Instead of letting the conditions on Earth, the majority, or the negatively oriented minority hold you back, understand that the power to advance is in your hands, as it always is regardless of the planetary situation. No one can hold back your spiritual progression but you.

It has been my honor and joy to bring forward the knowledge and wisdom in this awareness-expanding course for you, whomever you may be on planet Earth, or off planet. This awareness-expanding course is the only nonfictional book that I will write. I'll continue to utilize my particular skills and abilities to write fictional books filled with nonfictional material and wisdom to further my service-to-others actions. A book genre called: Truth in Fiction.

Since I am aware enough of my pre-incarnate plans, know that at any time before the micro-nova if I transition/die, am suicided, am disappeared, am seriously wounded, or come down with some illness such as cancer—no matter how convincing it may appear that it was an accident, natural, or whatever—it was due to the orders of highly negatively oriented humans that trickled on down to the human tool(s) who performed their bidding. If any of these things happen to me, it will further validate that the information in this course is very important and extremely beneficial for one to read and share with others. I have already experienced numerous adverse actions by their human tools because the highly negatively oriented humans have not been so happy with me since publishing my first truth in fiction book in 2020 that exposed their mentality, agendas, and the broken system they've engineered. The book was heavily shadow-banned and countless acts of online manipulation were used to hide its existence. They are now even less happy with me since bringing forward this awareness-expanding course. And 4th density negatives, and a 5th density negative being, knowing the probabilities of the future and the potentially large amount of positive polarity this book could generate, targeted me heavily in an attempt to stop me from completing this book. You're reading this, so it goes without saying they were not successful.

To all beings doing their part of service-to-others actions: Don't let a minor thing like the fear of transitioning stop you from doing what you incarnated to do, your goals or mission. You incarnated to do it, so not doing it would be somewhat of a wasted incarnation, most especially for wanderers. Negative-based programming and the social conditioning it shapes may attempt to convince you that you are not important and are simply ego-driven in your attempts to aid a large group or the entire planet. Everyone is important and everyone has unique skills and abilities to offer the whole. You incarnated on this planet at this high-vibratory time to progress spiritually and offer service-to-others actions that assist yourself and others in their advancement, so not doing your service would be a missed opportunity for you and others. To transition is to merely move onto the next adventure; it is nothing to fear and should produce no roadblocks in your plans.

In order to more fully absorb the information in this course, it is most beneficial to read this book at least twice. After reading this awareness-expanding course, you can do your part in not only doing the inner work and united meditations but also sharing this course with others. The highly negatively oriented humans and negative higher-density beings will do all in their power to stop the spread of information that threatens their power and control over the majority, so your assistance is greatly needed. This is a team effort. The act of sharing this course with others is a service-to-others act in itself, so the sharer gains positive polarity. Positively oriented beings learn information and share it with others because they care for others and may also know that the advancement of others also advances themselves as the vibration is raised for all of humanity. Each individual that's lifted raises the collective in part.

This course has been meticulously planned out, organized, and presented in a most effective and impactful manner, so please share it rather than attempting to teach it yourself. Such would be a huge disservice to the one attempting to learn. If after sharing the course the individual still doesn't understand something in it after they have finished the whole course and asks you for assistance, you may then offer understanding if you truly feel you have grasped the concept that is to be explained.

Thank you for showing your appreciation to my services by purchasing this book. The funds allow me to not only get by in the broken system but also to perform further service-to-others actions by writing truth in fiction novels.

Journey on, my fellow sparks. We are all One.

About the Wanderer/Author

Jasun Ether is a later 6th density wanderer/starseed who incarnated onto planet Earth with the mission to assist humanity in graduating to the 4th density by bringing through this course: The Cosmic Experience of One. Pertaining to Ether's truth in fiction books, his interest as an author is to produce entertaining novels that are filled with truth, meaning, and empowering ideas, and which help humanity raise its consciousness, one reader at a time.

Website: www.jasunetherbooks.com

www.ingramcontent.com/pod-product-compliance
Lightning Source LLC
LaVergne TN
LVHW041058080826
845145LV00007B/1625